Reform Rule in Czechoslovakia

Reform Rule in Czechoslovakia
THE DUBČEK ERA 1968–1969

GALIA GOLAN

LECTURER IN POLITICAL SCIENCE AND RUSSIAN STUDIES
AT THE HEBREW UNIVERSITY OF JERUSALEM

CAMBRIDGE
AT THE UNIVERSITY PRESS
1973

Published by the Syndics of the Cambridge University Press
Bentley House, 200 Euston Road, London NW1 2DB
American Branch: 32 East 57th Street, New York, N.Y.10022

© Cambridge University Press 1973

Library of Congress Catalogue Card Number: 72–83587

ISBN: 0 521 08586 1

Printed by offset in Great Britain by
Alden & Mowbray Ltd
at the Alden Press, Oxford

Contents

To my mother

Acknowledgments

Foremost among those who have generously and graciously given of their time and knowledge in helping me prepare this book were a large number of Czechs and Slovaks, most of whom would prefer to remain anonymous. Particularly helpful was the encounter with leading Czechoslovak reformers provided by the Universities of Reading and Glasgow at their 1971 seminar on the Czechoslovak reform movement. As always, the excellent resources of the Czechoslovak research unit of Radio Free Europe were of great assistance. I am also indebted to Professors Leonard Schapiro and Shlomo Avineri for their continued encouragement and advice, as well as Tatiana Hoffman and Yehuda Lahav for their comments and suggestions.

I would also like to thank Terry Bender, Peter Brod (in Munich), Ilana Diament, and my typists Malka Kroll, Shelley Einis, and Claire Lipton. I would particularly like to thank Michael Shafir for his preparation of the index. Thanks to the hospitality of my friends at Kibbutz Nahal Oz I was able to write part of the book in their peaceful surroundings, and the Eliezer Kaplan School of Economics and Social Sciences of the Hebrew University of Jerusalem generously provided me with the necessary research funds.

A word of thanks is also due to the staff of the Cambridge University Press for their patience and much appreciated advice.

Jerusalem   GALIA GOLAN
August 1972

I

The Beginnings of Reform Rule

The advent of a reform regime in Czechoslovakia was the result of many years of struggle, disappointments, setbacks, and half-fulfilled hopes. It had its roots in a movement which began, in fact, in the mid-1950s with the death of Stalin and Khrushchev's secret speech in 1956. It was then that many Czech and Slovak Communists, like so many of their colleagues elsewhere in the Communist world, began to question some of the methods if not the dubious achievements of their years in power. Some began to examine the idea of reform; intellectuals and students went so far as to demand it.[1] Yet these first signs of reform-mindedness in Czechoslovakia were of significance only insofar as they were the first seeds of a plant which was a long time in coming to fruition. The regime in fact succeeded in stifling these first efforts, thereby warding off reform for six years more; Czechoslovakia remained the 'model satellite' until 1963.

Background

It was perhaps strange that the one country in Eastern Europe with a democratic-humanitarian tradition of several hundred years, the one society which had known a genuine western-style democracy in this century and a pre-war legal Communist Party which itself was 'notorious' in Communist circles for its evolutionary–parliamentary bias, should be one of the most stubborn in throwing off the Stalinist practices condemned even in Russia by 1956. Yet there were a number of circumstances which combined to militate against de-Stalinization in Czechoslovakia in the 1950s. Among these was the rule of the *apparatchiks*, that is those people such as Party first secretary Antonín Novotný, who had risen to power during the massive purges in the 1949–54 period. It was through loyal and unquestioning obedience to the old methods that these people had survived and risen; they then continued to use these methods once in power. Given the purges and the atmosphere generated by them, more imaginative or progressive men than those of the *apparat* had little hope of gaining power or even influence. Moreover, this new leadership was

[1] At the 1956 Writers Union Congress and the students' 1956 Majales Festival.

dependent upon the old methods because of the basic instability of the regime. The leadership had been so involved in the past excesses of the Party that it probably could not survive (and therefore did not dare permit) genuine liberalization. Novotný himself, as well as most of the others in his regime, had been too directly involved in the preparation and perpetration of the purge trials – including the trials of the Slovak 'nationalists' which took place after the deaths of Stalin, Gottwald, and Beria – to risk a genuine review and rehabilitation which were part of 'de-Stalinization.'[1]

Another factor which helped the regime forestall liberalization was the relative economic stability of Czechoslovakia. After the economic problems of 1953 and certain concessions (although quickly rescinded), the standard of living in Czechoslovakia had risen at a relatively satisfactory rate. The economic successes of these years were later proven to be only partial and deceptive insofar as genuine progress within the framework of a viable economy was concerned, but at the time the regime could point to certain successes. This in fact led it triumphantly to declare the ascension to socialism in 1960 and the adoption of a socialist Constitution. Moreover, the average citizen experienced a certain improvement in his standard of living, especially in relation to the rest of Eastern Europe. In fact, Czechoslovakia had long been better off than its Eastern European allies, having emerged from World War Two with its highly developed industrial economy almost unscathed. Together with this relatively good economic position during the ensuing years, there was, however, also a dependence upon the Soviet Union for natural resources and, to a certain degree, as a market for Czechoslovak products.

Another factor which played a role, albeit a negative one, in the avoidance of liberalization in the 1950s was Czechoslovakia's geopolitical position and tradition. Of this the most significant element was, perhaps, the feeling of friendship (or at least good-natured tolerance) for the Russians. While these feelings should not be exaggerated, they did account for the *absence* of a strong anti-Russian tradition which might have acted as a stimulant for liberalization, as in the case of Poland and Hungary in 1956. Moreover, there was also the Czech tradition of passive rather than active resistance – the 'sit it out' attitude which characterized much of the period under Habsburg rule, for example. Still another factor which facilitated the regime's efforts to forestall liberalization was the serious minority problem in Czechoslovakia. The Czech–Slovak conflict often diverted and thereby dissipated what might have been a unified opposition within the Party.

[1] For a history of Novotný's positions on this subject, see 173–4

None of these factors was conclusive or static. Given different circumstances or a change in one or another of these factors, some obstacles disappeared or turned into stimulants rather than deterrents for reform.
Thus by the end of 1962 the situation was quite different and the factors
militating *for* liberalization were much stronger or had replaced those
which earlier constituted obstacles. For example, the economy was in a
nearly critical situation by 1962, and in August of that year the Third
Five-Year Plan had to be scrapped half-way through. The failure of the
plan, the continued deterioration of the economy, and the inability for
these reasons to promulgate more than *ad hoc* one-year plans all pointed
to the need for reform.

In addition, the chronic weakness of the regime was aggravated by a
power struggle – albeit between two conservatives – which impaired the
unity of the *apparat*. This struggle, between Novotný and his Interior
Minister Barák, did not render the alternative of de-Stalinization any
more attractive or 'safe' in the eyes of Novotný, but it did weaken his
ability to withstand pressures for change.[1] Despite Novotný's victory over
Barák, the Party was seriously split over the action against the slightly
more popular, yet conservative, competitor for power.[2] At the same time,
more progressive Party people were agitated by Novotný's efforts to stage
a show-trial, not only of Barák, but also of several liberals accused of
creating a 'pro-Titoist group,'[3] and this at a time when many countries of
Eastern Europe had renounced such methods and permitted rehabilitations.

A third factor operating in the direction of de-Stalinization came from
Moscow. The Twenty-Second Congress of the CPSU, with its opening
of the second wave of de-Stalinization, led to pressures on various Parties
in Eastern Europe, including the Czechoslovak Party, finally to begin to
take steps towards de-Stalinization. These pressures were also connected
with Soviet concern over the Czechoslovak economic situation and the

[1] This affair remains unclear, but apparently Barák (who also had a hand in the trials)
gathered materials on Novotný's role in the trials (which he had confiscated while
chairing a committee of investigation of the trials) for possible use in a power struggle.
It was later suggested that Novotný commandeered these materials, for they were later
found to be missing altogether. See Jiří Pelikán, *The Czechoslovak Political Trials*
(London, 1971), 218–19; *Reportér*, 5 June 1968. For suggestions of Soviet involvement
see William Griffith, *Albania and the Sino-Soviet Dispute* (Cambridge, Mass., 1963),
74 and Victor Velen, 'Czech Stalinists Die Hard,' *Foreign Affairs*, 43:1 (1964), 321–2.
[2] According to Novotný's own admission: *Usnesní a dokumenty ústředního výboru KSČ :
od celostátní konference KSČ 1960 do XII sjezdu KSČ*, II (Praha, 1963), 244–5.
[3] Pelikán, *Political Trials*, 28–9, 217–18.

possible failure of the latter to fulfill its obligations to the bloc. Moscow's past willingness to tolerate continued Stalinism in Prague may have been tempered by the increasing awareness that Czechoslovakia might no longer be able to 'return' the favor through its usual economic performance. Moscow may well have argued that the de-Stalinization demanded by the Twenty-Second CPSU Congress could provide the tools necessary to restore the Czechoslovak economy to good working order.

With the accumulation of pressures and objective factors, in 1962, many Slovaks saw that their specifically Slovak interests might be served by de-Stalinization or even by liberalization – and that the circumstances were now fortuitous for pressures in this direction together with likeminded Czechs. For the Slovaks the most immediate demand was the revision of past verdicts against the Slovak Communist Party leadership; thus the Slovaks' greatest interest in de-Stalinization lay in a review of the trials and rehabilitation of the former Slovak leaders, including Gustav Husák and Laco Novomeský, as well as Vladimír Clementis (posthumously).

It was this 'confluence' of factors: economic crisis, political instability, pressures from Moscow, and Slovak exploitation of the situation, which brought Novotný, reluctantly, to abandon some of his habitual caution and agree to a very limited de-Stalinization. Thus in August of 1962 he appointed a committee to review the trials, and at the December 1962 twelfth Party congress he announced both this decision and that of the Party to explore economic reforms. The overall conservative tone of the congress, however, was probably the result of efforts by Novotný to minimize the significance of these decisions and, perhaps, an indication that he was still thinking in terms of merely symbolic de-Stalinization. A decision to de-Stalinize for Novotný and indeed for most of the Party's leadership was akin to the opening of a Pandora's box. It could – and did – lead to a questioning not only of the specific contributions these people had made to the preparation of the trials, but a questioning of the practices and ideas of the whole 'Stalinist' period, practices and ideas which were still in use.

The first stage[1]

By taking these basic decisions in 1962, the Party did indeed open the floodgates to demands and criticism which led ultimately to a revolu-

[1] The following is a brief summary of a period which was of utmost importance in the development of reform; further details may be found in subsequent chapters and the

tionary reform program. Starting with demands for renunciation of the Stalinist malpractices responsible for the trials, intellectuals, mainly Slovaks, subjected every sphere of Czechoslovak society to severe criticism, in the name of anti-dogmatism. Everything from the economic system and the social services, to the misrepresentations of T. G. Masaryk and Kafka in Communist histories, and the lack of contact with the West, came under fire.[1] Demands for change were made concerning almost every aspect of the prevailing model of socialism, including the dictatorship of the Party and the all-pervasive nature of political–class considerations.

Most of these complaints and demands came from Party members writing in a controlled press – particularly in the specialized organs of the intellectuals such as the Czechoslovak Writers Union weekly *Literární noviny*, the Slovak Writers Union weekly *Kultúrny život*, the Committee for Socialist Culture weekly *Kulturní tvorba*, and the writers' monthlies *Plamen* and *Host do domu*.[2] The many congresses of 1963, particularly of the Czechoslovak Writers Union, the Slovak Writers Union, and the Slovak Journalists Union provided ample platforms for these demands, subsequently carried by the unions' organs. Moreover, this criticism often appeared even in the Party press, such as the theoretical monthly *Nová mysl* (particularly during the liberal editorship of Čestmír Císař) and the Slovak Party daily, *Pravda*.[3] Thus de-Stalinization was a Party affair, a movement for reform from within, spearheaded by Party intellectuals; and as this drive gained momentum, one change led to another. For example, in response to pressures from the liberals, Novotný agreed to certain personnel changes: the old Stalinist, Karol Bacílek, who had played an active role in the purges of the Slovaks, was replaced as Slovak Party first secretary in April 1963 by the moderate-liberal Alexander Dubček.[4]

author's *The Czechoslovak Reform Movement: Communism in Crisis 1962–1968* (Cambridge, 1971).
[1] The following intellectuals were among those linked with this phenomenon: Eduard Goldstücker, Karel Kosík, Zora Jesenská, Ladislav Mňačko, Karol Rosenbaum, Radoslav Selucký, Jiří Šotola, Pavol Števček, Ladislav Szántó.
[2] *Kulturní tvorba* was taken over by the Party in August 1964 because of these articles.
[3] Even the Party daily, *Rudé právo*, carried an occasional critical sally, for example its editorial on 20 August 1963.
[4] The term 'liberal' is applied more or less arbitrarily to indicate views or persons favoring a liberalization or democratization of the system (as distinct from Liberalism); it is employed throughout interchangeably with the term 'reformer' or 'reformist' as well as the term 'progressive' which is used in Czechoslovakia.

·Along with Bacílek, Pavol David and Bruno Köhler were also demoted. Novotný opposed Dubček's appointment, favoring Michal Chudík instead. (*Kulturní tvorba*, 11 April 1968.)

Dubček in turn accorded the Slovak press and Party press a large degree of freedom, evoking public censure from Novotný in June 1963.[1] This liberal press-policy had led to the publication on 3 June 1963 of the speech delivered by journalist–professor (and former *Pravda* editor), Miroslav Hysko, to the Slovak Journalists' congress in May 1963. In this speech Premier Viliam Široký came under sharp attack for his role in the purges of Slovak Communists. Široký did not survive this attack, sanctioned as it was by its publication in the official Slovak Party organ. Three months later he and his government were forced to resign and he was replaced by another Slovak, Jozef Lenárt, who was then more acceptable to both Slovaks and liberals.

This was but one manifestation of the increasing momentum of the reform drive. Novotný himself was pressured not only to rehabilitate past victims (whose return to at least semi-public life in turn prompted still further demands) and to purge some of those responsible for past injustices, but also to agree to genuine reforms which would guarantee that such miscarriages of justice would not recur. That he felt threatened by this review of the past and still more threatened by the demands for reform was evidenced, however, by such things as his reluctance to fully rehabilitate the Slovak Communists (by thoroughly invalidating the charges of 'bourgeois nationalism' put against them) or his defense of his own past in the form of references to his own near-arrest in the 1950s.[2] By December 1963 he was so embattled that it seemed he was about to be toppled by the liberals. At this time Khrushchev sent Leonid Brezhnev to Prague in the interest of securing political stability, a precondition, as it were, for restoring the formerly dynamic economy. Brezhnev apparently saved the faltering dogmatist, possibly by arranging a compromise. Novotný stayed in office, but apparently on condition that he accede to some of the liberals' demands, permit de-Stalinization, and institute reforms aimed particularly at revitalizing the economy.[3] The nature of the compromise became apparent over the following two years as reforms were introduced in one sphere after another of Czechoslovak society.

The Stalinist-type command-economy was one of the institutions which warranted reform, according to liberal economists. They argued that while this system had, perhaps, been suitable to the first stage of 'extensive'

[1] *Rudé právo*, 13 June 1963 (speech at Košice, which Bratislava television refused to telecast at the last moment).

[2] *Der Stern*, 10 October 1963.

[3] The first sign was the December 1963 central committee decision finally invalidating the changes of Slovak 'bourgeois nationalism.' (*Rudé právo*, 29 January 1964.)

part of the complex of 'transmission belts' for the benefit of the state and the Party, were to be freed of supervision from above and the role of serving the regime, becoming real interest groups representing their members.[1] Student leader Jiří Müller went so far as to suggest that mass organizations be permitted an independent political role.[2]

A minor reform in the health system gave patients the right to choose their own doctors, even if they were located in another district.[3] The educational reform was much more significant, for it was conceived to eliminate a large number of Soviet-designed practices which had destroyed the once exemplary quality of the Czechoslovak educational system.[4] The overburdening of students through their obligation to work in 'youth brigades' or to attend political events or meetings was to be discontinued. Teachers' tasks were to be de-politicized and the qualifications of the teachers raised, in part by the abandonment of the cadre system. Textbooks were also to be de-politicized and subject matter and teaching methods were to be modernized. The structure of the schools was to be changed to permit gifted students to receive greater attention and earlier specialization. A 'differentiated' approach was to replace the Soviet-type 'unified' system. The humanities were to be restored to their rightful place in balance with the natural sciences. The basic schools were to be extended from eight to nine years, with greater demands placed on the last two years. The high schools were to be de-technicalized and there was to be a return of the pre-Communist-type gymnasia for university-bound students and a system of technical and vocational secondary schools for others.

At the higher educational level, reforms reintroduced entrance examinations and pre-Communist degree titles and eliminated the cadre system. As in the pre-Communist system, the rector was to be elected by secret ballot (and not appointed by the state), and students were to gain a seat in the ruling body of the university. Studies were to be de-politicized, the humanities reinstated, and teaching methods and teacher qualifications upgraded. Education was to be given greater priority in the allocation of funds, and wage differentials under the new economic system would, it was hoped, encourage students to continue their studies and gain better specialization or higher degrees.[5]

---

[1] *Rudé právo*, 4 February 1965 and *Práca*, 25 January 1966.
[2] *Student*, 26 January 1966.
[3] *Sbírka zákonů*, No. 20/1966.
[4] Čestmír Císař, 'School and Life,' *Socialistická škola*, V:4 (1964), 193–6 and *Rudé právo*, 24 October 1964.
[5] *Sbírka zákonů*, No. 19/1966 and *Rudé právo*, 1 June 1965.

There were also signs of de-Stalinization in the attitude toward religion. The imprisoned Archbishop and several other persecuted clerics were released, although forced to retire. The various religious groups were given slightly greater freedom to publish and instruct without prejudice to their adherents. Dialogues between the state and the major faiths, between Catholic and Protestant leaders, and within the Jewish community, were permitted, as was greater contact between Czechoslovak religious groups and their counterparts abroad. Even anti-religious propaganda and instruction was revised to make up for the moral gap it was admitted socialism had left in the forming of the youth.[1]

The cultural world, too, underwent reform. Without formally ridding themselves of the state censor, the intellectuals continuously expanded the boundaries within which they could publish. With the aid of Party liberals, the Czechoslovak press, radio and television became forums for the exchange of ideas and even bold criticism. The change was clearly felt in films and the theatre, and in several books, commencing with Mňačko's controversial *Delayed Reportages*, which began to appear alongside avant-garde poetry. A press law, passed in 1966 to protect some of these newly won freedoms, was designed to give editors a legal basis for complaints against censorship, though it fell short of the intellectuals' demands.[2]

The reform movement could not help but affect the political–governmental sphere as well. Reforms were introduced in the legal and judiciary systems designed to give defendants greater rights and protection; the all-powerful Soviet-type prosecutor-general was downgraded in favor of greater rights for the defense attorney. Qualifications were raised for all persons connected with the law, from investigators to judges, thus doing away with the former system under which one- and two-year crash-courses made Party hacks into 'lawyers.' Citizens were given greater recourse to the courts even for administrative matters, and the judicial system was reorganized to free investigating organs from political interference.[3]

The government itself was reformed to accommodate the economic reforms and to improve the quality and nature of its work. Government

---

[1] See for example, Vítězslav Gardovský, 'Marxism and Atheism,' *Věda a život*, 2 (1966), 67–70 or J. Krejčí, 'Criteria of Scientific–Atheist Education,' *Nová mysl*, XXI:8 (1967), 17–19.

[2] *Sbírka zákonů*, No. 81/1966.

[3] Through new civil and penal codes, new rules of administrative procedure, new laws on judges and lawyers, and a new public prosecution act.

organs, from the cabinet down to the locally elected National Committees, were given greater responsibility and independence – on the top level, independence from the Party; on the lower levels, from the center (by means of financial autonomy).[1] The Slovak government regained its cabinet and some of its former authority; the role of the Slovak Board of Commissioners and the rights of other Slovak organs were redefined and upgraded. The role of the National Assembly was revised somewhat: the committees of the Assembly (and of the Slovak National Council) were given greater powers to initiate laws, amend or return government-proposed laws, review the constitutionality of laws and decrees, supervise implementation of laws through hearings and requests for reports, and oblige government members to appear with regard to legislation under consideration.[2] A new election law was passed which offered a certain amount of choice at the nominating level and room for more candidates than positions on the ballot.[3]

In the political sphere, there were demands for changes as radical as those secured in the economic sector. If the economists wanted a market system, the more politically oriented wanted democracy. Reformers demanded a National Assembly composed of persons truly representative of the people and of the conflicting interests within society. Opposition should not only be permitted but institutionalized and protected by law. While most considered the idea of western-style political parties out-moded, it was argued that the various groups or social organizations in society could serve much the same purpose – without the pre-socialist aspect of parties as representative of class interests. Some believed it was the duty of the Communist Party to be above politics and the task of the government to harmonize the conflicting interests, and to protect the long-range goals of socialism, as a sort of arbitrator or ideological body. Thus while Communism would remain the goal, above opposition and protected by the Party, the road to Communism and the policies and methods within socialist society would be debatable and democratically decided.

Although these ideas were merely discussed, they provoked strong demands for an end to the Communist monopoly of power as provided for

[1] For this and following see, *Rudé právo*, 23 December 1965; 28 March 1964; 29 May 1964; *Sbírka zákonů*, No. 124/1964.
[2] There were even occasions when the Assembly amended or even returned government bills (Prague radio, 12 April 1965 and 9 February 1966); *Rol'nícke noviny*, 14 December 1966; *Mladá fronta*, 1 March 1967; *Lidová demokracie*, 3 February 1967.
[3] *Sbírka zákonů*, Nos. 113–14/1967.

in the Constitution. The Party, therefore, decided to sponsor and enlarge a committee of experts, which had originated in the Czechoslovak Academy of Sciences, to study possible reforms of the political system. This committee, according to its chairman, Zdeněk Mlynář, and its young secretary, Petr Pithart, was commissioned to make proposals regarding such issues as the electoral system, the formulation of political policies, the place of social engineering and sociology, the relations between man and institutions, the function of law and public opinion, nationalities problems, and the role of the Party in a socialist society. The starting-point for the study was the 'necessity to analyze social reality as far as the division into social and common interest groups is concerned, and...to propose the [most] suitable forms for the movement of society.' The committee was to take into consideration the development of other political systems, 'including the plurality of parties in the West.' Of primary interest would be the question of substantive guarantees for the democratic formulation of policy and civil rights. The objective was to be the formulation of a model for a 'socialist' Constitution – despite the fact that Czechoslovakia already had a 'socialist' Constitution, that of 1960.[1]

The crisis

All of these reforms or steps toward reform were achieved only with great difficulty and lengthy debate, particularly within the Party. Novotný himself was not in favor of them, but was pressured into accepting them. He sought to limit these hard-won measures, if for no other reason than that his power base within the Party lay with the conservatives, particularly those middle-level functionaries who had the most to lose by the reforms. In effect, Novotný sought to block implementation of the reforms or to restrict them so that they could not have the originally intended effect. Therefore, the movement suffered many setbacks, such as numerous shifts in the editorial boards of the outspoken journals; the removal of liberal Milan Hübl as pro-rector of the Party college; the expulsion from the university and drafting of rebellious student leader Jiří Müller in 1966; the suppression of certain avant-garde films such as Věra Chytilová's *Daisies* in 1966; and the dispatch of Čestmír Císař to Bucharest as Ambassador in the same year.

The difficulties began to mount in 1967, however, when it became evident that Novotný was returning to former methods, successfully blocking implementation of enacted reforms, and trying to stifle the

[1] *Rudé právo*, 6 July 1967 and *Student*, 27 September 1967.

reform drive. The most serious problem, perhaps, was that of the economic reforms, since they were the most urgently needed. Party conservatives had succeeded in adding so many compromise measures and restrictions to the reforms – in the name of smoothing the transition to the new system – that, in fact, it was difficult to say that the new system had been introduced at all. Liberal economists persisted in demanding that the new system be implemented without hindrances and subterfuges, and they insisted that this could only be done if the regime were willing to abandon some of its controls. This had been recognized as early as the thirteenth Party congress in May 1966 when the official architect of the economic reforms, Ota Šik, explained (to the express displeasure of Novotný) that effective implementation of the economic reforms could not be achieved without political reform.[1]

At the same time, the Slovaks, many of whom had neglected the reform movement after having achieved some of their basic, Slovak-oriented demands, were reawakened by Novotný's efforts to turn back the clock. His ill-timed, tactless reference to nationalism as 'bourgeois' and 'reactionary' stirred the Slovaks to demands for greater autonomy and implementation of the measures already approved to enlarge the role of the Slovak organs. They argued for a federal system, and, thus, they too accepted the formerly debated conclusion that only political reform, in their sense a new Constitution, could assuage their grievances.[2] The youth, too, felt stifled by the conservative tack taken by the regime both in its punitive actions against student leaders and in its refusal to permit genuine reform of the youth organization (evidenced at the June 1967 ČSM congress). Thus in November 1967, when Novotný resorted to brutal police tactics to break up a peaceful youth demonstration against poor conditions in the Strahov hostel in Prague, students responded with their own demands for thoroughgoing political reform.

After a series of setbacks for the intellectuals as well, for example the total lack of implementation of the Press Law, the suppression of the young writers' journal *Tvář*, at the end of 1965, the arrest of two young intellectuals, and the muzzling of the liberal journals with regard to the Israeli–Arab conflict (with overtones of anti-semitism reminiscent of the 1950s), the writers came to their fourth congress pessimistic and bitter.[3]

[1] *Rudé právo*, 5 June 1966 and *Kultúrny život*, 5 July 1968.
[2] For example, *Kultúrny život*, 5 May 1967 (Roman Kaliský) or Vladimír Mináč, 'Slovakia and its Economic Life,' *Slovenské pohľady*, 83:1 (1967), 36–8.
[3] Slovak writer Ladislav Mňačko journeyed to Israel in protest against the regime's policies, in which he saw symptoms of Novotný's efforts to turn the clock back.

Nonetheless, they resumed their campaign for liberalization begun four years earlier at their third congress, as speech after speech criticized the regime, urged reform, and even demanded constitutional change in the direction of real democracy.[1] Novotný's response was to expel three of the more outspoken intellectuals from the Party, and in September the government seized the Writers Union weekly *Literární noviny*.[2] The intellectuals responded by refusing to write for the government journal, and the Slovak Writers Union, albeit belatedly, expressed its solidarity by protesting to Party ideology chief, Jiří Hendrych.[3]

These pressures from the various groups interested in reform, together with the Party liberals' growing realization that Novotný had returned to former methods and that there was no possibility of real reform under his leadership, led to the dispute of the October and December 1967 central committee plena and achieved the replacement of Novotný at the January plenum.[4] Novotný tried at the last minute to retain his position by calling for Russian aid (rendered effectively in 1963) and by organizing military backing. The Russians, in the form of a Brezhnev trip to Prague on 8 December 1967, were not willing this time to bring the necessary pressures to bear. Misreading the nature of the dispute in the Czechoslovak Party, they saw it as a conflict over personnel which could be resolved satisfactorily only with the removal of Novotný, since the vast majority seemed to oppose him. Believing (as did the Czechoslovak public) that the *apparatchik* Novotný was not the impressive leader upon which the system might stand or fall, and personally not particularly inclined toward him, Brezhnev limited himself to a mild expression of support for Novotný (in the interest of continuity) and left the matter up to Prague.[5] Novotný's other efforts failed, thanks particularly to the chief of the Main Political Directorate of the Army, General Prchlík, who sided with the reformers.[6]

The reformers themselves were never a fixed group in the Party, but

Mňačko's departure was the source of much dispute, particularly among his fellow-Communist writers in Slovakia.

[1] *IV. Sjezd svazu československých spisovatelů* (Praha, 1968) carries all the speeches.
[2] Ivan Klíma, Antonín Liehm, and Ludvík Vaculík were expelled; Jan Procházka was deprived of his candidate membership in the central committee.
[3] *Kultúrny život*, 3 November 1967.
[4] The most authoritative accounts of these plena may be found in Mencl and Ouředník, 'What Happened in January,' *Život strany*, nos. 14–19 (1968) and Pavel Tigrid, *Why Dubček Fell* (London, 1971).
[5] Relations between Brezhnev and Novotný were reportedly cool since the latter's angrily expressed opposition to the manner in which Khrushchev's ejection was handled in 1964.
[6] For details, see 183–4

men of diverse leanings who, whether for pragmatic, idealistic, or Slovak nationalist reasons, saw that the system simply was not working, or was not producing the type of society they had envisaged or sought. Among the most persistent and earliest fighters for reform were Communist veterans František Kriegel and František Vodsloň, joined by economist (and till relatively late considered a Stalinist[1]) Ota Šik, and Josef Smrkovský. Ideologist Václav Slavík, Moravian leader Josef Špaček, and intellectual Eduard Goldstücker also played important roles in promoting the reform cause in the Party. There were such men as Martin Vaculík, Jozef Lenárt and Drahomír Kolder who at one time or another, for various reasons, lent at least partial support. Vaculík and Lenárt, however, rallied to Novotný at the crucial plena, when in fact many opportunists and others who had personal accounts to settle with Novotný joined the liberal forces. The reformers had no particular candidate with which to replace Novotný as first secretary. Their struggle had been one *against* Novotný, *for* a program, a new style of Party work and new approach to the country's problems. It was this that the Russians failed to understand (as, indeed, did many Czechs and Slovaks). The choice of Dubček was in fact a compromise. He had been partially raised in Russia and his loyalty and acceptability to Moscow was above question. He was a Slovak, which would serve to engage the dissident Slovaks, yet he believed that Slovak rights could be best guaranteed through democratic reform of the whole society; he had shown himself a friend of liberal intellectuals and reform philosophers in Slovakia, yet he was not a 'radical.' Though he was no friend of the dogmatists, he had never openly attacked them,[2] and his election would not *ipso facto* alienate that segment of the Party except insofar as he represented an approach that was alien to them. He was a moderate rather than a liberal who could answer the needs of the majority of the Party without, it seemed, too sharply alienating the minority. Indeed, some supported his appointment because they thought him weak and therefore 'controllable'; some conservatives even thought that the fact that he was a Slovak would make him unacceptable and possibly sabotage the entire effort to replace Novotný. Just how loyal Dubček was to the reform program was to be seen only later, just as the full significance of the January change was discovered by many only later.[3]

[1] By Löbl in *Kultúrny život*, 5 October 1963.   [2] Until the crucial October plenum.
[3] For views on Dubček's selection see also Josef Smrkovský, 'Democracy Doesn't Come Overnight,' *My 1968*, v:4 (1968), 5–8; *Kulturní noviny*, 29 March 1968 (Šik); Miroslav Kusý, 'The Czechoslovak Political Crisis,' *Nová mysl*, xxii:11 (1968), 1315–28; 'Moravus,' 'Shawcross' Dubček – A Different Dubček,' *Survey*, 17:4 (1971), 203–17.

A beginning

The 1963-7 period had been a preparatory period, a first stage and a breakthrough for a new way of thinking within the Party. It had, however, constituted a 'revolution from above.' Popular discontent was a factor which influenced the regime – both because of the pressures this dissatisfaction created (in the form of complaints and occasional work stoppages and demonstrations) and because of the lack of support for and therefore effort in fulfilling regime programs, specifically in the area of labor productivity. But the public at large took little active interest in this movement; the man in the street tended to look upon the whole thing as Party in-fighting likely to have little, perhaps even a negative, effect upon his life. The workers by and large failed to grasp the significance of the movement; they tended to see only that side of the economic reforms which might deprive them of security, and they evinced little interest in the rest of the reforms. The only non-Party group which might be considered an exception to the above was the youth, in particular the students, who quite early in the process apparently grasped what was afoot in the Party.

Thus, following a few weeks of near silent stock-taking and organization, the regime undertook its first major task; this was to mobilize the popular support necessary for the implementation of the promised but little-known new policies. While a Party committee formally began work (on 6 February 1968) on a new Party program, reformers such as Šik appeared on radio and television to explain their plans, and gradually the public began to comprehend the possibilities of the situation. By March of 1968, the reform movement assumed an entirely new character. What had been almost a purely Party affair became a public cause, and the people with increasing confidence began to exert pressure to ensure fulfillment of the Party's promises. The 'focal point' shifted to the masses who, through spontaneous action, forced the regime's hand on a number of measures, converting the 'revolution from above' into a mass movement.

Few personnel changes were instituted in the beginning, probably out of a desire to create a minimum of dislocations and avoid an aura of purge. The Party presidium was supplemented by liberals Josef Špaček and Josef Borůvka, and men believed, at the time, to be at least moderates: Emil Rigo and Jan Piller. Vasil Bilak, Dubček's ideological chief in Slovakia, became Slovak first secretary, possibly because Dubček believed he could trust him because of his record of opposition to Novotný.[1]

---

[1] The Slovak presidium was expanded by three new members (Pecho, Harenčár, and Hruškovič).

By early spring, growing public demands led to more significant re-shuffling and indeed, a wave of resignations finally took place.[1] Most notable of these was the resignation of Novotný from his post as President on 22 March 1968 and the formation of a new government on 8 April 1968.

While the conversion to a mass movement greatly accelerated and to a large degree radicalized the liberalization process, it did not significantly alter the basically legalistic, methodical, institution-directed socialist thrust of the reform movement. Indeed, there were even complaints about this traditional Czech preoccupation with legality when it dictated tolerance of the continued presence of conservatives in the Party organs.[2] Dubček, however, was not willing to use illegal or undemocratic means to secure the democratic society he sought, and for this reason the convening of an extraordinary Party congress became one of the most pressing political issues of the spring. It was only at a congress that the Party could elect a new central committee and thereby secure the solid pro-reform majority needed for the tasks at hand. Another device considered, so as to avoid purges and arbitrary appointments, was the creation of a Czech Party (authorized as part of the new federalization plans), so as to counter the feet-dragging of some members of the reform regime. This, too, became a political issue, though it remained unresolved in 1968.

Aside from the specifically Slovak aspect, the movement-become-regime remained, as before, non-nationalistic, domestically oriented and pro-Soviet. In time, however, interference from the Soviet Union did become an issue, and the regime was forced increasingly to emphasize Czechoslovakia's specific conditions, as the fears of certain other socialist countries threatened to put a stop to this creation of a new model for socialism. The movement clearly went beyond the measures envisaged by the reform regime, which did indeed try to restrain the process, but it also created a degree of enthusiasm for socialism – albeit of a specific variety – unprecedented in Eastern Europe.

[1] Novotný's security chief, Miroslav Mamula, however, was replaced by Prchlík on 19 February 1968.

[2] Referred to by *Pravda* editor, Prague radio, 4 February 1968; Smrkovský, *Rudé právo*, 4 April 1968; and *Literární listy*, 30 May 1968, 11 July 1968, and 8 August 1968.

2

The Economy

The economic reforms, although an integral and crucial part of the Czechoslovak experiment, were not the major subject of debate in the eight months of the 'revival.' These reforms had already been mapped out in great detail, discussed and debated extensively in the previous period, and it had been recognized in the closing months of 1967 that basically what was needed was not a still newer program of economic reform but implementation of the one originally proposed. Moreover the reformers had concluded that no significant progress could be made in economic reform without prior political reform. There were, however, discussions as to improvements or changes in the economic reform program once the reformers came to power. In one area the new suggestions and revisions were designed to assure enterprise independence, and included changes in the organization of industry as envisioned by the pre-1968 reform and in foreign trade. In another area the new suggestions were designed to provide a greater role for the workers in the management of enterprises, i.e. some type of workers councils.

Demands for change in the reform

The major elements of the economic reforms were reviewed, on a number of open platforms such as radio and television in addition to the previously used specialized economic journals and Party organs, with an eye towards the revival of the spirit of the reformers' program. Together with declarations on the need for swift, thorough, and genuine implementation of the reform, those elements of the reform most connected with the idea of democratization were increasingly singled out.[1] It was repeatedly pointed

---

[1] See Dubček's speeches at the collective farm congress or his anniversary speech, 22 February 1968 (*Rudé právo*, 23 February 1968) or Šik (*Rudé právo*, 19 March 1968) or Černík (*Rudé právo*, 15 March 1968). Černík was relatively slow to admit the past failures (*viz.* his 22 March 1968 speech: 'we can state today that the results of 1966–7 indicate the unambiguously improving trends in the national economy.' *Práce*, 23 March 1968). Černík's role as a conservative brake on the economic reform program was noted by the National Assembly committee for plan and budget, despite Černík's recent switch to the liberals, in its 26–27 March 1968 meeting. (ČTK, 27 March 1968.)

out that the market could not work if there were not genuine enterprise independence which would permit greater responsibility and, therefore, initiative for the enterprise, as well as the sink-or-swim element, so necessary if the market were to determine the fate of an enterprise. There were those, such as Slovak economist Eugen Löbl, who had long been criticizing the new economic model for its organization of the economy into associations and trusts, i.e. basically monopolistic units which restricted the freedom of enterprise and of the market. Löbl continued this line of argument, favoring an end to monopolies and the creation of a market of competing enterprises. In order for plants to be competitive, he maintained (on Bratislava television, 21 March 1968), they would have to be independent to the extent of receiving the profits they earned and bearing their own losses, even to the point of closure. If economic criteria were thus to operate, enterprise independence should be further ensured by permitting enterprises to amalgamate or separate according to economic, rather than administrative, demands. If this were taken to its logical conclusion, one must permit the founding of small enterprises, preferably private, the flexibility and speedy adaptability of which were suitable for such spheres as hand-production, maintenance, repair shops, crafts and services. Löbl estimated that some 250 000 such smaller enterprises were needed to encourage craftsmanship and stimulate competition in the services, for example. Other economists, for example those interviewed by the journalists' weekly *Reportér* on 17 December 1966, had already made similar suggestions. Šik, however, expressed his opposition.[1]

Löbl maintained that an obstacle to the competitive market he envisaged was the concept of specialization which predominated in Czechoslovakia, i.e. the idea of one enterprise, one product. He pointed out in *Kultúrny život* of 9 February 1968 that Philips produced a whole range of products from refrigerators to television sets and even the old Baťa shoe company had produced a whole range of rubber products and operated their own export–import firms. Enforced specialization provided a measure of restriction on the enterprise, limiting it as to what it could or could not produce no matter what the enterprise directors' own economic calculations or initiative. A second, and presumably more critical, obstacle, according to Löbl, was the association directorate or management board devised by Šik. This in Löbl's eyes was nothing but 'superfluous,' a 'bulky bureaucratic...administrative barrier' which hampered development. Arguing that every cooperative, including consumer cooperatives, should be an independent enterprise, Löbl asserted that there should be

[1] *Zemědělské noviny*, 28 February 1967.

no central management. If so desired, enterprises could establish 'superior organizations' to handle such things as wholesale purchasing, market research and so forth, but these organizations should play no role in management. Rather than an organ of the ministries, as the association directorates had become under the new system, 'this higher organization would be an organ of the enterprises in their dealings with the ministries.'

A third obstacle to enterprise independence and, therefore, to a competitive market, according to Löbl, was the foreign trade monopoly. While in the pre-1968 reforms direct enterprise participation in foreign trade had been urged, the furthest the reformers had gotten in this area was the decision announced in December 1966 to create joint-stock companies of producers together with foreign trade enterprises, and to permit limited foreign currency bonuses for certain plants (and collective farms).[1] Even joint-stock companies still prevented independent enterprise decisions on what the enterprise need import and what it would export, and they still shielded the enterprise from the pressures of the world market. Therefore, both Löbl and Šik urged direct enterprise-to-enterprise foreign trading.[2] Other economists also pointed out that the use of four different exchange rates, or the lack of a 'realistic' exchange rate or a convertible currency, was also a barrier between the enterprise and world market.[3]

Many argued in favor of enterprise independence, some directly criticizing the association directorate system, others referring more vaguely to carry-overs from the former directive system and the need for changes in institutions.[4] The consumer cooperatives voiced their agreement with these objections by passing a resolution at the 27–28 March 1968 session of the central committee of the Union of Consumer Cooperatives. The resolution approved 'the principle that consumer cooperatives should become independent specialized organizations' and demanded 'the elimination of the distorting interference by state organs in the retail network, in wholesale trade, and in producer cooperatives.'[5] Šik himself favored the idea of enterprise independence and, as in the past, he argued that the criticism was directed against a distortion of rather than the original idea he had had in mind for the association–trust

---

[1] *Sbírka zákonů*, Nos. 125–7/1967 authorized the creation of three such companies, set up in 1968.
[2] *Kulturný život*, 9 February 1968; *Zemědělské noviny*, 28 February 1968.
[3] *Predvoj*, 8 February 1968 or Šik at 20 March 1968 rally.
[4] See for example Jan Lipavský in *Reportér*, 10 January 1968, or *Rudé právo*, 15 March 1968.
[5] Bratislava radio, 29 March 1968. The Union's central committee also passed a no-confidence vote regarding Interior Trade Minister Jindřich Uher.

system. Šik argued that his original proposal had been based on the assumption that the government ministries would not be a part of the system of management via the associations or trusts. He had been unable, however, to have his original ideas of enterprise independence included and the 'Principles' of the new system published in 1964 specified the associations and trusts (with their directorates) as links between the enterprises and the central (government) organs. In 1968 Šik bemoaned the 'rigid, monopolistic system' and urged that enterprises be free to organize in associations or trusts, or to remain 'under certain economic circumstances [unspecified] independent.'[1]

Šik blamed mainly the state and the economic institutions for the failure of the system to work as he had planned. His original intention had been that the ministries should concentrate on legislation relevant to their fields and refrain from making economic policy. The problem, he explained to the 20 March 1968 Prague rally, was that the government ministries were in themselves giant monopolies, 'conglomerations of departmental interests,' so that, on the one hand, they were not subject to economic criteria and, on the other, unable to direct and implement economic policy. What was needed, in Šik's view, was some central economic authority. This 'policy center' would direct national economic policy, through economic measures, in the interests of protecting the consumer and stimulating competition. In the reforms proposed in 1964, the central organs were to be responsible for long-range planning, certain national economic questions (major investments), regulation of competition, market prognosis and so forth.[2] These functions fell into the category of policy-making so that the innovation in the 1968 suggestion would appear to have been the transfer of these functions from the various ministries to one central body. Presumably the brief but disappointing experience of 1967 had revealed the need for a still more basic institutional change if the habits of the directive economy were to be changed, the enterprise freed, and the market permitted to function; the existing institutional structure had been proven unable to adapt itself to the spirit of the new system.

'Democratization of the economy' was to be applied within the enter-

---

[1] *Zemědělské noviny*, 28 February 1968.

[2] Originally Šik had agreed that the central organs should fix wage categories or limitations. In the 26 February talk, however, he urged the removal of limitations on wages and acceptance of the idea that wages would vary between enterprises, presumably because of the regime's attempts in 1967 to curb wage increases resulting from unexpected increases in profits.

The economy

prises, as well, in the form of greater worker participation in management. The idea had been raised in earlier years, specifically for Yugoslav-type workers councils or a return to the 1945–8 Czechoslovak works council (factory committees). Yet these ideas had been rejected as premature for the then current state of the economy.[1] The nucleus for some worker–management body had been created in the form of production committees, which were gradually to receive a certain voice in the administration of the enterprise, but the pre-1968 program had not specifically envisaged autonomy for these bodies. If, however, the workers' fate were dependent upon management's production decisions, it was natural that they should demand an effective voice.

Šik attacked the former system of selecting managers, arguing that it was impossible for a central body or a ministry to select a manager. He urged that representatives of workers, together with specialists (from institutes of learning and research, or banks) decide on managers, 'in a public selection procedure' (presumably elections in the enterprise). As envisaged by Šik, elected employees of the enterprise would sit on a collective organ *superior* to the enterprise itself, at a ratio of, perhaps, 1/3 workers to 2/3 outside specialists, and this organ would have the power to recall and appoint managers. He did not at this early stage, however, specify what other, if any, functions this body would have.

Earlier statements, in particular by Dubček himself, indicated that there was thinking in the direction of factory councils similar to those of the 1945–8 period, i.e. an elected, autonomous, legal body which would supervise the economic activity of the enterprise and participate in its administration. Calling for a democratization of economic administration, Dubček said on the 22 February 1968 anniversary:

'At long last we will also have to consistently implement the innumerable resolutions proclaiming the expansion of the working people's share in the actual administration of the economy. In this respect *we may draw valuable suggestions from the experience which our revolution gained in the years between 1945 and 1948* but which was forgotten in the following years.'

On the same occasion trade union chief Miroslav Pastyřík was even more explicit, revealing that the dissolution of the earlier factory councils was now considered a mistake. He admitted that these councils could hardly have continued to function effectively under the directive system intro-

[1] See for example Margita Piščová, 'About Some Problems of Transferring Certain State Functions to the Trade Union Organizations,' *Právnické štúdie*, XIII:4 (1965), 580–615.

duced by the Communists, but with the change in circumstances the production committees and the trade union enterprise committees might provide vehicles to worker participation in management.[1] While Pastyřík emphasized already existing institutions such as the production committees, his reference to the 1945–8 factory councils was an indication of the regime's thinking on the subject.

Demands for inner-enterprise democracy in agriculture were also raised, particularly at one of the dramatic events of the early days of the revival: the seventh congress of the cooperative farms (JZD). This congress, which took place in Prague from 1 to 3 February 1968, offered the first broad official podium for the new regime; it offered Dubček his first real opportunity for an 'inaugural' address, and the first occasion for an organization to test, officially and concretely, the reality of the promising atmosphere. The results were indeed encouraging as evidenced by the frank and critical contributions of the participants, and the rewriting, in an all-night session, of the congress resolution ending in a bold statement of the farmers' demands.[2] The congress resolved that democracy should be established within the JZDs, meaning, as was explained in a 16 February radio discussion with cooperative farmers, that members of collectives have the right freely to elect or recall their chairmen. The congress also sought full legal and economic independence for the collective farmer.[3]

Both these demands were connected with the reforms envisaged for agriculture under the new system of management and, in particular, the *organization* of agriculture under this system. Collective farms were to have received autonomy under the reforms – at least insofar as planning their own production and deliveries according to the market, based on contracts. Organizationally something similar to the association–trust system for industry had been set up for agriculture in the form of district agricultural associations (DAA). Autonomy had been merely illusory, however, for the DAAs, like the association management system in industry, were merely vehicles for a continuation of the former system of central control, previously administered through the agricultural production administrations (APA). While the DAAs were to have been voluntary, and were intended to be organs of the farmers and not of the government,

---

[1] *Práce*, 22 February 1968. The role of the trade unions will be discussed below.

[2] Prague radio, 3 February 1968. Atypical of the atmosphere of the congress was the banning of newsmen from the sessions. Slovak agricultural journalists later publicly held Agricultural Minister Karel Mestek responsible for this ban. (Bratislava radio, 26 March 1968.)

[3] Bratislava radio, 3 February 1968; Prague radio, 2 February 1968. The resolution also called for an agricultural union, discussed below.

here as in industry the habits of the old system had proved too strong. Moreover, the functioning of the market was even more seriously limited in agriculture than in industry, not only by the bureaucratic function of the DAA, but by restrictions, exceptions, and 'temporary measures,' such as subsidies, grants, taxes, and redistribution to help weaker farms, which had appeared even as part of the reform. The most serious obstacle to market-directed autonomy was, however, the continuation of the purchasing agencies – monopolistic bureaucratic units which stood between the farmer and the market. Alongside this monopoly, the monopoly on supplies and services for agriculture had also continued.

The resolution of the farmers' congress also included a demand for the same rights as those enjoyed by industrial workers, specifically in the realm of social security. Another issue, raised by Dubček himself, was that of the status and rights of the private sector in agriculture. The over 400 000 people involved in this sector, generally ignored by the regime and operating under severe handicaps, were recognized by Dubček at the congress as allies of the working class 'to whose needs we should pay attention.'[1] The type of attention which might be accorded this sector was outlined in an article which appeared, simultaneously with the congress, in *Predvoj*, the weekly of the Slovak Party central committee. It suggested that the system of state bonuses, as applied to state and collective farms, should be introduced in the private sector as well, perhaps in the form of tax reliefs, as a reward for farming unfertile land. Other forms of aid were suggested to ensure reinvestment so that this land would not go fallow. Investments could be stimulated through cheap credit and subsidies for construction; the state might assist in soil conservation schemes, road building, construction of buildings (or common use of buildings by whole villages or hamlets); boundary lines might be adjusted so that the private farmer's plots would be contiguous and not scattered hectares from each other. Another suggestion was to accord the private farm equal status with the JZD regarding such things as prices for machinery and repairs and to facilitate services for the private farmers, for example, by setting up repair and sale of second-hand machinery centers for them. Indeed, it was proposed that the JZDs should play a role in helping private farmers to increase production and to raise the level of their education. Finally, it was demanded, that just as collective farmers should receive the same social and health benefits as industrial workers, so too the private farmers, who hithertofore had been in a disadvantaged position with regard to health insurance, family allowances,

[1] Bratislava radio, 1 February 1968.

old-age pensions and the like. One concrete suggestion for aid to private farming was a plan to combine private farms with tourist facilities, the state helping to build such units. As early as the spring of 1968 the East Bohemian regional National Committee actually financed some seventy units in the Krkonese mountains to be leased to experienced farmers for this purpose.[1]

This attention to the private sector of agriculture was a notable innovation, for the economic reforms had almost entirely neglected this sector. Indeed agriculture itself had failed to receive as much attention in Šik's plans as industry, having been left for a later review despite the recognized fact that this was the weakest sector in the sagging Czechoslovak economy. The reforms which finally did appear for agriculture in 1966 had been marked by significant restrictive characteristics similar to those introduced in industry and so were repugnant to the spirit of the reforms. The task in agriculture, as in industry, was to eliminate the obstructionist measures introduced by the conservatives and so revise the original reforms as to ensure their implementation in the spirit originally envisaged by the reformers.

Enterprise independence and the market

The Party's new program, the Action Program, called for an end to 'administrative' measures and the measures restricting the implementation of the economic reforms.[2] It condemned the practice of 'perpetuating economic backwardness, together with pricing policies, subsidies, grants, and, most important of all, the system of surcharges in foreign trade' and the 'immense network of protectionism,' calling it 'senseless to paralyze an economic policy forever by taking things away from those who work efficiently and giving them to those who manage poorly.' The Action Program further asserted that 'enterprises confronted with a demanding market must be granted the freedom to decide on all problems concerning the immediate management of the enterprise and its operation, and they must be enabled to react in a creative manner to the demands of the market.' It specifically asserted that enterprises had the right to choose

[1] Prague radio, 10 February 1968. Each unit was to contain a three-room apartment plus 15 beds for tourists; sheds for 15 cows and a pigsty for 2 pigs; 20–28 hectares of meadows; and sufficient mechanization for a family of three to run. Each unit would make an annual payment of 60 000 crowns to the state after the initial year. The monthly income per unit was estimated at 1700–2000 crowns per person (as compared to 1200 per capita in the JZDs and 1600 in industry).
[2] The Action Program was published in *Rudé právo*, 10 April 1968.

their 'organizational allegiance.' Supra-enterprise organs, i.e. the association directorate, could not be organs of the state or the central authorities. Moreover, enterprises should have the right to group or regroup voluntarily, on the basis of their own economic interests.

The Party program stipulated, however, that the new policy of voluntary association should not be implemented until the government had set up appropriate regulations, so as to avoid the possible chaos of immediate departures from existing associations or trusts, or disruption of scheduled production. It was presumably this fear which prompted the new Premier, Černík, in his address to the National Assembly on 24 April 1968, to suggest that 'technical–economic efficiency' be used as a criterion for reorganization. The danger in such a proposal, however, was that it presumed once again some central determining factor and, therefore, determining body to regulate changes. Moreover, it would seem that such a criterion could be applied only *after* the economy had been rationalized according to the economic reform, i.e. finally based on market-determined economic values – something which admittedly was prevented by the very monopolistic organization of the economy. Even Šik, however, could see a certain danger in uncontrolled freedom to regroup or leave the existing associations. On Prague radio, 7 May 1968, he made known his fears of the possibility that successful component members of larger associations might wish to achieve autonomy in order to preserve their privileged position at the expense of other enterprises within an otherwise integrated production unit. Šik had long asserted that the disruption of 'rationalization' caused by freedom (whether of prices, operational decisions, or otherwise) would be offset and remedied by the logical functioning of the market. Here, however, he was faced with the possibility of an enterprise going under (because of economic pressures) as a result of an injustice. Šik's hesitation on this point bordered on recommending a policy of protecting weaker enterprises, at least if they were the result of a splitting off by their more successful components. Indeed the government did decide to limit this freedom by the establishment of criteria in the vein suggested by Černík. Organizational changes were to be permitted 'only if the independence of an enterprise results in improved conditions for economic competition, increased contribution to national revenue, and more effective participation in the international division of labor. Organizational changes must not lead to one-sided advantages at the cost of existing regional groupings or enterprises.'[1] Šik later asserted that any regrouping should be reviewed and considered by

[1] Prague radio (English), 26 April 1968.

all the enterprises in the association concerned, as well as by outside experts from, for example, the banks, government or trade unions.[1] Černík maintained, however, that the relevant ministry, with advice from independent experts including those of the unions, would make the final decision in the case of a dispute.[2]

These restrictions at least presumed economic rather than administrative criteria for association, even if full independence from the central authorities were not achieved. More important, the association or trust itself was to have a different function and character. Even before the Action Program, Černík explained in *Rudé právo* of 15 March that the 'relations of subordination and superiority...including the personal dependence of directors of enterprises on the superior organs' would have to be changed. Both the Action Program and the government session of 12 April 1968 affirmed that the organs of the associations or trusts would no longer be organs of the government but representatives or organs of the enterprises which more or less voluntarily composed them; they were not to be linked to the central organs, nor were they to interfere in the management of the enterprises.

This new character and function evolved from the new role envisaged for the government in the economy, and, as the idea of enterprise independence vis-à-vis the government became more certain, to retain the associations and trusts as organizational units became superfluous. The draft enterprise bill prepared in the first half of 1968, but presented by the government only in January 1969 (and never passed), provided explicitly for enterprise autonomy, at least organizationally, abolishing the trusts and associations, and with them the association directorates. The draft bill provided for three types of enterprises: social, public (state), and those based on shares. The social enterprise was described as 'an autonomous unit, managed within the framework of state economic policy, *exclusively* by the enterprise council and the director with his team of executives.'[3] The enterprise council and director would be 'exclusively responsible' for the management of the enterprise and 'for all its obligations towards its business partners, both at home and abroad.' The public or state enterprises, on the other hand, would be neither self-supporting nor autonomous. Responsibility for management would lie with the state or in certain cases the National Committees. These enterprises would be founded (by the state or National Committees) for such services as communica-

[1] ČTK, 25 May 1968.   [2] Prague radio, 24 April 1968.
[3] *Zemědělské noviny*, 31 January 1969 or *Rudé právo*, 21 February 1969. Enterprise councils and 'share' enterprises will be discussed below.

tions, railways, roads, waterways, and so forth. Thus production enterprises fell into the social enterprise category which presupposed a new role for the government in the economy.

According to the Action Program, the government would be limited, as originally envisaged by the reforms, to general economic policy, long-term planning, and protecting the consumers' (not the producers') interests. To do this without suppressing the various actors on the market, specifically the enterprises, a reorganization of the government's economic organs was introduced, the purpose of which was to limit the power of the economic ministries by subordinating them to an all-over economic policy board. At the same time, enterprise autonomy was to be maintained by limiting the board to economic rather than administrative instruments only.[1] Thus on 12 April 1968 the government created a National Economic Council, to be chaired, surprisingly, by Lubomír Štrougal, rather than Ota Šik.[2] A supra-ministerial organ, it would prepare government decisions on fundamental questions of the national economy, particularly in the areas of planning, budget, currency, and large-scale investments.[3] In other words it was to be responsible for the macro-aspects of the economy.

While it would appear contradictory to establish still another central organ in what was supposed to be a drive to limit central control, the logic of the move was to remove the various (and numerous) economic ministries from policy decisions, and to provide a measure of control over the powerful monopolies which these ministries constituted. In keeping with this, a government reorganization of 25 April 1968 provided for the coordination of the economic ministries by the Economic Council. It also abolished the former supra-ministerial commissions and created four new ministries: one for economic planning, one for technology, one for labor and social affairs, and one for prices (State Price Office). The reorganization did not, however, reduce the number of ministries, and such a measure continued to be urged.[4]

[1] Dubček's reiterated promises, in addition to those of the Action Program itself, to provide a complete renewal of the market and to eliminate the distortions that had entered the reforms in 1966–7, suggested that economic levers would not be once again misused.
[2] Štrougal was Novotný's Interior Minister in 1961–5 and head of the Party's economic commission. It was rumored that the more conservative Černík rejected Šik. Šik became Deputy Premier responsible for the economic reforms, however. (Prague radio, 16 April 1968.)
[3] ČTK, 12 April 1968.
[4] See, for example, *Pravda* (Bratislava), 3 May 1968 or *Rudé právo*, 3 July 1968.

Smrkovský explained in an interview with the Yugoslav paper *Borba* on 2 April 1968, that 'ministries would not be in command of the enterprises and their work,' rather enterprises and ministries were to be 'equal partners,' eliminating any attitude of superior and subordinate. The ministries would no longer be permitted to appoint management bodies or enterprise directors. Thus the ministries would be limited in interfering on an operational level, while subordinate to the Economic Council on the policy level. In regard to the jurisdiction of the state for the fixing of prices and wages, the Action Program clearly stated that 'rational price relations cannot be established and laid down by the state authority; one must give free rein to the influence of market forces in determining them.' This having been said, however, the Program went on to qualify that 'the central organs of management, while giving the necessary freedom of movement to internal prices, must regulate general economic relations to prevent an unprofitable rise of the price level and also to ensure a growth in real wages of at least 2.5 to 3 per cent per year.' The whole issue of prices and wages and the government's role must, however, be seen in the perspective of the first year of the new economic system. Inflationary trends had begun to appear, prompting accusations that the flexible price and wage policy of the new system was responsible. Šik retorted that the cause of the unfavorable trends was the fact that prices had *not* been reformed and freed, and that the numerous supplementary measures such as subsidies had so restricted the market mechanism that one could hardly speak of flexible prices or even flexible wages.

These problems of inflation and labor productivity, and so forth, had already been extensively debated in the pre-1968 period;[1] of interest to us here is whether or not the 1968 revival period saw any revision of the reform program with regard to the role of the center in determining wages and prices. The Action Program promised the elimination of protectionism and subsidies, in accord with the reform principles, and almost all government and Party statements claimed that the role of the market was to be strengthened so that prices and wages would be determined by supply and demand. The question raised, however, was that of the role to be played by the government in the formulation of economic policy, i.e. was the state plan to guide or merely follow market-determined relations. This was, in fact, the central question of the economic reform, for this issue of the plan and the market was crucial to almost every element of the reform, from prices and wages to enterprise independence and investments. Šik's program had mapped out the role of the

[1] See, for example, Klaus and Ježek in *Kulturní tvorba*, 15 December 1966.

31

central organs, but even so the role of the market in all-over planning was never entirely clear, and the creation of the National Economic Council did not clarify the issue.

One reform member of the government, Education Minister Vladimír Kadlec, explained the relationship of the plan to the market thus: the central organs, in the form of the plan, would determine the basic structure of the economy, i.e. the preference for consumer or industrial production. With this plan acting as an orientation guide, prices and the production of specific goods would be determined by the consumer through the market.[1] Šik, however, opposed the *a priori* fixing of structure or orientation and argued that one must move from the 'micro' to the 'macro,' i.e. follow the market entirely.[2] Economic Planning Minister František Vlasák also favored the liberalization of prices and the strengthening of the market (in *Rudé právo* of 21 June 1968), but several reservations were raised. In order to protect the consumer, certain 'rules of competition' would have to be worked out, such as legislation regarding advertising and so forth.[3] In addition to this, some control would have to be maintained to prevent inflation, and this through fiscal, credit, investments and wage policy.[4]

This last attitude towards control was indeed the one adopted in the Party program, for the effect freeing prices would have on wages was feared. Thus the Action Program concluded that while

'prices will be primarily the result of direct negotiations between trade and production enterprises...it will also be necessary to introduce effective central price control to prevent the free movement of prices from unfavorably affecting the population's living standard. The central agencies must plan the price level for sufficiently large groups of products, and must set the development of prices with a tolerance such that individual prices may react fairly to the market.'

The Action Program went on to stipulate that only the prices of 'the specific standards of certain basic needs' could be centrally set, but, for the rest, the central authorities should control prices only indirectly, i.e. through economic instruments. Unfortunately, some of the economic instruments referred to included subsidies to reduce prices – despite

---

[1] Cited in Harry Trend, 'Pre-August Trends in Czechoslovak Economic Organization and Policy – III,' RFE, 18 November 1968, 14.

[2] Prague radio, 20 May 1968 (speech to Czechoslovak Economic Association).

[3] *Noviny vnitřního obchodu,* 26 April 1968.

[4] State Price Office director Václav Hůla, ČTK, 4 June 1968.

the fact that the Action Program itself urged an end to the use of subsidies.

In early August 1968 the government issued a price directive outlining criteria for the retail and wholesale price changes designed to prepare the economy for the successful functioning of the market.[1] The new prices were to be determined primarily by the market, but they were also to be set so as to encourage the desired structural change. Although this was to be a once-for-all administrative change of prices, the directive did stipulate certain principles for pricing, generally: prices should be determined by supply and demand; price relations should reflect the technical and qualitative level of the product; and 'unwarranted' differentiation in profitability should be eliminated. This did not mean, however, that there was to be no profitability differentiation; indeed it was stipulated that the system of redistribution of profits to help weaker enterprises was to be abolished. World prices were to provide the upper limits for the domestic price levels, and the proportion between the three price categories (free, limited, fixed) was to be adjusted. Thus the free price category was to be increased to roughly 23 per cent (instead of the then current 6 per cent of all commodities), the limited category 55 per cent instead of the current 59 per cent, and the fixed category approximately 21 per cent instead of 35 per cent. The desired result was to be greater price flexibility, and price subsidies (as well as other obstacles to the play of the market such as the differentiated turnover tax) were to be gradually eliminated.

The general thrust of the Action Program, and of government pronouncements thereafter, was in the direction of freeing or strengthening the role of the market. It is in this light that one must see the pronouncements favoring enterprise independence, the end of producer and supplier monopolies, and the expansion of competition on the domestic market. This last goal, it was suggested, might be achieved in several ways, from creation of small enterprises to increased imports and changes in foreign trade organization and policy. With regard to small enterprises, the Action Program stated that one must envisage the creation of small and medium-sized enterprises 'primarily for the purpose of supplementing the range of production with a view toward the rapid enrichment of the market.' Room should be made for 'economic competition,' the Program continued, 'among enterprises of all kinds and forms of business, in the first place in the sphere of production and the sale of consumer goods and food products.' Specifically referring to the form of ownership envisaged, the Program asserted that 'small private enterprises are also justified in the

[1] See *Hospodářské noviny*, 9 August 1968.

sphere of services' and recommended that legal provisions be worked out for 'small-scale enterprises designed to fill the present gap in our market.' A commission for small-scale enterprises was subsequently set up under the chairmanship of Eugen Löbl, and proposals were worked out for presentation in August or September.

One of the problems encountered in earlier (1964) attempts to permit private enterprise, on a very limited scale, in the service sector, was the large degree of skepticism and fear on the part of prospective private owners. People would have to be convinced that they would not risk political or economic discrimination (higher purchase prices, taxes, etc.). That people would be willing and probably able to enter such businesses if these objective factors were acceptable, was demonstrated by the fact that 'moonlighting' had existed on a relatively lucrative basis for many years – throughout Eastern Europe. Löbl pointed out in the youth daily *Mladá fronta* of 19 June 1968, that the creation of private enterprises would permit the government to benefit from this formerly illegal and, therefore, tax-free business; it would encourage handicrafts and artisanry, and most important, it would help create a market which satisfied the demands of the consumer. The Löbl commission envisaged several types of private enterprises, the most radical of which would permit the hiring of more than six employees. The draft enterprise bill did indeed provide for an enterprise based on shares, which might be established as a 'common-interest enterprise to cover the needs of its founders, who may be any body corporate, the precondition being permission issued by the relevant bodies.'[1] All responsibility would rest with the founders, who would share in both the management *and results*, proportionately to their share in the investment. The tax laws were to be adjusted to accommodate such enterprises. Few details are available on this type of enterprise, but it would appear to provide the possibility of private enterprises envisaged by the Löbl commission as a part of the general category of small-scale enterprises. One must not exaggerate the private nature of ownership of these enterprises. While Löbl foresaw some 250 000 such enterprises, the total probably would not have exceeded the number of private enterprises existing in neighboring Poland. The important factor was the recognition of the fact that large enterprises were not the only valid approach to production, that there was a place and indeed a need for a variety of sizes of enterprise and forms of production even in a modern socialist economy.

[1] *Zemědělské noviny*, 31 January 1969.

Foreign trade

Competition on the domestic market was to be achieved not only by permitting producer competition in the market and the breaking-up of monopolies, but also by the linking of the domestic market to the world market. The Action Program strongly urged 'submitting our economy to the pressure of the world market,' for the reasons expressed by the reform economists and even the regime so many times before, i.e. to raise the technological level of domestic products, to improve the balance of trade, to bring domestic prices in line with world prices and achieve a convertible currency. The original reforms had proclaimed just this aim of improving domestic production by the introduction of an element of pressures for meeting world standards; it remained, however, to overcome the obstacles which stood in the way of implementation of this goal.

Reforms in the sphere of foreign trade concerned three issues: organization of foreign trade; prices and the achievement of convertible currency; and orientation of trade. The Action Program accepted the reformers' demand for an end to the foreign trade monopolies, first by permitting enterprises to choose the export–import firm (presumably from amongst the new joint-stock companies[1]) they wished to use, and, secondly, by permitting the enterprises to 'act independently on foreign markets.' As it had been agreed that all bureaucratic obstacles standing between the producer and the consumer, whether domestic or foreign, must be eliminated if the market were to operate positively, this organizational change was in keeping with the principle of enterprise independence. Thus the draft enterprise bill provided that the enterprise council and director, i.e. the autonomous management of the enterprise, would be exclusively responsible for the commercial obligations of the enterprise abroad as well as at home.[2] The first applications for such direct contacts were taken under consideration in October 1968, according to the Czechoslovak news agency, ČTK, 11 October 1968.

This organizational change did not provide the entire answer to the gap between domestic production and the influence of the world maraet. The Action Program called for creation of conditions that would make the Czechoslovak crown convertible, such as an adjustment of prices so as to bring domestic prices more in line with world prices. The inconvertibility

[1] Formed on the following division of interests: 60% to the producers, 30% to the foreign trade enterprise, 10% to the state. As late as 9 April 1969 Prague radio was still announcing their formation.
[2] *Zemědělské noviny*, 31 January 1969.

of the crown, which in itself was the result of the isolation of the domestic market and therefore of domestic prices from the world market, in turn provided an obstacle to Czechoslovakia's possibilities of trading on the world market. It had been because of this that a number of surcharges, discounts, subsidies and so forth had been introduced, thus further removing Czechoslovak industry from the pressures of the world market. These measures, both protectionist and restrictive, were to be gradually removed and convertibility sought with the change in domestic prices.[1]

The issue of convertibility, while most directly connected with price policy and domestic reform, involved also the related issue of trade orientation and Czechoslovakia's ability to compete on the world market. The lack of a convertible currency and of hard currency reserves limited Czechoslovakia to trading primarily with soft currency areas, and because even within these areas there existed no convertibility, barter trading was the rule. An unfavorable trade balance resulted for Czechoslovakia with regard to both trade areas: it had a deficit or unfavorable balance in the hard currency area and a surplus or favorable balance with the soft currency areas – a situation which further obliged it to trade with the soft currency areas.

The currency-orientation issue was also the result of political considerations, for the lack of hard currency reserves meant that trade with the West would need credits – in part long-term credits – which were politically undesirable.[2] For political reasons trade with the Communist countries (which were soft currency areas) was desirable, but this trade was not always economically beneficial to Czechoslovakia (e.g. Czechoslovakia was a creditor nation on this market), and, moreover, the state monopoly system for foreign trade within these countries limited trade to barter. Thus, even when the regime accepted the principles of the new system as early as 1965, calling for economic rather than political criteria for foreign trade, there existed serious economic obstacles. Czechoslovak goods could not compete on the western market, they could not earn hard currency, being of inferior technological standards. Credits were needed to permit the import of goods and techniques which could directly or indirectly serve to raise the standard of Czechoslovak goods. These had to come from the West, for it was the very eastern orientation of Czechoslovak trade that had led to an 'easy' or until recently 'sure' market which

[1] *Noviny zahraničního obchodu*, 19 June 1968.
[2] This issue was debated in the pre-1968 period, for the reform view by Jozef Lenárt, 'Economics, Production, Trade, and Management,' *Czechoslovak Foreign Trade*, 7:1(1967), 3–7, and against, by Oldřich Černík, *Rudé právo*, 3 August 1966, for example.

did little to encourage the raising of the quality of Czechoslovak goods and much to change the structure of the Czechoslovak economy away from goods suitable for the world market.

The orientation of Czechoslovak trade was much debated in the period of revival, for, together with the recognized need for a large hard currency credit, this appeared to be the major obstacle left to the desired connection of the domestic market with world standards. The issue did *not* start as an effort to gain economic independence, to disengage from the eastern bloc, from CEMA or the Soviet Union. The demands for a change in trade orientation were born of economic, not political considerations; if the placing of trade on an economic rather than political basis could have meant a continuation of the almost exclusive eastern orientation, the re-formers probably would have favored it. As it was, economic considerations did *not* favor this, and a situation was created in which economic considerations created demands which could easily and understandably be interpreted only politically and which, in time, could indeed be of grave political significance.

From the beginning Dubček asserted the new regime's intention not only of remaining loyal to CEMA and the Soviet Union but of intensifying economic cooperation with the USSR and Czechoslovakia's neighbors.[1] Nonetheless the Action Program was relatively clear:

'Cooperation with the Soviet Union and the other socialist states, particularly the states associated in CEMA, will also be the basis for development of international economic relations in the future. It must be realized, however, that in the future the success of this cooperation will, to an ever increasing extent, depend on the ability of our products to meet competition. The role of our country in developing an international division of labor will be-come more important in proportion to the general interchange-ability of our products. As regards relations within CEMA, we shall strive to see to it that economic calculation and mutual profitability of exchange are more fully emphasized.'

It appeared that Czechoslovakia hoped to solve at least part of its prob-lems within the framework of CEMA, particularly through a reform of CEMA, as Šik himself proclaimed at the March rally. Černík told the National Assembly session of 24 April 1968 that the problem with CEMA was not its plans for a socialist division of labor (to which Romania so objected), but that the division of labor was *insufficient*.

Czechoslovakia's efforts for a reform of CEMA had begun even prior to

[1] *Rudé právo*, 2 April 1968 (speech to central committee plenum).

1968, but these efforts were apparently earnestly pursued only in the post-January period.[1] It was announced by Prague radio on 12 April 1968, for example, that at a recent CEMA meeting Czechoslovakia had resisted efforts of 'many members...to force the ČSSR to sign a long-term agreement on transit fees.' The issue itself (Czechoslovakia opposed binding, long-term agreements) was less important than the fact that there was a conflict and that, because of Czechoslovak opposition, no agreement was reached. Czechoslovak CEMA representative Otakar Šimůnek, who was fighting for his own political life, revealed in *Rudé právo* of 13 April 1968 the existence of differences between Czechoslovakia and other CEMA members over such issues as direct enterprise contact in foreign trade, the suitability of Czechoslovakia's economic reforms as a model which might promote CEMA cooperation, multilateral consultations, and other questions connected with the reconciliation of internal economic reforms in some countries with the unreformed systems of others. Even Šimůnek, however, had to concede that 'insofar as the economic systems of management and organization in the socialist countries do not come closer together, we must soberly undertake evaluation of the prospects of further intensification of socialist integration.'

The Action Program asserted that, in addition to continued CEMA cooperation, Prague would

'also actively encourage the development of economic relations with any other country in the world that is interested, on the basis of equality of rights and mutual benefits and without discrimination.'

The program continued:

'We advocate the development of *progressive forms of international collaboration, particularly in production and pre-production operations*, exchange of scientific technical knowledge, exchange of licenses, and suitable collaboration with interested countries, *on loans and other financial matters.*'[2]

A sample of this new policy was the founding of a joint Yugoslav–Czechoslovak bank to provide the currency convertibility for the increased trade and cooperation agreed upon between the two countries even before 1968.[3] Negotiations for the bank probably began prior to 1968, as part of the pre-revival liberalization, but it may be assumed that objections made by conservatives were overcome and the agreement reached only after the change in regime, especially since the agreement

---

[1] See, for example, *Rudé právo*, 12, 24, 25 February 1966 or Prague radio, 29 March 1966.

[2] Emphasis mine.　　　　　　　　[3] *Borba* (Belgrade), 24 February 1968.

permitted the free setting of prices between the enterprises involved, using world prices as a basis.

In the spirit of the new policy, Prague opened talks with Austria. In what were the first direct contacts between the foreign ministers of the two countries in over thirty years (according to Prague radio, 21 June 1968), negotiations were begun for a settlement of outstanding Austrian claims regarding Czechoslovak nationalization after 1948. Prague also began to show interest in renewed membership in the International Monetary Fund and the International Bank for Reconstruction and Development.[1] Perhaps more controversially, Prague began looking for a hard currency loan. While Czechoslovak officials denied that such a loan was being sought in the West, Šik revealed in March 1968 that Czechoslovakia was considering acceptance of a foreign loan, and Černík told the National Assembly in late April that Czechoslovakia was considering accepting foreign loans so long as no political preconditions were posed – a clear sign that the sources considered were western. On 17 August 1968 Černík revealed in an interview to an Austrian television correspondent that Czechoslovakia was considering loans from both the World Bank and western firms. Indeed such loans were being urged by economists within Czechoslovakia, some pointing out that no political strings were being attached by the prospective creditors.[2]

Most of these statements were later denied by Czechoslovak officials, who were anxious to play down the political aspects of such moves, particularly in view of growing Soviet sensitivity on the subject. None of these moves, however, need have been at the expense of Czechoslovakia's allies or loyalty to the Soviet bloc, for even with western credits, Czechoslovakia was likely to continue to turn to the USSR as a vital soft currency supplier of raw materials and a major market for manufactured goods which were below western standards. Indeed, Czechoslovakia turned to the Soviet Union for a hard currency loan presumably as an alternative to a large one from the West.[3] While Czechoslovak leaders were reluctant to speak about this request as well, which was for hard currency (gold) worth $400 million, Dubček did reveal in a *Rudé právo* interview on 6 May that Prague had asked for Soviet assistance in Czechoslovakia's program to

---

[1] *The Economist*, 25 May 1968. Hungary and Romania had also been showing interest in membership. Czechoslovakia left the IMF in 1955.

[2] For example, *Reportér*, 29 May 1968; *Práce*, 5 April 1968 (interview with economist Hvezdoň Kočtúch).

[3] ČTK, 15 May 1968 (Smrkovský to the National Assembly on the trip by Czechoslovak leaders to Moscow, 4–6 May 1968).

reform her economy. The only direct Soviet response to this request revealed to the public, after the 10–12 June 1968 economic talks in Moscow, was that the Soviet Union would be willing to help by deliveries of installations – nothing was said publicly of the loan at the time.

One might have assumed that if Moscow was seriously concerned that western credits might lead Czechoslovakia to assume a more independent economic position vis-à-vis the East, it would have itself hastened to grant the loan when approached. The issue was not simple from the Russian point of view, however. To refuse the loan outright or try to use it as a lever to gain concessions from Prague risked pushing the Czechs into western arms; to grant only part of the loan would not have eliminated Czechoslovakia's need to seek credits in the West. On the other hand, the Soviet Union had never granted a hard currency loan of anything approaching this size to any of her allies. Czechoslovakia herself had in 1957 been the recipient of a Soviet gold-loan of $13.5 million, and the largest such loan granted by the USSR to date was $85 million (to East Germany also in 1957).[1] The only loan of this size ever granted to Czechoslovakia by the USSR was in soft currency. Thus it was not entirely clear that the Soviet Union could afford such a loan, especially since it would have reduced Soviet gold reserves by one-seventh.[2] On a more limited basis Moscow could and did show Prague how dependent the latter was on the Soviet Union by delaying grain deliveries, although only for a short period.[3] Such pressure, however, risked merely demonstrating to the Czechs the vulnerability of their position and the need for hard currency, for if grain were not forthcoming from the USSR, Czechoslovakia would, as in the early 1960s, be forced to turn to the West.

It is difficult to determine to what extent there were genuine Soviet fears of a change in Czechoslovak trade orientation, to what extent such fears were justified, and to what extent the Soviet Union created the very situation it claimed to fear through its own pressures and interference. On the one hand, there were countless statements by Dubček and other leading officials attesting to continued loyalty to CEMA, plus the very real economic basis for Czechoslovak cooperation with the Soviet Union and CEMA. On the other hand, it is undeniable that there were at least some demands for a reappraisal of Czechoslovak–Soviet trade relations,

[1] Marshall Goldman, *Soviet Foreign Aid* (New York, 1967), 24–5.
[2] rrg, 'Some Aspects of the Czechoslovak Request for a Soviet Loan,' RFE, 21 June 1968, 11.
[3] *Nová svoboda*, 28 March 1968.

not just from the point of view of achieving profitability, but also from the point of view of achieving a more independent economic position, or a less 'eastern' orientation. It was nothing new to have the Soviet price of crude oil or ores for Czechoslovakia questioned; indeed these issues were aired even on the radio in the 1963–7 period. Nor was it entirely new to hear demands for more beneficial trade agreements, although it did border on the radical when Czechoslovak supplies of uranium to the Soviet Union were questioned and declared harmful to Czechoslovakia's own *economic* interests.[1] But a number of articles urging a change in trade orientation struck a different note. An article in *Reportér* of 29 May 1968, for example, pointed out that it was important to accept a large loan only from an area that would permit repayment in exports to 'the most advanced markets in the world,' so that Czechoslovakia could thereby fulfill her export requirements at the same time. Without this, the argument continued, production would continue to lag and, protected from the competition of the world market, would remain behind world standards. The same article urged Czechoslovakia to negotiate a combination of loans 'evenly distributed among creditor nations, so as to make sure that Czechoslovakia will not become too dependent on any one of them.' Thus the author urged that the principle of not accepting any loan with political strings 'be applied to every potential creditor.'

Even these few more radical demands were not, however, based on a political or ideological rejection of cooperation with the Soviet Union; even one which hinted that it might be worthwhile to be politically independent of either bloc, based its argument on the demand for economic rather than political criteria for economic relations. There can be little doubt, however, of the political interpretation such economic changes might be given, and it is indeed difficult to know how impressed the Soviet Union was with such utterances. Given the misinformation Moscow had been receiving from its people in Czechoslovakia, it is difficult to know how much if at all the Soviet leaders overestimated the acceptance of such views among the reformers. If, however, the Soviets' major concern regarding the reformers was that they wanted a more independent economic policy, it seems likely that Moscow might have found methods other than military for coping with them; for example, the loan, fairer trading terms, possibly even limited reforms in CEMA. Moreover, Czechoslovak–Soviet talks might have focused on this issue, which as we shall see below, they did not.

[1] *Svoboda*, 21 and 22 April 1968; *Svobodné slovo*, 7 May 1968.

Workers councils

Thus far we have seen the innovations of the post-January period with regard to enterprise independence and the connected features which were designed to free the market from government controls and open it to the competition believed necessary for the progress of the Czechoslovak economy. Integrally connected with this was the issue of inner-enterprise democracy, the effort to find a form of worker participation in management commensurate with the responsibilities and freedom now given to the enterprises. The Action Program reflected earlier demands by calling for the establishment of 'democratic organs' with a 'defined authority' with regard to enterprise management. Such organs, consisting of elected representatives of the workers plus 'other representatives of certain sectors outside the enterprise' would appoint the enterprise director and executives who in turn would be responsible to 'these organs...for the overall results of their work.' Such organs were to be 'direct components of the managing mechanism of the enterprises, not social organizations – therefore, they cannot be identified with the trade unions.' The Action Program left the details to be worked out, urging the utilization of 'certain traditions of the factory councils of 1945–8, as well as modern business experience.' In effect the Action Program established the principle of some type of worker role in or control over management – interpreted variously over the following months.

The theoretical basis for workers councils was provided, after the Warsaw Pact invasion, by Rudolf Slánský, Jr, writing in the trade union daily, *Práce*, on 24 February 1969. Operating on the Marxist premise that he who owns the property has the power or control over it, Slánský argued that the state in the socialist society controlled the enterprise. The state, however, was not an abstraction but actual people who acted in its name, he explained. These people belonged to or were appointed by the state *apparat*. Thus the state *apparat*, exercising a monopoly of ownership of nationalized property possessed a monopoly of power. This monopoly should be abolished, specifically through the decentralization of proprietory rights of the state and a transfer of these rights to 'those in whose interest the socialist enterprises operate' – the producers. Slánský was quick to point out that it was not a question of ownership – clearly society 'owned' the property. It was a question of the exercise of these rights, i.e. the control and direction of the enterprises. This should be in the hands of those directly concerned – not of the state, which was one step removed and not always best able to know what was in the interests of the *enterprise* as distinct from all-over state interests. Thus the enterprise council, a group basically representing the enterprise collective rather than the state administration, should exercise *ownership rights* (for example, the right to appoint the manager, distribution of profits, approval of the concepts of the development of the enterprise), in much the same way as a board of directors exercises the rights and interests of the owner while entrusting management itself to persons specifically qualified for the task.

This theoretical explanation made an implicit distinction between state-owned property (or state capitalism) or what Marx once called the first stage of communism or even vulgar communism, and property owned by the workers (collectively) or by society. The Communist regimes had always operated on the principle that if property were owned by all, by society as a whole, then some organ representing or more accurately embodying society itself, must see to it that the interests of the owners (society) were furthered. This organ was the state (guided by the Party), a solution which left things in effect at the stage of state capitalism. The idea of the enterprise or workers council was simply that the workers (as communal owners) would exercise this function in place of the state. While it was granted that this system of separating the state and the enterprises might complicate the safeguarding of the interests of society as a whole, Slánský claimed that experience had shown that the state could not successfully ensure these interests for the simple reason that it could not successfully and efficiently run every single enterprise. It was better to permit those more directly involved to fulfill this function and, in so doing, accord the producers the ownership rights they were supposed to have gained in the act of expropriating the expropriators. The issue, therefore, came down to the simple question: in whose interests would the management of a given enterprise operate – the state's or the producers'. The management obviously was appointed by and operated in the interests of the owner; the Marxist answer as to which group, state or producers, should figure as the owner when 'society' was the owner, clearly was the producers, for society was but the producers.[1]

Šik favored much of Slánský's idea, particularly a council which operated similarly to a board of directors in the West. According to his interpretation the council would select the manager and express its opinion on management decisions without, however, assuming management's responsibility to decide. The council would be a consultative and

---

[1] While Marx's intentions for the state – insofar as one would continue to exist in a socialist society – are open to debate, the reformers did not go into the issue, merely operating towards a state with a minimum of functions, in the spirit, at least, of Marx.

controlling body which, 'in the interest of the whole society, controls the development, profitability, and prosperity of the enterprise as well as the ability of the management.'[1] It would have the right, for example, to veto large investments and to pass on structural matters and the important decision of mergers or association. In cases of disagreement between the management and the council the council could set up an organ to supervise management.[2] Here, as in his earlier suggestion, Šik abandoned his still earlier demand (of the reforms presented in 1964) for few restrictions on management and the possibility for managers to use their initiative and judgment. This reversal must be seen, however, in the context of the independent enterprise, for previously Šik was arguing for management freedom vis-à-vis the state administration, i.e. control from above and outside. Once enterprise independence was gained, the problem was no longer the same, and control from below and inside, as it were (at least in relation to the state), would not be considered an obstacle to initiative and responsibility – so long as it too refrained from interfering in day to day operations. Taking this less radical, control-orientation view of the councils, Černík pointed out that 'Production techniques are not matters for democratic decision but for technical calculation,' and that the intention was *not* to weaken management. In this spirit some suggested, on Prague radio, 11 April 1968, that the workers councils be limited to a mere inspection agency performing the function of a 'social supervision agency.' On the other hand, workers tended to demand still greater powers for the councils, up to and including appointing the pertinent economic minister and running the enterprises on a daily basis.

The differing interpretations as to the jurisdiction and powers of the councils could be seen in the varying views regarding the composition of these organs. Šik revised his original suggestion and, according to Prague radio, 20 May 1968, urged that 'the decisive' (presumably this meant 50 per cent or more) part of the members should be elected by and from among the workers of the enterprises (though they should have the 'moral and character qualities...[and] scientific knowledge' necessary for the job). From 10 to 30 per cent of the members should be drawn from outside but related organizations, such as the bank granting the enterprise its credits, experts, etc. This was the arrangement advocated by the trade unions also in their statement in *Práce* of 5 July 1968. Another view, however, urged that only 1/3 of the places on the council should go to worker representatives, 1/3 to management, and 1/3 to 'some neutral ele-

[1] *Rudé právo*, 7 April 1968.
[2] Speech to the Czechoslovak Economic Association.

ment,' i.e. outside experts, etc.[1] This view was defended on the grounds that worker interests as such should not be given a greater voice than those of the enterprise itself, especially since the workers had their trade unions to promote their interests. This conservative view more or less denied the theoretical arguments favoring the very existence of such councils. A still more conservative view was expressed by economics professor Pavel Hrubý, who advocated a small council consisting of only two representatives of the workers, a trade union representative, and three to four experts consisting of the director and his deputies or chief engineers.[2] He later urged that 'we Communists' retain 'the necessary influence...[and] turn them into bastions of socialism.'[3]

Šik's was the proposal adopted by the government presidium on 29 June 1968, to be begun on an experimental basis from 1 July 1968.[4] The only alteration was the inclusion of the manager on the council, which nonetheless retained the right to select and replace managers. The system thus experimentally introduced as well as that suggested by Šik had less of a 'worker' character than the councils of the 1945–8 period, which were composed entirely of elected workers and subject only to trade union approval of the lists of candidates. On the other hand, the new councils were to resemble the earlier boards with regard to function (with slightly more power, i.e. the right to appoint the manager). On both counts they differed from the Yugoslav system of worker-management. In fact this provisional 'final' product was just what the Action Program ordered: a concept which used something from the factory councils of 1945 and something from the western board of directors. It was the latter, however, that the new concept most resembled.

The draft of the enterprise law contained what was probably the final decision on the form of the enterprise councils. There were to be enterprise councils in all three types of enterprises (social, public, shareholder). In the social enterprise, which was to be the major type, the workers would elect representatives to 80 per cent of the places on the council, the remaining 20 per cent to go to outside experts, with one seat reserved for a representative of the state. Thus, instead of management being represented, one seat would be reserved for the state. In the other types of enterprises, only 1/3 of the board would be worker representatives,

---

[1] The view of the Committee for Scientific Management as reported by Eduard Vopička, Prague radio, 11 April 1968.

[2] *Práce*, 2 April 1968.   [3] Prague radio, 3 June 1968.

[4] *Pravda* (Bratislava), 30 June 1968. Second stage of implementation by 1 October 1968; final implementation 1 January 1969.

1/3 senior officials of the enterprise (management) and 1/3 representatives of the founders (the state in the case of the public enterprise, the corporate group in the case of the shareholders' enterprise). A dispute arose when the 1969 Czech government offered a much more conservative proposal calling for the councils in the social enterprises to take the same form as those in the other two types of enterprises and granting the state final authority in a large number of matters, such as the right to final approval over appointment of the manager, the right to annul important council decisions, and the right to control decisions on mergers, etc. This plan, reported in *Práce* of 18 February 1969, would in effect reduce the councils to mere control bodies with the real power, i.e. the exercise of ownership rights, remaining with the state. The Czech proposal represented the more conservative views expressed in the post-January period, and it may be assumed that the draft prepared by the Federal government more closely corresponded to the idea that would have been finally adopted had the Czechoslovak experiment been permitted to continue.

Agriculture

The Action Program suggested little in the way of concrete reforms in the agricultural sphere, although the major suggestions heard in the past were accepted in principle. As with industry, the primary concern of the reformers was to gain 'enterprise' independence to permit farmers to determine their own affairs, from management and day to day operations to competing on the market. Thus the Action Program said: 'It will be useful to make individual cooperatives independent, self-contained, and fully authorized economic and social organizations, to abolish the ineffective administrative centralization of cooperatives, and to superimpose on the cooperative enterprises only those organs which carry out activities that are economically useful to them.' Among the first concrete steps the Action Program envisaged to achieve the above goals were: permission for cooperative farms to engage in business activity in other sectors and, perhaps most important, 'the right and possibility of direct sales of part of the farm production to the people and to the retail trade system.' The reference here was to at least partial elimination of the monopolistic central purchasing agencies. By the same token, the Action Program gave reason to believe that the monopolistic supply organizations would also be decentralized or eliminated. In this regard, the Party called for a way to ensure a direct link between the farmer, the supplier, and the market, i.e. that the farmer might be able to play a more direct role in the marketing of his products and be in a better position with regard to those providing supplies and services to agriculture. In this connection farmers also wanted direct purchasing and marketing rights in foreign markets, which would further free them from the monopolistic position particularly of domestic suppliers.[1] No clear-cut decision on this matter was announced by the regime, however.

The Action Program statement regarding closer contacts between the producers and the market ended with a suggestion for new forms of contact, 'similar to the former agricultural cooperatives.' The reference here would appear to be to the former agricultural marketing cooperative, the functions of which were, conceivably, to be resumed by some supra-farm organization. The supra-enterprise organization already existing was the DAA, which was a territorial or vertical organization in practice exercising centralized administrative controls similar to those of the association or trust in industry. This form of organization was vertical rather than functional, and, therefore, not likely to be the type of organization the Action Program envisaged. It would seem that the Action Program foresaw either an entirely independent marketing enterprise for the farmers or, perhaps, the inclusion of this function in the all-state agricultural union, the formation of which was authorized by the Action Program but variously interpreted in the following months.

A state-wide conference of DAA chairmen, held in early April, maintained that the DAAs were an agency of the agricultural enterprises vis-à-vis the center – not the reverse.[2] The farmers, however, sought independent rights, both economic or social, through organizations of their own choosing, as we shall see in the discussions concerning an agricultural union. They wished to separate the state sphere of management from that of the enterprise (thus an elimination or downgrading of the former practices of the DAA), and to provide farmers with independent organs for the assertion of their rights and the independent settlement of certain of their economic problems, for example, by the setting up of an agricultural bank to grant credits.[3] The idea of voluntary economic union did take hold and by the end of the summer 67.3 per cent of all agricultural enterprises had

[1] See, for example, *Zemědělské noviny*, 26 March 1968. Such direct contacts had taken place under the pre-1968 reforms on an individual basis, within relatively stringent government limitations. This type of activity continued, and the Czechoslovak co-operative farmers delegation signed a protocol with representatives of the Norwegian cooperative center in Oslo, 10 June 1968, calling for the development of *direct mutual trade contracts*. (Prague radio, 10 June 1968.)

[2] *Zemědělské noviny*, 11 April 1968.

[3] See, for example, *Zemědělské noviny*, 3 July 1968, or Prague radio, 24 June 1968.

become members of some type of economic grouping.[1] This movement continued after the invasion and included one organization designed to convert the agricultural supply and procurement enterprises into economic cooperatives (i.e. a voluntary economic association), as well as an organization of Tractor Stations and an Association of Land Conservation Cooperatives.[2]

The Action Program contained the germ of still another innovation for agriculture by calling for greater cooperation with and help for the private farmers. In keeping with this an Agriculture and Food Ministry official announced, in a *Rudé právo* interview on 12 June 1968, that farmers interested in private farming might apply for return of their property confiscated 'on the basis of an incorrect interpretation of the 1955 government decree.' This was not intended as a return to private farming or abandonment of the idea of collectivized farming, as was clearly pointed out, for example, by Gustáv Husák in a speech in Bratislava. The intention, rather, was to remove the stigma attached to private farmers, in an effort to make use of and perpetuate the beneficial role they played in developing certain areas, e.g. land that would otherwise remain fallow.

In keeping with the Action Program the government prepared a set of proposals concerning private farms and their relationship with other agricultural units. These proposals, according to the Agricultural Ministry daily, *Zemědělské noviny* of 8 August 1968, provided private farmers the right to sell their produce, independently of central direction, under substantially the same conditions as the collective and state farms. The delivery quotas eliminated for the JZDs and the state farms under the reforms of 1966 were now to be eliminated for private farmers as well. As the reformers had demanded, private farmers were to be offered the same prices as other farmers for the purchase of supplies and services. Although they would not be included in the same bonus system as the other farmers (as had been suggested), they would be given some form of subsidy. These proposals were approved by the Economic Council on 6 August, to be submitted for final approval, and implemented as of 1 January 1969. According to *Zemědělské noviny* of 7 December 1968, the post-invasion regime intended to implement these proposals.

Slovakia

Dubček had been a supporter of the economic reform program before 1968, but this support had been somewhat equivocal insofar as economic

[1] *Zemědělské noviny*, 14 August 1968.
[2] Prague radio, 7 October 1968; *Zemědělské noviny*, 24 and 27 October 1968.

reform in Slovakia was concerned. In late 1967 he had proposed that subsidies and other such aid be provided by the state for Slovak enterprises – despite the principles of the new economic system – because of the disadvantaged position of Slovak enterprises if unfettered competition and the profitability criterion were introduced. Dubček's position was, not unexpectedly, reflected in the Action Program. The Program maintained that because Slovakia lagged behind the Czech lands, its economic level would have to be raised before the reforms could be thoroughly applied there. Otherwise, the argument went, the federalization of the country, sought by the Slovaks, could not be genuinely effected, for it would perpetuate the gap between the two nations. Moreover, it was a fact that earlier political decisions to raise the economic level of Slovakia had often conflicted with sound economic policy; thus Dubček's apprehensions that, left alone, existing Slovak enterprises could not survive economically. It was on this basis that the Action Program urged that the new economic system be worked out in such a way as to permit Slovakia to participate on 'an equal level.' In keeping with this thinking, the economic policy directive issued in August 1968 provided for a number of 'special' measures for Slovakia: exemptions from taxes for certain enterprises, maintenance of previously established favorable credit conditions, and subsidies.[1] Specifically, tax exemptions might be granted to enterprises which would suffer serious strain as a result of the introduction of the new economic system.

While such measures ran counter to the spirit of the new system, a deeper problem was at stake: federalization of Czechoslovakia – economically as well as politically. Federalization as a principle had indeed been accepted by the Action Program, and it was on the basis of this principle that symmetry (i.e. two equal national units) was advocated. Yet the same persons who argued for limitations of the economic reforms in Slovakia used the very reform system as the theoretical justification for federalization. These people argued that the heart of the economic reforms was decentralization, enterprise independence and autonomy, and in what better way to promise these things for Slovakia than by federalization? The standpoint of the committee of the Slovak Planning Commission, given in *Pravda* (Bratislava) of 19 May 1968, put it thus:

'It is not possible – as some prominent Czech economists and officials of central organs in Prague are doing – to demand in one breath high relative independence for individual enterprises and the integrated grouping of enterprises according to the work they

[1] *Hospodářské noviny*, 9 August 1968.

49

do, and to deny the right of relatively independent economic
policy of [the two] nations.'
The new economic system, therefore, implied federalization – just as
federalization implied the 'simultaneous implementation of the economic
system of management. . .the abolition of this old central administrative
structure,' according to *Rudé právo* of 3 July 1968. From this one can
only conclude that the special measures desired for Slovakia – in contradiction to the spirit of the reforms – would for these people simply fall
under the category of the 'decentralized organs,' i.e. those of Slovakia, to
administer the system as they saw fit, independently of the center in
Prague.

The issue in the eyes of Prague was not, however, how honestly one
aspect of the reforms would be implemented if other aspects were not
introduced. The real concern was integration versus autonomy in a
federated society. There was a certain apprehension on the part of some,
particularly the regime, that federalization might lead to atomization, to
two economies or as Zdeněk Fierlinger (about to be dropped from the
Party presidium) put it: 'some crude form of dualism.'[1] Dubček expressed
his own fears of this possibility in a Bratislava speech on 20 April:

'Besides the moral and political factor, the strongest binder of
Czechoslovak statehood, the prerequisite for the development of
the social productivity of labor and for economic efficiency, is and
should be industrial integration, and not autarchy, the self-
enclosure of the national economies. We should take this fact fully
into consideration also in our federal organization.'

The federated system which appeared in the form of a Constitutional
law in October 1968 tried to find a solution to this problem. The Federal
organs would take care of all-over economic policy such as monetary and
credit policy. According to pre-invasion proposals by economists, reported in *Rudé právo* on 18 May 1968, there should be a common currency, a common market, a unified price system and unified wage policy,
with Slovakia having the right, however, to draw up its own plan and
budget. Only the last was, apparently, changed by the post-invasion
Constitutional law, which said that the plan and budget would be worked
out 'in mutual coordination and cooperation' between the 'national states'
and the Federal government. Only after agreement could the 'national
state' adopt the plan by law.[2] It is difficult to know if the law adopted con-

---

[1] Prague radio, 2 April 1968. See also Finance Minister Sucharda at the April plenum
of the central committee, ČTK, 2 April 1968.
[2] *Sbírka zákonů* No. 143/1968.

formed totally to the system intended by the pre-August reform leaders; certainly it provided easy opportunity for renewed centralization, as was pointed out by some Slovaks, for example, in *Nové slovo*, 12 December 1968. Just how much autonomy Slovakia would have received in economic matters was something only practice would have revealed.

Reactions to the reforms

The economic reforms had become something of a political football in the time of Novotný and particularly in the early months of 1968. Among the political implications of the reforms, evident in the pre-1968 efforts to introduce the program, were the fear of Party appointees that they would lose their jobs if economic qualifications were given priority; and the fear of the conservatives that the economic reforms would necessitate political reforms (which was indeed the case as Šik had pointed out on several occasions), and diminished power or control in the hands of the central organs, specifically the Party. The workers had responded only half-heartedly to the economic reforms, and Novotný had long exploited worker disdain for intellectuals to set the former against the reform movement and, thereby, prevent the formation of a powerful alliance against his continued rule. Once the reformers succeeded in gaining power, Novotný and his supporters did not hesitate to continue to play this card, feeding workers' fears of job insecurity and wage reductions which might result from the new system. By exaggerating these 'negative' aspects of the economic reforms, the conservatives hoped to prove to the workers that the intellectuals (meaning the reformers) were riding rough-shod over the interests of the working class. Making a political issue of the economic reforms, the conservatives often referred to the disadvantaged position of workers with large families, pensioners, and others under the new system.[1]

On television and radio, and in interviews to the daily press, Šik termed these contentions sheer demagoguery and asked where these defenders of the workers' well-being had been when the economic situation was deteriorating, when he (and others) had proposed measures to raise the standard of living only to have them shelved by these very same people. He asserted that the Novotný regime had hidden from the public the fact that Czechoslovakia's standard of living was 25 per cent less than

---

[1] For example, Novotný's speech at the ČKD factory in Prague, 17 February 1968 (*Lidová demokracie*, 18 February 1968) or Oldřich Švestka in *Rudé právo*, 14 July 1968.

that of neighboring Austria, that the rate of increase of real wages in Czechoslovakia over the past ten years had been only one-half that of Austria and one-third that of West Germany. Indeed one of the best weapons the reformers had in their struggle against the conservative arguments was the free atmosphere of the spring of 1968. Day after day, on radio and television, as well as in the press, economists, officials, and laymen explained to the people into just what kind of situation the former regime had let the economy fall. There was no dearth of information, statistics, *exposés* and very frank analyses of the reasons for such a development. A fairly commonly expounded explanation was that Czechoslovakia at the end of World War Two had had the capacity for favorable development, but, according to *Mladá fronta* of 24 April 1968,

'the indiscriminate acceptance and implementation of...the model of the Soviet economy and Soviet political system, which hardly corresponded to the level and former relations and conditions of our economy and which at the same time was in contradiction to the development of the creative economic activity and the democratic traditions and psychological outlook of our people [had] led to the gradual alienation of our own sources and factors of economic prosperity.'

Löbl went further than most by arguing in *Literární listy* of 20 June 1968 that Soviet domination had obstructed development. Moscow had vetoed various projects because of their links with the West and jailed most of the country's experienced economists, according to the numerous examples provided by Löbl.

A more philosophical argument was presented which in time might have had an important influence on developments: the theory presented by Löbl in his book, published in Bratislava in early 1969, *Reflections on Intellectual Work and National Wealth*. Löbl's theory was that the advanced economies had undergone or were undergoing a new revolution, that of science and technology or what might be called an intellectual revolution. The basic element of the economy was no longer the physical means of production or physical labor but mental labor. Thus, an entirely new organization of society would have to be considered, based on this new reality. Specifically, Czechoslovakia would have to abandon the outdated principles of the industrial revolution and pass on to the scientific–technological revolution, making place for the enlarged role of the intellectuals. These were indeed the findings of the Academy of Science Commission headed by Radovan Richta, whose work was commissioned by the Party in 1966 as the foundation for the Mlynář committee for political reform.[1] They were developed in 1968 by Richta's own Party-appointed committee on the 'scientific–technological revolution,' which worked closely with the Mlynář team and whose ideas gained a certain influence outside purely intellectual circles. They were later heard from such people as the then South Moravian first secretary and later presidium member, Josef Špaček, in a Prague radio interview of 15 January 1968, and even found their way into the Action Program, which expressed a new respect for science and the work of intellectuals and white-collar workers. A trade union staff worker even went so far as to publish an article which placed in serious doubt the continued 'historical mission of the working class' as distinct from the intellectuals in the new age.[2]

In response to the conservatives' attacks on the economic reforms, Dubček frankly decried the efforts to split the intellectuals and the workers and offered the workers a chance finally to 'implement' their interests through democratization. According to *Rudé právo* of 5 March 1968, he told Kladno workers that the Party would endeavor to 'strengthen the democratic influence of the working people's collectives on the management of production.' This promise, repeated often, included in the Action Program and embodied in the official proposals for enterprise councils, may well be what finally convinced the workers of the beneficial nature of the economic reforms (in addition to the efforts at explanation by students and the mass media, as well as the new atmosphere itself in which the workers could test their freedom).

One such freedom which probably helped to convert the workers to the idea of reform was the new possibility of going out on strike. There were a number of short strikes, reported by the Czechoslovak media, from March through the summer, protesting such things as unprofitable production lines, poor wages, and unpopular or inefficient managers; many more strikes were threatened. There had always been isolated strikes in Czechoslovakia, and in the 1963–7 period one or two had even been reported by *Práce*. The interesting thing about the 1968 strikes, however, was not only that they were objectively – sometimes even sympathetically – reported by the official state and Party media, but that they often had the support of the local Party committee and sometimes even achieved their goals. One of the more interesting of these was the one-hour strike in an electrical instruments plant in Southern Bohemia. The production

[1] Richta's committee expressed its views in *Civilizace na rozcestí* (Praha, 1969). See also, Eugen Löbl, *Úvahy o duševnej práci a bohatstve národa*, 1 (Bratislava, 1969).
[2] Zdeněk Valenta, 'The Working Class and the Intelligentsia,' *Nová mysl*, XII:11(1968), 198–210.

line had been switched to a less lucrative one, meaning an income loss for the workers under the new system. It was a question of a policy desirable to the association of enterprises but not to the plant involved. A strike committee, with red armbands, was formed by the Party's plant committee and the trade union's plant committee; the workers demanded autonomy from their association directorate. Partial settlement came when the general manager of the Prague plants agreed to restore to the plant its original production line and to negotiate further details with representatives of the workers. The parent enterprise did not, however, agree to dissociation, despite the fact that other plants in the same association also requested independence. *Práce* on 27 March 1968 supported the workers' demands and reported the strike as a 'further step in the democratization process, which thus spreads from the field of politics into that of economics.' Another strike in Bohemia forced the resignation of a plant manager and his chief engineer; the workers complained that special bonuses had been unfairly distributed.[1] Some workers achieved their aims merely by threatening to strike, as was the case with Ruzyně International Airport electricians. The strike was threatened over work conditions and successful negotiations with the transport ministry brought favorable results, according to *Práce*, 24 April and 3 May 1968.

The steadily increasing number of strikes and threatened strikes brought official comment. Newly elected trade union chief Karel Poláček said in a press conference on 27 March 1968 that he approved of strikes if the workers' rights had been impaired. Vojtech Daubner, Slovak trade union chief, supported the workers' right to engage even in political strikes, e.g. a strike in defense of the freedom of the press.[2] Dubček himself did not reject the idea of the strike, though he termed it 'the maximum method of exerting pressure.'[3] Thus the legality of strikes as such was not questioned, but it remained to be seen if the regime would, nonetheless, tolerate any and all strikes or only those organized by the trade unions. For this and other matters concerning strikes a law was urged, which the trade unions began preparing.[4]

Yet another way in which worker opposition to the reforms was to be overcome was the promise of welfare benefits for those adversely affected by the introduction of the reforms. In *Rudé právo* of 15 March 1968 Černík answered the conservatives with the argument that progress would

---

[1] Czechoslovak television, 12 April 1968.　　　　[2] *Rudé právo*, 22 March 1968.
[3] *Rudé právo*, 19 June 1968.
[4] According to the deputy chairman of the ROH, Czechoslovak television, 21 May 1968.

not be at the expense of workers' security, for the government would see to jobs, retraining, and support for released workers. Some workers called on the government to fulfill this promise: miners, fearing a lay-off, held a conference of their trade union leaders and declared in their program that a worker might not be transferred to other work unless the employer provided him new training.[1] While there was much discussion of this issue of job security and retraining, no measures other than those already taken in 1967 (unemployment insurance) were introduced. Welfare benefits were, however, improved, presumably to cope with the increases in prices. ČTK announced on 16 June 1968 that as of 1 January 1969 all social security payments and pensions would be increased by an average of 8 per cent, the lowest pensions to be increased by roughly 18 per cent. It was also proposed by the trade unions that the tax on pensions be eliminated, and an effort was to be made to raise benefits for farmers to the level of the workers.[2] Family allowances were also to be raised, as was maternity pay. Presumably to upgrade social security matters, the Office of Social Security was abolished and a Ministry of Labor and Social Affairs was established on 29 April 1968. These improvements were to coincide with improved working conditions, e.g. a shorter working week was approved by the Economic Council and on 15 May the government approved a 5-day, 40-hour working week, to be introduced in the 1968–70 period. The workers' position was eased still further by an extension of rights granted in principle by the 1965 Labor Code – the right to choose one's job and to change jobs. In keeping with the Action Program the government announced on 16 April 1968 that it was preparing legislation which 'would enable everyone to find the employment' he wanted and considered suitable. There were to be no more directives to enterprises as to how many persons, or specifically women, they might employ or how many workers they must supply for recruitment drives. Nor would National Committees be authorized to restrict the number of workers permitted to leave agriculture.

It was not these promises of improved or increased welfare benefits that marked the revolutionary aspect of the policy towards workers, however. Although the conservatives strove to stir up worker opposition on just such specific and 'immediate' issues as these, the essential point was the democratization process: the right for workers to have a decisive say in matters concerning them. The workers eventually realized that the campaign designed to give the citizen a genuine voice in the determination of

[1] ČTK, 13 June 1968.
[2] Prague radio, 24 April 1968 (Černík to National Assembly).

laws, leaders, and policy would be of much greater and deeper significance to them, individually, than the relatively temporary hardships – or even improvements – in such things as welfare. Thus as in the early 'pre-revival liberalization' attention increasingly turned to the social and political institutions which patterned the society, and interest was concentrated on how to define each man's position in society and his relation to and the nature of the existing institutions.

3

Mass Organizations

The reformers had long been bringing pressure for changes in the nature of the mass organizations, and a movement towards change had indeed gotten under way in 1964–5, only to be stalemated in its incipient stage, by Novotný's tightening up of 1966–7. Once in power, however, the reformers turned to this as a major area in the introduction of democracy to Czechoslovakia's socialist society. The crucial issue when dealing with the mass organizations was the very definition or description of society with regard to interests and strata. At the April central committee plenum, which approved the Action Program, Dubček reiterated the already accepted view that there existed 'differentiated' interests in the albeit classless society.[1] The Action Program itself proclaimed that

'it is impossible to overlook or deny the various needs and interests proper to individuals and social groups according to the jobs they hold, their qualifications, age, sex, nationality, and so forth. We have often made this mistake in the past. Socialism can only develop by making consideration of the various interests of the people possible.'

The existing system of mass organizations did not provide this possibility. The harmonistic or 'homogeneous' view of society had both justified and facilitated the rule of the Party, so that, in fact, the mass organizations – not considered representatives of particular interests – had been mere 'transmission belts,' conveying the Party's will (which by definition expressed the unified will of the workers' society) downward and providing an organizational–operational framework for the implementation of this will from the lowest levels upwards. Thus much of the 'democratization' of these institutions was connected with the political reforms revolving around the role of the Party and the political role of the mass organizations, which we shall see below, but these organizations were also to be redefined and reorganized to serve a different social function.

Dubček favored what he called 'an open confrontation of interests and standpoints, and *institutional guarantees of this expression of interests*, of

[1] *Rudé právo*, 2 April 1968.

their evaluation and solution.'[1] Thus, it emerged that the mass (or 'social') organizations were to provide the institutional framework for the expression of varying, sometimes conflicting interests. The problem was, however, how to bring about this desired function, for, as was pointed out during a Prague radio round-table discussion on 28 February 1968, for example, the social organizations till then 'had no chance' to play any positive role or have any 'social effect,' because they had been 'plagued by formalism' and controlled by the Party. A primary requirement often demanded, therefore, was 'independence' for the social organizations. Smrkovský openly welcomed the idea of independent organizations acting as 'spokesmen of certain strata of society.' He told the April central committee plenum that he thought that 'nothing will happen to socialism if we have various independent organizations,' according to *Rudé právo*, 4 April 1968.

An integral part of independence was also the right to associate or dissociate at will, as advocated by the veteran Communist writer Zora Jesenská, who called for the 'greatest possible variety of societies, associations, and clubs whose origins are free and spontaneous...allowing every organic interest of society to have its natural representation and an unrestricted right to be heard.'[2] The Action Program too proclaimed the need to guarantee the 'constitutional rights of assembly and association,' so as to permit the emergence of 'voluntary organizations, group-interest associations, clubs, and so on...without...monopolization by any organization.' Although, theoretically, this was already a Constitutional right, numerous demands were heard for a law to protect this right, and National Assembly chairman Smrkovský recommended such to the National Assembly; the government then began work on an appropriate law.[3] Equally part of organization independence was internal freedom, specifically the demand that the Party refrain from interfering. This demand was raised by Smrkovský himself, who opposed the custom of Party appointments to key posts in the mass organizations, advocating the right of the organizations to elect their own officials.[4] In this connection, *Mladá fronta* of 24 March 1968 advocated a consistent rotation of functionaries. Internal freedom would mean, however, the freedom for dis-

[1] *Rudé právo*, 21 April 1968 (Bratislava speech 20 April 1968).
[2] *Kulturný život*, 5 April 1968.
[3] *Rudé právo*, 19, 25 April 1968. The demands sent to the National Assembly from the Prague rally of 20 March 1968 also included the right to free association (Prague radio, 20 March 1968).
[4] Prague radio, 2 February 1968.

sent within the organization and, as journalist Vladimír Diviš pointed out, in *Kulturní noviny* of 8 March 1968,

'we cannot but get used to the fact that there will exist, in the future, in our country, in the social organizations and institutions, two or more groups with different ideas, having the right to express these views publicly and to try to win support for them.'

This last idea, however, would necessarily pose some problems regarding organization independence and the scope of the activities of these organizations.

The Action Program called for a guarantee against 'bureaucratic restriction' of the organizations, presumably from above, but it was not clear if this were to include elimination of the restrictions on political activities by these organizations. This point was of significance, for the demanded right publicly to express dissenting views and to try to win support bordered on political activity. The same could be said for 'unrestricted' *representation* of the various strata of society, for as *Mladá fronta* of 2 April 1968 argued, 'effective social organizations' could only be those which accorded the individual 'the right to influence public affairs through the organization of which he is a member.' A *Rudé právo* editorial of 16 February 1968 squarely faced the question by attacking the view that social organizations were mere interest groups with 'no business meddling in serious political matters.' Mlynář, who headed the Party committee to look into political reforms and who was usually careful in his statements, also argued in *Rudé právo*, on 13 February 1968, that all components of society, including social or interest groups and every institutional component of society, including the state, the Party, and the social organizations 'must also be an independent political agent...in such a way that none of these components can assume the place of another or control it in such a way that the former regards the latter as a "lever of transmission", as an instrument and not as an independent political agent.' Dubček later clarified this point somewhat when, speaking specifically of the trade union movement, he said that the Party fully supported the central union organization 'as a representative of social interests as well as a *political representative* of the class and other working people.'[1] Thus it became necessary to delineate the political role of the social organizations as members of the National Front, placing the issue once again in the realm of political reforms. The non-political, theoretical points were being worked out by the Party-appointed committee under

[1] *Rudé právo*, 30 June 1968. Emphasis mine.

Radovan Richta in the field of the 'social and human relations of the scientific–technical revolution.'[1]

The trade union movement (ROH)

The trade union movement was relatively slow to respond to the new situation in Prague at the beginning of 1968, and the former line predominated for close to three months; this line consisted of conceiving of the trade unions as transmission belts for the will of the Party, designed to organize and ensure the implementation of the economic plan at the enterprise levels. There were numerous efforts towards change in this role in the 1963–7 period, but, even after January, ROH chairman Miroslav Pastyřík proclaimed that the major role of the trade unions was to 'unconditionally serve socialism' and rally the masses around the regime's economic program through propaganda and education, with the aim of 'contributing to the strengthening of ideological unity.'[2] A meeting of the central trade union council was to have been held on 20–21 February 1968 to outline a program for reforming and improving the ROH in the spirit of the revival. This meeting was, however, postponed, ostensibly because the government had failed to submit proposals, according to two leading ROH secretaries, in *Práce* of 2 March 1968. In response, complaints and criticism about this procrastination and ambiguity on the part of the ROH came from below. For example, the Party members of the Ústí nad Labem regional trade union council complained about the delay, calling for personnel changes among the leading functionaries of the ROH; an *aktiv* of chairmen of works committees of the ROH in the second Prague district criticized the ROH central council and leading officials for hesitating so long in explaining their stand; and the trade union committee of the Košice Iron Works declared that 'it was high time' that Pastyřík resigned as chairman of the ROH.[3] Such prodding from below was sorely felt by trade union leaders, as evidenced by the speech of one union leader to the April Party central committee plenum. He complained that in many plants the Communists had lost control, with workers on their own initiative replacing trade union functionaries and whole shop and plant committees. He blamed this on the hesitation and vacillation of the Communists in the unions, which had led in some places to the slogan 'trade unions without Communists.'[4]

[1] *Práce*, 5 April 1968. [2] *Práce*, 13 January 1968.
[3] See *Práce*, 5 March 1968; Prague radio, 13, 18 March 1968.
[4] *Rudé právo*, 7 April 1968.

The trade union movement (ROH)

The need for reform was recognized by the Party and eventually, even at the highest levels of the ROH. Slovak trade union council chairman Vojtech Daubner sharply criticized the former 'transmission belt' system, and the impotence of the union. According to the Slovak trade union daily, *Práca* of 28 January 1968, he called for healthy criticism to get the movement moving again. Dubček too criticized the former role of the ROH and called for a change in the unions' function and orientation so as to 'create free scope for the implementation of the workers' specific interests through the trade union organization.'[1] Finally, on 12 March 1968, the presidium of the ROH central council produced a communique which recognized the justice of many of the demands for change. At a meeting of the Communist members of the central council the same day, ROH chairman Pastyřík and two secretaries, Bedřich Kozelka and Václav Pašek, tendered their resignations. The ROH Party group, however, decided that Pastyřík's resignation should not be accepted, on the grounds that one who had lost the confidence of the people should be removed rather than permitted to resign.[2] Pastyřík was indeed dismissed at the plenum of the ROH central council held on 20–21 March 1968, despite the fact that on 14 March 1968 the Party presidium had agreed to accept his resignation.[3] The resignations of three more ROH secretaries, Antonín Krček, Emil Hammerník and Anna Karlovská were accepted. The choice of Pastyřík's replacement was not, however, a fortunate one, for there was strong worker opposition to the new man, Karel Poláček. Not only did many members consider Poláček unqualified, but many objected to his having been elected 'undemocratically,' by acclamation rather than by secret ballot. Poláček was not, however, resistant to the liberalization, and the trade union movement was reformed despite his election.[4]

A necessary step in the democratization of the trade union movement was the granting of independence with regard to the Party, demanded within the context of the new role for all mass organizations. There were direct workers' requests for unions which are not mere 'yes-men' but

---

[1] *Rudé právo*, 5 March 1968 (speech at Kladno Steel Works 2 March 1968).
[2] *Práce*, 12 March 1968, Prague radio, 14 March 1968.
[3] Prague radio, 22 March 1968; *Rok šedesátý osmý v usneseních a dokumentech ÚV KSČ* (Praha, 1969), 38.
[4] A strike by 70 000 workers was threatened if he were elected; three enterprises, including the Pilsen Škoda works (where Poláček began his career), expressed their opposition (ČTK 22 March 1968; *Rudé právo*, 7 April 1968.) He eventually became something of a hero for the workers (before he entered Husák's Party presidium in April 1969), but it was privately said that he had merely permitted his name to be used for progressive initiative on the part of the movement.

'have an identity of their own.' Party members of a regional trade union council demanded the creation of conditions which would enable the trade unions to pursue their own policy.[1] *Práce* editor-in-chief Ladislav Zajac explained on 25 February 1968 that 'the mechanism of socialist democracy can only function if all its components function independently.' The center should merely guide, plan for the future, and determine the general line, 'but it cannot act in the place of every component.' These had been the views advocated by Zdeněk Mlynář, who argued in a 28 February 1968 radio round-table discussion, that the unions should be free of outside hindrance, including outside appointment or selection of their officials. Reform leader Špaček gave this stand something of official Party weight in a *Rudé právo* interview of 16 March 1968. He called for a system in which the trade unions would not be mere 'implements of Party policy' but an 'objectively existing' component of the political system, i.e. organizations which fulfill certain functions 'independently of the Party.' Dubček himself sanctioned this idea when he declared at the state-wide trade union conference of 18–20 June 1968 that the ROH should become an autonomous movement and promised that neither the Party nor the state would interfere in its work. It was on the basis of this promise that the draft program which grew out of this conference proclaimed the ROH a 'unitary, voluntary, and independent organization composed of workers, technicians, intellectuals, and other employed people,' the main task of which was to serve as an interest organization, expressing the political goals of the working class and all workers, promoting their human and social rights, and defending the interests and needs of its members.[2]

Once independent of the Party, the trade union movement was to return to the original function of trade unions in a democracy: representation and defense of the interests of the working people. The Action Program recognized this new function but continued to construe it relatively conservatively: the trade unions were to defend the working peoples' interests in their employment and working conditions; at the same time the unions were to maintain their 'educative' function of 'orienting workers and employees toward a positive solution of the problems of socialist construction.' The Action Program did relieve the unions of the task of implementing economic directives of the Party, but, in fact, the role envisaged by the reform leaders was broader and two-fold in nature. According to Smrkovský, for example, in *Práce* of 26 May 1968, the unions' main task was indeed to protect the interests of the workers in-

[1] *Práce*, 13 March 1968; 5 March 1968.
[2] ČTK, 19 June 1968; see *Práce*, 5 July 1968 for draft program.

stead of acting in place of organs of management, but they were also to act as a political force.

With regard to the function of representing workers' interests at the enterprise level, the unions were to ensure that management operated in the interests of the workers. According to *Práce* of 20 June 1968, they were to seek improvements in the system of social security, job security, taxes, and wages, as well as contribute to settling questions of economic policy. With regard to the methods the unions might use to defend workers' interests, strikes were not ruled out, as we have seen. The new ROH chairman Poláček specifically said that strikes on such issues as wages, changes in production lines, etc. were legitimate, while Slovak trade union chairman Daubner explained that many of the strikes already occurring were the result of the failure of some managers to make production changes without discussing matters with the workers (or as Daubner was reported in *Pravda* (Bratislava) of 20 April 1968, because of managers who 'do not understand that there has been a change and that they must consider the trade union organization a serious partner.') The earlier-mentioned demands for the creation of a strike fund were indeed met by the new ROH draft program.

The relationship between the trade union organizations and the new enterprise councils was outlined in an ROH statement published in *Práce* on 5 July 1968. The ROH supported the creation of the councils, the elections for which it was to supervise in each enterprise, and according to *Práce* of 18 February 1969, it favored as large a representation of workers as possible on these councils. Dubček explained that the enterprise councils would not eliminate the need for the trade unions, but, rather, would free the trade union organizations, so that they might 'express, represent, and fight for the real social needs of the working people.'[1] It was thus that Dubček conceived the second aspect of the role of the trade union: a social–political role. Dubček spoke of the unions' political force, 'securing for themselves significant participation in political life by taking the initiative in settling burning social problems of the workers' and acting as a representative of both the social and political interests of the working people.[2] According to *Rudé právo* of 16 March 1968, Špaček too saw the unions as initiators of suggestions for the Party to consider, but Dubček indicated to the May plenum that he meant even more when he said that the 'trade unions should once more become the

[1] *Pravda* (Bratislava), 4 June 1968 (29 May 1968 speech to central committee).
[2] *Rudé právo*, 23 February 1968 (22 February 1968 speech in Prague); *Rudé právo*, 30 June 1968 (to a district Party conference).

important political force in the National Front which they were before February 1948.' According to Dubček, the trade unions were to play a 'double role' of implementing the workers' interests vis-à-vis the economic or enterprise organs and of representing the working-peoples' interests vis-à-vis the organs of state power. 'This task,' he added 'will inevitably bring about a new political consciousness and a new political activity on trade union matters, an activity without which the further advance of our socialist democracy cannot be conceived of.'[1]

Democratization of the inner life and structure of the movement itself was also sought and included the following demands: democratic elections at all levels, including election of the ROH chairman by an all-state congress; leaders exclusively responsible to the membership, i.e. subject to control from lower organizations, which in turn would mean better-informed lower organs, and decentralization in favor of the basic organizations so that the members could see and control the management of their contributions. Lower, basic organizations were to be freed from directives and supervision by superior trade union organs, and basic organs were to have the final responsibility and authority to decide their own affairs. At the same time, basic organs were to have a share in the determination of trade union policy through an upgrading of their status relative to the central organs and a downgrading of the ROH central council presidium and secretariat relative to the plenum of the central council. Federalization of the trade union movement was agreed upon in the draft program of the ROH, splitting the movement along national lines, with the basic organizations responsible to the national (Slovak or Czech) trade union organ, which in turn would independently work out its own program and policies. The ROH council was to remain as a unifying unit above the two national organizations for dealing with the state and with foreign trade union centers, and for protecting all-over union interests.[2]

While the reforms were designed to provide greater trade union autonomy and authority at the basic level, they were, nonetheless, based

---

[1] It was probably in connection with recognition of the trade unions as independent social organizations that ROH declared its intention to increase contacts with the international non-Communist trade union organizations, the International Confederation of Free Trade Unions and the International Confederation of Christian Trade Unions. (*Práce*, 12 March 1968, communique of ROH central council presidium.)

[2] These changes were advocated on a number of occasions, but the official pronouncements from which the above was taken were the communique, *Práce*, 12 March 1968 and the draft program, *Práce*, 5 July 1968. There were also demands for a Moravian Council, but these were rejected at the ROH conference in June (ČTK, 4 June 1968 and Prague radio, 17 June 1968).

on the principle of one factory, one trade union organization. This principle came into dispute as the result of numerous efforts to split off from existing trade unions and/or to create new trade unions, within and even outside the ROH. Such efforts were within the scope of the Action Program's proclamation for the freedom of association and against 'monopolization by any organization,' but they conflicted with both Party policy and actual law, pending new legislation in the spirit of the liberalization.[1] A test-case was an effort by railway workers to establish a Federation of Locomotive Crews, possibly to be outside the ROH monopoly. The Federation (as explained in *Literární listy*, 18 April 1968 and *Zítřek*, 11 December 1968) represented some 24 000 workers; it was formed at the end of April and requested membership in the ROH as a union distinct from the Union of Czechoslovak Railroad Workers. This violated the one factory, one trade union organization principle, and the new Federation was ignored by ROH organs. To press its point, the Federation called railway engineers out on what amounted to a go-slow strike.[2] The railroad management, irrespective of the ROH or government, entered into negotiations with the Federation, but the ROH began to use discriminatory measures against Federation members.[3] Under pressure the railroads ceased dealing with the Federation, and the Federation found itself isolated. It, therefore, decided to apply for registration as a voluntary social-interest group instead of a trade union, so as to bypass the ROH altogether. After the invasion the Ministry of Interior turned down this application, at which point the Federation declared itself an independent trade union, as we shall see below.

Although the Federation was not an isolated case (some thirty-seven requests for new unions within the ROH were made by June 1968), it was perhaps a special one in that some saw in it an effort to revive the pre-Communist professional club–union known as the Federation of Machine Drivers.[4] The regime, however, was not interested in anything which might disrupt the ROH movement or cause competition for representation of specific workers. Thus a meeting of the Party presidium on 11 June 1968 was willing to concede the autonomy of trade union organizations but came out strongly in favor of federated mass organizations

[1] The 1951 law on voluntary organizations (*Sbírka zákonů* No. 68/1951) precluded the formation of additional political parties, trade union organizations, cooperatives, churches, or religious organizations.

[2] In fact they simply refused to work overtime, thus crippling the railways in some cases.

[3] No vacation rooms at spas or recreation centers; no use of the cultural or social funds of the ROH, etc.

[4] Prague radio, 4 June 1968; see for example *Pravda* (Bratislava), 6 April 1968.

instead of splits into independent groups.[1] The trade union conference of 18–20 June 1968 did approve the creation of 'independent' unions for each industry and each of the two nations, within the ROH, but it ruled out competition by strongly condemning attempts at organizing trade unions according to 'narrow interests' which 'split and weaken the strength of the trade unions.'[2] Dubček supported this view in his call for a unified trade union movement at the same conference. It would appear from this issue that not all aspects of democracy had yet been accepted or worked out, despite the proclaimed intentions of democratizing the ROH both within and in relation to the rest of society. Important elements of the Party, apparently, were still wedded to the previous notions of unified mass organizations as easy to deal with, perhaps easy to handle. On the other hand, from May onwards, when the Party was dealing with this matter, it was under severe conservative pressures (from both inside and outside) and was, therefore, understandably cautious on certain issues such as the unity of the workers' movement.

The agricultural union

The creation of an agriculturalists' union suggested by the Seventh Cooperative Farm (JZD) Congress in February 1968 was fraught with a number of difficulties. The crux of the issue was whether the new union would merely represent a reorganization of agriculture, with the 'union' operating as an economic organization together with or in place of the DAAs, or if the union would constitute a social, perhaps even political, interest group. This issue must not be underrated, for in it was manifest the opposition of the conservatives to the idea of more and stronger interest groups in the National Front. More specifically, the conservatives saw in the suggested agriculturists' union an effort to recreate the strong (and right of center) pre-war agrarian movement–party or even the less influential peasants' unions of the post-1945 period. For example, the unpopular Agriculture and Food Minister Karel Mestek (who was replaced in March 1968) attacked the mass media for encouraging what might turn out to be demands for 'a resurrection of an agrarian and fascist party.'[3]

[1] *Rok šedesátý osmý*, 225.
[2] Prague radio (English), 20 June 1968; *Práce*, 6 Sept. 1968.
[3] Prague radio (English), 18 March 1968 (speech to Nymburk district Party conference). *Práce*, and later the agriculture writers of the Slovak Writers Union, sent an open letter to Mestek in which they objected to his statement (as well as to his deeds, such as the banning of journalists from the cooperative farmers congress).

The JZD congress created a drafting committee to work out proposals for the suggested organization, and at its meeting on 19 March 1968 this committee (according to Prague radio 19 March 1968) apparently dealt only with plans for an economic organization. Some 1300 delegates to a farmers' meeting in Jičín on 26 March 1968, however, passed a resolution favoring the immediate creation of a farmers' social-interest union, to which some sort of economic organization would later be added.[1] In response, the Ministry of Agriculture and Food, through a conference of DAAs, proposed the DAAs as the core of the new organization, and that it should be an economic-interest organization.[2] Those who wanted a social organization argued that an organization of enterprises was not enough, for interests such as those of the members of a collective and those of the managers were not always identical. Farmers believed that it was not sufficient that there was a trade union organization on state farms, theoretically to protect individuals' interests (wages, benefits, cultural needs). They argued that only a state-wide interest group, i.e. a group specifically representing the interests of farmers as farmers could effectively put forth and protect farmers' needs.[3] The new Minister of Agriculture and Food, Party presidium member Josef Borůvka, told *Zemědělské noviny*:

'We need both the social and economic organization of farmers...It is necessary that these million farmers be united before the elections to ensure that we have our representatives in all national councils and to elect our agricultural deputies to the National Assembly. Big things are involved: our full equality has been acknowledged and now appropriate conditions must be created.'

The farmers were intent upon a social–political interest-organization, which could operate as a pressure group, and at least in the Czech lands, they took matters into their own hands. Preparatory committees of a 'Farmers Union' spontaneously began to form in the spring of 1968. Representatives of these groups met in Prague on 6 May 1968 and drafted a Farmers Union program. The Union was to be an all-state mutual interest organization of all those engaged in agriculture (from collective and private farmers to workers in the agricultural services enterprises), according to *Zemědělské noviny* of 9 May 1968. The number of preparatory organizations continued to grow and, by mid-June, the number of per-

[1] *Zemědělské noviny*, 26 March 1968; Bratislava television, 29 March 1968.
[2] *Zemědělské noviny*, 11 April 1968.
[3] See *Zemědělské noviny*, 17 April 1968 for example, and interview with Josef Borůvka in ibid. 30 March 1968.

sons registered for membership was estimated at 250 000.[1] This force from below preempted the tasks of the JZD's draft committee, but it did help to bring the committee around to accepting the idea of a social-interest organization in addition to the economic organization. Moreover, the proposal finally prepared by the JZD committee envisaged a Union of Cooperative Farmers which would include private farmers as well, and in which membership would be individual – rather than by enterprise.[2]

A federal union was envisaged, consisting of an all-state parent organization with two independent national organizations, and the Slovaks apparently did not believe that the concepts of Czech and Slovak unions need be identical.[3] Thus, in Slovakia things developed somewhat differently, for the Slovaks made no attempt to set up separate organizations, i.e. one economic and one social–political but rather one all-inclusive union for Slovak farmers.[4] Moreover membership in the Slovak union was not to be individual but by farm or agricultural enterprise – a practice related to the limited horizons of the economic organization concept. In addition, whereas the Czech concept was the product of initiative from below and pressures on the centrally oriented organs (the JZD committee), the Slovak concept had no such spontaneous pressures on it; it was the product of the JZD committee and a committee of the Slovak Agriculture and Food Commissioner's Office.

The above proposals pertained only to persons involved in cooperative and private farming, despite the idea of all-inclusive Farmers Unions. The state farmers did not see fit to join such organizations, establishing their own Economic Union of State Farmers (which also included state agricultural organizations) on 20 August 1968.

The Party's position on the formation and nature of an agriculturists' union only gradually became clear. The Action Program favored the creation of a union but failed to specify its nature. At its 21–22 May 1968 meeting the Party presidium and secretariat endorsed the creation of a union with the following functions: to assert and defend the interests of cooperative farmers particularly with regard to problems of work conditions, social security, etc., as well as with regard to cultural–social

[1] Prague radio, 10 June 1968. Until an organization received its authorization from the Interior Ministry it could form and convene only what were called preparatory committees and process requests for future membership. The Czech union was officially constituted in December 1968.

[2] Prague radio, 24 June 1968; *Zemědělské noviny*, 3 July 1968.

[3] Hungarian farmers proffered suggestions for a Hungarian farmers union or at least a minorities section in the Slovak union. (*Új szó*, 16 July 1968.)

[4] *Rol'nícke noviny*, 6 July 1968 (draft statutes).

interests, and it approved the idea of National Front association for the union.[1] As with the trade unions, Dubček made it clear that what was envisaged was not only a social organization, already a step forward, but a dual functioned social–political organization, which, on the one hand, would see to farmers' rights and needs, and, on the other hand, act as a political force. Dubček expressed the union's tasks as

'not only defending the individual interests of the cooperative farmers in problems concerning compensation, and so forth, but also politically representing the cooperative farmers in the National Front.'[2]

President Svoboda stated it still more radically:

'The class of cooperative farmers has won the right...to share in deciding all important matters in the country...It will then be only a logical culmination of the principles of cooperation in our agriculture for the union of cooperative farmers to become the spokesman of this class and one of the important members in the new system of the National Front.'[3]

The youth movement (ČSM)

The youth had become an important issue as a result of the 1967 (Strahov) student demonstrations which served to increase the pressures on Novotný in his struggle to hold his position in the Party. The youth had indeed shown an interest in the liberalization movement before 1967, as was evidenced not only by the almost yearly May Day demonstrations by young workers and students but also by the demands they voiced in various journals and in the youth organization, ČSM. As Císař pointed out after his return from Romania to Party life, 'even in the past period the youth closed ranks with strata of other generations in an effort to blast the path toward progress.'[4] Nor was the youth entirely ignored in the pre-revival liberalization, as evidenced by the efforts at educational reform and the concern expressed by the Party – even by Novotný himself – over the need for organs through which the youth could more genuinely express themselves. It was not until the 'Strahov affair' however, that the regime began to consider this a group to which it would have to answer.

[1] *Rok šedesátý osmý*, 161.
[2] *Pravda* (Bratislava), 4 June 1968 (speech to May–June plenum). Dubček specifically included private farmers in the union.
[3] Prague radio (English), 9 July 1968 (to Nitra conference, 9–11 July 1968).
[4] *Mladá fronta*, 28 March 1968.

Dubček was early to acknowledge, in his 22 February anniversary speech, that 'among all the questions facing us today, that of the youth holds a special place.'

Indeed the youth themselves took advantage of the shock caused in many corners of the society by the Strahov affair and formed themselves into something of a vanguard of the 1968 revival. They organized any number of rallies and meetings to which they invited leading political, cultural, and economic figures to answer their outspoken questions.[1] This activity was led by but not limited to students, for the students themselves sought to counter the conservatives' efforts to drive a wedge between workers and the intelligentsia; they sent letters to factory workers explaining their demands, and arranged joint meetings and discussions.[2] The rallies themselves were by no means exclusively student affairs, no more than the earlier May Day demonstrations had been comprised exclusively of students. To aid the students in their effort to cement their relationship with young workers, *Práce* even castigated the efforts to paint the Strahov affair as a class battle (young intelligentsia against young workers (the police)[3]) and pointed out on 10 March 1968 that most of the active students were children of workers or Party officials.

Some sought to dismiss the problems raised by the youth as natural gaps in understanding between generations. In *Pravda* (Bratislava) of 8 March 1968, one indignant Party member castigated the young for condemning past Party actions, thus:

'It is true that we then proceeded harshly [in collectivization]. You, the young, now can easily speak of the law and its sections. But at that time, the towns had nothing to eat. If we had not been hard you could not be sitting here at all, or you would be crippled by rickets.'

Aside from this simplified version of the generation gap, others pointed out the distrust and disillusionment of the youth vis-à-vis the older generation. As *Práce* of 10 March 1968 put it,

'they saw at each step that the practice was different from what was preached and at the time of the exposure of the so-called personality cult the youth ceased to believe even the teachers,'

---

[1] The largest and perhaps most interesting of these was in Prague, 20 March 1968, into which some 16 000 young people crammed themselves, to question Smrkovský, Šik, Goldstücker and other. (Prague radio, 20 March 1968 and *Rudé právo*, 22 March 1968.)

[2] See *Mladá fronta*, 13 March 1968.

[3] Reference was to remarks made by conservative František Kolář in *Kulturní tvorba*, 16 November 1967.

or as Goldstücker explained in an interview to an Italian Communist
weekly *Rinascita* (19 April 1968),

'in general the young people are disillusioned by the evolution of
Czechoslovakia, and they turn their preference toward that which
has been painted in the darkest colors, i.e. toward democracy of the
pre-Munich period.'

The young did indeed distrust their elders, especially the Party members, and found few people they could believe in since so many of even
the reformers had Stalinist or opportunistic pasts. Moreover, repugnance
of the Communists' mistakes, distortions, injustices and terror had a
counterpart for non-Communists in the shameful capitulation to Munich,
which was blamed on the leaders of the First Republic. Thus Czech and
Slovak youth saw little to emulate in their elders and believed little of
what they were told. The resulting ambivalence even towards the reform
regime was made clear by student leader Luboš Holeček who said at the
20 March 1968 Prague rally that the present support for the progressives
should not be taken as something definitive. He warned that if the
'political monopoly of the Communist Party' failed to secure the activity
of the masses, the students would have to seek another system.

On the other hand, the youth's demands were not limited to strictly
youth needs and desires. They included such things as the basic civil
freedoms, reestablishment of the Constitutional court, separation of powers
within the government, an investigation into the death of Jan Masaryk,
solidarity with Polish and French students, and even changes in foreign
policy (relations with Israel, help for Biafra, more equal status vis-à-vis
the USSR).[1] Indeed, objectively speaking, there was no gap between the
demands of the young and those of the reformers among their elders. Šik
once pointed out that the 1967–8 revolution in the Party was instigated
by some of the oldest members (such as Vodsloň and Kriegel) and, therefore, could not be characterized as a battle of generations.[2] Moreover such
ideas as those of older Communists who favored federalization in recognition of Slovak nationalism were apparently shared by young Slovaks,
whose nationalism seemed as strong as that of their fathers.[3] Yet many
were to point out that, while the words might be the same and the

---

[1] See, for example, 'Manifesto of Prague Youth' in *Reportér*, 3 April 1968.

[2] *Pravda* (Bratislava), 29 February 1968 (radio interview, rebroadcast 26 February
1968).

[3] *Rol'nícke noviny*, 29 April 1968, pointed this out with pride, reporting a mass march of
youth to Devín commemorating the Štúr-led youth march some 132 years earlier.
The paper said that just as a hundred years earlier Slovak youth wanted 'a free Slovak
state,' i.e. a federated ČSSR.

slogans mutual, there was a large gulf between the generations as regards the meaning of such words as 'democracy,' 'rights,' and so forth. This was one of the reasons the youth questioned their elders so severely, demanding at every step actions rather than words.

The young people strove to operate as a pressure group, demanding and indeed maintaining enough independence so as to be an effective force. This was perhaps the greatest difference between youth's role in the pre-1968 struggle and after. So long as the struggle had remained within the Party, the youth, as a group basically outside the Party, could not exercise a leadership role of any importance. The best they could do was to attempt to awaken their own ranks and strive to have their own demands included among those of the Party progressives. When, after January 1968, the process became a public affair, so to speak, and the Party turned to the public for support and participation, the youth found that they had new possibilities. As the best-informed and most involved, organized group outside the Party – one of the few if not the only non-Party group to have early on grasped the possibilities of the pre-1968 struggle – they were natural leaders of the hitherto uninformed, uninvolved, or unconsulted masses, and a natural bridge between these and the Party reformers, with whom they had cooperated in the recent past. In this new capacity the youth were indeed a force, and both they and the new regime had to consider how best this force might be institutionally expressed or handled.

The Party was naturally concerned that 'the gigantic political activation of young people' would not be used against but rather for the Party, and a *Rudé právo* editorial of 22 March 1968 urged Communists to go among the youth, talk to them and try to win them over, by deeds as well as words, in the spirit of the 'post-January program of revival.' Dubček understood the problem, perhaps more deeply, and placed the emphasis on deeds. In his February speech he said

'I do not think we can win over the youth simply by constantly
telling them or even throwing constantly in their teeth all that has
been successfully achieved...youth's enthusiasm and ardour
cannot be exhausted by merely praising what has been realized.
Youth wants to create themselves, to enforce their longings and
ideals themselves – precisely as the older generation wanted to do
when they were young and when the revolution provided them
with all the possibilities for this. They must not get ready-made
things, gifts, or achievements but scope for their own initiative,
for their ideas, for arranging their own future life so as to accomplish their tasks as the generation of our times.'

Dubček urged, therefore, the creation of conditions which would permit the youth to express themselves as he described.

It had long since been recognized that ČSM was in need of reform, but the brief movement to bring about change had been abruptly halted in Novotný's tightening-up of 1966 and 1967. In December of 1966, one year after his suggestions for a federated youth organization (composed of individual students, worker, and farmer groups) capable of operating as an independent political body, student leader Jiří Müller had been expelled from both the university and ČSM and drafted into the Army. His closest colleague Luboš Holeček was expelled from the university and drafted several months later. The proposals adopted at the 1965 student conference were shelved and the group around Müller and Holeček known as the 'Prague radicals' was on the defensive.[1] None of this settled the problem, as the Strahov events had shown, and in 1968 the Party was forced once again to face the problem of ČSM. At this time, however, ČSM was all but disintegrating, as group after group demanded independence. The most important or at least controversial of these groups was that of the students.

Relations between ČSM and the students had become strained as a result of the Müller affair, but they became still more problematic after the Strahov events, for the ČSM central committee had supported the Party rather than the students in that complicated issue. The Prague students retaliated by proposing the formation of Academic Councils of Students, beginning with one at the Philosophy Faculty, which more or less supplanted the ČSM committees since they consisted basically of the same people. On 13 January 1968 the ČSM University Committee for the Prague District (VOV) called a meeting of students and ČSM officials from the various Prague faculties. At this meeting the students – and the ČSM university representatives (VOV) – aired their complaints against the ČSM central committee, and a decision was taken to organize a referendum in Prague on the question of creating an independent student organization. ČSM's reaction was to declare, in its weekly *Student* of 31 January 1968, that: it would not consider itself bound by any decision of this meeting or any future group; it would not permit the ČSM to be used to organize a referendum which would be extended to non-ČSM members. The ČSM presidium announced that if a group wanted to leave the Union it was free to do so, but ČSM would not consider membership in such a splinter group a substitute for membership in ČSM.

---

[1] See *Práce*, 29 February 1968; *Student*, 13 March 1968; *Literární listy*, 7 March 1968, for a history of the issue. They were not 'radical' in the sense of the New Left, however.

ČSM's position gradually evolved as it – and the regime – sought to accommodate the rebellious students. Müller was readmitted to ČSM by reversal of the ČSM's 22 December 1966 expulsion order, and both Holeček and Müller were readmitted to the university following their early release from the Army.[1] After pressures from the ČSM–VOV and from the Party's own university committee, the Strahov investigation was reopened. As a result, on 11 March the Ministry of Interior apologized to the students, and the Interior Minister Josef Kudrna condemned what he called the unnecessarily harsh behavior of the police.[2] University reaction in Prague to Kudrna's 'self-criticism' was not favorable; on 12 March 1968 the Party's university committee demanded Kudrna's resignation, and the students (VOV) refused to accept Kudrna's explanation.[3] After Kudrna's dismissal on 15 March 1968 the Ministry of Interior issued several more statements regretting the police intervention (actually admitting it had been illegal).[4] Josef Kozoušek, rector of the Technical Institute (to which Strahov belonged) resigned 'for health reasons' on 28 March 1968.

ČSM organized a group to study suggestions for a reorganization of the Union. This group, according to Prague radio, 20 March 1968, recommended the resignation of the ČSM's presidium and secretariat, which was implemented on 21 March 1968, and the creation of a federation to be composed of various youth groups according to age, social group, interest, and possibly nationality. Preparations were begun for a special congress, but student reaction was both skeptical and cynical, for ČSM was now offering federation – Müller's old suggestion – to ward off total student independence. As one observer pointed out, in *Práce* of 29 February 1968, ČSM's narrow-mindedness and conservativism had driven the students to much more radical demands – so that Müller's suggestions by that time seemed conservative. Moreover ČSM's promises to permit 'political polemics and discussion' could barely be believed.[5] The *Práce* article expressed a widely held reaction: 'What was unthinkable yesterday is being promised overnight...who can believe them?' Moreover, students wanted more than political discussions within ČSM, they wanted their

[1] *Mladá fronta*, 23 February 1968.
[2] ČTK, 11 March 1968; *Mladá fronta*, 12 March 1968. A similar act was the decision by the Presidium of the Supreme Court to review the proceedings against the youths involved in the 1966 May Day demonstrations. (ČTK, 23 March 1968.)
[3] ČTK, 11, 12 March 1968. The party group of the Writers Union also expressed dissatisfaction with Kudrna's statement. (Prague radio, 13 March 1968.)
[4] Prague radio, 16 March 1968 and *Rudé právo*, 19 March 1968.
[5] *Student*, 31 January 1968.

ideas to reach the public. Quoting Lenin, one article said the students form 'the most sensitive part of the intelligentsia,' but they had 'no platform from which to deliver meaningful judgments' and their already formulated demands, which could be in the interests of the whole of society.[1]

The students, like the workers and the farmers in many cases, took matters into their own hands. On 21 February 1968 the ČSM committee at the Philosophy Faculty resigned *en masse* in favor of the Academic Council of Students, which itself declared its intention to run candidates for the National Assembly and the Prague National Committee.[2] A few days later the ČSM group at the Journalism Faculty relinquished responsibility for all but the 35 ČSM members at the Faculty; representatives to the Academic Council of Students were to be elected after a week's campaign (*all* students having the right to vote).[3] These actions were repeated elsewhere and on 19 March 1968 representatives of 17 of Prague's 24 faculties created a preparatory committee for a Union of University Students. The 'Prague radicals' leader Luboš Holeček was a member of this committee although he and the still powerful Jiří Müller and their colleagues from the VOV were neither decided nor united as to their attitude regarding a union, even one which would be an improvement over ČSM. They were wary of creating another *apparat* or bureaucracy; they sought freedom for the expression of the existing plurality of views, rather than another organization which might claim a monopoly on the expression of students' political views.[4] Thus, while losing little of their extraordinary prestige or influence among the students, they did not assume a leadership role in the founding of the new organization.

The 19 March 1968 Prague student assembly also formulated an Action Program for the emerging student organization. The program, based on the United Nations Declaration of Human Rights, proposed: support for the progressive forces and demands for personnel changes in the Party; rehabilitations; legal guarantees of civil rights; and postponement of elections pending amendment to the election law. The proposals, according to Prague radio, 19 March 1968, also condemned efforts to stir up differences between the students and other youth groups, i.e. the workers.

[1] Josef Wagner, in *Student*, 7 February 1968.
[2] Prague radio, 28 February and 1 March 1968.
[3] *Mladá fronta*, 5 March 1968, which also published journalist students' demands for a new Press Law and the reopening of *Tvář*, as well as freedom of information and so forth.
[4] See Holeček in 'Conversation about the Student Movement,' *Host do domu*, XVII:8 (1969), 20–4.

A national meeting of university students was held on 22–23 March 1968 in Brno, where local students had also spontaneously broken with ČSM. This meeting, according to Prague radio, 23 March 1968, resolved to hold elections throughout the country's faculties for representatives to a state-wide student conference in May 1968 which would decide upon the creation of a nationally federated student union outside ČSM. It also called on the public to support the demand for a postponement of the elections, a new electoral law, and the shortening of students' military service from one year to only three to six months.

In interviews to *Mladá fronta*, 1 and 15 March 1968, the students explained their actions as a total rejection of any solution or arrangement within the ČSM. They considered ČSM a moribund organization, membership in which had tended to be only a formal necessity and an organization which, in any case, had lost the confidence of the students. Most seemed to want student self-government at the lower levels, working up to a union of students with (genuine) representation in the International Union of Students. In speaking of a unified or all-state federated student organization, they were careful to add that this must be a real federation, with representatives genuinely representing their 'constituents,' keeping them informed and leading them without directing them. Moreover decisions should not be obligatory on those dissenting from union decisions.

The situation among the youth was far from clear, however, for any number of student groups were being constituted spontaneously, and in some cases (such as that of the Agricultural School in Prague), in opposition to the idea of any overall union. There was also the extreme radical group known as the Movement of Revolutionary Youth, centered in the Prague Philosophy Faculty, which somewhat resembled Poland's Kuroń and Modzelewski in its extreme emphasis upon communist revolution. Moreover, requests for autonomy, within or outside ČSM, rapidly appeared from other segments of the youth. For example, on the initiative of the young workers in the largest factories in central Bohemia, a state-wide meeting was held in Prague on 24 March 1968 to discuss the creation of a Union of Working Youth. The meeting (according to Prague radio, 24 March 1968) suggested that the working youth be organized from the bottom up, with councils at district and regional levels and one at the center. The councils 'would not, however have the right to control directly or to interfere in the individual groups' affairs.'

Slovak youth also wanted their own organization, and although this demand was met by the federalization of ČSM, there were demands for a union of Slovak farm youth; there were also demands for independent youth unions for the Hungarian, Ukrainian and Polish minorities.[1] The children's organization, the Pioneers, also demanded autonomy, raising its age-limit to permit membership for people over 15, to include, for example, its adult leaders who indeed promptly joined. Both the Pioneers and the youth section of Svazarm (the Union for Cooperation with the Army) called for the rehabilitation of Junák (the Boy Scouts), and Svazarm's youth committee proclaimed itself a preparatory center for the Boy Scouts.[2] According to *Mlada fronta* of 3 April 1968, young soldiers and secondary pupils also wanted independent organizations, for which they set up preparatory committees. The Socialist Party created its own youth group when it set up a preparatory committee for an Association of Socialist Youth on 4 April 1968; the Catholic Church sought the re-establishment of Catholic Scouts, or youth clubs and 'Orel' (a Catholic physical culture group); the Protestants began reactivation of the YMCA and YWCA.[3]

Responding directly to the students' activities Goldstücker and Čestmír Císař both admitted to radio interviewers (on 3 February and 8 April respectively) that ČSM did not provide room for the students. Smrkovský, admitting that the ČSM was undergoing 'a grave crisis,' told the April central committee plenum that, even if one did not consider the creation of an independent student organization 'expedient' or wise, one could not say that 'by itself an independent student organization is something anti-socialist or that its existence violates the principles of socialism.' The same plenum also heard pleas by such progressives as Šik and Dubček himself for unity in the youth movement, but Šik admitted that such unity, if enforced, might well 'encourage certain oppositional trends among youth.' He suggested that the Party simply advise the youth that experience had taught that splits weaken, a unified union would be stronger.[4] The Action Program conceded the need for an independent youth movement – independent from Party control and outside interference – and on these grounds the Party opposed the creation of youth movements attached to other parties.[5] If this argument were offered as the reason other parties should not have youth groups, it could easily have

[1] For example, Bratislava radio, 15 January 1968; 23 March 1968; *Új szo*, 15 March 1968. [2] Prague radio, 1, 20 March 1968.
[3] *Mladá fronta*, 5 April 1968, *Tribuna*, 5 February 1969.
[4] For youth views on this idea see *Mladá fronta*, 3 April 1968, which also recommended the creation of a Youth Ministry. In January 1969 a Ministry of Youth and Physical Culture was indeed set up.
[5] *Rudé právo*, 24 May 1968 (21–22 May presidium session).

been argued that the ČSM should no longer be the Communist Party youth organization. Without clarifying this point, however, the Party went on to declare its opposition to youth organizations independent of a federated ČSM, and thus insisted upon the continued monopolization of the youth movement, in clear contradiction to the Action Program's stand on the freedom of association.

Despite the Party's position, and in the midst of disputes among the students themselves over the need for and nature of a union (as a social-interest organization or as a political organization), the Union of University Students (SVS) for Bohemia and Moravia was founded in Olomouc on 26 May 1968. On 25 May 1968 a Union of Students of Slovakia (ZVS) was also founded. A Czechoslovak Student Center was set up as a co-ordinating body for dissemination of information and representation abroad, consisting of four representatives from each national union, but it had no decision-making powers. Its chairman and vice-chairman were to be alternately (tenure of one year) a Czech and a Slovak. A significant difference between the two independent organizations was that ZVS proclaimed its adherence to the principle of democratic centralism and sought membership in the National Front. The Czech students did not wish to have union decisions binding upon members and, therefore, opposed the principle of democratic centralism. They were still undecided on the issue of the National Front and accepted Jiří Müller's suggestion that this question be settled only at the union's next annual conference.

Membership in the SVS was by faculty rather than individual and, until the group's registration with the Ministry of Interior after the invasion, only 11 of the 63 faculties in Bohemia and Moravia were members. This lack of membership was by no means a sign of student indifference. On the contrary, it was probably the result of the fact that students were more directly involved in the political developments of those enthusiastic months than at any time in the history of the country. Thus as individuals and small groups, often focused around their faculties or clubs, they played a large role in bringing the workers into the reform movement (in the early months), and in the pressing of specific issues, through rallies, petitions, and articles in their publication *Student*.[1] It was probably because of this lack of interest in organizations as such that the Party presidium's admonition against a split of ČSM in June went unheeded. ČSM had in fact ceased to exist and the Party could not or was not willing to do much more than proffer its opinion.

---

[1] *Student* also left ČSM and on 3 April declared itself 'The Weekly Journal of the Young Intelligentsia.'

Associations, clubs and other mass organizations

The ČSM and the ROH were not the only mass organizations to find themselves faced with rebellious groups. Svazarm too suffered from this reaction against the over-centralization and administrative rule of the past. Although it retired its entire leadership, offered reform and opened its ranks to interests representing all sports, it suffered defections from numerous groups, for example Moravian aviation enthusiasts.[1] An independent Aeroclub of Moravia was founded on 17 March 1968, with invitations to Bohemian and Slovak air enthusiasts to follow them out of Svazarm, together to form a Central Aeroclub of Czechoslovakia; motorists too left to set up the Auto Club of Czechoslovakia. Although Svazarm declared it would be the parent organization of the revived Boy Scouts (Junák), Junák was reestablished as an independent organization on 29 March 1968.[2] It did not apply for registration as a new organization on the grounds that it had never ceased to exist, though prevented from functioning after 1948. Similarly suppressed after 1948, the Sokol organization also requested reestablishment. According to Prague radio of 19 June, however, it was informed that it must join the unified gymnastic organization: the Czechoslovak Association for Physical Culture. Presumably aware of the national–political–cultural importance Sokol had played in Czech history and tradition, the regime was reluctant to permit its independent revival.

A number of entirely new, still more controversial groups also formed. Czechoslovak scientists decided that, in the past, they had been unjustly denied the right to a union. As they explained in *Literární listy* of 11 April 1968, 'precisely in modern society, the weight of scientific thinking and scientific erudition is to be a basic force no less significant than the material contribution of scientific work.' Yet, they claimed, while they were scattered, they could not make their views felt nor properly support artists, for example, at critical moments. Therefore, a group of leading scientists and thinkers convened on 26 March 1968 to establish a preparatory committee for an independent Union of Scientific Workers. Among the founders were such people as Goldstücker, Šik, Charles

[1] *Zemědělské noviny*, 27 March 1968 and Prague radio, 30 March 1968. The leadership of numerous other organizations such as the Czechoslovak Women's Union and even the Union of Fire Brigades also resigned. (Prague radio, 27, 22 March 1968.)
[2] Junák had been repressed and the leaders jailed subsequent to the 1948 Communist takeover. In an emotional ceremony, the original pre-1948 leaders were reinstated. (*Lidová demokracie*, 30 March 1968.)

University rector Oldřich Starý, philosopher Karel Kosík and numerous leading academicians. As Goldstücker explained, the Union would have the two-fold task of representing the interests and needs of scientists on the one hand, and participating as a force in society and in the National Front, on the other.

The Union of Anti-Fascist Fighters also came under attack particularly for the persecution of people who had fought on the western front, in Tito's partisans, and in western armies. After putting forth a number of demands for improvements in the Union, World War Two veterans decided to form an 'association of soldiers who fought abroad,' the main task of which would be to see to the rehabilitation of those of their ranks persecuted after 1948.[1] Similar, in a sense, but much more controversial, was the club formed by former victims of the purges. This group called itself 'Club 231' (K-231) after the number of the paragraph of the Penal Code under which they had been punished. As with the veterans, the main purpose was to work towards full rehabilitation of former victims. The preparatory meeting was held on 31 March 1968 and attended by several thousands, by no means exclusively non-Communists – although the man elected acting chairman was Karel Nigrin, once a high official in Beneš' London-based government during the war.

K-231 ran into difficulties with the authorities, probably because it posed a direct threat – at least of discomfort – to those responsible for and involved in the trials. The club's constituent assembly was indefinitely postponed, as the government claimed that it had failed to meet the necessary requirements for registration. When chairman Nigrin tried to publicize the club's proposed program, neither the television nor ČTK would comply; finally Nigrin published the story of the club's difficulties in *Svobodné slovo* (organ of the Czechoslovak Socialist Party), on 21 May 1968. He claimed that pressures by conservatives had caused persecution, while Prague radio (24 May 1968) itself said that the difficulties may have been because the club was considered too close to a political party and, as we have seen, pending a new law, the creation of such groups as unions, political parties, and religious groups was forbidden. In fact the conservatives had launched a campaign against K-231, claiming that persons legitimately tried as fascists or anti-Communists were among the members of the club, and that the club sought rehabilitation of such 'justly' punished people.[2] Conservative fears were understandable when one con-

[1] Prague radio, 16, 29, 30 March 1968.
[2] See, for example, Jaroslav Prášek in *Reportér*, 12 June 1968.

sidered that the club claimed that some 128 000 persons had been sentenced on the basis of Law 231.[1] The regime refused registration for the club and even Dubček felt compelled to recognize the justice of certain fears. At the 29 May 1968 central committee plenum he said:

'There do not even lack attempts to create a legal basis for their ["relics of defeated bourgeois classes"] activities in some organizations which are now spontaneously emerging, particularly in the K-231, where people who have been justly condemned for anti-state activities also operate.'

After negotiations in mid-June, the organization was, however, to be permitted to continue until the implementation of the rehabilitations.[2]

A widely popular and apparently successful group was the Club for Committed Non-Party Members (KAN). This group was started on 5 April 1968 by 144 people, mainly members of the Czechoslovak Academy of Sciences. Their purpose, according to two of its founders, reported in *Literární listy*, 11 April 1968, was 'to offer citizens without party affiliation the possibility of active participation in political life.' The club program stated that they accepted socialism as a given, but wanted to actively join the struggle for democratic socialism 'because we feel that the only method corresponding to the traditions of our nation is democracy.' The program proclaimed the respect of each individual's sovereignty and right to be what he wishes,

'rejecting any manipulation of man by man...In the long run the club intends to strive to secure for its members, who have no political affiliation, an equal position in their work with members of the Communist Party, especially in view of the fact that there is no organization associating politically unorganized citizens.'

The club proposed to do this, among other ways, by putting up its own candidates for the National Assembly, according to Prague radio, 16 April 1968. Shortly after it was formed KAN recommended that the Social Democratic Party be re-formed.[3] The Communist Party rejected the request and, instead, decided to commemorate 27 June 1968 as the anniversary of the Social Democratic Party's merger (submergence) with the Communist Party.[4] KAN groups were formed in a number of communities, among workers and intellectuals alike. While they had difficulty getting officials to listen to them, they began to represent a certain force

[1] Ibid.
[2] Jaroslav Brodsky, 'Czechoslovakia's 231 Club,' *East Europe*, 18:6(1969), 25.
[3] Prague radio, 24 April 1968.
[4] *Rudé právo*, 24 May 1968; *Rok šedesátý osmý*, 160, 225; and below, 155–6.

which could – and in many people's eyes already did – constitute a political party.[1]

Still other similar groups included such associations as the League for Engaged Action, the Club of Critical Thought, The League for Human Rights, and the Circle of Independent Writers. Prague radio (18 April 1968) explained that the League for Engaged Action was to be a political club for youth. The Club of Critical Thought was to provide a platform 'for developing critical ideas so as to make them a lasting component of our social and political life,' according to *Zemědělské noviny* of 16 March 1968. Among the participants at the first meeting of the latter were Party writers Klíma, Vaculík, Kohout, Hamšík, Kundera, scientist–poet Milan Holub and philosopher Karel Kosík. The purpose of the League for Human Rights was to protect civil rights, but while the League was one of the rare groups to be granted a license, its Slovak counterpart, the Slovak Organization for the Protection of Human Rights, was denied a license by the Ministry of Interior – reflecting perhaps the relative strength of conservatives in Slovakia.[2]

The Circle of Independent Writers was formed by non-Party members of the Czechoslovak Writers Union on 29 March 1968. One of the purposes of the group according to its 'Declaration' in *Literární listy* of 4 July 1968, was to put non-Party people on an equal footing with the Party contingent in the Writers Union. For example, the Party group always discussed programs and resolutions before their presentation to the Union; non-Communists wanted the same right so as to share in the decisions of the Union more fully and on an equal basis. Like KAN, they too wanted also to provide a framework within which non-Party people could contribute to political developments. Their program sought cultural freedom; freedom of expression and speech 'for every shade of philosophy and aesthetics;' equal participation of Party and non-Party members alike in the editing of journals, management of publishing houses, etc. They intended to act as 'a mutual moral check' to prevent a return to the type of cultural narrow-mindedness and dictatorship of the 1950s. Established on the initiative of the young writer Alexandr Kliment and playwright Václav Havel, this group differed from the others mentioned in that it did not seek independence or association outside the Writers Union.

These and the many other groups, clubs, and associations which sprang

[1] See for example A. J. Liehm in *Literární listy*, 27 June 1968.
[2] Prague radio, 8, 18 June 1968. After Husák came to power in 1969 the Association's license was revoked by the Czech government. (Prague radio, 28 May 1969.)

up in the spring of 1968 were seen by many as the core of new political parties or as units which could act in the place of political parties, fulfilling the role of non-Party (non-Communist Party) opposition.[1] Yet, these groups did not have as much success with the legal authorities as the Action Program and numerous promises might have led one to believe. Granting both the short time the experiment was allowed to function and the serious pressures on the reformers from outside and from the conservatives, one might, nonetheless, have hoped for more positive early results. By 18 June 1968 some seventy requests for registration had been received by the Ministry of Interior, but only one had been accepted, with decisions on most of the others delayed indefinitely.[2] Crucial, perhaps, to the development the reformers wanted was the never-enacted bill on the freedom of association – a matter pointed out in many circles.

[1] See Ivan Sviták's lecture to KAN in *Student*, 30 April 1968.
[2] Prague radio, 18 June 1968. The one exception was the Czech League for Human Rights. Only eleven had submitted the required draft statutes, however. Both the regime and the organizations may have been awaiting the Party congress before moving on this issue.

4

Religious and National Minorities

During the period of pre-1968 thaw, a certain liberalization of religious life and a change in the official attitude towards religion had been tentatively begun. This process was given a great push forward by the advent of the reformers to power in January 1968. Indeed, perhaps for the first time, a genuine effort was made by the Czechoslovak Communists to come to grips with the existence of such minorities and furthermore to extend to them the liberties proclaimed by the reform movement. The Action Program expressed this, in but a single sentence, thus: 'The liberties guaranteed by the spirit of this law [freedom of assembly and association] must also be fully applicable in line with the Constitution to various religious faiths and denominations.' Amplifying on this somewhat, Husák commented on the possibility of reopening formerly banned churches, expressing the regime's willingness to afford the possibility for each citizen 'freely to adhere to that religious orientation he finds suitable for himself.'[1] A clearer sign that the regime intended to deal more fairly with religious groups however, was, the removal of Stalinist Karel Hrůza on 25 March 1968 from his job as director of the Ministry of Culture and Information's secretariat for church affairs. The choice for his replacement, Dr Erika Kadlecová, was cause for optimism. Dr Kadlecová was a sociologist, head of the Department of Theory and Sociology of Religion in the Czechoslovak Academy of Sciences (ČSAV) Sociology Institute, and had a record of being fair and objective in her approach to the problem. In response to a question referring to the 'millions of believers in Eastern Europe living in conditions of fear and conflict between their position as citizens and their position as believers,' Dr Kadlecová said: 'We are fully aware of this, and we want to provide room for the religious needs of the believers in this country.'[2] This stood in promising contrast to her predecessor, who claimed in an interview to *Lidová demokracie* on 13 March 1968 that he had never had any 'intimation' that there was anything but religious freedom in Czechoslovakia.

[1] Gustav Husák, 'Word for the Present Day,' *Nová mysl*, XXII:6(1968), 659–63.
[2] Prague radio (English), 7 April 1968.

The Catholic Church

Internal pressures for changes regarding the Church emerged only gradually as part of the general demands for a redress of past errors and democratization of Czechoslovak society. The Church itself, however, which nominally counted its adherents at 75 per cent of the population, began in early 1968 to present its grievances.[1] This was done by Bishop František Tomášek, a formerly persecuted prelate who had been permitted to replace the regime-appointed apostolic administrator in Prague only in 1965, in exchange for Archbishop Beran's removal to Rome.[2] In Beran's absence, his former protégé Tomášek became the Church spokesman in Czechoslovakia.

One of the most pressing problems in the eyes of Tomášek was the naming of religious leaders to the many dioceses left under regime-appointed apostolic administrators. Despite the relatively large number of dioceses (four in Bohemia, two in Moravia, seven in Slovakia), there were only four bishops (three in Slovakia, none in Moravia, and only one, Tomášek, in Bohemia).[3] While it was the Vatican which nominated the bishops, approval had to be granted by the Czechoslovak government in order for them to assume their tasks. While, according to both Tomášek and Kadlecová, this matter was to be settled in the course of negotiations between the Vatican and Prague, the regime did permit the reinstatement of Karel Skoupý as Bishop of Brno, Josef Hloucha as Bishop of České Budějovice, and Štěpán Trochta as Bishop of Litoměřice.[4] Bishop Eduard Nécsei of Nitra was named archbishop by Pope Paul VI, making him the highest-ranking prelate in Czechoslovakia pending Cardinal Beran's possible return.

Beran's return was indeed demanded by the Church, but according to both Beran and Tomášek this was a matter for decision by the Vatican and the Czechoslovak government.[5] Vatican–Prague talks were due to begin at the end of the summer, and Tomášek said that he hoped the

[1] The semi-official census of 1950 listed 75.4% of the population as Roman Catholic. 'Report on Czechoslovakia,' RFE, 1961, 37–44.

[2] The Vatican continued to list Beran as the 'impeded' archbishop of Prague, while Prague persisted in referring to him as the 'former' archbishop of Prague.

[3] Vienna radio, 27 March 1968 (Tomášek interview); Tomášek in *Reportér*, 12 June 1968.

[4] Ibid. and Prague radio, 18 and 23 May 1968.

[5] See Tomášek interview, Vienna radio, 27 March 1968 and interview in *Student*, 7 May 1968. This was the first time Beran was publicly to state his views in Czechoslovakia since his arrest in 1949.

Yugoslav–Vatican agreement might serve as a model for a Czech agreement. While Dr Kadlecová did not comment on the prospects for renewal of diplomatic relations between the two 'states,' she did say that 'as long as the Vatican provides scope for the Catholics to be good citizens of a socialist state, and the Church does not attempt to influence politically their attitudes and decisions, there is no reason that mutual relations should remain strained.'[1] Direct and frequent contact with the Vatican was in fact, reestablished in 1968 with Tomášek traveling to Rome several times, as did a number of other bishops. The Vatican, for its part, was apparently willing to show greater understanding on certain issues, such as matching the borders of dioceses to the borders of the country (so that certain parishes in Slovakia would no longer be under the archbishopric of Hungary). The creation of a Slovak archbishopric was being initiated, and, presumably, the naming of Nécsei archbishop was for this purpose.

A second important problem for the Church was that of religious education. Tomášek condemned as insufficient the current system of religious lessons *after* hours, up to the seventh grade, and only upon written request from the parents. This system also often provoked discrimination against religious children, or their parents, with regard to employment, according to Tomášek, so that most pupils were fearful of registering for such classes. Tomášek, therefore, urged the referral of religious education of the young to the Churches themselves.[2] The Church was in fact granted this significant reform by a decree of the Ministry of Education and Culture which went into effect for the school year 1968–9, placing religious instruction in the hands of the Churches.[3] While this did not mean that the Churches could run parochial schools or that religious instruction would become a part of the regular curriculum, religious instruction would be freed of state or 'administrative' interference, to be planned and administered by the Churches themselves. Tomášek also urged the possibility of sending pupils who wished eventually to prepare for the priesthood to what used to be called a 'small seminary,' i.e. a secondary school with extensive teaching of religion and Latin. There were also demands with regards to the seminaries themselves. All but two seminaries had been abolished by the Communists and these two, one in Litoměřice and one in Bratislava, were limited by a *numerus clausus*. If the situation were to continue, Tomášek argued, the number of

[1] Prague radio (English), 7 April 1968.
[2] Vienna radio, 27 March 1968. See also letter to Dubček published in *Literární listy*, 21 March 1968, signed by 83 Catholics sentenced in the 1950s.
[3] *Lidová demokracie*, 9 July 1968 and *Katolické noviny*, 15 September 1968.

The Catholic Church

priests in Czechoslovakia would drop by 50 per cent within the next ten years. Without the *numerus clausus*, which was in fact being abolished, the two seminaries could not handle the number of students who wished to enter. The regime, therefore, agreed to the reopening of the Theological Faculty in Olomouc, closed by the government in 1950, and was considering the opening of still another Faculty in Košice.[1]

Connected with the shortage of clergy in Czechoslovakia was the problem of the priests and members of religious orders arrested in the 1950s, for whom release and full rehabilitation were demanded.[2] Between May and July of 1968 some 100 priests were in fact released from prison, allegedly the last of those held.[3] Tomášek estimated that some 1500 were still awaiting rehabilitation. Dr Kadlecová had come out in favor of rehabilitations, but she admitted that the process was slow, and an estimated 1000 priests were still forced to work as laborers.[4] Still more difficult was the rehabilitation of former members of religious orders, for there was the question of permitting the reappearance of these orders. Tomášek argued that as the monasteries and convents were not closed by law but by administrative order, rehabilitations 'carried out truly to the end' would necessitate their reopening, and he pointed to the valuable services the orders had rendered in the past, e.g. in hospitals, homes for the old, and so forth. Some of the press supported this by providing a platform for Tomášek and other Catholic leaders and by articles such as the one in *Literární listy* of 25 July 1968, entitled 'Women in Black,' on behalf of nuns. In April a delegation of religious organizations submitted a resolution to the government demanding the reopening of the orders. Five months after the invasion the Prosecutor-General's Office announced that it saw no obstacle to the restoration of cloisters and convents.

Demands for rehabilitations of lay Catholics, combined with demands for a Catholic press, bore fruits for Catholic cultural life. Former political prisoners joined the staffs of the various Catholic journals, raising their standards and giving them a new vitality. The regime permitted these

[1] *Reportér*, 12 June 1968 and *Lidová demokracie*, 21 May 1968. Rather than reinstatement as a Faculty of the University of Olomouc it was eventually downgraded as a branch of the Faculty of Theology of Litoměřice.
[2] For example, at a meeting in Brno of 157 professors and teachers of Christian religion, *Nový život*, 6 June 1968.
[3] *Lidová demokracie*, 4 July 1968. *L'ud*, 1 February 1969 said that the last had been released in July 1968. Hrůza said that from 1961 to 1966 some 302 priests had returned to their ecclesiastical functions and in 1967 approximately 80.
[4] *Lidová demokracie*, 7 April 1968; *Lidová demokracie*, 16 March 1968; *Lidová demokracie*, 6 November 1968.

journals to increase their circulation and, judging by their content, apparently gave them a free hand.[1] The program of the publishing house of the Catholic Peoples Party also reflected the new situation, as its lists included numerous previously 'banned' Catholic writers and scholars, domestic and foreign. These developments were also due in part to the jettisoning of 'regime' clerics in favor of persons loyal to the Church. Thus the Communist-created and Communist-dominated Peace Movement of the Catholic Clergy, headed by the excommunicated priest and regime puppet Josef Plojhar, was abolished. This organization had come under open criticism from such groups as the theological students at Litoměřice, who adopted a resolution asserting that the organization was not a voluntary one based on democratic principles and from the start had been dominated by individuals who did not have the confidence of the clergy and of the believers.[2] At an historic meeting in May 1968, called the Velehrad Conference, attended by no less than twelve bishops, the 'Peace Priests' were converted into a new organization, presided over by Bishop Tomášek and called the Work of Council Renewal.[3] This placed at least the representation of the Church in Czechoslovakia, vis-à-vis the state, back in the hands of genuine servants of the Church.

Tomášek had other, broader ideas on this subject, which he raised in his *Reportér* article. He advocated a change in the existing laws concerning religion, calling them long-since obsolete and undemocratic. He believed that 'the harsh supervision of the state over the Church' should be changed into 'routine supervision, as is done abroad.' The clergyman should be subordinated only to his bishop with regard to Church matters (after swearing allegiance to the state). With regard to the economic side of state control of the Church, Tomášek saw two possibilities: the state might contribute a certain sum to individual dioceses and the bishop would have the right to decide on its use and distribution; or there could be a complete separation of church and state, with all costs borne by the Church. Presumably the Church preferred the second alternative, although the first possibility – which had better chances of acceptance – would also have marked a significant step forward.

Barring such independence both the regime and the Church expressed a

[1] Figures released in 1969 indicate that the Slovak-language weekly *Katolické noviny* doubled its circulation to 80 000 copies and the Czech version increased from 35 000 to 142 000 copies. Most notable of the journals was a new Catholic monthly, *Via*, which began in May 1968.

[2] Prague radio (English), 20 March 1968.

[3] 'The Velehrad Conference,' *Nový život*, 7–8 (July 1968), 179. After the invasion the Ministry of Interior turned down this organization's application for registration.

willingness to enter a 'dialogue,' in hopes of enlarging mutual under-standing and tolerance. In Prague, The Ecumenical Movement of Students and Intelligentsia was founded and organized debates on the subject of 'Faith and Socialism.'[1] Other formal debates took place between Church and socialist leaders and leading intellectuals of both types. Catholic authorities were even permitted to publish in non-religious journals.[2] Císař explained to the central committee the need for such a dialogue, since, he claimed, there were two philosophical systems in the world 'which may give claim to offer comprehensive satisfaction to the spiritual needs of man: Marxism and Christianity.' Both, he said, were engaged in debates on the sense of life, the mission of man, and the development of society. 'In our country too this dialogue is taking place,' Císař continued, 'because aside from the strong scientific and atheistic traditions we also have Catholic and Protestant traditions as well as those of the Czech Brethren.' It remained to be seen just how far the Party would be willing to let these traditions and this dialogue influence society, but the change in attitude was a promising sign.

Other Christian religions

One of the more outstanding events of the democratization process with respect to religion was the restoration of the Catholic Church of the Old Slavonic Rite (Uniates). Part of this Church had fallen under the Soviet Union when the latter annexed Czechoslovak Sub-Carpathian Ruthenia after World War Two; the part left in Czechoslovakia was banned in April 1950 (as its counterpart in the Ukraine had been earlier), with due arrests of bishops and priests.[3] On 10 April 1968 Uniate clergyman, hoping to serve a flock numbering perhaps 100 000, met in Košice and resolved to have their Church rehabilitated, according to *L'ud* of 14 April 1968. Ladislav Holdoš, one of the Slovak Communists rehabilitated in the 1960s and once Slovak Commissioner for Church Affairs, wrote an open letter supporting this move, and Husák too spoke of the injustice of the persecution this Church had suffered.[4]

On 13 June 1968 the government accepted the Church's appeal and gave permission for some 170 priests to officiate under the same condi-tions as priests of other Churches.[5] The revival of the Uniates did not,

[1] Antonín Kratochvíl, 'The Cultural Scene in Czechoslovakia,' RFE, 13 August 1968.
[2] See, for example, Tomášek in *Literární listy*, 21 March 1968 or Nécsei, *Kultúrny život*, 12 April 1968.
[3] By order of Husák and Holdoš.
[4] Husák, *Nová mysl*, XXII:6 (1968), 661–2.
[5] *Smena*, 16 June 1968.

however, go entirely smoothly, for the Orthodox Church in Slovakia was a bitter enemy of the Uniates, and had received much of the latter's property in the 1950s. While the property of the Orthodox Church was to be divided between the two groups, either by mutual agreement or government decision, in some villages Orthodox believers 'stood guard' at their churches barring Uniate entry.[1] In some cases churches were actually barricaded and fights broke out, according to *Práce* of 12 June 1968. There was, however, a political aspect to this conflict. As *Svobodné slovo* on 30 January 1969 said: 'Czechoslovak Orthodoxy is oriented towards its Russian origins,' and the Uniates had been banned in the Soviet Union because of their link not only with Rome but also with West Ukrainian separatism or Ukrainian nationalism. It was therefore little wonder that as Soviet interference in the Czechoslovak democratization process intensified, in no small part due to the dangerous repercussion of Czechoslovak events on the neighboring Ukraine, the Orthodox began to get their way over the Uniates.

Another Church suppressed after 1948, the Old Catholic Church, was also rehabilitated. This sect, which broke from Rome in the late nineteenth century, numbered no more than an estimated 5000 believers and six priests as of 1966 – one-quarter the number of believers prior to World War Two.[2] From about 1965 on news about the Old Catholic Church began to appear, sparsely, in various religious journals in Czechoslovakia, and in late 1968 the Ministry of Culture and Information announced its decision to accord state recognition to the bishop of the Church. Other Christian sects were not so fortunate. Those directly connected with the US or Britain such as the Mormons, Jehovah's Witnesses, Nazarenes, Salvation Army, the Holy Grail, and Christ's Followers remained under ban. The Freemasons, too, were still banned.

The Protestant Churches of Czechoslovakia also benefited from the liberalization. Of particular interest to them was the placing of religious education in the hands of the Churches, and they also participated actively in the Marxist–Christian dialogue, having in fact been one of the early initiators of the movement. In what may have been both self-criticism and a warning to the regime, a 'Resolution of Protestant Ministers' supported the 'widespread purification of our democracy.'[3] This perhaps unfortunate choice of accommodating phraseology was typical of the

[1] Government ordinance No. 70/13 June 1968.
[2] Antonín Kratochvíl, 'The Influence of the Liberalization and Occupation on the Development of Religious Life,' RFE, 13 March 1969, 13.
[3] *Lidová demokracie*, 12 April 1968.

Protestant Churches in Czechoslovakia until 1968, but the resolution went on to chastise just this 'accommodation,' or as they called it the 'indifference regarding public affairs' into which they had fallen. The ministers admitted their former mistakes which had caused their complicity in the past evils of the regime and asserted their determination to 'make a new start toward helping our fellow citizens and toward responsibility safeguarding our newly found freedom.' At a two-day conference of the Ecumenical Council of Churches in Czechoslovakia a letter was sent to regime leaders which echoed this determination to protect believers by an active participation in the 'revitalization process,' according to *Lidová democracie*, 20 April 1968.

The Jewish community

The position of the relatively few (16 000) Jews in Czechoslovakia was a sensitive political issue bound much more intricately and delicately to de-Stalinization than the issue of religion or the position of the Church. Although the Czechs themselves, unlike the Slovaks, were not particularly virulent anti-semites (being a basically anti-clerical people, with their Hussite tradition of tolerance), the Czechoslovak Party in conjunction with Stalin's anti-semitic campaign, had conducted a vicious purge of Jewish Communists with the notorious trial of the Jewish secretary-general of the Party Rudolf Slánský in 1952. Aside from the trials against the Slovak 'nationalists,' almost all the trials of the 1949–54 period contained the charge of Zionism or cosmopolitanism, and various international Jewish agencies were directly implicated for allegedly organizing espionage and other acts against the state of Czechoslovakia. The entire era of Stalinist 'excesses' was so permeated with official anti-semitism that any redress of past errors had necessarily to involve the position of the Jews not only as a religious community but as a national community as well. Therefore, what perceptible changes did come about for the Jews during the 1963–7 de-Stalinization period were the rehabilitation of Jewish Communists persecuted in the Slánský trials, an improvement in the cultural activities, including the formation of study groups comprising some one hundred Jewish youths, permission for one person to prepare for the rabbinate (in Hungary), and the long-demanded renewal of contact with at least some international Jewish organizations.[1] This slight amelioration in the life of the Jews was brought to an abrupt halt, how-

[1] See 'Czechoslovakia,' *Jews in Eastern Europe*, II:2 (1963), 74 and ibid. II:4 (1964), 62–3; and Alexander Chaim, *Die Toten Gemeinden* (Wien, 1966).

ever, by the Arab–Israeli War of 1967. The Jewish youth discussion clubs were closed, planned celebrations of the community's millennium were interrupted, and contacts with outside Jewish organizations were demonstrably halted by the murder of the American Charles Jordan, deputy chairman of the Joint Distribution Committee, on his visit to Prague in August 1967.

As the process of democratization got under way in 1968 the Jewish community was encouraged by the new attitude towards religion – and towards the past. As the Jews had suffered as both a religious and national group, it was in the name of both that the leader of the Jewish community, Rabbi Feder (who was then over ninety and has since died) issued a statement of demands to the new regime, published in *Literární listy* on 30 May 1968. The Jewish community demanded public condemnation of the anti-semitism of the trials and purges of the 1950s; thorough rehabilitation, meaning retribution for administrative as well as court actions 'which frequently affected Jews in a particularly harsh manner,' and elimination of racial discrimination in social and health legislation. The statement requested that in the future international political events (read, Israel) not be used 'as a pretext for disturbing the position of the Jewish community,' that contacts with outside Jewish organizations 'not be inhibited;' that 'at long last' the community might celebrate the millennium of Czech Jewry and the 700th Anniversary of Prague's Alte-Neue Synagogue, with extensive foreign participation. Finally, the community asked to be permitted to provide religious education of the young without interference 'through administrative measures.'

The regime's response was relatively favorable: rehabilitations of a sort occurred insofar as Jews were permitted to assume positions not only in the areas of culture and education but in foreign trade and the foreign service as well. Contact with world Jewry was resumed and, for example, František Fuchs, the head of Bohemian–Moravian Jewry and Benjamin Eichler of Slovakia were permitted to attend the World Jewish Congress meeting in Geneva in July 1968.[1] With regard to the millennium and anniversary celebrations, the request for foreign participation was in direct response to earlier regime efforts to limit the festivities to Czechs and Slovaks only, so as to avoid the participation of Israeli or world Jewish leaders. This order was rescinded and invitations did go abroad, but the celebrations were in fact indefinitely postponed – scheduled as

[1] Rabbi Katz of Slovakia (the only other rabbi in Czechoslovakia) settled in Israel in the fall of 1968. The student permitted in the pre-1967 period to pursue rabbinical studies in Hungary had not, by 1972, returned to Czechoslovakia.

they were for 30 August–1 September. The decree which placed religious instruction in the exclusive province of the Churches applied to the Jews as well, thus answering one of their demands. This concession could not, however, be fully implemented by the Jewish community because of the lack of qualified teachers – a result of the past regimes' restrictive policies.

The issue of anti-semitism was a much more difficult one to handle. While the Party never specifically condemned the anti-semitic aspects of the 1949–54 trials, it did, nonetheless, permit the publication of books and articles which did mention this. It also 'stressed,' in the Action Program, that it would 'fight against every manifestation of anti-semitism or racism.' It sought to implement this by, for example, abolishing government discrimination against Jews in areas more or less closed to them since the purges (such as foreign trade and foreign office). Yet anti-semitism as a sentiment, expressly stirred up by the Novotný regime as recently as the 1967 Arab–Israeli War, was not an easy thing to eliminate. Although the regime was generally prepared to make amends, the conservatives did not hesitate to use anti-semitism in their attacks on the reformers. Just as they tried to exploit worker distrust of intellectuals to block the liberalization, so too they tried to play on anti-Jewish sentiments among the people to alienate them from the reformers (whom they claimed were Jewish). This campaign was manifest in letters received by the press and by leading Jewish reformers, such as Goldstücker, calling the Jews 'parasites' and accusing them of trying to disrupt socialism with this 'so-called' demo-cratization drive.[1] Many papers, mass organizations, groups, and indi-viduals dissociated themselves from and condemned these attacks, and numerous articles appeared on the topic of Jews and anti-semitism in Czechoslovakia.[2]

A still more complicated aspect of the problem was the government's policy towards Israel, an issue colored by anti-semitism in 1967 but, nonetheless, connected more directly with Czechoslovak independence in foreign policy. A second aspect was the revival of Slovak nationalism, traditionally anti-semitic, and led by such people as Husák and Novo-meský who as individuals were never particularly tolerant towards Jews. Indeed among the complicated issues involved in the split which took

---

[1] See *Rudé právo*, 23 June 1968 or *Práce*, 5 May 1968. See also Institute of Jewish Affairs, 'The Use of Anti-Semitism Against Czechoslovakia' (London, 1968), 12–15.

[2] See for example *Kultúrny život*, 7 and 21 June 1968; or *Reportér*, 24 July 1968. The 'reappearance' of virulent anti-semitic, 'nazi-like' attacks was one of the reasons for the concern over increasing conservative activity which prompted the writing of the famous '2,000 Words' in June, according to one of the co-signers of that document, Charles University rector Oldřich Starý. (*Práce*, 29 June 1968.)

place among Slovak intellectuals in the spring of 1968 were those of Israel and Slovak writer Ladislav Mňačko's protest trip to Israel in 1967, arguments over which had definite overtones of anti-semitism. The signs of dormant anti-semitism which appeared in 1968 were relatively limited, however, and generally condemned by the Czech (if not as widely by the Slovak) population. Indeed even the anti-semitic outburst in neighboring Poland was condemned by Czech reformers.

The Hungarian and Ukrainian minorities

The Hungarian minority in Czechoslovakia had felt dissatisfied and deprived of rights under both the pre-Communist and Communist regimes. While numerous theses were put forward in 1968 as to who had been responsible for this and which regime had treated the Hungarians worse, the fact was that the injustices had continued into the 1960s. It also emerged that, no matter what the fine points of historical declarations and situations, the culprits in the lives of the Hungarians were the Slovaks (be they Communist or 'bourgeois') and their 're-Slovakization' campaigns.[1] Indeed no improvement had been felt even in the pre-1968 liberalization, for that period had been marked by the strengthening of Slovak nationalism. The 1968 democratization, however, brought with it the promise if not of total solution of the more general nationalities problems in Czechoslovakia, at least of a clearer understanding of the situation and efforts towards a more equitable arrangement.

Each of the recognized national minorities in Czechoslovakia, the Hungarians, the Poles, and the Ukrainians, had been permitted by the Communists to form cultural associations, but, like the mass organizations, these were no more than 'transmission belts' for the Party's policies and mere facades of national representation or expression. Insofar as it was useful to the regime, they were considered the organs of these various nationalities (rather than as simply cultural associations), but, on the other hand, the regime never permitted them to act officially this way, i.e. to represent their national groups in the National Front, to administer their affairs, or to operate as political–social units.

The Hungarian organization, Csemadok,[2] had thus, like others, been

---

[1] Even the number of Hungarians in Czechoslovakia remained disputed; the approximate figure offered by the Czechoslovak Hungarians was slightly more than 700 000 though many claimed only 600 000, and the official figure was 560 000. (*Új szo*, 18 April 1968; *Statistická ročenka Československé socialistické republiky* (Praha, 1967).)

[2] The Cultural Association of the Hungarian Working People in Czechoslovakia.

relatively discredited in the eyes of the Hungarians, and demands for its reorganization, revitalization, and restaffing were heard with the beginning of democratization, in the Hungarian-language daily *Új szó*, 12 and 14 April 1968. Yet the organization managed to redeem itself by taking the initiative in presenting demands for the amelioration of the position of the Hungarian minority – an action clearly beyond its former scope and inclinations. The Csemadok 'Standpoint,' subtitled 'Proposal for the Solution of the Nationality Question,' published by *Új szó* on 15 March 1968, pointed out that none of the proposals so far suggested, nor the Constitution, offered equality of nationalities. Indeed the legal position of nationalities was not defined by law. Thus, while favoring federalization, Csemadok demanded a Constitutional law defining the 'politico-legal' position of the nationalities, especially with regard to their self-government. The Hungarians wanted nationality agencies and institutions to represent all nationalities in the state and local government organs as well as mass organizations. For example, it was suggested that the Slovak National Council have a Nationality Committee (composed of representatives of the various nationalities, as well as experts and SNC deputies), and a Commissioner for Nationalities, in addition to nationality committees at the district and federal government levels and proportional representation in all SNC organs. A second major demand was territorial reorganization to affect the mixed nationalities districts, many of which were administratively created (with assimilation in mind) in the reorganization of 1960. Csemadok advocated 'compact units – homogeneous from the nationality point of view,' with Constitutional guarantees for the rights of minorities in the irredeemably mixed communities.

The above measures were considered immediately necessary, but provisional, pending amendments to the Constitution which would create 'institutions...and guarantee the most effective administration of social and national equality, based on the principle of self-government.' Csemadok proposed that all laws and decrees passed after 1945 concerning the Hungarian minority be revised, and that 'all discriminatory laws be abrogated.' Favoring education of nationalities in their native tongue, until then guaranteed only at the primary school level (though offered, at a low standard, at the secondary level), Csemadok demanded that the administration of Hungarian schools be put under the jurisdiction of Hungarian educational institutes. It sought equal opportunities for employment and continuation of studies; increased opportunities for higher education, with proportional admission by nationality guaranteed by law; and 'the rapid resolution of the whole problem of study in neighboring

Hungary.' In the area of culture, Csemadok urged the recognition of the national aspect of the various cultures, i.e. the link with the national culture of another state, and treatment of these cultures as individual and independent – not merely as translations of Czech and Slovak culture.

Two other Hungarian organizations joined their more specific demands to the Csemadok appeal: the Hungarian section of the Slovak Union of Writers and the Party organization at *Új szó*. The Hungarian writers criticized the 'demagogic or opportunistic attitude adopted by the majority of Hungarian functionaries,' which had succeeded in stifling the initiatives of the writers who over the years had tried to speak up for Hungarian rights.[1] They demanded a 'cultural policy in accordance with the principle of self-government' and recommended, among other things, an independent Hungarian book and newspaper publishing house, a second Hungarian daily, a cultural–political weekly, and Hungarian television programs. The writers' demands went further than Csemadok in that they specifically sought revision of the post-war indictment of Czechoslovakia's Hungarians as responsible for the 1938 dismemberment of the Republic. They demanded the full rehabilitation of all persons who suffered persecution under this charge, the official and public annulment of the policy of re-Slovakization (including renaming of villages in Hungarian ethnic areas), and the abandoning of the charge of 'bourgeois nationalism.'

The 'Standpoint' of the Communists in the Hungarian-language daily *Új szó* (2 April 1968) admitted the justice of the charges levied against it for conformism, lack of boldness, and lack of initiative, and it revealed that 'for years' the editorial offices had been divided over the issue of liberalization. The paper supported both the Csemadok and writers' demands, adding certain of its own grievances, particularly over freedom of the Hungarian-language press. This press was indeed filled with demands and discussions of demands in the early spring of 1968, the overall themes being the need for self-rule and clarification of the legal status of the Hungarian minority. According to the Constitution of 1960, Czechoslovakia was a unified state of two fraternal nations, Czechs and Slovaks, enjoying equal rights. The cultural development of other nationalities was to be guaranteed by the Slovak National Council, but, as it was pointed out by *Új szó* on 19 March 1968, that organ itself had been so emasculated that it could barely promote Slovak rights much less those of other nationalities. The Constitution did not consider the national

---

[1] This and the following are taken from the 'Standpoint of the Leadership of the Hungarian Section of the Slovak Writers Union,' *Új szó*, 24 March 1968.

minorities more than cultural entities; it did *not* consider them social elements with rights equal to those of the two dominant groups.[1] Thus the Constitution itself provided neither the principle nor the mechanism of self-rule. There were those who suggested that Csemadok fulfil this function, but, in effect, what was desired by the Hungarians was that Csemadok assume the role of a social or pressure group to pursue the provision of state organs or executive bodies for the Hungarian minority.[2]

This was indeed an appeal for more than cultural freedom, but, as *Új szó* pointed out on 2 April 1968, the demand for administrative reorganization to create Hungarian regions or districts was not designed to achieve even regional autonomy, since nationally mixed areas would always exist and protection of Hungarian minority rights would always be necessary. State agencies or organs of the nationalities could not be territorially delineated; they would have to represent the interests of all of the groups including those in 'non-Hungarian' districts. Yet it was the protection of the rights of the minority as a *social* (meaning socio-political) – not regional or merely cultural – group that was desired. Democracy, the paper argued, demanded more than linguistic or cultural rights, it demanded equal rights in all areas, and this could only be achieved if the nationality were regarded as a *social* group. Self-rule, i.e. organs to represent, promote, protect, generally care for Hungarian (or any nationality) needs would provide the nationality with control over its own affairs, including political, administrative, and economic matters. Thus a Csemadok central committee resolution demanded 'Constitutional recognition of the Hungarian minority *as a political agent* with the same rights as the Czech and Slovak national groups.'[3]

The Hungarian problem was historically one of the more difficult nationality problems in Eastern Europe, and it was symbolic of the conflict in Czechoslovakia that the very document Hungarians condemned as the official sanction for their suffering – the 1945 Košice Program – was the very document held up by their rivals, the Slovaks, as the basis for a just settlement of the Slovak problem.[4] The Hungarian minority directly challenged the Slovaks to grant the Hungarians what they, the Slovaks, were demanding vis-à-vis the Czechs, and the Hungarians did not hesitate to use the Slovaks' own arguments in this challenge, even quoting the Slovak nationalist hero L'udovít Štúr, in an *Új szó* article of 28 March 1968. The Slovaks, however, were not moved. From the outset, the

---

[1] *Új szó*, 19 March 1968.   [2] Ibid.; *Új szó*, 12 April 1968.
[3] *Pravda* (Bratislava), 24 May 1968.
[4] See *Új szó*, 19, 24 March 1968 or *Kultúrny život*, 12 April 1968.

Slovak press withheld publication of the Hungarians' demands. A situation therefore developed in which rumors exceeded imagination, and the now blossoming Slovak nationalism came into conflict with the re-emerging Hungarian nationalism, as both nationalities sought to exploit the 'democratization' to rectify wrongs they felt had been done to them. It was only after numerous complaints that *Pravda* finally published, on 24 May 1968, excerpts from the Csemadok statements.[1] In southern Slovakia, the area of greatest conflict because of its high concentration of Hungarians, the Slovaks sought to defend themselves against Hungarian demands by creating local *Matica Slovenská* (Slovak cultural) groups to counter the local Csemadok clubs.[2] Bratislava students even staged marches to villages in south-west Slovakia for the purpose of encouraging an 'awakening of national pride in Slovaks living in southern Slovakia', according to *Práca* of 13 May 1968. Such actions were by way of defense against the feared but little-known demands of the Hungarians and were designed to demonstrate Slovak sovereignty even over areas predominately Hungarian in population.

Slovak reaction to the Hungarians' demands took many forms, one of which was a resolution by thirty-eight Slovaks condemning the Csemadok resolution as nationalist, chauvinist, and even irredentist. Condemned as 'irredentist' were comments of Csemadok chairman Július Lörincz that 'In 1918 nobody asked us with whom we wanted to join forces. We did not attach ourselves voluntarily to Czechoslovakia, we were annexed by Czechoslovakia.'[3] Letters published on 21 May 1968 by the Slovak trade union daily *Práca* expressed resentment of the Hungarians' demands ('if they don't feel their rights are respected here they should leave for Hungary'), one of which, from a basic Party organization in Slovakia, said that Csemadok's demands smacked of 'a Magyarization of southern Slovakia and even an effort to break up the unity of the Czechoslovak Socialist Republic.' A common Slovak counter-argument to the Hungarians was that presented by Ivan Hargas in the Slovak Communist Party central committee weekly, *Predvoj*, on 4 April 1968, claiming that the Hungarians in Slovakia were much better off than the Slovaks in Hungary. Hungarians saw in this both an erroneous analogy and a thinly veiled hint to them that they were not wanted in Slovakia.[4] Indeed,

[1] Hungarian complaints about this appeared in *Új szó*, 18, 28 April 1968.
[2] Matica slovenská is a Slovak cultural organization long identified with Slovak nationalist sentiments. Such groups were set up in Galanta, Dunajská Streda, and Komárno districts, for example.
[3] See *Práca*, 21 May 1968; *Rol'nícke noviny*, 17 April 1968; *Új szó*, 27 March 1968.
[4] See *Új szó*, 18 April 1968 and *Hét*, 21 April 1968.

according to *Práca* of 21 May 1968, the cry 'Hungarians to the other side of the Danube' was heard upon occasion.

Negative Slovak reaction even found its way on to the pages of the liberal Slovak Writers Union weekly *Kultúrny život*. Articles by Michal Gafrik (19 April 1968) and Rudolf Olšinský (12 April 1968) referred to the danger to Slovaks from the 'chauvinism of the Hungarians' and to the Republic as a whole from this 'revival' of 'revanchist' ideas. Olšinský even recalled the struggle of the Slovaks against the Hungarian majority 'which lasted for a thousand years,' saying that even recent events, such as the 1956 revolution in Hungary, contained demands for annexation of southern Slovakia to Hungary – demands supported by some Hungarians living in Slovakia.

Not all Slovak reaction was negative. The well-known Slovak Communist writer Zora Jesenská came out strongly for the rights of the Hungarian minority, recognizing the principle of self-administration and admitting the injustice of the Košice Program with regard to the minorities.[1] Some tried to minimize the whole conflict by saying that only extremists, on both sides, were making demands and accusations.[2] Others, like the Slovak Party daily on 11 June 1968, tried to smooth the waters by claiming it unfair 'to blame all Hungarians indiscriminately for local excesses,' to demand to know what they were doing during the Slovak National Uprising, or to argue that things were better for Hungarians in Czechoslovakia than for Slovaks in Hungary 'under Horthy's regime.' The paper, in what greatly resembled a facetious tone, pointed out that when written down and signed, such views might be interpreted by Hungarians as belittling or offensive. *Pravda* did refer, however, to 'justified claims' on the part of the Hungarians, although it did not specify which claims it considered justified.

The position taken by the Party was not entirely unambiguous. In a *Kultúrny život* article on 9 February 1968, Husák condemned the postwar re-Slovakization policy and strongly denied that the Slovak Communists had advocated the deportation policy authorized by the Košice Program. This denial was prompted by questions which had appeared in the Hungarian-language press as to the role of the Slovak nationalist leaders (Husák, Novomeský, Okáli) in the injustices perpetrated against the Hungarians. The Czechoslovak Party had itself, in the Action Program, declared the necessity for 'constitutional and legal guarantees of complete and genuine political and economic, and cultural equality of

[1] *Új szó*, 12 April 1968 interview. See also Jesenská in *Kultúrny život*, 5 April 1968.
[2] *Új szó*, 11 June 1968 (article by two Slovaks).

rights.' It also agreed to the creation of state organs at all levels for nationality affairs, giving the nationalities the right 'in an independent and autonomous manner to decide on the matters that concern them.' To accommodate this, preparations began on the demanded nationalities law. Despite this, however, the Slovak Party did not propose any of the many specific demands pressed by the Hungarians. It was the Slovak Party which had held up publication of the Hungarians' demands in any language but Hungarian, on the grounds that they might produce an unfavorable reaction among Slovaks.[1] The long-awaited Slovak Communist Party Action Program, printed in *Pravda* of 29 May 1968, only repeated the Czechoslovak program's suggestion for nationalities offices at all levels, without referring in any way to the other guarantees and reforms requested by the Hungarians. The Slovak Party central committee 'Standpoint,' published the day after its Action Program, even warned Csemadok and the Ukrainian cultural association that their purpose was merely 'a cultural–educational one.' While it urged them to take a 'creative part' in the work of the National Committees, trade union movement, ČSM and other organizations, this may have been a warning not to demand independent organizations of their own – as indeed Csemadok had. Lörincz himself maintained Csemadok's stand at the Czechoslovak Party May–June central committee plenum but, apparently under pressure, he somewhat defensively condemned extremist excesses.[2]

The fate of the 57 000 Ukrainians was linked with that of the Hungarians, though theirs was not as serious an internal problem. The traditional Slovak–Hungarian rivalry, the disputed territory, and the connection of the issue with rehabilitated Slovaks now in power prevented any early liberal solution for the Hungarians. Slovak nationalism, nonetheless, was bound to impair the democratization process for the other minorities in Slovakia as well, the major differences being the size of the other minorities and the depth of the mutual animosity. As we have seen, the Ukrainian problem was both a religious as well as minority issue centered around the Uniate Church, and it carried with it international implications. A national reawakening of the Ukrainian minority in Czechoslovakia threatened a counterpart reaction from the inhabitants of today's western Ukraine, and its banned Uniate Church.

As in the case of the Hungarians, it was the Ukrainian cultural association which, though discredited in the past, led the revival of Ukrainian hopes and demands. The issues were similar: there were demands for a raising of the standard of living (the first most tentative or innocuous

[1] *Új szó*, 5 May 1968.   [2] *Pravda* (Bratislava), 6 June 1968.

100

demand), Constitutional reform guaranteeing full and equal rights to the minorities, and organs to serve and properly represent the Ukrainians.[1] The central committee of the Ukrainian association listed its grievances (published in the Hungarian daily, on 30 March 1968), starting with the failure of the Košice Program and the Gottwald government to recognize the Ukrainian National Council. The Association's 'Decision' pointed out the deterioration of the Ukrainians' position from 1948 to the present, i.e. the liquidation of the Ukrainian National Council, the closing of the Ukrainian Office of Education in the Slovak National Council, the abolition of the Ukrainian Supervisory Authority for Culture and Adult Education and of the Carpathian Youth Association. The poor conditions in which the Ukrainians lived, combined with the government's assimilation policy (which included trials of 'bourgeois nationalists') had led to the emigration and dispersion of many Ukrainians, the Association complained.

According to the Party weekly, *Život strany* of 19 February 1969, there was talk within the organization of proposing the creation of an autonomous Ruthenian region, but such reports may have been fabricated against Ukrainian interests. The cultural association did state, however, that it did not consider itself 'adequate for representing' the minority, because it could not guarantee equal rights. It, therefore, demanded the revival of the Ukrainian National Council to provide nationality self-government. The Union suggested cooperation with Csemadok for the working out of proposals for these changes.

The Ukrainian section of the Slovak Writers Union supported the above demands, condemning the 'solutions,' enforced in the past, of such sensitive national issues as religion, the very name of the minority, and so forth.[2] As in the case of the Hungarians, though slightly less so, there was negative Slovak reaction to the Ukrainian demands as well. Accused of irredentism and trying to break up the Republic, the central committee of the cultural association issued another statement at the end of May, condemning extremist elements even within its own ranks, but also condemning insulting and slanderous charges against it in the Slovak press.[3] Some Ukrainian teachers even threatened to strike over the proposed appointment of a Slovak chairman of the educational department of a predominantly Ukrainian district.[4] The Ukrainians generally empha-

[1] *Pravda* (Bratislava), 10 February 1968 (at the 9 February session of the Ukrainian cultural association); Prague radio, 20, 22 March 1968.
[2] *Rudé právo*, 7 April 1968.　　　　[3] *Pravda* (Bratislava), 29 May 1968.
[4] *Život strany*, 19 February 1969.

sized and depended upon the principles declared in the Action Program until such time as a better guarantee, i.e. Constitutional and institutional reform, would be adopted. The results, however, were dependent – for all the minorities – on just how successful democratization would be in overcoming the divisive effects of the traditional but newly crystallized feelings of nationalism, particularly of the powerful Slovaks. While this problem has traditionally been one of the most difficult to solve in Eastern Europe, it was one which the democratization process 'from below' clearly could not leave entirely untouched and indeed was to have been handled by the new Constitution – which unfortunately did not go beyond the drafting stage while the reformers were in power.[1] The 'National Minorities Bill' passed after the invasion did provide for such things as proportional representation for the Hungarians, Ukrainians, Poles, and Germans in all political and state organs but it did not go beyond the socio-cultural rights already granted.[2]

[1] Expressing the interests of the 130 000 Germans still living in Czechoslovakia, on 23 May 1968 the Germans of the town of Varnsdorf demanded the right to their own cultural life, similar to the rights of the Sorbs in East Germany. (*ČSSR: The Road to Democratic Socialism* (Prague, 1968), 81–2.)

[2] *Sbírka zákonů*, No. 143/1968. This very objection was raised by the Csemadok central committee at its December 1968 conference. (Bratislava radio, 18 December 1968.)

5

The Cultural Sphere

The cultural sphere was the major area in which the demands for and effects of the democratization were felt. As in the 1963–7 period, it was the intellectuals who expressed the pressures for change, and it was they who were most sensitive to each change, retreat, or step forward in the process, for freedom of expression stood at the crux of democratization. It was both as organized interest groups and individually that the intellectuals experienced and demanded modifications in the regime's cultural policies, concentrating their efforts eventually on the issue of freedom of expression.[1]

The unions

There were two immediate matters the Writers Union had to settle once the change in Party leadership took place: the Czechoslovak Writers Union had been without elected officers since its controversial congress in June 1967 and without its weekly journal, taken over by the government in the wake of that congress. On 24 January 1968, the central committee of the Writers Union met and elected Eduard Goldstücker their chairman, with Miroslav Válek (Slovak Writers Union chairman) and Jan Procházka as deputies. This decision was a compromise, however, for reform writers had long been demanding Procházka as chairman, despite regime opposition to his selection at the June congress. Procházka had been stripped of his candidate central committee membership in the Party in September 1967 because of his comments to the congress. In the aftermath of this and Party disciplinary action against other writers, Goldstücker, a moderate, emerged as the only candidate upon which both the

---

[1] There were also further reforms proposed for the educational sphere; these can be found in the Ministry of Education's Action Program, *Učitelské noviny*, XVIII:26 (1968), 5–7. They included greater differentiation of studies particularly at the secondary level, introduction of a four-year general high school, elimination of the government's right to veto elected rectors, and the conversion of the Institute of Marxism–Leninism for the Institutes of Higher Learning to the Institute of Social–Political Sciences.

writers and the regime could agree, but it was only in January that Gold-stücker himself agreed to take the job – and then only temporarily.[1] The reformers did succeed in having Milan Kundera named to the Union presidium, Party intervention having prevented his reelection to this position at the June congress.

The January 1968 meeting also decided upon the progressive Karel Kostroun to replace Jiří Hájek who had strongly supported the regime against the reformers, both during and following the 1967 writers congress), as editor-in-chief of the monthly *Plamen*. The reformers' control of the journal was further guaranteed by the naming of novelist Josef Škvorecký as chairman of the editorial board. Of greater moment was the announcement that the Union would once again be able to publish a weekly. Presumably to save face for the Party, *Literární noviny* was not to be returned to the Union; rather a new journal was to be started: *Literární listy*. As if to demonstrate the rescinding of the disciplinary nature of the earlier appropriation of *Literární noviny*, both the name and the editor-ship of the latter were changed, so that it would appear simply as a journal of the Ministry of Culture and Information. The new name was *Kulturní noviny*, and its editor was Vladimír Diviš, military journalist. The Union's new journal, *Literární listy*, was to be edited by *Literární noviny*'s last editor before takeover, the liberal novelist Dušan Hamšík. He chose for his board of editors *Literární noviny*'s former editors.

While publication of *Literární listy* had been approved by the regime in principle, the journal did not receive its license when requested and was repeatedly denied access to *Literární noviny*'s editorial offices. These complications ostensibly arose over practical questions of size and circula-tion of the planned weekly, but the underlying source of the difficulties was more likely the continuation in office of such conservatives as Karel Hoffman as Minister of Culture and Information and Jiří Hendrych as Party ideology chief. It was only after the Czech section of the Writers Union decided on 14 February 1968 to take the matter to the National Assembly that the government agreed to a 12-page weekly of 120 000 circulation.[2] Goldstücker had at an early stage said that the journal would not limit itself to literary matters as distinct from political questions and that one of the main tasks would be to bridge the gap between the intel-lectuals and the workers in an effort to eliminate the 'artificially created'

[1] Goldstücker interview to Prague radio, 25 January 1968.
[2] *Práce*, 1 February 1968; *Lidová demokracie*, 15 February 1968; Prague radio, 21 February 1968. In fact, circulation rose to 400 000 by the summer of 1968, the largest circulation among the non-daily papers.

dispute.[1] The latter was a reference to Novotný's often successful strategy in the past and the conservatives' renewed efforts in early 1968. As in the recent past, however, at least the press organs of the workers seemed to sympathize with the intellectuals, as evidenced by favorable publicity given the struggle for the birth of *Literární listy* by the trade union dailies *Práce* and *Práca*. On 29 February 1968 *Literární listy* appeared with an 'introductory' issue; the first issue appeared on 1 March 1968.

Among the other concrete issues pursued by the writers was the release of the young writer Jan Beneš, imprisoned in 1967. They secured his pardon after petitioning the President of the Republic, who granted it on 21 March 1968 in what was one of Novotný's last acts as President.[2] The Union also secured Party rehabilitation of the writers purged or disciplined as a result of the June 1967 congress (Ivan Klíma, A. J. Liehm, Pavel Kohout, Ludvík Vaculík, and Jan Procházka).[3] Another demand was for the revival of the young writers' literary journal *Tvář*, suppressed in 1966; *Tvář* did reappear in November 1968. The Union's central committee also decided to publish a daily to be called *Lidové noviny*, with *Literární listy* appearing as the Sunday supplement. This was in a sense a revival of the Brno daily of the same name, founded in 1892 and known for its Masaryk-influenced democratic orientation. It had been suppressed in 1952. Scheduled to appear in October 1968 under the editorship of A. J. Liehm, it never came out.

Within the Union itself a rehabilitation commission, under senior poet Jaroslav Seifert, was charged with reexamining all the cases of persecuted writers, with the goal of bringing about their full and genuine rehabilitation, as long demanded by reform-minded writers. According to *Lidová demokracie* of 28 April 1968, the commission also sought to push forward the cases of writers still awaiting retrial, and rehabilitations of persons purged from the Union, Union organs, and literary life in, for example, the 1959 moves directed against the liberals of 1956, or people who suffered in connection with the suppression of the journal *Květen* (something of a predecessor to *Tvář*). The commission also looked into the question of pensions for persecuted writers and the return of their works to libraries and shops. The commission's report came out strongly against the conservative literary 'boss' Ladislav Štoll, calling his works

[1] Interviews to *Práce*, 1 February 1968 and Prague radio, 21 February 1968.
[2] Prague radio, 22 March 1968.
[3] Czechoslovak television, 4 February 1968 (Goldstücker interview). *Rok šedesátý osmý*, 42. Disciplinary proceedings against Milan Kundera were also dropped.

'harmful' to Czech literature. As a result Štoll was dismissed from his position as director of the ČSAV Institute for Czech Literature and his editorships of the literary journals *Česká literatura* and *Estetika*.[1]

A second development within the Union was the creation of the Circle of Independent Writers. The Circle was favorably received by reform-minded Party writers, who called on Communist writers to see in it a challenge and a healthy opposition.[2] In this spirit the Union's journals were open to the views and articles of this group, just as they were to writers who were Party-members.

The writers' demands went beyond the scope of purely Union matters, as was to be expected. At their 29 March 1968 plenum, they urged post-ponement of the National Assembly elections pending a new election law, and they recommended the creation of a rehabilitation committee in the National Assembly.[3] Moreover they decided to call an extraordinary congress of the Union, inviting émigré Czech writers, and at this congress to nominate five candidates to stand for the National Assembly.[4] Such an action would make the Writers Union a genuine interest group with a political role in the National Front like that demanded by other mass and independent organizations. In fact, however, the Union foresaw itself as a voluntary syndicate whose members would be free to form any political party and whose task would be to protect writers' rights, particularly their freedom of expression.

A split within the Czechoslovak Writers Union had more or less taken place already in 1967, and the Slovaks did not in effect take part in the Czechoslovak Writers Union plenum of 29 March 1968. Most of the Slovaks had left the June 1967 Writers Union congress, after some of them, together with a number of Czechs, had issued a letter protesting the political turn the Congress had taken. In the closing months of 1967 the Slovak writers, nonetheless, once again closed ranks with the Czechs, letting the latter use the Slovak Union's weekly after *Literární noviny* was appropriated by the government. Once the reformers came to power, however, this division within the ranks of the writers began to show once again, and the source of the problem became apparent: a split amongst the Slovak writers themselves.

[1] Prague radio, 8 April 1968.   [2] See Pavel Kohout in *Literární listy*, 16 May 1968.

[3] *Literární listy*, 4 April 1969. The Communist group in the union also sent a letter to the district Party conference calling for the resignation of Novotný (ČTK, 16 March 1968). Seventeen Moravian writers sent a letter to liberal presidium member Špaček expressing no confidence in Karel Hoffman (ČTK, 3 April 1968).

[4] Goldstücker interview, *l'Unità* (Rome), 25 April 1968. Postponed and delayed re-peatedly after the invasion, it finally took place in 1969.

The unions

For the Slovaks who had stood in the forefront of the struggle for de-Stalinization since 1963, there were *two* issues: de-Stalinization and Slovak rights. So long as these two coincided, as indeed they did for a number of years, few distinctions could be discerned within the ranks of the Slovak 'liberals.' In time, however, it became apparent that for many Slovaks de-Stalinization meant mainly repudiation of those facets of Stalinism which had affected the Slovaks, such as the trials of the 1950s, certain types of centralism, and Novotný. As the advocates of de-Stalinization moved on to demand democratization, these Slovaks remained behind – on the now distinct second issue: Slovak rights. Thus there was a split between those Slovaks who favored democratization as the foremost issue and key to change, including any guarantee of Slovak rights or federalization of the Republic, and those Slovaks who favored federalization, i.e. Slovak rights, as the foremost issue – not necessarily at the expense of democratization but not necessarily connected with it.[1] The behaviour of the Slovaks at the 1967 Writers Union congress was but a hint at this split; disputes which arose within the Slovak Writers Union weekly *Kultúrny život* in 1968 brought it clearly into the open.

The dispute within *Kultúrny život* centered on such issues as the Israeli–Arab conflict and the Mňačko affair,[2] but these merely reflected the major issue: *Kultúrny život* had become 'influenced' by Prague – more interested in politics than in Slovaks, as one faction would have put it. This faction, which became known as the 'federalists,' included writers Novomeský, Válek (chairman of the Slovak Writers Union since May 1967), Vojtech Mihálik (Válek's predecessor), and it was under the ideological leadership of the rehabilitated Gustav Husák. The second faction, known as the 'democratists,' included such writers as Pavol Števček, Dominik Tatarka, Zora Jesenská, and Anton Hykisch. These writers, it must be remembered, were among those who, like Dubček, had fought hard and courageously for the rehabilitation of the Slovak 'nationalists' Husák, Novomeský, and others in the 1963–6 period. The break finally came during a dispute over articles *Kultúrny život* published (on 15 March 1968) favorable to Mňačko, including one by Mňačko himself, with which Novomeský then chairman of the *Kultúrny život* editorial

---

[1] Dubček was clearly a Slovak of the first group. A third group to be found in Slovakia was the Slovak Stalinists, who for obvious reasons received no sympathy from either the more moderate but nationalist Slovaks or the reformers. Perhaps the best description of the dispute can be found in *Reportér*, 15 May 1968 (Zdeněk Eis) or 26 June 1968 (Stanislav Budín).

[2] See footnotes, 15–16.

board, took issue. The argument then went on to matters of principle, for Novomeský had refused to publish articles critical of Slovak Party figures Matej Lúčan, Michal Pecho, and Vasil Bil'ak, who had been instrumental in disciplinary and repressive measures taken against *Kultúrny život*, and its liberal editor, Pavol Števček, in 1963–4. In response to these disputes, Novomeský left *Kultúrny život* on 14 March 1968 to write for the Slovak Party weekly *Predvoj*; he was followed by Válek and Mihálik. Together with Husák, they converted *Predvoj* into *Nové slovo*, a revival of Husák's 1944–8 journal, so that they had an organ which clearly pleaded the Slovak cause, without the distractions of other issues.[1]

After the split, which became the source of much dispute at the 30 April 1968 conference of Slovak Writers, a person's position on Mňačko and Israel became something of a test of his position vis-à-vis democratization[2]. This may not have been a particularly legitimate gauge, and, indeed, some accused Husák and Novomeský of introducing these subordinate matters to blur the real issue.[3] Yet there did appear to be certain differences in principles between people (like Husák and Bil'ak) who condemned Mňačko on the grounds that he had exaggerated the existence of anti-semitism in Czechoslovakia and its connection with a possible return to the 1950s,[4] and those people who defended Mňačko on the grounds of freedom of speech and civil rights, or Israel on the grounds that the people's will should determine the government's policies.

One of the first points on the agenda of the Journalists Union was dis-avowal of the position taken by the Union's congress in late 1967, specifically the inclusion in that congress's resolution of a regime-dictated condemnation of the June 1967 writers congress.[5] It was with this purpose in mind that the journalists suggested a meeting with the writers – only to have *Literární listy* editor Hamšík suggest, in the 1 March 1968 issue, that such a request smacked of opportunism unless journalist chairman Adolf Hradecký were to resign. The matter was settled, probably to the satisfaction of the writers, at a joint meeting in March of the central committees of the Czechoslovak Union of Journalists

[1] *Nové slovo* appeared on 23 May 1968, with an editorial by Husák and a photo of the first issue edited by Husák in 1944.
[2] See *Kultúrny život*, 10, 17, 24 May 1968; 7 June 1968.
[3] *Reportér*, 15 May 1968.
[4] Husák to Bratislava youth rally, 19 March 1968 (Bratislava television, 20 March 1968); Bil'ak to Bratislava Party conference (ČTK, 16 March 1968). The anti-semitism issue was a particularly sensitive one for such nationalists as Husák.
[5] *Mladá fronta*, 20, 23 February 1968.

and the Slovak Union of Journalists. At this meeting, Hradecký and the entire presidium of the Czechoslovak Journalists Union resigned. The new presidium, elected by secret ballot, left the selection of a chairman until a new congress of the Union, but it elected Bohumil Marčák temporary chairman and Stanislav Budín to fill Hradecký's position as editor-in-chief of the Union's journal *Reportér*. The central committees of the two Unions then admitted that the previous congress had committed 'a grave political error' in actively supporting the Party's condemnation of the writers. They revealed that this action had been dictated by the Party and accepted without either protest or debate by the union.[1]

It was also decided to revise the Union's stand regarding the Slovak Journalists Union conference of 1963. The reference was to the reservations the Union was forced to make to the speech of Miroslav Hysko at the Slovak conference. The journalists also decided on two organizational changes: to establish a 'symmetrical model,' i.e. to have two independent unions, one Slovak, one Czech, with joint all-state organs, and to establish a Prague organization within the Czech Union. The last was founded on 1 April 1968 and promptly proposed that the entire Czechoslovak government submit its resignation.[2]

After a campaign within the Union, an extraordinary congress was held (21–23 June 1968) which strongly condemned the 1967 journalists congress and passed a declaration supporting Dubček. It adopted a new set of Union statutes, creating a 'Center of Czechoslovak Journalists' as a 'voluntary, creative interest organization' which would act as a state-wide organ with two national components: the Union of Czech Journalists and the Union of Slovak Journalists.[3] This was in fact the first *official* split of any organization along national lines. The reform-minded journalist Vladimír Kašpar was elected chairman of the 'Center.' The Slovak Union promptly sent a letter to the Slovak Party expressing 'no-confidence' in Vasil Bil'ak (then Slovak Party first secretary), Stefan Brenčič (Slovak Commissioner for Culture and Information), and Matej Lúčan (Slovak Commissioner for Education), because of their negative attitudes to the press.[4] Nonetheless, radio commentaries on 23 June 1968 said that despite these changes, the congress had not lived up to expectations, had not been democratic, and had not been interesting, with the exception of speeches by Liehm and a few others.

[1] *Rudé právo*, 22 March 1968; ČTK, 29 March 1968.
[2] Prague radio, 1 April 1968. The North Moravian regional committee of the union authorized the creation of a Polish Journalists club at its May meeting.
[3] *Rudé právo*, 24 June 1968 and *Reportér*, 3 July 1968.   [4] *Kultúrny život*, 28 June 1968.

A number of creative unions (the Union of Theatre Artists, Union of Creative Artists, Union of Film and Television Artists) criticized the Ministry of Culture and Information and demanded independence as organizations even to the point of membership in the National Front with representatives in the National Assembly.[1] This resembled the demands of the Writers Union, and was in line with the sentiments of the Slovak Writers Union chairman, who argued that artists' unions must be controlled by their own agencies, thus eliminating the administrative control of culture.[2] Even the employees (including Communists) of the Culture and Information Ministry issued a statement urging full respect for the 'independent status' of the associations of artists, writers, and so forth.[3] This sentiment was particularly underlined at the national conference of the Union of Film and Television Artists held on 29–30 March 1968, covered in the Union's journal on 4 April 1968. The Union urged the passing of a law which would guarantee the right of every artist to perform his creative work, and that the artists' associations would be responsible for providing or guaranteeing the necessary social means for fostering and disseminating this work. This Union also decided to propose a law which would gurantee the independence of Czechoslovak television from state and political organs. Such a law was to go hand in hand with a proposed law for the abolition of censorship, the major concern of this as well as of the other unions in the cultural sphere.

An *aktiv* of Communists working in the cultural sphere was founded in Prague by Goldstücker on 5 June 1968 (officially, 22 June 1968). This group, for example, sent a resolution on 30 July to the Czechoslovak delegation in Cierna under the title of a slogan to become famous during the invasion 'We are Thinking of You, Think of Us.' On 6 May 1968 the various creative unions officially founded a Coordinating Committee consisting of representatives of the following Czechoslovak unions: Architects; Music Hall Performers and Artists; Film and Television Artists; Theatre and Radio Artists; Composers; Scientific Workers; Writers; Journalists; and Painters and Sculptors. This group generally gave added weight to the demands of the intellectuals, supporting, among other things, the '2,000 Words' published at the end of June 1968. Its most significant activities came after the invasion, however.

[1] Prague radio, 16 March 1968; *Rudé právo*, 13 March 1968; ČTK, 10, 12, 18 March 1968.
[2] *Večerník*, 14 February 1968.
[3] ČTK, 23 March 1968.

Censorship

The issue of censorship concerned on the one hand the flow of information, or the right of the citizen to be fully informed, and on the other hand the freedom of the individual to express himself as he pleased. Censorship interfered in the democratic process both by preventing people being fully informed, therefore rendering their participation futile from the outset, and by limiting this participation by restricting what they might safely say. It had been on both these points that intellectuals had criticized the implementation of the Press Law in 1967, i.e. information was not made available *and* people were not permitted to publish their views freely.

The campaign against censorship, particularly on the first point, began immediately after the historic Party plena, for the information released on even these revolutionary events was scant and vague. The widespread complaints with regard to this 'oversight' were eventually recognized by the Party, which, in time, released more information.[1] The matter was one of principle, however, and Party members such as the South Moravian Jaroslav Šabata pointed out, for example, that sociology regarded information and publicity as more important than the act of voting in a system of democratic decision-making.[2] This view was early echoed in a number of quarters, such as the Bratislava trade union paper *Práca* which argued on 9 February 1968 that the unity so often sought by the Party could be achieved, among other ways, by informing the public fully and speedily on Party proposals and decisions, in order to make possible 'the confrontation of opinions and the assessment of various proposals.' Leading Slovak officials and thinkers expressed the same view in the Slovak Party daily on 2 February 1968, arguing that 'the unobstructed flow of information from top to bottom and bottom to top is indispensable for a stable healthy social organism.' Philosopher Jan Uher put forward the argument that scientific information theory 'opposes the vigilent monopoly on information which intentionally gives society only what it sees fit (not because technical reasons prevent them from supplying all information), not what a healthy, stable development of the social organism requires.' A one-time liberally inclined philosopher, Ladislav Szántó, considered the information given to society insufficient, the result of the fact that top Party officials regarded the masses as 'immature

[1] *Rudé právo*, 20 March 1968 (the paper itself admitted the mistake); ČTK, 15 March 1968 (the Party history institute); *Rudé právo*, 11 March 1968 (Kolder); and many of the speeches to the April central committee plenum (*Rudé právo*, 2–13 April 1968).
[2] Prague radio, 2 February 1968.

people who had to be protected from the truth, especially if it were disagreeable.' By way of illustration, *Práce* of 13 March 1968 mentioned that such things as three crashes of Czechoslovak passenger planes received scanty reporting in Czechoslovakia and the public was never informed of the results of the investigations. In this and so many other cases, *Práce* argued, there was never the possibility of people exerting pressures for a calling to task of those responsible for the tragedies; the mass media had no control function whatsoever. This situation had not been in any way remedied by the 1966 Press Law, it was pointed out at a Journalists Union meeting, for although the law enjoined institutions and organizations to provide the media with information, there were no sanctions written into the law for cases of non-compliance.[1]

Objections were also raised to the prohibitions against receipt of non-Communist sources. Thus the continued jamming of the broadcasts of Radio Free Europe was criticized on the grounds that this interfered with the citizen's right to exercise his own judgment.[2] It was pointed out in *Reportér* (27 March 1968) that the two foreign press centers opened (one in Prague and one in Bratislava) were supremely inadequate to the demand. *Reportér* also criticized (7 February 1968) the procedure through which media in Czechoslovakia received foreign journals or papers. Delays and bureaucracy characterized this 'flow' of information, as did limitations on the placement of orders and the foreign currency allotted for this. It was a major accomplishment when the Journalists Union reached an agreement with the Central Publications Board (the censor) which permitted editorial offices subscribing to foreign papers to receive them without the delay of their first passing the censor.[3]

Control from above of information clearly limited the possibilities for discussion, for it created restrictions on what could and what could not be said or published. Intellectual after intellectual, citizen after citizen, expressed the need to shake loose all the limitations on expression. Communist writer Pavel Kohout asserted in *Literární listy* of 16 May 1968 that

'the first absolutely imperative prerequisite is that nothing be *taboo* and everything can be discussed freely... At the Fourth [Writers] Congress I claimed for the citizens the right to ask questions and to receive answers. This right must never again be curtailed – in time or essence. If only a single theme is exempted from discussion, there can be no guarantee that another will not be added tomorrow and still another the day after tomorrow.'

---

[1] *Mladá fronta*, 6 March 1968.   [2] Prague radio, 12 March 1968.
[3] *Mladá fronta*, 6 March 1968.

Writer Ludvík Vaculík issued much the same warning, in *Literární listy* of 1 March 1968, using the example of the Austro-Hungarian 'toleranz patent.' The writers did not want 'tolerance' or a liberal cultural policy from the regime: they wanted complete freedom or the equivalent to no policy, i.e. no government direction in cultural affairs. If a government could say what was tolerable, by implication it also had the right to say what was *not* tolerable. A government did not have the right to give this mark of approval, for that would mean it also had the right to withdraw it. Indeed, this had been the case during the controlled 1963–7 thaw, as pointed out even then by Slovak philosopher Július Strinka in his plea for institutionalized (protected and guaranteed) criticism.[1]

The call for free exchange of ideas was made in radio and television discussions too, and even in such 'non-cultural' organs as the agricultural weekly, demonstrating that this was not an issue that interested only the intellectuals.[2] It was argued that fear had caused people to become silent, and continued fear, in many cases, led to continued silence. People were skeptical of the latest Party pronouncements, and only a program which guaranteed 'a free exchange of views and standpoints and discussion' could provide the basis for a democratization, *Práce* of 13 March 1968 claimed. This meant that media must be permitted to say what they wished, for

> 'any restriction on information, any approval of the truth from
> above, any method other than that of confronting differing views
> ...would be equal to returning hundreds of thousands of people to
> the sad and extremely unsocialist conviction that the best thing to
> do is to be silent and keep one's thoughts to oneself.'

Thus independence of the media became the heart of the issue. There were polemics between reformers and conservatives over the right of the editor himself to determine what he would or would not print, and who should in fact determine just this point. Even the Party daily – which remained under the conservative Oldřich Švestka (though his subordinates had to resign in the pressures for liberalization) – in an editorial on 19 March 1968 declared the need for independence to inform as it saw fit. As a Party paper *Rudé právo* could not claim total independence, but it did seek freedom from arbitrary control by individuals or departments which had usurped the central committee's more general responsibility for the paper. Independence for the radio and television was also demanded.

[1] *Kultúrny život*, 26 November 1965.
[2] For example, television round-table, 29 February 1968 and *Zemědělské noviny*, 5 March 1968.

The management of the radio expressed its belief that incorporation into the Ministry of Culture and Information would not permit 'appropriate independence' and recommended two independent broadcasting networks (along national lines), with a joint organ for foreign broadcasting.[1] The same idea was presented for television. It was clear to most, however, that independence of the media and freedom of expression were possible only with a revision or abrogation of the 1966 Press Law, and it was to this end that most intellectuals and artists worked.

The demand for the total abolition of censorship began to gain publicity in radio and television discussions in February 1968. In one of these programs Zdeněk Mlynář volunteered the opinion that 'our socialist society requires no preliminary censorship' since violations of state secrets were already provided for by the penal code and interference in the expression of different views was not justifiable. Ludvík Vaculík, in another of these talks on 20 February 1968, pointed out that the writers had as early as their 1967 congress demanded either the proper implementation of the Press Law or a new law altogether. The Writers Union, at least as represented by its new chairman, Goldstücker, began the revival period with the minimum demand: proper implementation of both the letter and the spirit of the Press Law. Specifically, Goldstücker meant that pre-publication censorship should be binding only with regard to revelation of state secrets; otherwise the censor could only *warn* the editor, not suspend publication.[2] Slovak Writers Union chairman Miroslav Válek, who was not considered more of a progressive than Goldstücker, favored amendment of the law to exclude 'any type of censorship...from the sphere of the cultural press.'[3]

The Journalists Union began working on the draft of a new bill, and the government, on the recommendation of the Party presidium, collaborated in this effort. The Party organization of the Central Publications Board (CPB) itself called for the abolition of 'political' censorship, and on 4 March 1968 the Party presidium rescinded its directive for preliminary

[1] Prague radio, 26 March 1968. If not independent at least an autonomous administration through elected officials subject only to the Press Law, was urged. (Petr Pithart, *Literární listy*, 20 June 1968.)

[2] *Práce*, 1 February 1968 and Prague radio, 21 February 1968 (interview). The law in fact called only for the censor to point out any potential violation of economic, state, or social secrets or material harmful to society. A subsequent Party presidium directive (August 1966), however, ordered suspension of publication rather than mere warning. (*Mladá fronta*, 6 March 1968.)

[3] *Večerník*, 14 February 1968.

political censorship and removed the CPB from the jurisdiction of the Ministry of the Interior, in effect suspending censorship.[1]

With the *de facto* suspension of censorship a campaign began for the enactment of a law banning preliminary censorship altogether. The Party organization of the Ministry of Culture and Information, for example, called for such a law, as did the director of the Writers Union publishing house, Jan Pilař.[2] Pilař, who was also not considered particularly progressive, said that publishers should be given the right to decide what they want to publish, permitting only artistic criteria to decide. The Conference of the Film and Television Artists Union also called for a law abolishing censorship. The demands for a new law were published on the pages of almost all the journals, especially *Kultúrny život* and *Literární listy*, which publicized numerous examples of censorship which had occurred even after 4 March 1968. One of these, by writer Ivan Klíma, expressed the demands more specifically, calling for amendment to the law which, Klíma claimed, permitted 'covert control of the press, discontinuation of existing periodicals, and refusal to grant permission to new ones.'[3] Many writers still believed that some type of censorship would be continued, and that the best that could be hoped for was that 'the whole institution of the freedom of the press be based on the relevant law,' with rights to litigate against administrative measures and so forth, as Klíma put it. This in effect might have meant only a slight improvement over the legal framework secured for the functions of the censor in the enactment of the 1966 law, for then too writers had argued for laws, so as to provide both a limit on the censor and recourse to the courts against the censor. The crux of the matter, however, was the law's provisions regarding censorship of 'all material harmful to society,' as distinct from state secrets. These were the provisions which, in practice, served as the basis for what was considered 'political censorship,' and the comments which accompanied the the writers' demands left no doubt as to the spirit in which they viewed such an amendment. As Klíma said, freedom of the press was the most important factor in freedom of expression and the 'law stipulating and guaranteeing this freedom is the criterion of the level of freedom achieved

[1] Prague radio, 14 March 1968; *Rok šedesátý osmý*, 32–3.

[2] ČTK, 23, 25 March 1968.

[3] *Literární listy*, 11 April 1968. In this vein a letter to the editor, *Literární listy*, 28 March 1968, described a telegram refused by the Post Office as 'ambiguous.' It read ' "Long Live Joseph and his government. That is democracy." ' It was sent on the name's day of a friend named Joseph. 'Where is freedom of speech and expression?,' the letter-writer, Dr Jan Říha, asked.

by any society. A rapid amendment of the Press Law will provide evidence of the sincerity of the changes taking place in our society.'

The regime's position on this issue was not entirely clear, for it was subject to the changing situation and pressures. Although the early actions of the regime were limited, e.g. Hendrych remained as ideological commission chairman and Hoffman remained as Minister of Information and Culture, by March there were positive changes. One of the new, reformist members of the Party presidium, Josef Špaček, who as South Moravian first secretary in the pre-1968 period had permitted a loosening of restrictions on intellectual life in the Brno area, replaced Hendrych on 5 March 1968. Čestmír Císař was returned to his former position of Party secretary responsible for education and culture, from which he had been removed in 1963 (prior to other demotions in 1965) for his permissiveness regarding the publication of reform demands. Miroslav Galuška, demoted in 1964 for his liberal editorship of the weekly *Kulturní tvorba*, was named Minister of Culture and Information in the new government of April 1968. Moreover, the early policy statements promised cultural freedom, and the regime set out to implement this policy by withdrawing all-inclusive directives from the mass media and informally suspending censorship, as we have seen.

One of the earliest remarks on behalf of the new leadership with regard to freedom of expression came from Josef Smrkovský. In a radio interview on 2 February 1968, he called for a new information policy which would avoid secrets about the work of the Party and the state and would keep the people properly informed. Špaček also favored dissemination of more information, pointing out that people often received better information faster through broadcasts and telecasts from abroad.[1] Dubček revealed his own opinion in his 22 February 1968 speech. He said that the regime would have to eliminate anything and everything which might hamper artistic and scientific creativity or create tension. Yet at this early stage Dubček added the caveat: 'At the same time the Party cannot give up the right or the duty to see to it that artistic creation also effectively aids the forming of socialist man.'

Among the 'new men' Smrkovský and Špaček continued to expound the most liberal line on this subject. Smrkovský, in at least two additional interviews, agreed upon the need for leaders to appear on the mass media to 'inform the nation,' and he attacked the 'anonymity' of government and Party representatives. He asserted that to deprive journalists of the right to comment freely on current developments would be tantamount

---

[1] *Obrana lidu*, 10 February 1968.

to destroying the reason for their existence, and together with Špaček he defended the media against conservative criticism which had already begun to be heard.[1] Smrkovský altered his stand somewhat in the late spring but he never abandoned his support for the principle of freedom of expression. Špaček urged that 'unlimited scope' be given to art and science, that no limitations or directives be issued regarding them and that, instead, both areas, including the press, should be used to provide contrasting views and alternative solutions.[2]

The Action Program condemned any effort to 'coercively prescribe' what people would be allowed or not allowed to know, what they might or might not be able to express openly, when and where public opinion could have a say and when not. Thus the Program called for the Press Law to state more clearly what information might be banned by state organs and 'to preclude the possibility of advanced censorship.' More specifically, the Program asserted:

'We must put an end to delayed, distorted, and incomplete information; we must eliminate unwarranted hiding of political and economic facts; we must publish annual reports on enterprise operations; we must also publish alternative proposals for various steps and solutions.'

The Program also proclaimed the need for representatives of state and social organizations to hold regular press conferences to keep the public informed, and to submit their views to public discussion. Minority views as well, according to the Action Program, were to be given the possibility of free expression. The need for an expanded import and sale of foreign newspapers was also recognized.

Dubček himself asserted, and from all reports sincerely believed, that socialism could not develop 'without a high degree of public involvement, without freedom of speech, without democracy in the widest sense.'[3] He called for a law guaranteeing the freedom of speech, and institutional guarantees for 'an open confrontation of interests and standpoints.' He believed that only thus could the differing views and interests in society, the existence of which had now been accepted, be understood, evaluated, and, possibly, solved.

In June the Party entrusted Galuška with the task of drafting a new press law for submission by the end of August. In the meantime the Party authorized the liquidation of the CPB (the censor), and the National

[1] Prague radio, 11 and 20 March 1968.   [2] *Rudé právo*, 16 March 1968 (interview).
[3] *Rudé právo*, 21 April 1968 (20 April 1968 speech at Bratislava).

Assembly passed an amendment to the Press Law.[1] In effect, pending a new law, these measures were designed officially to eliminate preliminary censorship, placing responsibility for protecting state, economic, and official secrets on the shoulders of the editors and media themselves.

While this amendment to the Press Law was a significant step forward (or backward, since it reinstated the pre-1948 situation[2]), it did not abolish censorship as such and, therefore, did not meet the maximum demands of the reformers. The journalists favored the original government draft of the bill, which, unlike the bill passed by the National Assembly, contained no clauses which would permit post-publication censorship, according to *Reportér* of 26 June 1968. The journalists also objected that the law applied only to censorship by 'state agencies.' They claimed, justifiably in view of past experience, that neither the Party nor the National Front was a state agency and, therefore, the law provided no protection against an effort by either of these to interfere in the freedom of expression. Still according to *Reportér*, the journalists defined censorship as '*any* action against freedom of speech and pictorial representation,' while the law pertained only to such action if committed by a state agency. Moreover, the state alone was to compile a list of what constituted a state, economic, or official secret, and this list, according to complaints by the journalists and Minister Galuška, consisted of more than 400 pages.[3] Moreover, they complained, this government decision would be final; there was no possibility of recourse to the courts in a censorship case which applied to a matter decreed secret by the government. The editor-in-chief was to ban the dissemination of any such material and was to be held responsible through post-publication censorship, the institutions issuing information in no way being held even co-responsible.

There were still other problems connected with this issue, and perhaps the reason that the regime did not produce a satisfactory press bill was that the media had not waited for the new law or even for the Party's final decision. As early as January, but particularly from February and

[1] Prague radio, 13 June 1968; *Rudé právo*, 25 June 1968. *Sbírka zákonů* No. 84/1968. Thirty deputies voted against the amendment. Commenting on this, one journalist said: 'The last time preliminary censorship was abolished, in 1867, the Emperor himself was not as afraid of the freedom of the press as were these deputies.' (*Lidová demokracie*, 27 June 1968, Zdeněk Veselý.)

[2] *Sbírka zákonů* No. 121/1920, in force until 1948.

[3] In a strong speech to the journalists' congress A. J. Liehm said: 'Any attempt, however, to replace censorship by a list of many pages of facts to be kept secret in the interest of individual departments and institutions will end in an all-out fiasco. We will simply take such a list and burn it publicly.' (*Mladá fronta*, 25 June 1968.)

March onwards, they had taken full advantage of the promises of freedom, indeed taking matters into their own hands by publishing and broadcasting without apparent regard for limitations. Just as in the 1963 revolt of the intellectuals almost no area of society went untouched by the writers' criticism, so in 1968 no subject was *taboo* in the hands of the mass media. Radio and television, in particular, took the lead in '*exposés*' of past errors, open and critical discussions, and full reporting of anything and everything known to them (including a wide use of information gleaned and quoted from western media). The journals by no means lagged behind in this new process, but the vanguard shifted from the specialized journals (of the writers or the journalists) to the mass media.

This phenomenon may have been a reflection of the changed situation: before 1968 the reformers' struggle was conducted almost exclusively within the Party and by Party members. Only a certain segment of society understood or even knew what was going on, and the discussions and pressures, significant though they were, remained within the somewhat elitist circles of the intelligentsia and its own organs. While there were reforms in the radio and television prior to 1968, these had been relatively limited and were insufficient to make of these media the progressive instruments those of the intellectuals had already become. After 1968, however, the matter became public, so to speak. Having won their struggle for the official adoption of their ideas (by their successful ascent to power), the Party reformers now sought to include the public in the struggle to implement and carry through the liberalization. Indeed the public, after January, began to grasp what had happened within the Party and, perhaps for the first time, saw the positive possibilities of the situation. Thus, the initiative gradually passed from a small group to the masses, and the major spokesmen as well as the stage for the views expressed passed from the specialized journals to the mass media. Indeed, it was traditional in Eastern Europe for the intelligentsia to play a leading role, through its own media, given the status of the intelligentsia in Eastern Europe pre-World War Two. It was also natural, however, that in the second half of the twentieth century this role would be complemented, if not supplanted by the mass media. The Communists had, of course, never underestimated the importance of the mass media, but it was just this importance which led them to maintain even more strict control over them, making it more difficult for radio and television to play the type of role played by the journals.

As had been the case with the journals in the pre-1968 period, so too with the mass media in the post-January 1968 period, it was difficult to tell which came first: a loosening of regime controls or initiative from the media themselves. It had long been the case with intellectuals under the Communist regimes, at least since 1956, that they would exploit the slightest possibility to push against the limits encompassing them and imposed upon them from above. Thus in 1968 the mass media exploited every crack in the Party's cultural and information policy – acting as if every promise were already law (much the way the workers, farmers, and students did) – to express their views and thereby become both the leaders and representatives of the public. They became in a literal sense the 'media of the masses.' The explanation of this process is probably no different from that of the increased power of the journals in the earlier period: reformers within the organizations were strong enough to prevail, reformers in the highest ranks of the Party were numerous and/or strong enough to protect or condone this.[1] From this a certain process developed whereby the limits were continuously pushed outward, in large part due to pressures from below demanding that the media say more, reveal more, do more.

The regime was by no means oblivious to this whole process. Indeed the new leaders had been brought to power on the wave of such a process, but not unlike Novotný before them many were uncomfortable about the instability of a situation which was beyond the Party's control and direction. This discomfort was accentuated by the outright fears and complaints of less liberal Party members and officials – as well as by the pressures from certain of Czechoslovakia's allies. The Party daily, *Rudé právo*, as early as 10 February 1968, published an article criticizing the 'mud-slinging' and emphasis on past mistakes apparent in the mass media. Kolder, who had wavered opportunistically between the reform and conservative forces in the past, and once a protégé of Novotný (but nonetheless opposed him in the crucial plena of 1967), took the more conservative position on this issue. Speaking to a Party group on the need to provide more information, Kolder said that while repression of justified criticism would not be permitted,

'we cannot allow the press, radio, and television to become tribunes for views running counter to the entire line of socialist construction.

[1] Momentum from below was particularly apparent in the radio, for the conservative director, Miloš Marko, was not replaced until 25 July 1968. He had in fact become no more than a figurehead, the tone for the radio being set by the more radical heads of departments and certain liberals such as Igor Kratochvíl, who returned in the spring having been ousted in 1961 as part of the 'Yugoslav group.' Outstanding commentators also had contacts with regime reformers such as Smrkovský, Špaček, Šimon and others.

It is inconceivable that internal Party affairs, which are the subject of intra-party discussion, should appear in mass communication media...The Party backs the democratization process; it is not admissible, however, for this process to take a haphazard course, and it is impossible to conceive democratization one-sidedly and separately from the strengthening of socialist discipline and the indispensable state discipline.'[1]

Other Party members also expressed their concern over the situation at the April plenum of the central committee. One local official complained of the harm being done the Party and Party discipline by the 'sensationalist' reports in the press about the 1950s. At the same meeting the conservative Pavel Auersperg, formerly chief of the central committee ideology department and, then, still candidate member of the central committee, also criticized 'some of the most striking extremes' of the mass media, which included plain 'mudslinging,' according to *Rudé právo* of 4 April 1968. While Auersperg was particularly critical of comments directed against him, his remarks did reflect the growing concern on the part of many. Vasil Bil'ak, former Slovak Party ideological chief and Dubček's replacement as first secretary of the Slovak Party, also took a not unexpected conservative position on this issue at the April plenum. Recognizing the positive role the media were playing, he sought to reveal 'the other side of the coin,' noting 'shortcomings in these media, where some workers, whose experience of life and politics is small, try to present even serious matters in a one-sided and sensational manner,' according to Bratislava radio, 9 April 1968. He launched into a lengthy tirade urging discipline, attacking television in particular, and implicitly criticizing the Party decision to suspend censorship. He called it 'naive' to demand that the Party give up its right to determine what should or should not be published, saying 'Nowhere in the whole world, and in no civilized country, can as much democracy and freedom of the press be found... as can be found at present in this country.' He called on Communists working in the mass media to remember that radio and television were 'instruments of the state policies and have not ceased to be instruments of the ideology and policies of the socialist state.'

The reformers themselves began to show a certain uneasiness in this sphere, however. Smrkovský, one of the staunchest supporters of the

---

[1] *Rudé právo*, 10 March 1968. ČTK, Czechoslovak television, *Mladá fronta*, and *Práce* carried a paragraph excluded from the original *Rudé právo* version of this very speech. *Rudé právo* corrected itself the following day and in turn pointed out parts left out by ČTK and the others. (*Rudé právo*, 11 March 1968.) .

principle of freedom of speech, generally defended the media, but on at
least one occasion he criticized them for dwelling on the evils of the past
rather than suggesting constructive measures for the future.[1] Císař, an
early supporter of liberalization in the cultural sphere, also saw fit to
plead for restraint, becoming increasingly critical of the media. He
divided the work of the media into two periods (as did many others)
claiming that unlimited criticism had served a positive role in the first
period, that of introducing democratization. The media had then
'mobilized the broadest strata of the people and enlisted them for political
activity.' It was the second stage which became troublesome, according to
Císař, for the press

'began to accelerate the pace of opening and bringing up problems
and the readers began to be flooded with a continuous flow of
information, in particular on discovered facts, criticism, and
sensations. Quantity began to outweigh quality and hastiness
created half-truths, speculations, and even fabrications...the flood
of often unselective criticism of the past activity of the Party and
the state began to cause in the minds of people a general
discrediting of the period of socialist construction.'

Going into some detail of the evils of this second period, Císař praised the
fact that in some offices responsibility and discipline were replacing this
dangerous 'spontaneity and sensation-mongering.' He, nonetheless,
called on the media to look upon their responsibilities more seriously, to
exercise greater discretion and discipline, to desist from provocative or
unqualified statements, and to present as such views which departed
from the official standpoint, rather than leave them uncommented upon.[2]
In an interview given to the Hungarian weekly *Élet és irodalom* on 4
May 1968, Císař said somewhat ominously that the policy for the arts
had to provide little or no control and expanded freedom, but that 'other
rules apply to the press.' Even Josef Špaček, who like Smrkovský had
defended freedom of speech even against the renewed attacks in March,
by May was subtly warning the media to remember that they had a *dual*
role: to present suggestions 'from below,' but also to 'carry policy from
the top down...to create public opinion.' This task, he said, was 'naturally
more difficult than limiting efforts to the exposure of past errors.'[3]
While it may be assumed that at least Špaček and Smrkovský – who

[1] *Práca*, 30 April 1968.
[2] Prague radio, 2 April 1968 (interview), Prague radio, 8 April 1968 (remarks to a Prague
meeting), and *Rudé právo*, 30 May 1968.
[3] *Rudé právo*, 23 May 1968.

felt it necessary to express certain public warnings – continued to defend the principles of free speech in Party debates, there were also those who openly defended the media against *all* attacks. For example the reformer Bohumil Šimon, candidate presidium member and head of the Prague city Party committee, praised the fairness displayed by the media in presenting both sides of issues, and he warned against justifying the fears of those whose distrust of both the Party and the present democratization was deep – and not without foundation.[1] *Mladá fronta* of 12 March 1968 also warned against a return to old practices when people harboring different opinions or acting contrary to the wishes 'of some groups of people or an individual in power were immediately suspected of anti-Marxist and anti-socialist intentions, accused of attempts to restore capitalism, and liquidated by violence.' The agricultural paper *Zemědělské noviny* defended the media on 12 March 1968, critizing the remarks of *Rudé právo* against them, saying: 'The mistakes – and in the last few days also the mud – were not created by newspapers, which merely write about mistakes.' The same paper later, on 9 June 1968, came out again on behalf of the media, answering 'indignant and even malicious voices to the effect that there has been enough freedom of the press.' It claimed that such comments came from officials and anonymous letters, people who were 'simply confused by the new freedom which replaces authority with abundance of views and therefore the need to think; some are simply jealous that they no longer hold the monopoly on information; some would indeed like to return to the former system of controlling what may or may not be said.' The paper pointed out that it was not a very large step from pointing out excesses to 'advising' what subjects should be avoided, thus returning to the former system.

Dubček most likely found it difficult to weave a just policy out of the contradictory views, given the pressures and concern felt even by many of the new regime. His speech to the 29 May – 1 June 1968 central committee plenum clearly showed his own concern and the position the Party was taking, although the outside pressures of this time probably also played a role in the shaping of this new policy. While he praised the work of the media, Dubček devoted most of his remarks concerning this area to criticism. In his speech, carried by *Pravda* (Bratislava), 4 June 1968, he analyzed the reasons for the wave of criticism of the media, explaining that the media did not realize the power they had to influence opinion – in this particular situation – against the Party. By the 'biased stressing of mistakes,' they had created a distrust and uncertainty

[1] *Rudé právo*, 6 June 1968 (to 29 May – 1 June central committee plenum).

among the public regarding Party policy, he explained. Failure of the media to respond quickly to 'anti-socialist' attacks from abroad was also a problem.

Dubček said that journalists should bear in mind the rapidly changing objective political situation, and not just their own subjective desires. 'An ill-considered, although well-meant, utterance may objectively harm the revival and play into the hands of both rightist opposition elements and dogmatic forces.' Dubček went on to say that he believed it correct to provide the media with freedom of expression and, indeed, the amendment to the Press Law was about to be passed, but, he said,

'no one must confuse this with the right to express subjective views before millions of viewers, listeners, or readers without due consideration of the social effect. The government is responsible for the state information media: ČTK, radio, and television.'

He called on Communist journalists to assume greater responsibility for the defense of socialist values:

'We will rely on both the Communists on the editorial boards and on the activity of the National Front, whose groups should influence their press organs in the spirit of the National Front policy.'

This reference to the National Front demonstrated just how far the regime had come, nonetheless, in the democratization, for it recognized that the Party could (or should) no longer dictate to other groups, and that many groups or social organizations were no longer dominated by Communists. Therefore the appeal to follow 'National Front' policy, i.e. an effort to find some authority among the diversity the Party had itself sanctioned.

Dubček's warning could not have been misunderstood, for just two weeks prior to the plenum the conservatives had succeeded in introducing (though not in having passed) to the National Assembly a bill which would limit the media. While the bill itself was more a reflection of the outside pressures – it concerned the dissemination of material which might be harmful to Czechoslovakia's relations with her allies – it, nonetheless, demonstrated the current danger of a return to repression.[1] The bill was proposed by Vilém Nový, the conservative who had resigned from his job as rector of the Party college at the request of the students and teachers in March 1968. He was supported by several other conservatives in the Assembly, but as the bill was presented to the foreign relations committee it stood little chance of success, for the chairman of that committee was Jiří Pelikán, reform-minded director of Czechoslovak

[1] Prague radio, 15 May 1968.

television. At the May–June plenum, however, Černík announced that the government had decided on certain measures designed to 'guide' the media. According to these decisions, Černík explained, the media were to publish 'official documents, information and viewpoints without polemical commentaries.' Declaring that a return to censorship was not being attempted, Černík announced that a 'program board' would be created to supervise broadcasting. This board was to be appointed by the government and consist of fifty per cent radio and television personnel and fifty per cent National Front and state representatives.[1] This announcement, combined with Dubček's warning at the plenum, was sufficient to cause the reformers serious concern, as pressures from outside for a more restrictive policy grew.

Certain intellectuals, in part out of skepticism and distrust, had warned of this eventuality long before. Their plea also reflected one of the principles that had motivated the intellectuals from the beginning of their struggle in 1963: there had to be institutionalized changes and changes in the institutions if there were to be any real guarantees for the gains made. Such a warning was early voiced in *Kultúrny život* of 2 February 1968, by liberal Slovak journalist Pavol Števček who himself had suffered from the vicissitudes of earlier thaws. Philosopher Ivan Sviták was a constant skeptic in these months, pointing out on numerous occasions that no structural changes had been introduced to provide a significant guarantee against what he called 'the mechanism of totalitarian dictatorship.'[2] Sviták's thesis, as explained for example at the Film and Television Artists conference, was:

'The bureaucracy of a totalitarian dictatorship accepts personnel changes easily while it is afraid of structural changes, against which it will defend itself to the utmost. Therefore we must demand structural changes and not be satisfied with an exchange of persons ...the present political changes are so far only the change of ideologies of one and the same elite in power...its maximal program of democratization is our minimal program of true democracy.'

Sviták pointed out that the only area in which hopes were being fulfilled was that of freedom of expression, for the only change instituted was the abolition of preliminary censorship. Because this was the only real concession made to date, Sviták pointed out in *Student* of 10 April 1968, it was on this issue that one must expect 'the counter attacks of the conservative forces...These forces will call for restraint; they will offer new

[1] *Rudé právo*, 7 June 1968.   [2] *Student*, 20 March 1968.

economic reforms and new persons instead of fundamental political changes.'

Sviták's prognosis, however radical in the eyes of most reformers, was indeed accurate, and people in the literary and mass media world began to fight this dangerous new phenomenon. In an early move some twenty-three editors of *Nová svoboda*, all members of the Party, signed a resolution rejecting the accusations against the mass media as attempts by 'the conservative faction of the political "apparat"...to preserve their shaky positions.'[1] Poet Lumir Čivrný, for example, was not so confident that only a faction was involved but implied, in *Pràce* of 24 March 1968, that in fact the regime was using the carrot and stick method, i.e. first offering freedom of expression and then limiting the areas to be publicly discussed, referring to 'socialist discipline and public restraint.' This was of particular concern, he asserted, considering that such was the method when only supply of information was involved; what then would be the case when the public tried to exercise its rights of control and recall of its elected representatives and so forth? In a similar vein another intellectual, Zdeněk Veselý, referred, in *Lidová demokracie*, 28 April 1968, to having freedom of the press only 'on parole,' since, without a new law, censorship could be reinstated in a moment. The vulnerability in this area was but a sign of the vulnerability of the whole democratization process, for until there were deeds, i.e. laws and institutional changes, one had freedom and democracy only on the word of honor of certain leaders.

It was in May and after, however, that the intellectuals' proddings became an expression of genuine concern and dismay over what they saw as 'the slowing down of the democratization process.'[2] Cases of continued censorship were reported, the most grievous having been orders to editorial boards to refrain from publishing statements by or about the former Social Democratic Party, which was demanding reinstatement.[3] Similar orders were reported with regard to K-231 and KAN. In addition to this muzzling, there were rumors among the intellectuals that the regime was trying to engineer changes in the editorial board of *Student* because the weekly was 'becoming uncomfortable to certain quarters.'

In a sign of the newly achieved cooperation between workers and intellectuals, workers committees were formed in the Ostrava industrial center, among the shipyard workers, and elsewhere (with the support of

[1] ČTK, 13 March 1968.
[2] Declaration of the central committee of the Union of Film and Television Artists meeting, Prague, 17 May 1968. (*Filmové a televizní noviny*, II:11 (1968), 8.)
[3] See *Literární listy*, 30 May 1968 and 20 June 1968.

and sometimes on the initiative of the ROH) for the defense of freedom of the press. Workers threatened to strike if freedom of the press were not respected, thus apparently agreeing with the intellectuals that attempts to muzzle the press represented a danger to the whole democratization process.[1] Petr Pithart, in a similar vein to the declaration of the Union of Film and Television Artists, saw such attempts as 'the most significant symptom of the slowing down and retarding of the Czechoslovak revolution.'[2] A return to censorship, according to *Zemědělské noviny* of 9 June 1968, would mean a return to the situation in which differences in opinions were not permitted, and decisions from above were final. Jiří Lederer argued in *Literární listy* that this meant efforts to limit the possibility of public policy-making, upon which the very 'hope of democracy' was based. The references to 'anti-socialist' and 'anti-communist' forces in Party proceedings were considered ominous signs that the conservative forces were gaining strength, in particular when viewed in conjunction with the 'return to "smoke-filled room" politics by the Party leadership.'[3]

This concern culminated at the end of June 1968 with a declaration signed by a selected list of workers, artists, scientists, writers, farmers, sportsmen, and engineers, known as the '2,000 Words.' It was published simultaneously by the youth daily *Mladá fronta*, the trade union daily *Práce*, the agricultural daily *Zemědělské noviny*, and the writers' weekly *Literární listy*, on 27 June 1968. This matter-of-fact declaration neither praised nor condemned the present situation but, rather, pointed out that the democratization process had entered a crucial stage which demanded a concerted effort by the people to secure their rights. While the document was moderate and practical both in tone and content, demanding nothing more (and even less) than that which had already been demanded on many public platforms, it was to be of extraordinary perhaps even tragic significance. The declaration, in the eyes of some, was a call for 'action from below,' which threatened, if not already demonstrated, the weakening of Party control over events. At the very least, the regime feared that the Soviet Union and other sources of pressure on Prague would interpret the document this way, and, therefore, made what it was later to admit as a

---

[1] See *Práce*, 13 June 1968; *Literární listy*, 30 May 1968 (Jiří Lederer). These committees were apparently created on the initiative of the workers, for Lederer called for co-operation between them and the intellectuals, suggesting that such cooperation did not exist on a practical level.

[2] *Literární listy*, 20 June 1968.

[3] *Reportér*, 29 May 1968 (Jiří Ruml) and *Filmové a televizní noviny*, II:11 (1968), 8.

tactical error.[1] At an emergency presidium meeting it condemned the declaration, and in so doing contributed to the attention, importance, influence, and support accorded the document, particularly in Czechoslovakia.[2]

Some of the signers of the document (Charles University rector Oldřich Starý, Academician Otto Wichterle, engineer–writer Jiří Hanzelka, and scientist–poet Miroslav Holub) met with National Front chairman František Kriegel to explain the document. They explained that the growing power of the conservatives, evidenced by such things as the anti-semitic, 'nazi-like' letters recently sent to Goldstücker, was underestimated. At the same time, they said, the declaration, and particularly 40 words of the 2,000 Words, was being grossly misinterpreted. Reporting the meeting, *Práce* (29 June 1968) regretted that a less liberal opponent to the declaration (Kriegel was one of the earliest and most consistent fighters for reform) had not appeared for the discussion, for the arguments of more conservative critics of the '2,000 Words' would have revealed some of the conservative line against which the declaration had come to protest. That line was expressed, for example, by conservative National Assembly members who termed the document 'an open call for counter-revolution.'[3] Kriegel himself told a Prague district Party conference, that he did not consider the document counter-revolutionary, and that many of the signatories were quite honorable people whom he knew personally. He did add, however, that the content of certain passages could provoke dangerous reactions among the public.[4] That meeting itself, as many others like it, heard numerous suggestions that a stand be taken expressing opposition to the Party presidium's condemnation of the document and its ignoring of the declaration's 'sound core.' At another district Party meeting in Prague, Ota Šik also supported the legitimacy of the declaration's intentions and allegations, as did Jihlava Party secretary Jaroslav Šebesta, who publicly opposed the presidium condemnation, and reformer Josef Špaček.[5] While conservatives such as Jan Piller and Alois Indra

[1] Even the Yugoslavs, who gradually expressed sympathy with it, saw in it 'anarchist' elements. (*Borba*, 1 July 1968.) Their concern was the implied threat to use violence, but, in fact, the only phrase containing this threat was part of an offer to stand behind the government, even with arms, in its efforts to withstand outside pressures.

[2] *Rok šedesátý osmý*, 228–30.

[3] Prague radio, 26 June 1968. Slovak deputy Major-General Samuel Kodaj.

[4] Reported in *Zemědělské noviny*, 30 June 1968.

[5] *Zemědělské noviny*, 30 June 1968 (Šik); Prague radio, 6 July 1968 (Šebesta and Špaček). After initial opposition Smrkovský too expressed support for '2,000 Words' in a *Rudé právo* article entitled '1,000 Words'.

supported the presidium condemnation, and the Slovak Communist Party presidium issued one of its own, the Slovak Party organ itself ran a commentary on 3 July 1968 by historian Samo Falt'an opposing the summary dismissal of the declaration.[1] The Party meetings exhibited mixed reactions, ranging from outright support for the declaration to outright condemnation. The media, however, reported an avalanche of letters, telephone calls, and 'resolutions,' the majority of which supported the '2,000 Words,' including support from 1000 employees of the Tesla factory in Prague, 500 workers in a Prague plant, and workers in Brno.[2]

The '2,000 Words' was in a sense the intellectuals' supreme effort to bring about change in the pre-invasion period. It caused much more of a sensation – and crisis – than expected, and it marked the beginning (though not the cause) of the final stage of what proved to be irreversible pressures on Czechoslovakia from outside. All subsequent efforts concentrated on resisting these pressures, and the intellectuals, artists, and mass media closed ranks behind the Party leadership in this struggle. This is not to say that they did not keep up their own battle for freedom of expression, for it was clear that a return to censorship was part of – perhaps the major part of – the Soviet, East German, and Polish demands on Czechoslovakia. They, therefore, made every effort to concede the responsible demands of the regime without conceding their own basic rights, and they continued to play a major role in the attempt to keep the public fully informed.

It is difficult to know just what stand the Party would finally have taken on the issue of the freedom of expression had it not been harassed for at least one-half of those eight months of 'revival' by outside and conservative pressures. There can be little doubt that the media did go further than even the reformers had wished, but there is also reason to believe that most reform leaders were committed to the principle of a free public exchange of views. Indeed Šik repeated this as late as the beginning of August, and the fact that for some time after the invasion the writers, at least, succeeded in publishing much of what they had to say, testified to the fact that Dubček, Smrkovský, Špaček and the genuine liberals in the Party were opposed to denying this freedom.

[1] Prague radio, 29 June 1968 (Indra at Hodonín and telegram to district and regional Committees); Bratislava radio, 1 July 1968 (Piller at Kladno meeting); Bratislava radio, 2 July 1968 (presidium statement).
[2] According to Prague radio, 2 July 1968; *Práce*, 6 July 1968; and even *Rudé právo*, 6 July 1968.

6

Political Reform and the Party

The focus of attention in 1968 was upon the political sphere, specifically on the questions of the concentration of power in the hands of the Party and the right to opposition, for freedom of association and freedom of expression could only be valid – and of interest – if there were freedom to oppose, i.e. an end to the monopolistic power of the Party. There were many suggestions as to how this power might be curbed and best used, some centering on the element of popular control, others on a separation of Party and government functions, others on the right to opposition by forces outside the Party, still others on the right to opposition within the Party itself. Implicit in all of these suggestions was revision of the concept of the leading role of the Party with the establishment of democracy.

The leading role of the Party

The very earliest discussions in 1968 on the Party's role did little more than affirm points conceded earlier, for example, the idea that the leading role of the Party did *not* mean that the Party should interfere in day to day matters of the economy and management. This was the principle implicit to the economic reforms. According to *Rudé právo* of 12 January 1968, the Party's task was to provide coordination for society's activities, concerning itself only with the general aims of society, leaving the concrete decisions for daily activities to the various groups in society. The Party should provide no more than a programmatic statement and, also, create conditions for the settlement of conflicts which might arise as a result of leaving matters to the various groups in society. Thus the possibility of conflicting interests was recognized (as it had been in earlier Party proposals for reform), with the Party to serve as an arbitrator of sorts.

Both the programmatic role and that of arbitrator were inconsistent with the accepted theoretical basis for the role of the Party. As Zdeněk Mlynář, chairman of the Party committee for political reform, pointed out in *Rudé právo* of 13 January 1968, the role of the Party had originally been worked out to suit the stage of the dictatorship of the proletariat, i.e. to fit the struggle of the working class *against* all other classes and, in keeping with this, to consolidate the 'centralist command system of economic management' which replaced private ownership. Therefore, Mlynář explained, 'for many years the political system in this country was deliberately adjusted to conform to the demand that *a single interest*, embodied in the form of directives issued by the center, should be made to prevail without any resistance.' Thus not only did the Party interfere in and regulate all aspects of society from the center, it also regarded any 'interest' or opinion beyond the appropriate directive as an obstacle to unity. Slovak Party central committee member Ondrej Repka added, in *Roľnícke noviny* of 20 January 1968, that the Party had seen itself as infallible and therefore conceived its leading role as that of dictating. People's participation had been limited to carrying out directions, Mlynář pointed out. This in turn had led to a concentration of power and decision-making by the few, and, according to Repka, the famed unity became no more than a 'sterile and false' unity imposed from above.

If the existence of legitimate conflicts in socialist society – once classes in the Marxist sense were eliminated – were recognized, Repka argued, the Party would have to adjust its concept of unity to one based on 'a permanent clash of views.' Its leading role would have to be conceived as mediating between these conflicting views, by permitting genuine and active participation through free discussion and, as Mlynář put it, by recognizing each of the components of the society's political life as independent entities so that they could make their own contribution to the solution of problems and provide an element of control. Thus the Party should see itself, according to reform leader Václav Slavík, as 'merely a component, albeit the principal one, of the entire political and managerial system,' a co-participant with the other groups in society.[1] As such, it was argued, the Party should no longer dictate to or even through the other organizations in society, whether the government, the mass organizations, the schools, the factories, or the cultural–artistic world. Mlynář had pointed out that the all-pervasive role of the Party had been designed for the struggle for the new system against hostile classes and private property. Such controls were neither necessary nor appropriate in a classless socialist society. Psychology lecturer and Brno Party activist Jaroslav Šabata argued on Brno radio, 7 February 1968, that not only was the Party 'not identical with the organs and institutions which govern or should govern,' but it could not even claim to represent all citizens. The people were represented by their official elected bodies. Thus, it was argued that the Party's leading role should not be achieved by the direction and control

[1] *Rudé právo*, 30 January 1968.

of the non-Party institutions and offices but by the influence of Communists in these bodies. Yet this too should not be achieved by way of directives or the imposition of Party people on to these groups or by the 'cadre system' whereby the Party approved appointments. The task of the Party should be, rather, that of an *avant-garde* or example for the other groups, achieving its leading role by virtue of the success of this example and its proponents.

These concepts of the Party, as mediator rather than dictator, as co-participant and independent component rather than controller of the political scene, were seen by their advocates as ultimately conducive to the strengthening rather than the weakening of the Party's leading role. Both Slavík and Repka contended that if the Party sought unity through conflicts of views and discussions, it would be required repeatedly to invigorate its own arguments, constantly adjust and rejuvenate its own views to meet the challenge of others. Thus, instead of dogmatism, a living, suitable (to the conditions and demands of society) program would ensure the Party's leading role. In effect the Party's authority as the leading force in the country, written into the Constitution as a recognition of past achievements, would no longer be merely formal. It would be constantly 're-earned.'[1] Slavík went so far as to say: 'These words of the Constitution are valid only if the Party fights and proves them by action,' according to *Práce* of 7 February 1968. Others too, such as Smrkovský and Slovak presidium member Miloslav Hruškovič, expressed regret over the Constitutional preference for the Party.[2] The reformers concluded that the Party must constantly re-win its right to this role by seeking and fulfilling the public's trust.[3]

In his earliest pronouncement on the subject, Dubček quoted Gottwald in calling for an end to direct management by the Party and 'administrative and commandeering methods.' He called for a broad programmatic role for the Party, providing room for the institutions of society to decide on their own plans and activities and for 'the confrontation and exchange of opinions.'[4] Dubček also advocated the idea that the Party must con-

---

[1] *Rudé právo*, 10 January 1968 (conservative ideologist Jan Fojtík). In this article Fojtík reverted to the conservative idea that the Party's job is to ensure that decisions in each sphere (economic, governmental, social) correspond to all-socialist interests and not to narrow 'subjective' ones.

[2] Czechoslovak television, 29 February 1968; Josef Smrkovský, 'Democracy Does Not Come Overnight,' *My 68*, v:4 (1968), 6.

[3] *Práce*, 7 February 1968 (Slavík); *Rudé právo*, 8 February 1968. See also *Práce*, 14 March 1968 (Radoslav Selucký).

[4] *Rudé právo*, 23 February 1968 (22 February speech, in the presence of visiting leaders such as Brezhnev). See also *Rudé právo*, 5 March 1968 (speech at Kladno, 2 March).

stantly renew its mandate from the people. In his 2 March speech at Kladno he said:

'The Party's leading role can only stem from, originate, and be maintained to the extent to which it [the Party] is regarded by our people as their political leader. It is impossible for us to achieve this by a resolution. This position of our Party is not established or maintained on the basis of power but on the basis of correct policy. The policy which creates the Party's leading role must not lead to the citizens standing outside the Party – and of these there is a majority in our society – getting the feeling that they are restricted in their rights and freedoms by the Party's leading role; on the contrary, they must see the role of the Party as the guarantee of their rights, freedoms, and interests.'

In the weeks prior to the Action Program, the essence of the new interpretation of the Party's role was that the Party would no longer maintain a monopoly of power over decision-making; it would, rather, pursue its goals through equal competition in offices, factories, and institutions through people of all interests and backgrounds. The Party's abandonment of its monopoly would mean abandonment of the favored position accorded to it by the Constitution. It would have to share power, permit a clash of ideas and interests, and implicit in this, permit criticism, division of powers, and controls.[1] A more radical view, however, was that of philosopher Ivan Sviták, expelled from the Party in 1965 for exceeding the limits of that precarious period of thaw. He claimed that the leading role of the Party had no theoretical support in the works of Karl Marx; the idea had come from Lenin to accommodate 'the fact that in Russia the workers' class formed a negligible fraction of the illiterate masses under czarist despotism,' and had been institutionalized by Stalin. Sviták considered this phenomenon totally 'unsuitable for democratic countries in which there are no illiterate people.'[2] Unlike moderates such as Goldstücker, Sviták rejected the very *idea* of the leading role of the Party for Czechoslovakia, apparently at any stage. Most Party members merely rejected the idea for a *socialist* society; Goldstücker even justified the dictatorship and terror following the 'revolution' as the necessary and

---

[1] See, for example, Prague radio, 20 March 1968 (Prague rally); *Reportér*, 6 March 1968; *Rudé právo*, 29 March 1968 (Smrkovský); *Rudé právo*, 2–11 April 1968 (speeches by Dubček, Špaček, Slavík, Smrkovský and others); *Práce*, 5 April 1968; *Rudé právo*, 6 April 1968 (central committee resolution).

[2] 'A Conference Marked by the Sign of the Times,' *Filmové a televizní noviny*, 11:7 (1968), 7.

natural development of all revolutions, and he merely called for a new stage now that the revolution had thoroughly secured itself.[1] Moreover, the most common Party position was not that the concept of the leading role of the Party was unjustified but that it had merely been distorted over the years. If, however, this distortion meant the concentration of power and decision-making in the hands of the Party, the remedy – as advocated by Dubček himself – was an end to this monopoly, a sharing in power, and withdrawal from day to day decision-making (or direct management). The 'leading' role of the Party might then be both vague and vulnerable, for it could be difficult to delineate clearly between 'sharing power' and 'leading.' This was indeed to become the crux of the problem.

The Action Program fully endorsed the idea of the leading role of the Party, though it redefined this role in keeping with the theory that a distortion had set in. This distortion, the Program explained, was the result of the 'false thesis that the Party is the instrument of the dictatorship of the proletariat.'[2] Presumably this was a rejection of Stalin's institutionalization of the leading role of the Party, based on Lenin's original concept that the Party was not only the vanguard of the working class but also the very embodiment of the proletariat. It was the Leninist concept of the Party which had led to the assumption that the Party should rule in the name of the proletariat in the period of the dictatorship of the proletariat, however long, or short, Lenin anticipated that period to be. According to the Action Program, the state, plus the economic and social institutions, were the instruments of the proletariat. The Party's leading role consisted of other functions, primarily to 'encourage initiative, to point out the paths and realistic possibilities of Communist prospects, and by systematic persuasion and the personal example of Communists, to win over the working people to these prospects,' as determined by 'the programmatic nature of Party activity.'

Thus the Program declared that the Party should not 'rule over society,' but 'continuously earn [its leading role] by deeds;' 'the aim of the Party is not to become a universal administration;' it should provide only guidelines rather than concrete decisions. By the same token, the Party should not replace or dominate the social and political institutions of the society (e.g. the National Front) for they, not the Party, represented the varied interests and groups in society. The Party, nonetheless, should play the role of arbitrator for the varying interests, seeking 'a method of satisfying

[1] Prague radio, 20 March 1968 (Prague rally).
[2] The term 'instrument of the dictatorship of the proletariat' is from Stalin's *Problems of Leninism*.

various interests that will not threaten the long-term interests of society as a whole.' However, the Program also added:

'Through its members, organizations, and organs, the Party must perform the practical organizational function of a political force in society. The political–organizational activity of the Party *coordinates the practical efforts of the people to ensure that the line and program of the Party are implemented in all sectors, that is, in the social, economic, and cultural life of society.*'[1]

This statement would seem to mitigate all that had gone before it on non-interference in social and cultural institutions, and so forth. The key to this apparent paradox lay, perhaps, in the fact that the Action Program called for a change in the *methods* used by the Party in executing its role. Instead of commanding, the Party was to exercise its authority informally, by way of persuasion and example, free of imposition (i.e. an end of the cadre system and the practice of controlling the various institutions through Communists placed in their leading organs). To clarify this the Action Program contained Dubček's statement of one month earlier:

'Party policy must not lead to non-Communists getting the impression that their rights and freedom are limited by the role of the Party. On the contrary, they must see in the activity of the Party a guarantee of their rights, freedom, and interests.'

The Party's position on its 'leading role' changed but little in the course of the disputes and pressures of the following months. The only significant alteration was proposed in an interview to the Hungarian weekly *Élet és irodalom* of 4 May 1968 by Čestmír Císař. Císař suggested that the Party abandon its monopoly on ideology as well as on decision-making. While this idea may have been implicit in the newly recognized rights of the groups in society, it was the first 'official' suggestion that the Party's role was not necessarily to be 'keeper of the faith.' Because, according to Císař, there were non-Marxist socialist views in Czechoslovakia as well as non-Communist Marxist views, the Party must struggle as one among many for the support of the public even in the ideological sphere. Indeed a leading law professor had said earlier, in a discussion conducted by *Reportér* of 14 February, that the existence of a 'state ideology' written into the Constitution, befitted a society based on religion.

Democratization of the Party

There were those who believed that the best way to control the power of

[1] Emphasis mine.

the Party, or to prevent a distortion of the Party's leading role (assuming that the Party would maintain its leading role), would be to change the Party itself, its internal *modus operandi*, and perhaps its structure and composition. If the leading role of the Party until 1968 had been based on acceptance or even distortion of a Soviet concept designed for specific conditions at a specific stage of development, so too, it was argued, the concept of the internal Party mechanism was based on a model devised for the specific conditions of Russia in a specific period. While this explanation was discussed but little – Party leaders preferred to refer simply to mistaken interpretation or distorted application of legitimate principles – an article which appeared during the crucial central committee plena of late 1967 delicately implied that democratic centralism as designed by Lenin – with its emphasis upon strict division of labor and centralized decision-making – was intended *only* for the conditions prevailing in Russia at the time of the revolution, and was intended even there to give way to a different working concept once the Party was in power.[1] The article, by a lecturer at the Party's higher school, even presented some of Trotsky's warnings of the potential dangers of the Leninist concept. The problem lay not only with Lenin's concept, the author argued, but with the fact that it was blindly copied by Parties outside Russia without much attention to the differences in conditions. Moreover, the very essence of Lenin's idea of adapting practice to circumstances was lost, for instead of providing a basis for the evolution of the concept of the Party, Lenin's ideas became the basis of a dogma.

Whether implicitly or explicitly accepting this idea, Party members, after the January plenum, began to present proposals for democracy within the Party through adjustment of the concept of democratic centralism, at least as applied prior to 1968. Amongst the earliest demands were that Party proceedings be published and that lower Party organizations be provided greater information instead of being presented with a *fait accompli* from above. While these demands began as complaints over the lack of information regarding the October–January plena, they rapidly became part of the more general proposals for inner-Party democracy.[2] *Rudé právo* of 5 March 1968 reported that at the March 1968 Party conferences there was an almost universal demand to improve the system of information within the Party, and complaints were heard that Party

[1] Kůš, Vladimír, 'Characteristic Features of Lenin's Organizational Principles at the Time of Their Origin,' *Příspěvky k dějinám KSČ*, vii:6 (1967), 856–77.

[2] See, for example, *Rudé právo*, 19, 30 January 1968; *Pravda* (Bratislava), 22 January 1968; *Rovnost*, 2 February 1968.

members had to learn of important events from the *foreign* press or from rumors and gossip.[1] This issue was considered particularly important for it was but one manifestation of the Party's tendency to command rather than lead, from the top downwards. Communists demanded that less emphasis be placed on discipline and more on participation. Specifically, as reform leader Špaček pointed out, there should be a two-way flow of information and proposals, with unobstructed suggestions from below including criticism and 'corrective suggestions to Party policy,' as well as suggestions from the central committee downwards so that the basic unit might 'arrive independently at its position on the basic questions of Party policy.'[2] This idea meant not only prevention of 'exaggerated centralization,' as Dubček said in his 22 February speech, but the opening of channels from the bottom *to* the top.

Open channels and genuine participation of members at all levels implied, however, the more controversial issue of criticism. In the past, dissenting or critical views were generally suppressed. Šik offered his own personal example to illustrate this phenomenon, pointing out not only that he had been denied the right to speak before Party gatherings but that critical comments had more often than not been labeled 'revisionism,' then 'liberalism,' or with regard to Slovaks, 'nationalism,' so that fear prevented people from speaking their mind.[3] Smrkovský urged that conflicting views within the Party be settled by argument and discussion rather than by authoritative pronouncements or the obligation of passive assent 'so often called discipline.'[4] Many quoted Italian Communist leader Togliatti's condemnation of the doctrine of monolithic unity under which ' "disagreement became the number one enemy" ' within the Party.[5] These arguments generally implied the right of minority views not only to be expressed but to be defended. It was pointed out in *Pravda* (Bratislava), on 7 February 1968 that in Lenin's day 'there were vivid discussions in the Party, no one was afraid of voting, on each issue majorities and minorities formed up, and final unity did not have to be identical with unanimous views.' The question was to what degree the

---

[1] *Pravda* (Bratislava), 12 March 1968 (comments at a Slovak Party district meeting) or Prague radio, 7 February 1968.

[2] Prague radio, 17 March 1968 (Špaček speech at Brno). Workers' complaints regarding this lack of participation were raised, for example, by Communists in Avia factory, regarding the Party decision against the 1967 writers congress (ČTK, 26 February 1968).

[3] *Pravda* (Bratislava), 29 February 1968 (radio interview, 21 and 26 February 1968).

[4] *Práce*, 21 January 1968 or Smrkovský, *My 68*, v:4 (1968), 6.

[5] For example, Rudolf Hoffman, *Pravda* (Bratislava), 7 February 1968.

ban on 'factions' and the required 'final unity' coincided with what Togliatti had recommended: the publication of dissenting views and arguments and continued pursuit of such views. Indeed even before the Party formulated a clear position, unity was 'undermined' by the free exchange of views Party members participated in, not only on Party platforms but in the mass media as well. It was often difficult to determine when these views were 'critical' of already accepted Party decisions and when 'justifiable' as pre-decision discussions. Špaček even advocated at the April plenum the formation of a journal of 'free Marxist theoretical, political thinking...not bound by the obligation of expressing the official views of the central committee.'

Free discussion should include criticism of leading functionaries as well as proposals and decisions, it was pointed out by such people as Šik, for individuals should be held responsible for their decisions. An atmosphere free of fear would have to be created, however, so that one might speak out. It would also help if there were the possibility for an honorable retirement even including the right to return to active Party work instead of the former system of total condemnation, ostracism, and worse.[1] It was in connection with the groundswell of demands for Novotný's resignation from the Presidency that these proposals were put forth for an institutionally based, qualitatively new way of changing leaders. Smrkovský, at the April plenum, argued that even Novotný should be permitted to retire with a pension and not suffer the type of eclipse that Novotný himself had forced on others in the past. Increasing demands for the removal of conservatives often contradicted this new spirit, but it was pointed out that the demanded summary dismissal of people like Lenárt, Kolder, and Martin Vaculík or even Hendrych just because they supported a different line would be tantamount to returning to former methods.[2]

Objective criteria were sought for determining personnel changes, and the constant verification of decisions in practice was urged by *Pravda* (Bratislava) of 7 February 1968. Quoting Lenin, one Party daily argued that no decisions or conclusions could be considered irrevocable; Marxism should be used as a scientific method which supplied a framework for correction of errors and 'the continuous control of decisions,' not as a dogma. The introduction of modern scientific methods was advocated,

---

[1] *Pravda* (Bratislava), 29 February 1968 (Šik); *Rudé právo*, 10 January 1968 (editorial) and 8 February 1968; *Práce*, 21 January 1968 (Smrkovský).

[2] For example, Czechoslovak television speech by *Pravda* editor Ondrej Klokoč, reported in *Pravda* (Bratislava), 4 February 1968.

and Špaček, at the April plenum, for example, pointed to the absence of central committee commissions 'for observation and investigation of concrete socio-political parties and social organizations,' which were necessary to provide the basis for the scientific solution of problems. Agreeing, Dubček urged as early as his 22 February address that 'professional qualities and enlightenment...[should] be very prominent in the working out of the line of the Party's policy,' based on the 'numerous cadres of scientific workers and experienced practitioners able to suggest well-founded and well-thought-out solutions.'

Many maintained that personnel changes alone, even democratically achieved, would not be sufficient to ensure inner-Party democracy. As one theoretist, Ivan Cigánik, explained, in *Pravda* (Bratislava) of 14 March 1968: 'The democratization process will grow lasting roots in our Party only when it is no longer guaranteed merely by outstanding progressive individuals but when effective methods and measures...are formulated in the statutes and become habitual.' Such methods should include rule by as broad a group as possible, elected by the largest possible proportion of the membership. The elected body, notably the central committee, should control the organs it creates, such as the secretariat and presidium, not vice-versa.[1] For this to be effective, however, the central committee and all Party officials should themselves be democratically elected. This would mean not just the introduction of a secret ballot and elimination of the practice of demanding unanimous or near-unanimous selection, but also a change in the system of selecting candidates. Outgoing election commissions should not be the ones to decide on their own replacements, it was argued; there should be a campaign period, and potential candidates should face Party groups and explain their views. The Slovak Party daily of 14 March 1968 argued that there should be publication of prospective candidates' views and the whole procedure should be handled openly and democratically. Indeed many of these demands were implemented in an *ad hoc* fashion at the March Party conferences at which Party members repeatedly stopped speakers to criticize or question and often changed the lists composed by the election commissions and so forth.[2] It was even admitted by Prague radio on 18 March 1968 that in one case (Karlové Vary) the list of candidates imposed by the members upon the election commission 'shocked

[1] *Rudé právo*, 8 February 1968 (editorial). See also Prague radio, 20 March 1968 (Šik to rally); discussion in *Reportér*, 6 March 1968; Prague radio, 7 February 1968 and *Pravda* (Bratislava), 5 April 1968.
[2] Reports on Prague radio, 17–18 March 1968.

the working presidium of the conference speechless; not a single secretary of the district committee [was] on the list.'

The Action Program endorsed almost all of the demands connected with democratization of Party life. It called for democratic discussion and secret voting for all important questions and appointments and stronger working contacts between the Party and the scientific world, with the latter providing alternative proposals. The rights and responsibilities of each of the Party's organs were to be clearly defined, particularly to clarify relations between the elected organs and the *apparat*, and measures were to be worked out to provide 'regular rotation of leading functionaries.' Members were to have easier access to information so that participation in decision-making might be broader, and the role of the elected organs was to be strengthened. The Program further stipulated that 'the clash of opinions is a necessary manifestation of responsible efforts to seek the best solution and to enforce the new against the outdated.' Supporting the idea of internal criticism in an atmosphere free of distrust, the Program nonetheless *retained* the principle of Party discipline: once a decision was made, it was encumbent upon all, including the dissenters, to implement it. Nothing was said in the Program about publication of or persistence in dissenting views.

Once the reformers had won their battle, in May 1968, for the early convening of an extraordinary Party congress, Party meetings concentrated on election of delegates to the congress and formulation of the new Party statutes.[1] The pressures which accompanied these summer meetings hindered a great deal of the work, but even with the limitations thus imposed the draft of the Party statutes to be presented to the congress was much more than a mere revision of the old set of rules.[2] A qualitatively new document, the statutes consisted of a less detailed, more general outline of rules and regulations, with the emphasis more on rights of members than on obligations, and more emphasis on active and critical participation in decision-making than on discipline. The new document was permeated with such words as humanitarian, democratic, and critical – a decided departure from the former one. More than a new tone and emphasis were provided, however, for specific 'guarantees' had been demanded. Therefore, beginning with application for membership and ending with resignation, the life of the Party member was to be changed. Considerably less space was given to the pre-requirements for acceptance

[1] See 19, 218–20. On 1 June the central committee resolved to hold the fourteenth congress on 9 September 1968. *Rok šedesátý osmý*, 218–19.

[2] Draft statutes were published *Rudé právo*, 10 August 1968 (see *Rok šedesátý osmý*, 271–90).

to the Party, simplifying the procedure, and the special clauses concerning former members of non-Communist parties were dropped. For the first time the right to resign from the Party, or any of its offices, was written into the statutes. Moreover, the penalty system was simplified, according an offender the right to be present at all proceedings concerning him. The new statutes also contained the one liberal innovation of the former rules (introduced at the 1966 Party congress): punishment or expulsion must be decided upon by the basic Party organization. However, the new document also maintained the former caveat on this clause: 'In cases where the Party primary organization refuses to expel a member from the Party in spite of serious breaches of the program and statutes, the decision on his expulsion can be made by a higher Party organ.' Greater attention was accorded, however, to the appeal procedure and rehabilitation.

The most significant innovation of the new rules lay in the rights of members, specifically the right not only to criticize (promised at least theoretically by the old rules as well) but to express and *persist* in dissenting views. Specifically, the

'minority has the right: to formulate its standpoints and request
that they be recorded; and to persist in its view and to request
from the relevant Party organization or organ a repeated evaluation
of its, the minority's, standpoints on the basis of new information
and to request verification of a decree that has been accepted.'

No more than argumentation might be used against supporters of minority views; thus an atmosphere of security was to be created for the expression of dissenting views. This progressive clause was, however, followed by a potentially dangerous, highly vague formulation which guaranteed this limitation to persuasion *only* in the case that the dissenters 'are not in fundamental conflict with the program and statutes of the Party.' It is surprising that with all their experiences of past abuses, the framers of what was meant to be a liberal provision inserted (even in their earliest drafts) this vague caveat so reminiscent of loopholes which had in the past neatly sufficed as justification for the suppression of 'undesirable' minority views. Nor did the provisions on this matter specify just how much and in what ways one might safely 'persist in' or propagate the dissenting views,[1] although the original draft did permit publication of the minority opinion along with that of the majority.[2] The drafting com-

[1] Another clause (19*d*) did give each member the right to express openly and critically at Party meetings *and in the Party press* his opinion on the activity of the Party and its organs and members irrespective of the office they hold.
[2] For original draft, prepared by a group under Military–Political Academy researcher

mittee, under conservative Indra, eliminated this clause, but both the original and final drafts stipulated that dissenters could *not* form an 'organized grouping' or 'organize minority supporters outside the framework of the statutes.'[1] The first draft did permit temporary groupings for the purpose of discussion and even preparation of alternative proposals, but the final draft dropped the words 'temporarily associate,' limited cooperation to members involved in similar spheres (e.g. within the cultural sphere), and demanded prior approval for such contacts.[2] Thus the Leninist ban on factions was to continue, even if the very significant rights to dissent and horizontal contact were granted.

To facilitate participation, the statutes did call for 'the mutual exchange of internal Party information between all levels; the accessibility of information and documents of Party organizations and organs to their members; an exchange of views and information between the Party and the public at large by means of the communications media.' Party members were given the right to express even critical views of all persons, organs, or matters concerning the Party, and to discuss important issues before decisions were taken by the higher authorities. While the lower organs were still bound by the decisions of the higher organs, they were to be independent in policy decisions in their own spheres of action, so long as they did not conflict with the general Party line. This innovation meant freedom from the *apparat* for Party units in mass organizations, etc.

Together with the rights to dissent and criticism, other changes were introduced which could serve as limitations on Party organs and officials. Party rule at all levels was to be based on scientific analyses, the use of experts, and constant verification of policies in practice. Going beyond the 'scientific outlook' of Marxism–Leninism, the statutes called for the use 'of the latest information obtained from the social sciences' as well as 'confrontation of views and evaluations of various suggestions from Communists and non-Communists' and 'the systematic use of specialist expertise and scientific research in decision-making and propaganda.'

All Party organs were to be elected by secret ballot, with uniform voting procedures. People were to be chosen for office,

'who, on the basis of their political, professional, and moral qualities and experiences in Party and public activity, have

Miroslav Havlíček, see Jiří Pelikán, *The Secret Vysočany Congress* (London, 1971), 130–84.

[1] In an interview Martin Vaculík said that an 'organized grouping' was a permanent organization as distinct from temporary groupings on specific issues (*Večerní Praha*, 1 August 1968).   [2] Original draft required only prior notification.

personal authority and the confidence of the workers...Quality is the only valid criterion in choosing and recommending candidates and applicants for Party, public, and economic functions.' Unlike the former statutes, which urged the maintenance of 'the continuity of leadership' and the election of 'the best-tried warriors for Party policies...irrespective of their present functions,' the new statutes specifically condemned the practice of combining important Party jobs in one person, and limited the terms of office.[1] Officials above the basic level could not be elected to more than three consecutive two-year terms or more than two consecutive four-year terms. Only a two-thirds majority in the Party organ involved could authorize an exceptional additional term. Moreover, the elected organs would maintain authority over the organs they themselves appointed or elected, such as the Party *apparat*, including the Party secretariat and presidium of each of the two national Parties (Czech and Slovak, in accord with the federalization of the country). The Party *apparat* was specifically forbidden to take over the authority of Party organizations or of Communists in various state, economic, or social organizations and institutions. By the same token, the control and auditing commissions, originally designed to maintain Party discipline and ensure all-over implementation of Party decisions, were made independent of the rest of the Party *apparat*, responsible only to the organs which elected them.

While the major flaw of democratic centralism, the emphasis on centralism, was theoretically remedied by the innovations promising greater independence, participation, and control from below, no change was made in the basically Leninist concentric structure of the Party. Aside from the elimination of the *regional* Party organization, presumably rendered superfluous by the federation of the Party, no structural changes were envisaged. The existing structure, with Party organizations corresponding to each economic, social, and political component of society, did contain the now recognized danger of Party interference in or assumption of the functions of these organizations.[2] The reformers may have believed, however, that the new principles of withdrawing the Party from direct involvement in the other spheres of society would be sufficient guarantee against this danger. Moreover, the new statutes, born as they were in an atmosphere of intensive pressures from conservatives and Soviet fears that the Party was abandoning its leading role, were but a

[1] For old statutes see *Rudé právo*, 8 June 1966.
[2] See Vaculík in *Večerní Praha*, 1 August 1968 for discussion of alternative structural changes.

first step towards total reform. What may have been denied organizationally, however, was, as we shall see, advocated explicitly both by the statutes and other elements of the political reforms.

Separation of the Party and the state

The removal of Novotný from the post of Party first secretary was accomplished in the name of separating the top two functions in the country and thereby preventing too great a concentration of power in the hands of one man. Having created this precedent, albeit for purely political–tactical reasons, the Party was rapidly faced with demands that the 'separation of powers' accomplished at the January plenum be carried to its logical conclusion by full separation of powers throughout the political structure, with regard to institutions also, above and beyond mere personnel changes.[1] While the achievement of independence from Party domination in the economic, social, and cultural spheres was to be provided by the reforms in these areas, the major area left was the state itself and the removal of the Party from the life of the political institutions.

In keeping with their view of the Party's role as programmatic, and limited to long-range guidance, many reformers felt that responsibility for the administration of state affairs was to be left to the government. Smrkovský, for example, told a Prague radio interviewer on 2 February 1968, that the government should be responsible only to the National Assembly, according to the Constitution, and, therefore, should not be subject to direct management by the Party. The latter practice was criticized even by Drahomír Kolder (presumably in an effort to 'change with the times'), on the grounds that the merging of the Party and state apparatus or functions stifled the initiative of government institutions and obscured not only their authority but also their sense of or actual responsibility for their own activities.[2] Dubček too condemned the merging of functions, commenting on 22 February that 'socially beneficial initiative' in the state organs was prevented from developing because of the concept of 'direct management.' He added, in this speech and again at the April central committee plenum, that this had the negative effect not only of weakening the authority of the state organs but of rendering their activities mere formalities. The practice was also criticized on the grounds, which

[1] See, for example, *Rudé právo*, 2 April 1968 (Dubček to plenum); *Práce*, 21 January 1968 (Smrkovský); *Zemědělské noviny*, 9 January 1968 (editorial); Sviták, *Student*, 10 April 1968.
[2] *Rudé právo*, 18 February 1968. See also *Rudé právo* editorial, 8 February 1968.

we have seen above, that there was no theoretical basis for such a concentration of powers, the Party was not the instrument of the proletariat,
and it could not even claim to represent all citizens (in the sense of a
mandate) since it had not consulted the people nor was it answerable to
them.[1]

The first step was to be a separation of powers and elimination of any
concentration of powers in the hands of any one organism. It was pointed
out that the liberal concept of separation of powers (checks and balances)
had been considered irrelevant for a society which was expected to move
rapidly to a society free of state agencies.[2] The transition period had
proved, however, to be extended, and, according to the new Party Higher
School rector Milan Hübl, the executive, legislative, and judiciary powers
had remained concentrated in one agency: the Party. Mlynář argued in
Rudé právo of 13 February 1968, that only the independent existence of
each component of political life and the clear division of powers could
provide the necessary safeguards against monopolization of power and,
therefore, mutual controls. In this spirit Smrkovský recommended the
separation of executive, legislative, and judiciary powers 'open in every
respect to control and criticism.'[3] Part of this control was to come from
the promised freedom of expression, but guarantees were sought, in the
form of institutional, Constitutional, and legal provisions for controlling
power. Dubček himself admitted this to the April plenum:

'No democracy – and thus not even our socialist democracy – can
live for long on the fact that opinions can be freely expressed, that
criticism is permitted. That in itself is only decisive if free and
sound criticism removes old obstacles from the road of social
progress. In order to live and rule democratically in our society
even then, when the obstacles have been eliminated everywhere
and for good, we must have a well-thought-out and well-functioning
system of institutions, organs, and organizations, which will
work in a new and effective way, where new policy will be pursued, and these bodies will be permanently under democratic supervision of citizens.'

Thus the goal was not just a separation of powers but the guarantee
that power would never be permitted to be *over* the people.[4] Power

[1] Brno radio, 7 February 1968 (Šabata); Prague radio, 17 February 1968; Action Program; Jesenská, *Kultúrny život*, 5 April 1968.
[2] Milan Hübl in *Kultúrny život*, 5 January 1968. See also Hanzelka's contribution to
Reportér discussion, 6 March 1968.
[3] Smrkovský, *My 68*, v:4 (1968), 6.
[4] See, for example, *Práce*, 21 January 1968 (Smrkovský).

should be in some way under the control of the people. This could be accomplished, most believed, by the 'proper' functioning of the various agencies of the people: the elected organs, the social-interest organizations, and the National Front, while the organs of the government, selected and/or run by these agencies, would be independent, free of bureaucratic methods, and responsible to the public or its agencies. There were several requisites for such a system, including open competition for positions, a broad system of information, free elections, protection of minority rights, and the protection of the individual's civil rights. The first step, however, was the independent operation of each component of the political system by limiting the Party to the more general tasks envisaged for it.

The Action Program proclaimed the independence of the political components, each with its clearly defined area of responsibility, and limited the Party to an indirect role, through members who hold positions in the government, without use even of the 'cadre system.'[1] Government positions were, however, to be accorded only qualified persons in accordance with a procedure providing for honorable recall of unqualified or no longer qualified persons. The new Party statutes also upheld the withdrawal of the Party from the functioning of the government, prohibiting the concentration of important state and Party positions in the same individual.[2] The most important Action Program declaration with regard to the government was, however, the following:

'Party decisions bind Communists in these (state, economic, and social organizations), but *the policy and management, and also the responsibility, of the state, economic, and social organs and organizations are independent.*'

The only organ to which the government must answer would be the National Assembly. The Action Program did not specifically place the government subordinate even to the *policy* laid down by the Party (or by any organ), although Dubček did say in his speech to the central committee plenum which approved the Action Program that the government must ensure the needs of the Republic 'expressed in the policy of the Communist Party.'

[1] 'the Presidium of the Czechoslovak Communist Party decided that the decisions on class and political qualification were no longer to be considered in the selection and placement of workers and that the conclusions of this verification were to be stricken from the cadre records, or eventually be reviewed.' (*Rudé právo*, 24 May 1968.)

[2] 'Not to amalgamate leading party, state, and public functions which, if joined, could lead to a privileged position of an individual and would weaken control over this individual.'

7

Political Reform and the Government

Elected organs

Popular participation was seen as a necessary, perhaps the best, guarantee against concentration of power. Dubček often emphasized that democratization could only be accomplished and maintained with 'a high degree of public involvement' and participation of the people.[1] Others too expressed the belief that 'the only effective safeguard is the organized public,' and that 'Through their deputies...the representative bodies,' the elected organs, specifically the parliament, should 'control how the government and its organs fulfill their tasks.'[2] Czechoslovakia, as many, such as Peter Colotka in *Život* of 17 April 1968, were to point out, 'In the past...belonged among the countries with the most developed parliamentary democracy.' Yet under the Communists the elected organs had become a mere formality. There had been efforts in 1964 and 1965 to increase the role of the elected organs, particularly the National Assembly, but the basically conservative Party leadership of those years had obstructed implementation of any significant reform. Therefore, despite some legal and even practical changes in the work of these bodies, the situation had changed but little.

Basic to any reform of the elected organs was the resolution of a fundamental contradiction. According to the Constitution, and reiterated by a Party resolution in May 1964, the National Assembly was the supreme organ of state power in the country. Yet the Assembly was subordinate to the Party not only in practice but even by explicit order of the 1966 Party statutes. As pointed out by reformers such as Colotka and Štefan Sádovský, the National Assembly thus became no more than a rubber-stamp for the wishes of the Party, as dictated through the intermediary of the government.[3] This necessarily weakened the Assembly's relationship to the government, even though according to the Constitution the govern-

[1] For example, *Rudé právo*, 21 April 1968 (speech of 20 April).
[2] *Mladá fronta*, 2 April 1968 (editorial); or *Rudé právo*, 29 March 1968 (interview with Smrkovský).
[3] Colotka, *Život*, 17 April 1968; *Rudé právo*, 13 April 1968 (Štefan Sádovský to April plenum).

ment was responsible to the Assembly. The Party had in fact assumed the functions of both the executive and the legislature insofar as it dominated the one and dictated to the other. Assembly deputies themselves pointed to what they termed the 'incorrect implementation of the Party's leading role in all spheres of our political life and particularly in the replacement of the supreme body of representatives,' as the main source of the incapacitation of the elected organs.[1]

While the Party was to abandon its domination of the government, and Dubček advocated restoration of the 'traditional position and authority' of the Presidency,[2] reformers such as Smrkovský urged that it express its 'leading role' in the elected organs in a new way: through the influence of Communist members elected to these organs – no more, no less. Communist delegates might form a delegates' club to better coordinate their efforts, but they were to be regarded merely as one of many elements in the Assembly, having no more rights than other deputies to submit proposals or to strive to gain a majority.[3] Communist deputies would also have to defer to the majority's decision, presumably even if it were unfavorable to the Party. Like every one else in the elected organs, they would have the right to publicize and try to achieve public backing for their proposals. Indeed it was one of the reformers' demands that Assembly sessions should be public, with only security matters subject to secret votes.[4]

The change in the Party's relationship to the executive and legislative organs might also permit restoration of the Constitutionally provided relationship of the government to the legislature. Assembly deputies called for implementation of the earlier reforms which had provided, for example, for the appearance of government members before Assembly committees and their submission of reports on the implementation of Assembly decisions.[5] It was suggested that the government be elected by

---

[1] *Pravda* (Bratislava), 28 March 1968 (National Assembly Plan and Budget Committee meeting).

[2] *Rok šedesátý osmý*, 48.

[3] See *Rudé právo*, 13 April 1968 (Sádovský speech), 2 April 1968 (Dubček speech), 13 April 1968 (interview with Smrkovský). The Federal Assembly created on 1 January 1969 did indeed organize delegates according to parties and other groupings under the National Front (ČTK, 23 January 1969).

[4] Ibid. or Václav Kraus, in *Práce*, 22 June 1968.

[5] *Pravda* (Bratislava), 28 March 1969. Černík was singled out for criticism for his past indifference towards the assembly in his role as State Planning Commission chairman and for his 'former concepts in the development of our national economy.' See also, Michal Lakatoš, *Kulturní noviny*, 26 April 1968.

the National Assembly rather than appointed by the President, and that it be subject to recall by the Assembly. This return to the practice of no-confidence votes was urged by future Assembly chairman Smrkovský on Prague radio, 2 February 1968, even if it required a change in the Constitution. More specific proposals included demands for qualified persons both as deputies and consultants to the National Assembly, and greater authority for Assembly committees along the lines of the unimplemented pre-1968 reforms.[1]

The Action Program endorsed most of these suggestions, calling for a National Assembly 'which will truly make laws and decide important political questions, and not just approve drafts submitted to it.' The Program advocated the strengthening of the control function of the Assembly vis-à-vis the government (and 'all areas of public life'), including the subordination of the control apparatus, presumably the control commissions, to the Assembly. While the Program contained nothing on votes of confidence or public proceedings, it did say that the Assembly must be restored its Constitutional position as the supreme organ of state power and must establish closer ties with 'the public opinion of the citizenry' – though how it did not say, in either case.

Suggestions prepared by Mlynář's committee for discussion at the fourteenth Party congress included a radical change in the National Assembly which would resemble the structure introduced in Yugoslavia (and proposed by Mlynář as early as 1965). In addition to a chamber of deputies chosen by territorial constituencies and a chamber of equal numbers of deputies from the two major nations (envisaged by the forthcoming federalization), there might be chambers selected along professional lines and elected by the enterprises or institutions engaged in these professions, e.g. an industrial chamber, an agricultural chamber, and so forth, having control over bills relating to their specific fields. This proposal was envisaged for adoption probably only after federalization and workers councils had taken root, by 1970 or so, when the new Constitution was to be ready.[2]

The National Committees were dealt with only in general terms. Although the local representatives of the state organs of power, their primary function, according to the Action Program, was to provide local self-administration. They too were to be relieved of their functions as mere transmission belts for the Party's will as expressed by the government or National Assembly. Just how much power or independence they

[1] Ibid. and Colotka, *Život*, 17 April 1968; Czechoslovak television, 29 February 1968.
[2] Pelikán, *The Secret Vysočany Congress* (London, 1971), 233-4.

would have vis-à-vis the central authorities, however, was not stipulated. Presumably the pre-1968 reform granting the National Committees a degree of financial autonomy was considered a major contributing factor to this somewhat amorphous autonomy. This lack of attention to local government may have been the result of a traditional Czech tendency (exhibited in the first Republic) against strong local government. It is more likely, however, that the workers councils were seen as the major organ of decentralized or local rule, and, therefore, took precedence over work on reforms of the National Committees. There was, nonetheless, a distinct difference in emphasis between the Yugoslavs' purposeful decentralization in the interests of the withering away of the state, and the Czechoslovak concern for controls on power and traditional parliamentary democracy.

It was clear to most that the success of the changes planned for the elected organs would be dependent upon the *method* of representation or, specifically, on election procedures. The then current system was criticized, from the first stages of the procedure to the last, and demands were heard for an entirely new electoral law. It was urged that selection of nominees to be proposed to the National Front election commission should be conducted at a plenum of the organization-members of the National Front, and not, as was the custom, at meetings of small groups of functionaries of these organizations. Thus, *Pravda* (Bratislava) of 28 February 1968 argued, the principle of the widest possible participation in the selection of candidates should be observed, and, according to *Rudé právo* of 16 February as well, applied also to the composition of the National Front election commission itself, usually monopolized by the Communist Party. It was also suggested, for example by Vodsloň and Šebesta in television and radio talks, that individuals should be able to present themselves as candidates – without benefit of *any* organization. Another suggestion was to publicize the work of the election commissions so that people might know the deadline for proposing candidates, and such practices as predetermining the number of women, of Slovaks, of youth and so forth to be among the candidates, might be eliminated.[1]

The fact that the election commissions determined the order of candidates on the ballot was considered a serious obstacle to democracy, for although there were more candidates on the list than positions, as a result of the 1964–7 electoral laws, the order of the candidates, not the number of

---

[1] Czechoslovak television, 29 February 1968; *Rudé právo*, 16 February 1968; *Pravda* (Bratislava), 28 February 1968; Prague radio, 17 February 1968.

votes they received (provided it was over 50 per cent of votes cast), determined who would be elected. Thus, as Vodsloň pointed out on television on 29 February 1968, a candidate who was, for example, third on the list and received 65 per cent of the votes might be elected while a candidate who was ninth on the list and received 90 per cent of the votes would not be elected if only six seats were open. The element of choice was further weakened by the fact that the voter really knew nothing of the various candidates. To remedy this, it was suggested that the names of the components of the National Front represented be listed beside each candidate's name and that there be election campaigns in which candidates would publicly present their views.[1]

Indeed, it was pointed out, the very act of voting had become a mere formality: one did not know anything about the candidates, one could not really determine who would be elected, and one could not actually do anything at the polls because of the custom of demonstrative voting. The voting act had become a symbol of a person's support of socialism, and if one failed to turn out for the elections or dared to inspect the ballot – much less cross out a name or try to enter the uninviting booth supplied – one was considered 'anti-socialist.' This whole procedure of 'forced voting,' whereby voting was a duty rather than a right, and turnouts of 99.9 per cent were reached, was, as Slovak presidium member Hruškovič said on television on 29 February 1968, 'ridiculous.'

The net result of this procedure was that the candidate elected had no sense of responsibility to his constituents, for his 'election' had little to do with them. Therefore deputies rarely appeared before their constituents, and there was no channel for popular control. It was suggested that some form of recall of deputies be permitted, and, as recommended for the Party, that resignation be considered an honorable step rather than a disgrace.[2] The critics' views were perhaps summed up in one citizen's letter:

'As long as the elections are not free and secret, as long as I cannot select without haste and freely between citizens A and B, as long as there is not another, much wider possibility of choice of representatives, it will not be possible to talk about elections. It

[1] For these and other comments on the election system, see Prague radio, 28 February 1968; *Kulturní noviny*, 24 February 1968; Czechoslovak television, 29 February 1968.
[2] Prague radio, 28 February 1968. It was even pointed out that the electorate probably no longer knew 'how' to say anything, i.e. it would have to be taught how to exercise its democratic rights in free elections without fear. (Prague radio, 17 February 1968 and Pithart, Prague radio, 7 February 1968.)

will be at most a formal act, the abolition of which would save the treasury a great deal of money.'[1]

With these ideas in mind, the demand arose for postponement of the National Committee elections scheduled for 19 May 1968, and amendment of the election law, if not a new law altogether. At the March Party conferences many condemned the present laws as 'outdated by the current democratization process,' according to ČTK, 17 March 1968, and conference after conference urged postponement. A public opinion poll at the end of March revealed that some 79 per cent of interviewed persons favored postponement, and such organs as Csemadok, the Czechoslovak Lawyers Association, the agricultural daily *Zemědělské noviny* and the massive 20 March youth rally in Prague went on record as opposing elections under the current laws.[2] To this groundswell were added the proposals of three National Assembly committees and even the Slovak election commission, according to Bratislava radio, 27 March 1968. At its meeting of 25 March the Party presidium decided to postpone the elections by approximately one month, but the Party's election commission recommended to the central committee session of early April that the elections be postponed until the fall. This suggestion was accepted, and work on new electoral laws was intensified.[3]

There were also voices raised, for example in the 29 February 1968 television discussion, concerning the election of the President who, under the Czechoslovak parliamentary system, was elected by the National Assembly. Suggestions for the introduction of popular election would have meant a change in the Constitution *and* Czechoslovak tradition; they apparently did not receive much support. It was urged, however, that the present system should be used democratically; that the National Assembly must have a genuine choice and freedom of expression, and that a qualified person be chosen. Thus in the days following Novotný's resignation the names of several candidates were heard, in particular General Ludvík Svoboda, Josef Smrkovský, and Čestmír Císař. The ČSM presidium passed a resolution favoring Císař as 'its' candidate, as did groups of students and high-school pupils, not necessarily because they opposed Svoboda but because they wanted more than one candidate, in the interests of democracy. On 26 March the Czechoslovak news service reported in English that Císař had actually accepted the youth nomination, though he never formally offered himself as a

---

[1] In *Kulturní noviny*, 24 February 1968.
[2] ČTK, 26 March 1968 (Czechoslovak Academy of Sciences poll).
[3] *Rok šedesátý osmý*, 44–7; *Rudé právo*, 6 April 1968.

candidate or campaigned. On 28 March 1968 the Party central committee selected Svoboda as the Party candidate, and two days later the National Assembly elected him, by a secret ballot of 282 votes for, 6 against.[1] On the day of the elections students staged a demonstration for Císař, who then appealed to the crowds to accept the regime's choice. In answer to subsequent objections that the selection had not been democratic, the Party, in the person of Alois Indra, defended its right, as the politically most significant sector of the society, to propose the candidates for head of state.[2]

The Action Program did not mention the issue of Presidential selection, and one may assume that the regime intended to continue the traditional parliamentary selection system. The Program devoted little space to the election problem at all, merely affirming the need to postpone the National Committee elections and to draft a new law. This new law should, the Program asserted, 'adjust' the principles upon which elections were prepared (including the nominating procedure), and be carried out, in keeping with the 'new political position of the National Front and of the elected organs themselves.' This indeed was the crux of the matter, since the efficacy of any elections would depend a great deal on the institution of the National Front and the idea of single-list elections.

The National Front and the possibility of opposition

It was recognized at an early stage that the National Front had become no more than a formality, still another 'transmission belt.' It consisted of the various mass organizations and the remodeled remnants of certain political parties from the 1945–8 period. If the mass organizations were nothing but transmission belts for the Party, the political parties had even less of a role to play. As pointed out in 1968, they did little more than say 'amen' to the decisions of the Communist Party, even to the extent of receiving orders directly at the latter's central committee plena.[3] In 1959, in accordance with a Party central committee resolution, the National Front itself had been placed under the direction of the Party.[4] As a result the National Front presidium rarely met, its functions were taken over by the Party presidium, and even the top jobs were merged, i.e. the chairman of the

[1] Prague radio, 30 March 1968. One vote was invalidated.
[2] Prague radio, 8 April 1968 (at a Prague Party meeting).
[3] See letter from the National Front to Dubček, ČTK, 18 March 1968; Czechoslovak television, 29 February 1968; Jiří Lederer in *Literární listy*, 21 March 1968; Prague radio, 18 March 1968.   [4] *Rudé právo*, 25 April 1959.

National Front presidium was the Czechoslovak Party first secretary. The Party's 'guidance' of the National Front was codified in the most recent (1966) Party statutes. Yet theoretically the National Front existed to provide the overall platform of the government and the framework for both elections and the decision of power within the government. It was on these very functions that the debates for reform of the institution centered.

A basic step for reform of the National Front was to grant it greater policy-making powers by strengthening it vis-à-vis the Party, or in effect rendering it independent of the Party. As such it should be able to present its views and proposals prior to decisions by the highest organs of the country and, at the least, co-participate with the Party in the shaping of the country's policies.[1] An early sign that the Party was willing to free the National Front from its direct control was the election on 8 April 1968 of new chairmen of the Czechoslovak and Slovak National Fronts (František Kriegel and Ondrej Klokoč respectively), instead of the former merger of Party and National Front chairmen. Yet for this to be effective, it was pointed out that the National Front had to be changed internally as well. Within the Front the Party would have to see itself as only one of many, equal, components, each able to submit its ideas. Thus, the National Front would cease to be an instrument of the Party externally, and a rubber-stamp for the Party internally.

Such reforms, according to Mlynář, would permit a clash of views within the National Front, making it a platform for the various and even conflicting groups in society.[2] Each group would have the right to defend its views, so that the possibility for competition and bargaining would exist at least within the Front. According to Mlynář it would, therefore, be necessary not only to strengthen the role of the social organizations but also that of the other members of the National Front: the political parties. This meant, as Mlynář admitted, the end of the monopoly of a single (the Communist) party, albeit only *within* the National Front. This too would entail a change in the Constitution, for this document not only explicitly asserted a favored position for the Communist Party, but excluded any mention of other political parties when describing the components of the National Front.

[1] See Prague radio discussion, 7 March 1968; central committee resolution, *Rudé právo*, 6 April 1968; Kliment, *Literární listy*, 4 July 1968.

[2] *Rudé právo*, 26 March 1968; Prague radio (English), 18 April 1968 (interview with Mlynář); *Rudé právo*, 5 April 1968 (Mlynář to April plenum); see also Selucký, *Práce*, 11 April 1968.

The reform leaders recognized that a pre-requirement for 'pluralism' within the National Front was the rejuvenation of the already existing parties, so as to render them capable of expressing an independent opinion. A turnover of personnel was necessary since the regime had at an early date placed trusted puppets in the leading positions of the non-Communist parties. The presidium of the Czech People's Party resigned, under strong pressures from within, and Antonín Pospíšil was elected, by secret ballot, to replace the excommunicated priest Josef Plojhar as chairman.[1] The new chairman was not much more of an independent than Plojhar and Plojhar himself was kept on as honorary chairman as well as the People's Party candidate for its seat in the new cabinet. Nonetheless vociferous objections published in the People's Party daily *Lidová demokracie*, forced Plojhar's removal from the honorary post and as the party's nominee for the government. The Slovak non-Communist parties (Freedom Party, Democratic Party) and the other Czech non-Communist party, the Czech Socialists, also replaced their leading functionaries.[2] The two Czech parties began to demand a larger role in the National Front, and, eventually, they even dared to criticize the slow pace of liberalization.[3] Once the regime lifted the ceiling on membership in these non-Communist parties their ranks swelled by some thousands, and, as reported in *Lidová demokracie* of 12 April 1968, they were permitted to form local organizations.

There was also an effort to restore the former Social Democratic Party, which was merged with the Communists in June 1948. Pressures for this came from below, with such things as a letter to the youth daily on 29 March claiming that the 1948 merger had been accomplished without members of the party having been consulted. Restoration of the Social Democrats also became one of the KAN demands. In early June a preparatory committee was set up for the reinstitution of the party, and the basis laid for the subsequent formation of some 120 to 300 branches, despite the fact that at its May presidium meeting the Communist Party rejected the proposal on the grounds that it would split the unity of the working class.[4] Reinstitution of the Social Democratic Party was a development of a different nature than the revival of the recognized parties,

---

[1] *Lidová demokracie*, 1 April 1968. Plojhar was Minister of Health but even the Communists in this Ministry opposed his continuation in view of his conservative attitude.

[2] ČTK, 7 May 1968; *Svobodné slovo*, 8 April 1968, 8 June 1968.

[3] *Rudé právo*, 11 June 1968.

[4] *Rudé právo*, 24 May 1968 and *Svobodné slovo*, 7 June 1968. Number of branches from Czech source who prefers to remain anonymous.

for the Social Democrats had been a serious contender for the workers' support in pre-war Czechoslovakia, and, as a second Marxist party it was often perceived by Communists as a much more serious threat than other potentially even more well-supported parties.

The idea of a plurality of political parties within the framework of the National Front found a number of supporters, such as veteran Communist Zora Jesenská, who argued in *Kultúrny život* of 5 April 1968 that there was 'nothing incompatible with socialism' about the existence of 'real political parties' in the National Front. Even the radical thinker Michal Lakatoš admitted in *Kulturní noviny* of 5 April 1968 that a 'rebirth of the National Front' might be the only possibility for pluralism, given the historical position of the National Front and 'our present complicated conditions.' Yet the parties in the National Front should be entirely autonomous and able, along with all components of the National Front, to try to form public opinion and win supporters to their ideas. Only thus, Lakatoš argued, could these groups genuinely represent the varied interests of the people, struggle for them in the elected bodies and champion them in the formulation of the state's policies.[1]

National Front chairman Kriegel agreed in *Rudé právo* of 19 June that the determination of state policy should be gradually shifted from the Communist Party to the National Front, the latter being the organization of the different interest groups, in which varying viewpoints could be aired and conflicting ideas welded into compromises. And to safeguard this function new statutes were being worked out for the National Front. Kriegel went on, however, to limit the freedom of operation of the National Front by demanding that members 'respect the principles on which the National Front is based,' i.e. anti-fascism, anti-racism, communism (and anti-anti-communism), alliance with the Soviet Union and the other socialist countries. These conditions were perhaps minimal, since all discussions of pluralism in the National Front were premised on the idea of *socialist* democracy, i.e. the continuation of socialism in Czechoslovakia. Yet any restriction was a potentially dangerous idea. One could but remember that the interpretation of what constituted anti-communism or fascism or opposition to the socialist alliance had in the past been most flexible and frequently misused.

Many people, however, were not satisfied with the institution of the National Front, whether as an organ strengthened vis-à-vis the Party, as the Action Program advocated, or as a platform for independent, competing views, as many reformers proposed. To understand their criticism

[1] Lakatoš in *Kulturní noviny*, 24 February 1968.

The National Front and the possibility of opposition

it may be helpful to bear in mind the difference between the 'National Front' of the 1945–8 period and that of the post-1948 era. The former was a broad coalition of all political parties reinstated after the war. Although there was no opposition or parties outside this coalition, the 1945–8 National Front in Czechoslovakia had not foregone the parliamentary system of competing parties. Elections had been held on a party basis and places distributed according to the percentage of votes received. It was the Communists who had urged the inclusion of the mass organizations in the National Front, perhaps because they were unsure of their influence over the other left-wing parties in 1946–7. There are those who criticize even the pre-1948 National Front, but it was still far different from the united-list device used by the Communists in most of the other East European countries to neutralize non-Communist parties on the Communists' way to power.[1]

The major flaw in the National Front, in the eyes of its critics, was the impossibility of genuine opposition – an impossibility which denied the parties any sense as 'parties' and, therefore, in effect ruled out meaningful pluralism. As political scientist and Party member Petr Pithart pointed out in *Literární listy* of 1 May 1968, the Action Program explicitly pro-hibited the division of the National Front into ruling and opposition parties and it did not permit an opposition line or a political struggle for power in the state.[2] Yet, Pithart argued, the very business of politics, as well as the *raison d'être* of a political party was the struggle for power, for its candidate and program. Moreover, he said, 'it is a symptom of the democratic nature of such a struggle that it must be accepted as natural that the power thus acquired may be lost in the same way.' If this prin-ciple were not recognized, i.e. if the parties could not present the voter with alternatives to the ruling party – either in candidates or ideas – the parties in essence differed little from the special-interest organizations. While these organs could, possibly, defend the interests of certain groups, they were not, as playwright Václav Havel pointed out in *Literární listy* of 4 April, based on political convictions or goals, and they could hardly provide the alternatives to power which were necessary to a pluralistic system. Moreover, the control function of a pluralistic system was also thereby lost, for the National Front, with its unified list and plat-

---

[1] Otto Friedman, *The Break-up of Czech Democracy* (London, 1950), because there was no opposition outside the Front or the government.

[2] 'The Czechoslovak Communist Party regards the National Front as a political platform, which does not divide the political parties into government and the opposition, in the sense that opposition would be created to the state policy as the policy of the National Front and a struggle for political power in the state.' (*Rudé právo*, 10 April 1968, Action Program.)

form, in effect neutralized the parties, no matter what the alleged intention. Pithart argued that even if the Action Program promised new methods for asserting the leading role of the Communist Party (persuasion instead of dictatorship), it hardly provided for any genuine change because it provided no mechanism for the situation in which the Party might *not* succeed in 'earning' its leading position. As journalist Jiří Hanák put it in *Reportér* of 24 April 1968: what would happen if 'some eight million people in the country do not wish to be led by the Communist Party but by a Monarch of the dynasty of the Přemysl-ides. What then?' The Action Program expressly prohibited such a situation, but the arbitrary exclusion of this possibility was reminiscent of the former system.

Going further than most reformers, Pithart argued that the Party was making the National Front into some sort of *deus ex machina*, having responsibility for the formulation of state policy (instead of this being with the Communist Party). If this were the case, what was the parliament supposed to do?, Pithart asked.

'If the essential problems are settled within the National Front
first (generally out of sight of the public, for it is easier to pursue
cabinet politics in such political groupings than in parliamentary
lobbies), parliament will be – as before – merely an ornament,
a decorative setting for the formulation of laws and for the battle
of dwarfs fighting over the crumbs left by the National Front.'[1]

Moreover, the National Front was not an *elected* organ; not even the political parties in it were represented according to voting strength. The only criterion for influence within the National Front would appear to be membership strength, but this would hardly be a legitimate criterion since people might well be members in more than one organization and thus represented in the National Front several times. Indeed the Communists in them, as Havel pointed out, would be bound by Party discipline to uphold the Party line even within these organizations. Since the National Front presented a unified list for the elections (of the National Assembly and the National Committees), the situation would merely be perpetuated. Thus the National Front, as presented by the Party, would not permit the development either of a representative democracy or of a pluralistic political system.

Pithart's analysis was supported by a number of others who saw in the

[1] It was argued that this had been a major flaw in the 1945–8 concept of the National Front as well and that the use of parliament might have prevented the Communist victory in February 1948. (*Dějiny a současnost*, XI:1 (1968), 24.)

National Front nothing but a device to 'improve' the rule of one party without providing any real pluralism.[1] The 'parties' of the National Front could not serve the purpose of parties because 'they have never presented a platform of their own,' and could not, because of the National Front concept, present an independent list of candidates. Thus the National Front was rejected as the sought-after 'control on power' or mechanism to break up the monopoly on power – just as freedom of expression, democratization of the Party, strengthened social organizations, a division of executive and legislative powers and so forth, were considered necessary but insufficient for genuine democracy.[2] The only and best form of control, according to most of the conclusions of the reformers – and the population at large – was the existence of more than one party, i.e. a genuine competition for power. Letters to the editors of various journals reflected a decided interest in an opposition party as a guarantee against 'deformations and excesses.'[3] The existence of a possibly more desirable alternative would force the ruling party to 'watch itself,' to improve its program, and to conform to the wishes of the people, for fear of its being replaced.[4] Others argued that only a two-party or multi-party system could provide for the genuine political representation of all the people, since four-fifths of the population were *not* members of the Communist Party and, therefore, not genuinely represented, politically.[5] Nobody had the right to speak for the non-Communists except the non-Communists themselves, it was argued, but only organized groups could hope to put forth their interests successfully. While an individual might be permitted to present himself as an unaffiliated candidate, without an *apparat*, and lacking funds, propaganda facilities and so forth, it would be unrealistic to see him as a serious competitor against the Party amongst the electorate. The realization of this may indeed have been the major reason for the creation of such organizations as KAN.[6]

If non-Communists were to have an effective role they would have to be recognized morally as well as politically, according to Havel and writer

---

[1] For example, *Kultúrny život*, 12 April 1968 (Števček); *Literární listy*, 21 March 1968 (Battek); *Echo*, 30 June 1968 (Moravčík).

[2] For example, *Literární listy*, 4 April 1968 (Havel) and 26 June 1968 (Pithart).

[3] See, for example, *Literární listy*, 14 March 1968.

[4] See on this subject: *Literární listy*, 1 May and 20 June 1968; *Reportér*, 10 April 1968; Prague radio discussion, 28 February 1968.

[5] For example, *Kultúrny život*, 12 April 1968 and 31 May 1968 (Hykisch), or *Literární listy*, 21 March 1968.

[6] *Svobodné slovo*, 22 March 1968; *Reportér*, 24 April 1968; *Literární listy*, 4 and 11 April 1968; *Kultúrny život*, 29 March 1968.

Alexandr Kliment in *Literární listy* of 14 March 1968. They had been so atomized and abused over the preceding twenty years that they lacked the respect necessary to operate as genuine competitors. Moreover, if genuine pluralism were to be introduced, both the public and above all the Party would have to 'get used to the very concept of "opposition," ' Kliment said. Many argued that the Communists must overcome their image of opposition as a destructive force which seeks to destroy the state and to establish itself as the permanent power. This, both Kliment and Pithart maintained, was a hangover from Stalinism. In effect, the existence of an opposition would strengthen the state and benefit society, for it would provide the control and representative elements necessary to democracy. Even the Party would profit from the existence of an alternative and a challenge. As Communist writer Hykisch exclaimed in *Kultúrny život* of 31 May 1968, 'Government by a single party is a biological absurdity, for it means, organically, the government of a people of a single type, from top to bottom...Imagine the kind of people who join the ruling party: most are guided by pure self-interest.' Writer Pavel Kohout pointed out (*Literární listy* of 16 May 1968) that the Communists in the Writers Union had never been so productive as since the formation of a circle of non-party writers within the Union. Far from being interested only in 'reaction,' it was an opposition group which had provided the thrust forward in the Party itself in January 1968. One old-time Communist declared, according to *Reportér* of 24 April 1968, 'The Party need not fear competition.' Speaking of himself, he said:

'The author of these lines is a Communist who years ago joined the Party without any reservations and who has derived no advantage from his membership – apart from the one advantage that, as a Party member, he was always right – even if he was wrong. This advantage I should like to get rid of; of course not by leaving the Party. I trust that as a Communist I should always be able to hold my own in any discussion with any adversary...Naturally it would have to be an adversary with equal rights, that is to say, it would have to be a political adversary.'

As to the basis upon which opposition parties might be founded, almost all the protagonists were agreed that pluralism could only be within the framework of socialism.[1] Although such theoreticians as Pithart allowed that the 'very concept of socialism would have to be the subject of discussion,' socialism as such would not be placed in question but

---

[1] See, for example, Mlýnková and Rybáček on KAN in *Literární listy*, 11 April 1968.

rather the *type* of socialism.[1] If it were to be the type of socialism which would provide for pluralism, it would have to recognize that no one party could monopolize or lay claim to exclusive rights to the mutual, all-over goal of socialism.[2] The problem thus revolved not so much around the effect that genuine pluralism would have on the maintenance of socialism but the effect it would have on the leading role of the Communist Party. There were those, such as the above-quoted Communist, who believed that genuine democracy was more important than arbitrary protection of the Party's role, and that the Party *could* prove itself within a free competition. They demanded only that this competition be within the general framework of socialism, which meant in Czechoslovakia of 1968, a society freed of class conflicts and class exploitation. The parties that would make up this pluralistic system would (and could) not be a threat to this; they would not be instruments of specific classes with economic and social programs dictated by their class interests.

Some envisaged a second Marxist party, along the lines of the former Social Democrats, others an undefined 'loyal opposition.' Some favored arriving at pluralism through the building-up of the newly formed clubs of non-party people until these might be used as parties.[3] Mlynář, for example, preferred some sort of pluralism beyond the traditional idea of parties, based on the division of labor in society, an idea which resembled the Yugoslav system though it bordered on the corporate system of Italian fascism.[4] Pithart, however, responded to this in *Literární listy* of 20 June 1968, with the suggestion that one might learn from the recent past and not aim too high. He believed it best to pass through the stage of political parties before trying to introduce something entirely new and 'ideal,' such as some sort of 'direct formation of a general will without the medium of political parties.'

A number of Party theoreticians and the leadership itself shared to some degree the fears of the conservatives (and of Moscow) that the Party could *not* maintain its position in a genuinely pluralist system. While the Party agreed to become a partner with the various elements of the National Front and to permit them independence and a voice in policy formulation, it was not willing to permit a competitor for power. This was made entirely clear by the Action Program, and subsequent demands for the opposition expressly forbidden by the Action Program led to further clarifications of the leadership's position.

Looking at the anti-conservative camp we can find among certain

---

[1] Pithart in *Literární listy*, 1 May 1968.   [2] Kliment in *Literární listy*, 14 March 1968.
[3] See *Student*, 18 April 1968 (Sviták).   [4] Prague radio, 17 May 1968.

leading figures as early as March disapproval of the idea of an opposition party or parties. In what was otherwise a liberal article in *Život* of 17 April 1968, leading Slovak Peter Colotka said that he did not believe that political parties were the key element in democracy. He believed it sufficient that the social organizations within the National Front be 'given room to solve all the problems which exist' among their members, without being mere transmission belts for the Party. Husák recognized that the western Communist Parties accepted the idea of other parties and he agreed that 'one single party is no longer an axiom of Marxist doctrine.' Yet he opposed the idea of an opposition party, for the present, arguing that opposition could be expressed within the existing institutions: the state organs, the social organizations, and even through public opinion.[1]

These early Slovak views were moderate, possibly an effort to appear reasonable and open to all suggestions; they did not reject the idea in such a categorical way as might have alienated the public. Goldstücker, who had the reputation of being a much more honest man than Husák, did express himself more directly. In a number of interviews to both western and Czechoslovak papers, he dismissed the idea of political parties as a purely bourgeois phenomenon and an anomaly for a socialist society, for he accorded them the classical Marxist definition: representatives of class interests.[2] Goldstücker admitted that controls to prevent dictatorship were necessary, but he saw these in the possibility of people expressing differing opinions. Thus he believed that this possibility should be provided within the Communist Party. As to the idea, however, of an opposition which might suggest 'an alternative on the road to socialism, and...' discharge the function of the control on power,' he said to *Pravda* (Bratislava) of 13 April 1968: 'I think that not even such a party as this should be created.' He believed that any conflict of ideas should be within the National Front, but he expressly ruled out any struggle for the power in the state within that body. Mlynář too ruled out the idea of an opposition which strove to gain power in the state or oppose the state policy. Opposition within the National Front, in the form of independent groups, was only to act as a control through the clash of views within the Front. Mlynář also opposed a multi-party system on the grounds that parties would prevent the expression of group interests according to occupation.[3]

[1] Prague radio, 20 March 1968 (Prague rally); Bratislava television, 19 March 1968 (Bratislava rally); *Lidová demokracie*, 22 March 1968 (interview).
[2] ASHAI (Japan), 22 March 1968; *Volkstimme* (Vienna), 12 April 1968.
[3] *Reportér*, 6 March 1968 (discussion); *Rudé právo*, 26 March, 16 May, 6 June 1968; Prague radio (English), 18 April 1968.

Goldstücker, and to some degree Mlynář, maintained that sufficient controls on power could be achieved by the change of the Party's leading role from decree to persuasion, with 'the function of power' transferred to the state, National Front, and elected organs. Josef Špaček, one of the more consistently liberal of the reformers, also rejected the idea of opposition at an early date. He said in an interview to *Rudé právo* on 16 March, that one should not be bound by the only existing example of democracy, i.e. the bourgeois example with its party and parliamentary system. Rather Czechoslovakia should 'elaborate a guarantee of socialist democracy under the existence of one leading party.' Špaček called for democratization of the Party and responsiveness to the people's wishes as a means of improving and consolidating the leading role of the Party, in answer to the idea that the Party must abandon this role if so demanded by a non-Party majority.[1]

By May the Party was on the defensive and showing signs of succumbing to those elements – domestic and foreign – which feared the growing demands for genuine pluralism. As we have seen, Špaček spoke in terms of rebuilding the authority of the Party against possibilities of spontaneity and anarchy. Yet he nonetheless favored a liberal rather than repressive way of achieving this consolidation. An article in the Party journal also reflected the leadership's nervousness, condemning the idea of an opposition party as 'unsuitable for our country.' The author, one of the journal's editors, said that given the past errors of the Communist Party, if an opposition party were permitted, it would perforce become anti-Communist 'regardless of the subjective ideas and aims of its founders.' As this 'would certainly not promote the cause of socialism in our country' it was clear 'that Communists should publicly argue with anyone who proposes the foundation of an opposition party.'[2] The nervousness was also reflected in the efforts by the Party in the late spring to muzzle the press, and to curb the creation of political or quasi-political groupings, e.g. the attacks, by Dubček himself, on K-231; the ban on the restoration of the Social Democratic Party, and, perhaps the clearest of such measures, the Ministry of Interior announcement on Prague radio (24 May) that 'organized activity purporting to be that of a political party' would be considered illegal. This announcement was based on the application of the still-existing laws against additional political groupings (or union, etc.), rather than the spirit of the Action Program which was supposed to lead to new laws. Yet at approximately the same time the majority of Party members (55.5 per cent), polled in May 1968, expressed their preference

[1] *Rudé právo*, 23 May 1968.   [2] Karel Vlč, *Život strany*, 11 (1968), 36.

for a multi-party over a one-party system (the figure was approximately 90 per cent for non-Party members interviewed, as published by *Rudé právo*, 27 June 1968).

The 28 May–1 June central committee plenum demonstrated the dilemma faced by the reformers on this issue. Some, like Bohumil Šimon, were convinced that the Party could successfully compete with other programs and work out concepts acceptable to a majority of the population.[1] The general tone of the plenum, however, was for a regaining of control over matters and a reassertion of Party leadership, albeit through persuasion rather than by force. Císař and Štefan Sádovský, both new Party secretaries, condemned the suggestions for parties outside the National Front or opposition to the Communist Party. Císař called these an effort 'to dredge up old and outdated bourgeois democratic orders,' the advocates of which

> 'imagine that alongside the Communist Party, which rules today, opposition parties will begin to develop with a fully independent program of perhaps whatever kind and that there will be necessarily competition for victory, a struggle in which the Communist Party may even be defeated in so-called free elections and replaced in its ruling position by the former opposition forces. However, our long-term development does not provide for the renewal of the old "party system." '

Slovak National Front chairman Ondrej Klokoč, a reformer, echoed the earlier arguments of Goldstücker and Mlynář, claiming that 'what is expected of the new political parties can be far better fulfilled by the social and group interest organizations' and by the 'confrontation of alternative proposals within the Communist Party itself.'[2] Šik saw the solution not in an opposition party but in democratic self-management.[3]

Dubček on a number of occasions addressed himself directly to the question of parties, saying in a speech on 20 April that the question of 'state, politics, and power in conjunction with the development of socialism and communism' could be solved, 'not by forming opposition parties, but on the basis of the internal process of revival within the party.'[4] At the May–June plenum, favoring the participation of the people in the making of policy through their organizations in the National Front, he stipulated that 'it would be a *distortion* to maintain that the Party does *not* express the

---

[1] *Rudé právo*, 6 June 1968 (for this and following speeches to plenum).
[2] *Pravda* (Bratislava), 13 June 1968.
[3] *Zemědělské noviny*, 30 June 1968 (to a Prague Party meeting).
[4] *Rudé právo*, 21 April 1968.

interests of society.'[1] Thus Dubček was willing to grant these organizations the privilege of partnership with the Party but not the possibility of trying or even claiming to compete with it for the role of representative of the majority of the people's wishes.

'The basic difference between bourgeois parliamentarianism and socialist democracy [he explained], is the fact that relations between the political parties which preserve the foundations of the National Front must be relations of partnership and cooperation, not relationships of struggle for the repartition of power in the state – a struggle which is typical of the bourgeois political system.'

Moreover, the National Front should not be a coalition of political parties only but should provide an outlet for people of no party affiliation, by including the social organizations. According to Dubček's formulation, however, there existed barely any difference between the parties and the social organizations. Not only was the element of competition for power to be completely absent, but the right to an independent program within the National Front was neutralized by the fact that, according to Dubček,

'the confrontation of views (within the National Front) must be based on the common socialist program. *The leading role of the Czechoslovak Communist Party guarantees this program* because there is no other realistic program for the building of socialism but the Marxist program, a program which leans on scientific knowledge and on the most progressive social interest.'

The most progressive social interest, according to Dubček's earlier formulation, was expressed by the Communist Party.

Thus, wittingly or not, Dubček reinstated the very concept of infallibility of the Party which his program had sought to undo. He expressly closed the door to the possibility of any other valid program and thus closed the door to any hope for a genuine influence of non-Communists upon policy-making. He ruled out, emphatically, the creation of parties outside the National Front 'because this is the road toward a renewal of the power struggle.' He warned that

'our Party will oppose such efforts by every possible means because under our present conditions – independently of the desires of those people who advocate such views – such efforts would finally result in an attempt first to undermine the position of the Czechoslovak Communist Party in the society, and finally also to reverse socialist development.'

He argued that there would be enough room for mutual opposition within

[1] *Pravda* (Bratislava), 4 June 1968 (emphasis mine).

the National Front but that the new organizations to be authorized under the eventual law for freedom of association would not be permitted to oppose the program of the National Front. Dubček had already said, however, that the only program open for acceptance by the National Front was that of the Communist Party, so there seemed little hope that either the law on association or the 'change' in the National Front would promote meaningful pluralism. Indeed in the same speech Dubček said that the new law on association would have to provide safeguards against the creation of groups having 'no responsibilities to the state or to the principles of the National Front,' such as the K-231.

While there was no subsequent change in his position regarding opposition parties, Dubček did, in following weeks, revert to emphasizing the Party's need to *prove* that its program was the only valid one for socialism and its need to win majority support for this nonetheless indisputable fact. Using almost identical words on two succeeding days, Dubček said:

> 'In our country there is no other alternative to socialism than the Marxist program of socialist development which our Party upholds. Nor is there any other political force, loyal to revolutionary traditions, which would be a guarantee of the socialist process of democratization. That is why we are righteously defending the leading role of the Party in society. We know that it is not given automatically. We want to contend for it.'[1]

Yet by 'contend,' Dubček meant not against other contenders, nor that this role would be abandoned if not won, but merely that the Party would try to earn it, by practice, rather than merely decree it. Differing views would no longer be suppressed; they could be heard and legally represented, but the only possibility they might have of becoming policy would depend on the ability of their proponents to convince the Party to accept them. While persuasion was indeed a step forward insofar as the Party's methods were concerned, it could hardly be a potent instrument in the hands of powerless non-Party groups which lacked the possibility of presenting the electors with an alternative to the Communists or of offering a real challenge to the Communists' grip on power. Moreover, since the Party did not recognize the validity of any but its own program as genuinely socialist, it made little difference if, in the confrontation of views it was so generously permitting, it gained or did not gain a majority. Aside from interests of 'good will' or conscience, there was no need for

[1] *Rudé právo*, 1 July 1968 (speech to Líšeň peace rally); *Rudé právo*, 30 June 1968 (speech to Prague district Party meeting).

the Party to heed the majority any more than it had in the past, and it stated, *a priori*, that it would not heed an opinion which might threaten its own right to rule. Thus the system as envisaged by Dubček had no guarantees, particularly no guarantee that the Party would not once again misuse its power. In fact it offered only the semblance of democracy; it might have been more accurate for the Party to have admitted that what it was striving for was not democracy but liberalization.[1]

Whether the result of outside pressures or of apprehensions amongst the reformers themselves that the new mass movement was getting out of hand, the above points were incorporated into the policy declaration of the National Front of 15 June 1968 as the basis for the planned law and statutes of that institution. There was to be no competition for a re-division of political power in the state within the National Front, no political groupings or program outside the Front, and no additional political parties even within the Front.[2] The program adopted by the National Front was the Communist Party's Action Program. A few weeks later the Party presidium passed a resolution to accept a National Front law which would ban political organizations whose activities were not in harmony with the 'socialist platform of our political system' or the program of the National Front, i.e. any political organization outside the National Front or unwilling to accept the policies adopted by the Front.[3]

The materials prepared by the Mlynář team for the Party congress expressly recommended retention of what they termed the 'monopolistic position of the National Front' as outlined above so as to prevent the 'highly probable' conflict over the hegemony of the Communist Party.[4] This, however, was to be a temporary measure prior to the new Constitution which was to make the final decision on the 'openness' of the political system, based on the experience of the intervening two years. Even in this interim period, however, there was to be an effort to reduce the negative

---

[1] The author was told privately that some people who realized the implications of the Party's stand began to work on entirely new ideas for a one-party system, e.g. the idea of an open mass party.

[2] *Rudé právo*, 16 June 1968.

[3] *Rok šedesátý osmý*, 247 (explained by Dubček speech, Prague radio, 11 October 1968). The law (No. 128/1968) was passed on 13 September 1968 and defined political parties and organizations carrying out political functions thus: 'An organization which groups together members and followers on the basis of a world outlook or on the basis of some other common political program, primarily in order to be politically active amongst the citizens and thus take part in the formulation of policy and in the state power exercised by the representative bodies.'

[4] For this and the following, see Pelikán, *Vysočany Congress*, 235–7, and Ivan Bystřina, 'Change in the Political Structure and Infra-Structure,' unpublished paper (1971).

features of the one-list National Front system. Although no list outside that of the National Front might be presented to voters, the common list would present the titles of the organization or party represented by each candidate, permitting the voter to select the organization or party he wanted (with all the candidates it presented); places in the body to be elected would then be divided proportionally amongst the components of the National Front according to the votes received. Thus the 1945–8 system was restored in part. In addition, however, a certain percentage of places (a suggested 25 per cent) were to be put aside for candidates to be selected by the voter as individuals (regardless of organization or party), on the basis of a simple majority. Thus the system would favor that party which, although it might not do well as an organization, could achieve more seats through the direct election of individuals by the old one-list, absolute-majority system. A concomitant suggestion was to permit entirely independent candidates to appear on the list provided they had a certain minimum of electors' signatures. The Congress materials expressly acknowledged, however, that it picked this combination of a proportional and absolute-majority voting system so as to prevent the Communist Party becoming a minority party.

The Prague city Party committee, under reformer Bohumil Šimon, planned to present an alternative proposal to the congress which sought to increase direct public participation. It recommended plebiscites and referenda on the important political decisions and urged the choice, at elections, between alternative programs as well as alternative candidates, albeit ('at the present') on the basis of the National Front.[1]

Legal–judicial system

An area considered of utmost importance in terms of preventing the misuse of power – even if full democracy were still debatable – was that of the legal and security organs. A large number of suggestions had been made in the 1963–7 period particularly concerning the legal system and a number of changes had even been introduced in the areas of court procedure, defense, lawyers, the law, and investigatory procedures. In the 1968 period, however, interest in this area was both generated by and focused on revelations concerning the purge trials of 1949–54. The Party had never fully come to grips with these trials; although a review of the trials was the issue which had opened de-Stalinization in Czechoslovakia

[1] 'Stanovisko komunistů mimořádné městské konference k obecným politickým problémům,' unpublished paper (Praha, 1968).

in 1963, only partial rehabilitations had been granted by Novotný. Almost nothing concerning the trials had been revealed to the public, nor had anyone been publicly and specifically punished for his role in them.[1] In 1968 revelations about past errors were authorized in connection with the 'telling of the truth' about Novotný and the methods of the Stalinists. As a result, public attention began to focus on efforts by the media to reveal and understand as much as possible about the trials, presumably in the interests of finding the key to their prevention in the future. There were interviews with trial victims or their survivors, articles describing the methods (including torture and drugs) used by the investigators, and even interviews with persons one way or another responsible for these parodies of justice.[2] Not only the famous 1949–54 cases were rehashed but also the fate of non-Communists such as Bohumil Laušman and later political prisoners such as the former Communist Interior Minister Rudolf Barák.[3] Even the strange circumstances of the death of Jan Masaryk were aired, and the Prosecutor's Office was led to open an investigation.[4] There were those who openly implied that there may have been foreign (Soviet) involvement in Masaryk's death, and the question of suicide/murder was once again raised.[5] While this question was not answered authoritatively, a 'rehabilitation' of both Masaryks did take place, symbolically, by pilgrimages to their graves – including the placing of a wreath on the grave of T. G. Masaryk by the new president Svoboda.[6]

[1] Viliam Široký, Karol Bacílek, Bruno Köhler, Pavol David, Josef Urválek, and a few others were demoted or purged but there was no official linking of them with the trials. Only a *Rudé právo* editorial of 14 May 1963 hinted at the connection.

[2] For example, *Smena*, 28 April 1968; *Rol'nícke noviny*, 26 March 1968; *Lidová demokracie*, 22 March 1968; *Mladá fronta*, 29 March 1968; *Rudé právo*, 7 June 1968 (on use of drugs); 14 April 1968 (interview with Urválek); *Reportér*, 28 February 1968; 10, 17 April 1968; 15 May 1968; 5 June 1968; *Literární listy*, 28 March 1968; 25 April 1968; *Student*, 6, 20, 27 March 1968; 3, 10 April 1968.

[3] *Práce*, 19 May 1968 (on Laušman). On Barák: *Kulturní noviny*, 5 April 1968; *Reportér*, 5 June 1968, for example.

[4] ČTK, 3 April 1968. Václav Kadlčák, who had given evidence in this investigation under the name of 'Major Chlumský' pointing towards political murder, was brought to trial in February 1969 for providing false information. In the midst of the proceedings he was injured in an auto crash, in which mysterious bullet holes were found in his car. (*Mladá fronta*, 12 February 1969 and Prague radio, 19 February 1969.)

[5] *Student*, 3 April 1968 (*Sviták*); *Reportér*, 6 March and 17 April 1968; *Zemědělské noviny*, 8 March 1968; Prague radio, 27 March 1968, for example.

[6] Prague radio, 6 March 1968; Prague radio, 13 April 1968. Other past leaders and events formerly discredited were also reevaluated. For example, articles on M. R. Štefánik in *Reportér*, 24 April 1968; *Kultúrny život*, 8 March 1968; 22 March 1968;

The role of the Soviet Union was brought out in connection with the trials as well, although nothing more than presumptions were actually published. Those who stood to suffer from their past involvement understandably sought to place everything on orders from Moscow or on the Soviet advisors themselves.[1] Thus agents of Beria and even Mikoyan were blamed for the trials, the latter as a result of his trip to Prague in November of 1951. Historian Karel Kaplan, secretary of the Party's newly created Piller committee to review the trials, wrote a scholarly, and possibly authoritative series of articles on the reasons for and mechanism behind the trials. On the specific charges against the secretary-general of the Party, Slánský, Kaplan pointed out that Stalin had earlier agreed with Gottwald that Slánský was not guilty of more than certain administrative mistakes and should not be arrested but merely transferred to another job – which he was. Kaplan hypothesized that the building of the case against Slánský was, therefore, either the independent action of the Soviet advisors (with or without the knowledge of Stalin's wishes) *or* the independent initiative of Czech security forces, with cooperation from the Soviet advisors.[2]

Kaplan documented the connection between the purges in Eastern Europe and the founding of the Cominform in 1947, Zhdanovism, and the consolidation of the 'socialist camp,' demonstrating how Tito was both victim and then cause of the development of this process. Kaplan also demonstrated the direct connection between the trials in Hungary and Bulgaria and later Poland (with demands for similar action in Czechoslovakia too), with internal pressures created by the enforced implementation of the Cominform line in agriculture, the economy, and other areas (often called the 'Sovietization' of Eastern Europe). Tracing the almost organic development of the investigations and arrests, Kaplan was puzzled by the change in accusations and the introduction of the anti-Zionist, anti-semitic element. His only explanation of this – and that of the Piller report – was the shift in Soviet policy regarding Israel in, he claimed, 1949.

Among the major contributing factors to the trials, in addition to the international factors and the internal (economic) pressures, and Stalin's

3 May 1968; or the Czech Legion in World War One in *Reportér*, 1 May 1968; *Student*, 20 March 1968.

[1] *Smena*, 28 April 1968 (Bacílek); *Rudé právo*, 14 April 1968 (Urválek).

[2] Karel Kaplan, 'Thoughts About the Political Trials,' *Nová mysl*, XXII-6-8(1968), 765–94, 906–40, 1054–78. The Report of the committee (under Jan Piller) was not published in Czechoslovakia. It has appeared in English in the West: Jiří Pelikán, *The Czechoslovak Political Trials 1950–1954* (London 1970).

ideological basis for the trials (the intensification of the class struggle), Kaplan counted also the political system itself. He argued that as the Party assumed a monopoly on power it came to rely more and more on its security organs until these in turn assumed a role of extreme, eventually supreme, importance. As he described it, the first cases were handled mainly by the Party organs, with the participation of security forces; then came joint Party–security solutions; and finally a 'purely security solution, in the case of Slánský.' It was not that the security organs 'took over,' but rather that the Party became more and more dependent upon them. Moreover, there was no control or protection against misuse of the concentration of power in the hands of the Party, the 'fogging' of individual responsibility, and the concept of discipline which prevented any rebellion even of persons certain of foul play. This was not to mention the atmosphere of fear and mutual distrust caused by the procedure if not by the system itself as it became more and more dictatorial.

As to the reasons that the Czechoslovak trials were longer (they continued even after the deaths of Stalin and Beria), more extensive (it is said that some half a million Communists were purged), and extreme (eleven of the leading figures were executed) than those of the rest of Eastern Europe, Kaplan said only that one reason might be that these trials came last.[1] Presumably his explanation of the organic nature of the system could also serve as an explanation, for when Novotný came to power in 1953 he seemed merely to carry on a process begun before him (though not without his direct participation). He may have done so out of fear of halting the machine or simply because he himself had risen as part of the purges and, as his contribution demonstrated, he regarded this as the most efficacious means of ruling. A possible explanation for the cruelty and extent of the trials, implicit in Kaplan's articles, might be the fact that Prague had been singled out as the center of the anti-socialist forces in Eastern Europe. This choice of Prague may have been connected (though this was not suggested by Kaplan) with the large size of the Party, the large number of former Social Democrats, fellow-travelers, and others brought into the Party during its bid for popular election in the 1945–7 period, as well as the Czechoslovak Communist Party's own 'evolutionary' or democratic past tendencies. These factors may have led Moscow to seek a more thorough cleansing and a more striking lesson for this Party. Indeed the Cominform's disdain for Gottwald's 'Czechoslovak way to socialism' would support this hypothesis. In the numerous analyses of the trials which appeared in Czechoslovakia in 1968, however, relatively

[1] Kaplan, *Nová mysl*, XXII:8(1968), 1054.

little attention was paid to the unique characteristics of Czechoslovakia's purges.

Kaplan, and others, were careful to point out that to accuse 'the system' was not to ignore the responsible organs, offices, people, and institutions within this system. Many critics in fact sought to determine and replace those persons responsible. This effort, while a legitimate element of the rectification process, was not devoid of certain personal account-settling, while, for political reasons, most people demanded that the conservatives, held responsible for the trials or for having condoned them, be removed from positions of power, and/or punished. A particular target was, understandably, Novotný, and his principal accuser was Gustáv Husák, Novotný's own most important victim.[1] Husák did not call for punishment of Novotný, but he did unequivocally state that Novotný should not remain in the Party. The other leading Party functionaries who had a hand in the trials (Kopřiva, Bacílek, P. David, Široký, and so forth), were similarly criticized, but, at the same time, a campaign was waged against those in the other organs responsible for the injustices, e.g. Ministry of Interior and Ministry of Justice officials as well as security officers and prison officials.[2] Party historian Milan Hübl said that he did not believe that persons 'directly, or indirectly connected with the trials should be able to hold public office,' while Löbl said: 'why should only the accusers be punished; why not the defense, why not the judges, why not the investigators, all those who knew, before the trial started, that the accusations were a *fraud*, and the condemned innocent?'[3]

An editorial in *Student* of 6 March 1968 listed the officials (lawyers, judges, prosecutor) at the Slánský trial and demanded they be 'called to account,' singling out for special criticism Josef Urválek and Václav Škoda,[4] respectively Prosecutor-General and Justice Minister for many of the trials. Although Urválek had been forced to resign ('for reasons of health') as a result of the 1963 rehabilitations, he had not been publicly called to account in any way nor had he admitted his responsibility or lost his Party membership. Škoda was currently deputy chairman of the National Assembly.

[1] See, for example, Husák in *Nové slovo*, 6 June 1968 or *Kulturní tvorba*, 13 June 1968.
[2] For example, *Lidová demokracie*, 27 March 1968.
[3] Prague radio, 20 February 1968. In one poll, 58% of those interviewed believed that those responsible for the trials should themselves be tried; 37% thought they should be dismissed from their jobs; only 3% thought the past should be forgotten, and 2% had no opinion. (*Lidová demokracie*, 4 May 1968.)
[4] See also ČTK, 15, 19 March 1968 (Ústí nad Labem Party conference of jurists and judges); *Rudé právo*, 17 April 1968; *Rol'nícke noviny*, 19 March 1968.

Some Party people actually encouraged this criticism of legal organs and officials on the grounds (and in the *hopes*) that the Party alone might not be held responsible for the past.[1] The regime was, however, sensitive to the above demands and a number of personnel actions did take place. For example, Interior Minister Kudrna was dismissed in March 1968, to be replaced by Josef Pavel, a victim of the trials. Pavel, in turn, conducted personnel changes in the Ministry, though he merely demoted most. The only high official to be dismissed altogether from the Ministry appears to have been deputy Minister Jindřich Kotál, who had been deputy to both Kopřiva and Bacílek, successive security chiefs during the period of the trials. A new chief justice was named, replacing Josef Litera (Urválek's replacement in 1963), by Otomar Boček, whose past was thoroughly uncompromised. Prosecutor-General Jan Bartuška was replaced by the uncompromised attorney Miloš Čeřovský on 9 April; Čeřovský set up a commission to check the possible responsibility of any Prosecutor's Office workers for the injustices of the 1950s, and carried out personnel changes, replacing two deputies and the chief military prosecutor.[2] The Justice Ministry too changed hands, Bohuslav Kučera replacing Alois Neuman (who claimed to have had no knowledge of the past illegalities). Stronger action was taken at the May–June central committee plenum, when, in response to the public and internal Party pressures, the new leadership suspended Karol Bacílek, Pavol David, Bruno Köhler, Štefan Rais, Viliam Široký, Josef Urválek, and Antonín Novotný from Party membership pending clarification of their responsibility in the trials.[3]

Another issue aired in connection with the trials was the long-standing demand for rehabilitations of the victims. Despite rehabilitations and revisions throughout East Europe, Novotný had resisted demands for rehabilitations until 1963. In 1955 Novotný did permit the creation of a committee to review the trials, exclusive of the Slánský trial itself, under the chairmanship of Rudolf Barák. While some revisions of sentences took place in 1956 as a result (*re:* Goldstücker, Pavel, Smrkovský, and London) the charges, particularly those of the Slánský trial and of the Slovak 'bourgeois nationalists' (against Husák, Novomeský, etc.) were

---

[1] For example, speech by Michal Pecho, Slovak Party secretary, 26 March 1968 (Bratislava television, 26 March 1968). Husák said that he believed it was enough that these functionaries were bothered by their consciences. 'I do not think I want to make a fuss and embitter their lives even more.' (Prague radio, 20 March 1968.)

[2] *Rudé právo*, 20 April 1968 (Čeřovský interview).

[3] *Rok šedesátý osmý*, 164.

upheld.[1] In April 1956 a second commission was created, again under Barák, to study the Slánský trial itself. This commission's report concluded that there had been no basis to the charges pressed at the trial. Despite this Novotný – and Barák – at the June 1956 Party conference upheld the trial and even added some charges to the original. The Party's reaction to both commissions was to place all the blame of the trials on Slánský – without, however, rehabilitating the others. On 30 September 1957 Barák's final report to the central committee reaffirmed this stand. It also revealed that of 6698 requests for reinvestigation, 263 cases were reopened (2.6%) and of these only 50 verdicts were quashed. Of the remaining 213 cases the 'original guilt was reestablished' but the sentences were lowered.[2] With this the matter was dropped until August 1962, when the politburo, followed by the Twelfth Party Congress, authorized a third commission, this time under Drahomír Kolder (Barák being in prison). The Kolder commission reviewed the same material as the two previous commissions, minus material Novotný had removed after Barák's arrest.[3] It rejected Barák's findings on the grounds, according to Kolder, that his objectivity had probably been affected by the fact that he himself already held the position of Interior Minister in 1953 and 1954. The results of the Kolder commission as we have seen revised the former conclusions, although Slánský and six others continued to be regarded as guilty of Party violations, and no clear invalidation of the charges of Slovak 'bourgeois nationalism' was announced. The latter was left for the 'Barnabité Commission,' which led the December 1963 central committee meeting finally to exonerate the Slovaks.

As pointed out by this history of the reviews, revealed publicly for the first time by Kaplan and Kolder, only a limited number of cases were reopened, even under the 1962 mandate. Thousands of Party members and non-Communists had yet to have their cases reviewed; even in the cases already covered, Party rehabilitation had often been denied, and full, public rehabilitation and indemnification had been accorded to very few.[4] Public demands were, therefore, raised for full-scale reviews and rehabilitations, not only of Party members but of the tens of thousands of non-Party members persecuted, including farmers arrested during collec-

[1] Kaplan, *Nová mysl*, XXII:8, 1070–1; Husák, *Nové slovo*, 6 June 1968.
[2] Quoted by Kolder in speech to the April plenum (*Rudé právo*, 6 April 1968).
[3] This was referred to obliquely by Kolder in 1968, who said that he had found nothing to prove an 'active negative role' by Novotný but that 'the records were in a terrible state.' (*Rudé právo*, 6 April 1968. See chapter 1.)
[4] Husák claimed that rehabilitation would affect between 30 000 and 40 000 people. (*Rudé právo*, 15 March 1968.)

tivization, members of minorities, clergymen, writers and so forth.[1] In a May 1968 poll some 90 per cent of those questioned believed there should be rehabilitations of those unjustly punished in the past, according to *Lidová demokracie* of 4 May 1968. The demands were often specific, calling for appropriate jobs and indemnification for those harmed, as well as for a rehabilitation law to provide for indemnification.[2] Husák and Smrkovský (both former victims who had refused to 'confess') were among the most active pursuers of rehabilitations, and Smrkovský called for speedy review of *every* case, non-Communist and Communist alike.[3]

As early as February 1968 the idea of an indemnity law, the draft of which had been begun as early as 1966, was revived.[4] After much prompting, including a threat by Smrkovský to bring a vote of no-confidence against the Justice Minister in the National Assembly if a draft bill were not soon presented, a law on judicial rehabilitations was finally passed by the Assembly on 25 June 1968.[5] The law, the first of its kind in the Soviet bloc, provided for appeals (even on behalf of deceased persons) on *all* sentences, including non-political cases, handed down from October 1948 to 1965. Review teams consisting of three persons (five for the Supreme Court) would be formed in each court, with persons involved in the trials in any way to be excluded from these review boards. The reviews were to be open to the public, their costs covered by the state, and decisions open to appeal. The law called for rehabilitations for individuals rather than blanket rehabilitations for groups (Church orders, etc.). This was a drawback in the eyes of many who believed that individual revisions would take too long; they advocated such blanket measures, for example, as cancellation of all decisions of the State Court (which heard only political cases) from 1948 to 1959.[6] The only exception to the above procedure applied to tradesmen and private farmers sentenced for minor offenses;

---

[1] *Pravda* (Bratislava), 8 March 1968; *Práca*, 10 April 1968; *Práce*, 22 February 1968; *Rudé právo*, 20 February 1968.

[2] Prague radio, 21 March 1968; ČTK, 22 March 1968. *Pravda* (Bratislava), 8 March 1968, said that the rehabilitation of peasants was being held up because of the cost involved.

[3] Smrkovský, *My 68*, v:4(1968), 6.

[4] *Literární noviny*, 27 January 1968. The 1964 civil code had deferred this matter to a new law on indemnification. (*Sbírka zákonů*, No. 40/1964 Para. 426.)

[5] *Pravda* (Bratislava), 30 April 1968 (Smrkovský interview); (*Sbírka zákonů* No. 82/ passed 25 June 1968.) The law on extra-judicial rehabilitation, approved by the government on 25 July 1968 was never passed because of the invasion. See ČTK, 26 March 1969.

[6] *Zemědělské noviny*, 14 March 1968 (interview with officials of the Prosecutor-General's Office). Smrkovský mentioned both ways. (*Rudé právo*, 4 April 1968, speech to plenum.)

their sentences were quashed by the law itself. Indemnification did not, however, provide for return of their nationalized properties. In general the indemnification provisions allowed a maximum compensation of 20 000 crowns for loss of income during imprisonment. Further compensation could be demanded for disability caused by imprisonment, legal costs, fines, and material losses. Direct cash payments, however, would not exceed 20 000 crowns; above this figure state bonds redeemable at the rate of 5 000 crowns per year could be issued.[1]

The law also provided for dismissal from office of persons responsible for miscarriages of justice. These cases were to be determined by a screening commission which would examine the roles played by the security forces, prosecutors, interrogators, judges, and prison staff. Legal action might be initiated against those who had violated the law, but owing to the statute of limitations this would probably affect only those charged with murder (i.e. responsibility for actions which resulted in death). This point had been criticized by legal experts and K-231 prior to the passage of the law, on the grounds that the regime was resorting to 'legal purism' regarding a period when legality itself had been suspended so that appeals could not be submitted within the 'legal' time-limits.[2] The cases of persons interned without trial, mainly the thousands sent to labor camps, would be handled by a new law on administrative rehabilitations.

Even prior to the law, however, courts reviewed cases and granted appeals for retrials, as in the case of the 1950 political trial against Viliam Žingor (executed) 'and collaborators,' or the 1954 'conviction' of an eleven-man group of Social Democrats. New trials were ordered on the grounds that the original depositions had been extracted by force.[3] Rudolf Barák was released and, in July 1968, the Supreme Court quashed his original sentence. On the anniversary of the liberation of Prague, President Svoboda declared an amnesty which for the first time included political prisoners, some 500 of approximately 700 being released immediately.[4] The amnesty also affected some 100 000 people who had illegally left the country or stayed abroad since 1948.[5] Rehabilitation

---

[1] Worker's average monthly wage: 1500 crowns.
[2] See *Literární listy*, 30 May 1968 or *Rudé právo*, 5 May 1968.
[3] Prague radio, 28 March 1968; ČTK, 1 April 1968.
[4] Prague radio, 9 May 1968. It is not known exactly how many political prisoners were held. A Ministry of Interior official in March 1968 said 3.5% of all prisoners were political. (*Lidová demokracie*, 14 March 1968.)
[5] This action facilitated the efforts conducted by writers and scholars to persuade noted Czech and Slovak émigrés to return. (Such 'invitations' were made to Professors Táborský and Ducháček, for example.) *Literární listy* published a letter from Táborský

commissions were also set up in various ministries, offices, factories, and organizations to process requests and internal restoration of rights, and a commission was established at the Ministry of Interior to investigate prison practices.[1]

The Party too set up a rehabilitation commission, at its April central committee plenum, headed by Jan Piller and authorized to review all important cases of the 1949–54 period, from the point of view of Party violations. This commission decided to recommend to the fourteenth congress the full rehabilitation of Slánský, Šling, Reicin, Šváb, Outrata, Fischl, Lewinter, Landa, and Taussigová (i.e. those held guilty by the Kolder review).[2] Although the invasion prevented official Party action, symbolic public rehabilitation was accorded by Svoboda when, in honor of May Day 1968, he restored to Slánský and Šling (posthumously) their former honors and bestowed new awards upon them and a long list of other persecuted Party members.

Despite these actions a definite change in emphasis could be noted in Party comments as the public *exposés* on the trials and other injustices began to show signs of hurting the Party's reputation. More conservative leaders, such as Indra, had from the outset cautioned that rehabilitations should not be accorded to all, indiscriminately, thereby permitting 'inimical elements' to profit from the Party's 'purification process.'[3] At the April Slovak central committee plenum Bil'ak warned not to 'expect any rehabilitation of those class-enemy and anti-social elements to which the revolutionary measures of the state power apply by law.'[4] The dispute over K-231 revolved, in part, around the same concern that genuine enemies ('anti-socialists') were trying to profit from the rehabilitations, the more cautious (as *Reportér* of 12 June 1968 explained), arguing that not all the charges had been without foundation. Responding to both internal and external pressures, Dubček even supported this view to some

in its 2 May issue, and émigré editor of *Svědectví* Pavel Tigrid was interviewed on a number of occasions. A group even went to interview RFE in July 1968. (U.S., 'Interview with Pavel Tigrid,' *Host do domu*, XV:7(1968), 46–7; *Student*, 24 July 1968.)

[1] A curious incident occurred, possibly in connection with the rehabilitation procedure. Judge Brešt'anský, deputy chairman of the Supreme Court, was found dead in a wood 30 kilometers from Prague. The papers said he committed suicide by hanging, after reports had been printed of his disappearance. Brešt'anský reportedly had been authorized to look into the trials. (*Práce*, 28 March 1968 and ČTK, 2 April 1968.) He himself, however, had been criticized for his role in the 1950s. (*Rudé právo*, 23 March 1968.)

[2] Pelikán, *Trials*, 296.   [3] Prague radio, 8 April 1968.
[4] *Pravda* (Bratislava), 10 April 1968.

degree, when in his speech to the May–June plenum he admitted the need to curb 'anti-socialist' elements which might take advantage of the democratization process. Thus reform leaders gradually tried to swing attention from the past to problems of the present and future. Various reformers, such as Smrkovský, warned that one should not become obsessed with the past, and, together with Dubček, maintained that there — were good Communists and bad; only certain people and not the Party as such were responsible for the past errors.[1] Dubček strongly urged the Party to dissociate itself from the Stalinists so as to overcome the severe criticism being levied. It was for this reason that he agreed to suspend Bacílek, Köhler, and other long-since demonstrated Stalinists, despite his aversion to compounding past illegalities with new purges.[2] Sensitive to the increasing criticism, Dubček was probably anxious not only to demonstrate that the Party would not continue to tolerate in its ranks those responsible for the trials, but also to use these people as scapegoats so as to redeem the Party from the discredit into which it had fallen.

The demands connected with the trials sought also to change the legal–security system which, in the past, had been unable to control power – indeed had even contributed to the misuse of power. The new system proposed by the reformers consistently proclaimed the rule of law as the very basis of democracy. It was argued that it was not enough to make personnel changes or to bring defects out into the open; only the preparation of new and democratic norms could prevent a repetition of the past.[3] Dubček too urged the formulation of new laws as the essential guarantee of democracy, and he, as well as most reform groups, advocated laws protecting individual civil rights, including free speech, freedom of association, freedom of travel and residence abroad, and so forth. Yet a central problem was the guarantee that the new laws – assuming their promulgation – would be implemented, i.e. that legality would be observed. Therefore attention was focused on reforms which would permit the functioning of the legal–security apparatus in the interests of the individual citizen and his rights.

There were basically three institutions involved: the judiciary (the Ministry of Justice), the security organs (the Ministry of Interior) and the Office of the Prosecutor-General. As we have seen among the proposals for the separation of the Party and the government there were the demands for

---

[1] *Mladá fronta*, 5 April 1968; *Práca*, 30 April 1968; *Rudé právo*, 4 April 1968 (speeches to April plenum).

[2] *Pravda* (Bratislava), 4 June 1968 (Dubček to May plenum).

[3] Czechoslovak television, 29 February 1968; *Student*, 7 May 1968.

a separation of executive, legislative, and judiciary powers. An independent judiciary was considered an essential element to the rule of law, both as a protector of the legal process and as a control on the other branches of power.[1] Independence of the judiciary vis-à-vis the legislative branch (the right of review of laws, exercised by the Constitutional Court in pre-1948 Czechoslovakia), and independence from politics (appointment by the highest state organs instead of election), were demanded but also independence vis-à-vis the Party. Judges and the courts should, it was argued, be free of the supervision and interference of the central committee's eighth department (for security affairs), headed from 1960 to 1968 by Miroslav Mamula.[2] Even the much-criticized Mamula himself admitted, in *Reportér* of 5 June 1968, to Party interference in and manipulation of the judiciary, for example in the form of dictating judges' verdicts. Smrkovský pointed out to a district Party conference, according to Prague radio, 18 March 1968, that 'the powers of comrade Mamula were greater than those held by two ministers and the entire government together, with all the tragic consequences.'

Independent investigatory organs and reforms of the institution of the Prosecutor-General were also demanded. Reforms had already been initiated in this area and investigatory organs had been promised independence, but as in all other spheres, these pre-1968 reforms had foundered on the essential element of the Party's willingness to relinquish controls. The Prosecutor-General's Office too was subject to the central committee's eighth department and this was criticized no less than the similar subjection of the judiciary.[3] Subordination of the courts to the Prosecutor-General's Office was also criticized, but the new Prosecutor-General Miloš Čeřovský said in a *Rudé právo* interview (20 April) that the most serious problem was the Party-enforced 'fictitious unity,' which demanded total agreement between the Party, the Ministry of Interior, and the Prosecutor, at the expense of considerations of law. No disagreement with the Party and security organs was possible; the Prosecutor could but comply. This was in direct violation of the Constitution, which held the Office of the Prosecutor-General responsible to the National

---

[1] Colotka, *Život*, 17 April 1968; *Rudé právo*, 13 February 1968 (Mlynář).

[2] *Rudé právo*, 23 March 1968 (Communist *aktiv* of the Ministry of Justice); Prague radio, 23 April 1968 (interview with Justice Minister Kučera); *Práce*, 16 March 1968.

[3] See, for example, *Rudé právo*, 13 March 1968 (letter from Communist teachers at Charles University Law Faculty); *Zemědělské noviny*, 14 March 1968 (interview with Prosecutor-General's Office officials); *Rudé právo*, 20 April 1968 (interview with the new Prosecutor-General).

Assembly alone. Yet, as was pointed out by many, the National Assembly had no committee for security matters. This left responsibility for assuming the observance of legality with the Prosecutor's Office itself, a task which was seriously complicated by the fact that the Prosecutor was also a 'party' in criminal cases. Čeřovský recommended that some sort of independent authority should take over this control responsibility from the Prosecutor-General's Office.[1]

While the problem of the subordination of justice to the central committee's eighth department might have been worked out as part of the separation of the Party and the government, there remained the issue of the strength and role of the state security organs themselves. While the Party to some degree adopted the line that the security organs in the past had set themselves above the Party, there was the concomitant theory that the security organs had been misused by the Party or certain Party officials. Therefore it was deemed necessary both to remove the security forces from direct Party control, and to find a way of controlling the activities of the security forces. It was Lt.-General Václav Prchlík, Mamula's replacement as head of the eighth department, who himself led the efforts to have this department abandon its ubiquitous and nefarious role. Prchlík favored the creation of a central committee defense and security commission similar to the ideological, legal, and economic commissions, to provide objective and scientific information concerning activities in this area, according to an interview in *Práce* of 21 April 1968. Rather than recommending still another instrument of Party control over these areas, Prchlík saw in this commission a means of breaking up the concentration of power *within* the Party over these matters. More important, he championed what he called the integration of the security forces 'into the social system and state structure.'[2] The state organs, specifically a National Assembly committee for defense and security matters, together with the government, should determine the policy and duties of the security organs – not the Party (whether directly through its eighth department or indirectly through its adherents within these bodies), according to Prchlík and the new Interior Minister Pavel in *Práce* of 11 April 1968. It was Prchlík's major success that he brought about the abolition of the eighth department; unfortunately with this he lost his own position as a last-minute concession to the Russians.

Most reformers favored Prchlík's idea of a National Assembly commit-

---

[1] As late as March 1969 establishment was urged of the pre-1950 institution of examining magistrates (*Práce*, 18 March 1969).

[2] *Rudé právo*, 7 April 1968 (Prchlík to April plenum); *Práce*, 21 April 1968.

tee on defense and security, for this would in effect provide a certain degree of public control over security organs through the people's representatives.[1] The National Assembly itself decided to create such a committee on 29 March 1968. Another element of public control recommended was for greater publicity and availability of information for public scrutiny regarding the security organs' activities. It was further recommended that precise regulations be laid down concerning the jurisdiction and powers of the security organs, including laws specifically protecting civil rights.[2]

The Interior Ministry itself was to be reformed in the interests of curbing its powers. Interior Minister Pavel suggested, for example, that the sub-department concerned with pursuing 'enemies within the Party' should be abolished. Pavel also suggested separating state and public security organs, and he recommended that, to prevent too great a concentration of powers in the Ministry, certain of its functions, such as the investigatory organs and the prison system, should be shifted to the Justice Ministry. An Interior Ministry official did point out in *Kulturní tvorba* of 13 June 1968, that 'the most serious illegal acts were committed roughly up to 1953 when the prison system was still under the jurisdiction of the Justice Ministry,' but this transfer was made in December 1968.

The Interior Ministry was critized over such specific issues as the behaviour of the police in the Strahov affair and such restrictions of civil rights as the maintenance of an armed, closed border, and the Ministry's rules on travel abroad.[3] The continued presence of Soviet advisors in the security apparatus was also criticized, although little or almost no discussion of this delicate issue reached the public.[4] Only the numerous personnel and organizational changes, designed to increase public control over these organs gave any indication that Czechoslovakia was rebuilding a security system under its own supervision. It would, for example, be difficult for the Soviets to continue to give orders to an apparatus removed from the supervision of the Party and subject to scrutiny by genuine popular representatives in the National Assembly, though such outside interference might be maintained, at least partially,

[1] See Prague radio, 11 March 1968 (interview with Viktor Knapp, Chairman of the National Assembly law and Constitution committee); *Lidová demokracie*, 12 April 1968 (interview with Josef Pavel).

[2] *Rudé právo*, 7 April 1968 (Prchlík to April plenum) and *Pravda* (Bratislava), 11 June 1968.

[3] See *Práce*, 16 March 1968.   [4] *Pravda* (Bratislava), 11 June 1968.

if the necessary personnel changes were not initiated. The difficult task of removing Soviet agents from the security forces was apparently begun (some thirty agents reportedly were relieved) but had only barely progressed by the time of the invasion, when first deputy Interior Minister Šalgovič provided cooperation with the invading forces. A thorough reorganization of the secret police was, however, reportedly decided upon by the Party presidium just prior to the invasion.

Two other elements of the security establishment which came under scrutiny were the militia and the Army, the very existence of the militia being challenged. It was pointed out that the militia was an armed force of a political party – the exclusive privilege of the Communist Party. Even if the constitutionality of such a force were not questioned, claimed *Mladá fronta* of 25 April 1968, it had outlived even its original justification as an instrument of the proletariat against the other hostile classes. Moreover, this power had been misused by the Party for repressive actions, it was argued even in the Party central committee, and as a potential power in case of trouble.[1] There were suggestions that the militia should be subordinated to the Defense Ministry or that other parties might be permitted to maintain such forces.[2] Both Smrkovský and Dubček, accompanied by the Slovaks, came to the defense of the militia, claiming that such a force could never be used 'against the people.'[3] While such statements may have been designed to win the militia organizations with their several hundreds of thousands of members over to the reformers, there was also an effort by the leadership, for example in Dubček's 21 April speech, to present the militia in this 'new' stage as a part of the forces for protection against external threat, rather than against elements inside the country. Even the militia chief characterized the militia's 'new role' this way.[4] On 20 June, however, a state-wide meeting of the militia issued a conservative statement, dispatching it to the USSR, and thereby permitting itself to be used by the latter in the pressures against the Czechoslovak reformers.[5] The Russians' particular

[1] Bratislava television, 27 May 1968.
[2] *Svobodné slovo*, 19 July 1968. See also letter to *Student*, 12 June 1968 and Škutina in *Literárni listy*, 20 June 1968.
[3] *Práce*, 26 May 1968; Prague radio, 19 June 1968 (Dubček at militia rally); *Rudé právo*, 2 April 1968 (Dubček to April plenum); Slovak May 1968 central committee resolution.   [4] Bratislava television, 27 May 1968.
[5] *Pravda* (Moscow), 21 June 1968; *Rudé právo*, 25 June 1968. See response in the form of letters from Soviet workers, *Pravda* (Moscow), 29 June 1968. *Pravda* (Moscow), 22 May 1968, reported receiving resolutions from individual militia groups in Czechoslovakia as well.

sensitivity to the militia issue may have been because the militia was the public arm or at least a symbol of the general security apparatus, over which Moscow undoubtedly wished to retain its control, as well as the symbolic instrument of 'workers' power' in Czechoslovakia. By July, however, as the crisis developed between Prague and her allies, the chief of the Czechoslovak militia expressed solidarity with the reform regime against 'interference in internal affairs.'[1] Nonetheless, the late summer saw a massive signature campaign throughout the country urging the dissolution of the militia.

On 25 February 1968, General Jan Šejna, then chief of the Party group in the Defense Ministry, crossed the Slovak–Hungarian border and fled to the US, according to the Yugoslav news agency on 2 March 1968. Announcing his flight, Prague radio (27 February) said that Šejna had been implicated in a case of misappropriation of some 300 000 crowns' worth of seeds and had been about to be arrested. This 'explanation' was not generally accepted, however, and the National Assembly presidium demanded an investigation, which was undertaken by the Party.[2] Almost simultaneously with these announcements, Prague radio (14 March 1968) reported the suicide of another general, deputy Defense Minister Vladimír Janko. The flight of Šejna (and probably the suicide of Janko) was generally connected with semi-confirmed rumors that Novotný had tried to use the Army in an effort to stay in power during the January 1968 plenum. The Yugoslavs stated clearly that Šejna had been connected with the anti-reform resistance within the Czechoslovak Army, and, therefore, probably fled in fear of repercussions.[3] General Prchlík revealed that Šejna had indeed been one of the initiators of a letter sent by the Communist group of the Defense Ministry to the central committee during its crucial December meeting.[4] The letter apparently contained an implied threat by the Army to intervene on Novotný's behalf and in fact certain units of the Army had actually been placed on alert, certain officers, including Šejna, planning to intervene if the Party's deliberations went against Novotný.[5] A number of interviews led to the conclusion that the

[1] Czechoslovak television, 8 July 1968. Reportedly only reluctantly, however.
[2] It was, however, upheld by the report of the investigation, published 11 June 1968, which said Šejna received no help from any foreign government in his flight.
[3] *Vjesnik* (Zagreb), 3 March 1968.
[4] *Rudé právo*, 19 March 1968. (Rumors about this letter and attempted interference had already been circulating following an article in the Defense Ministry's weekly *Obrana lidu*, 24 February 1968.)
[5] Bratislava television, 27 March 1968; *Zemědělské noviny*, 30 March 1968.

Party organization in the units involved (in Bohemia) prevented an intervention.

While the details were never fully clarified, the rumors, and then admissions of at least plans to intervene, publicly raised the issue of political use of the Army. Thus in this sphere too, the connection of the Party and the Army, and the possibility of control, were debated. The question of the Party was particularly pertinent as it was revealed on television on 26 March, that Šejna, Janko, and others had been striving to stop the reformers on the basis of a report circulated by Mamula, chief of the eighth department, who had urged action to save Novotný. As it appeared, the Communists in the Defense Ministry, subordinate only to the Party's eighth department, were thwarted by the Army's Main Political Directorate, headed by Prchlík. Prchlík, as we have seen, urged an end to this direct Party control of the security forces, including the Army, advocating the same controls as suggested for the other security forces: the creation of a central committee commission and a National Assembly committee on defense and security, and a withdrawal of the Party from direct control of the Army (even to the extent of manipulation via Communists in the Defense Ministry or the Political Directorate of the Army).[1] Prchlík even supported the idea that Party units within the Army should be elected organizations.[2]

Specific individuals and the Army's Main Political Directorate itself were subjected to extensive criticism, particularly once the Šejna case had brought to light the potential threat from conservatives in the Army. Moreover, aside from Prchlík and one or two others, the Army and Defense Ministry failed until March openly to support the reform movement. Defense Minister Lomský, who refused to dissociate himself from Šejna, was forced to resign on 3 April. He was replaced by Martin Dzúr and personnel changes were conducted in the Ministry. In addition, a new chief of staff was appointed to replace General Otakar Rytíř, also a Novotný supporter.

Conservatives were predictably disturbed by the attacks on the security organs, and Indra, for example, continued the line that only increased Party controls could guarantee an improvement in the work of the public and state security organs.[3] Slovak security organs rejected any criticism pointing out that they had had no role in the Šejna affair and vehemently dissociated themselves from the past malpractices.[4] From a more liberal

---

[1] *Práce*, 21 April 1968; ČTK, 19 March 1968.
[2] *Rudé právo*, 7 April 1968.   [3] Prague radio, 8 April 1968.
[4] *Pravda* (Bratislava), 12 April 1968 (statement by Slovak Party security department); *Pravda* (Bratislava), 3 April 1968 (statement by chief of Bratislava region security forces).

position, however, Smrkovský expressed certain apprehensions about the criticism, urging people at the 20 March Prague rally to respect the decent and necessary work conducted by the security forces. As the pressures grew, Party statements became more conservative on this score. Mlynář, for example, in his speech to the May plenum, opposed the 'attempts to disintegrate the security and justice apparatus of our state,' and warned against crippling the security forces, especially counter-intelligence, from operating against justifiedly suspected persons. Dubček himself, at the May plenum, called for a strengthening of the security organs and pledged support of the militia as 'one of the guarantees of the socialist nature of society.' Nonetheless, he added that these organs must be strengthened only within the spirit of the Action Program.

The Action Program condemned the 'excessive concentration of functions' in the Interior Ministry and called for such things as a transfer of the prison administration to another body, and a clear delineation of the jurisdiction of the courts in investigations. It recommended the division of the security forces, as suggested earlier by Pavel, into an independent organ for public security (police and public order) and one for state security (foreign intelligence). The state security organs were 'not to be used to resolve domestic political questions and conflicts of socialist society.' The Program urged legal norms to provide 'clearer definition of the control of security by the government as a whole and by the National Assembly.' It also called for a strengthening of the role of the courts, though not for independent courts. Despite the harder line at the May plenum, the abolition of the eighth department (whose responsibilities covered the administration of justice and the Prosecutor-General's Office as well as the security organs) demonstrated the reform regime's willingness to free these organs from at least direct Party control. While the Action Program in numerous clauses called for the protection of individual and civil rights, including the right to travel and reside abroad, and the right to an equal legal position vis-à-vis state and other institutions, no more than the rehabilitation law (and the amendment to the law on censorship) were actually passed, the rest being frozen in the draft stage by the August invasion.[1] Pending legislation these rights were often granted on an *ad hoc* basis and the necessity of transferring controls from the Party to the elected organs of the government was recognized, so as to provide the element of Constitutional and public control necessary to the rule of law.

[1] The idea of a return to a Constitutional Court was incorporated into the new Constitutional Law passed in October 1968, restoring the principles of judicial review and protection of Constitutional rights.

8

Political Reform and Slovakia

The Slovak issue was one of the contributing factors to Novotný's downfall and a source of contention and disappointment in Czechoslovakia since the two nations came together in 1918. It had been the Slovaks who spearheaded the movement for reform in 1962–3, and, while their own ranks were far from united on the question of democratization, it was to be expected that any political reform must include a change in the role and position of the Slovak organs. Pressures in late 1967 had indicated, however, that in all probability an entirely new approach to any used previously in Czechoslovakia would have to be found for a solution of the 'Slovak question.'[1]

Before any serious changes could be worked out, there was a certain need to demonstrate that the Slovak demands were not some sort of reversion to 'bourgeois nationalism' or, worse still, separatism and, yet, to convince the Czechs of the necessity and legitimacy of a new Czech–Slovak arrangement. Husák, principal spokesman of the Slovaks, admitted that a certain reeducation of the Czechs was necessary, for, he said, the Czech public had been purposely misinformed. It had been told that the leaders of the Slovak Communist Party in the 1940s were separatists, and in the minds of the public Husák, Clementis, and company were probably no different from the earlier, Fascist separatists. For thirteen years, he said (according to Bratislava television, 20 March 1968), a campaign had been waged against Slovak nationalism and when, in 1963–4, this policy was revised, the public, particularly the Czech public, was barely informed of it. Therefore, the lack of understanding persisted, and the Czechs tended to look upon Slovak demands as requests for favoritism and handouts, he told *Lidová demokracie* of 22 March 1968.

Smrkovský, a Czech, confirmed the existence of Czech prejudices and even the reasons given by Husák, pointing out that these prejudices were primarily the result of what he called Czech chauvinism, and of the misconception that matters had been settled by the Košice Program and

---

[1] For a biased but roughly accurate history of the Slovak issue in the 1960s, see Pecho in *Tvorba*, 7–15 October 1969. See also Golan, *The Czechoslovak Reform Movement*.

the economic development of Slovakia.[1] Others pointed out that when one sought to discuss this issue in Prague one was met, at best, with polite but bored tolerance. Many Czechs, because of a lack of understanding, felt that Slovaks were hypersensitive about their rights, a Slovak writer pointed out.[2] This lack of understanding, he explained, was caused by the *absence* of any national feeling on the part of the Czechs: the young Czech was universalist, European, no longer a minority with a 'nationalist' consciousness, no longer confronted in his own lands with other minorities (the Germans having been expelled after World War Two), and, therefore, unaware of the feelings of a nationality group. The underestimation of nationalism as 'beneath the dignity of educated European intellectuals' was termed a 'catastrophic error.' Universalism was a Stalinist distortion of Marxism, full of illusions and 'utopian projects,' the article continued. Such theories or disdain for nationalism simply did not stand up to the test of reality, for today more than ever before nationalist feelings were coming to the fore, even in the freed African states and in the most economically advanced countries. Reality would lead to the conclusion that nationalism was not a phenomenon connected necessarily or exclusively with material, economic, or class factors.

The intention was to redeem nationalism in the eyes of Marxists by returning to the use of Lenin's formulations, dismissing the system used in Czechoslovakia after the Communist takeover as a Stalinist distortion. The national question, it was argued, could be settled in a socialist state only by the use of the Marxist–Leninist recognition of the right to self-determination for all peoples. For example, Slovak economist Pavlenda maintained, in *Pravda* (Bratislava) of 2 March 1968, that the *form* of the solution to nationalist problems might vary with different periods but never the content, i.e. the principle of self-determination. Slovak Party secretary Michal Pecho, in *Predvoj* of 22 February 1968, called 'attempts to suppress, even under socialism, the national interests of a smaller nation' a 'vulgar distortion of the Leninist program.' And Dubček said in his 22 February speech that underestimation of national needs and interests was 'completely contradictory to our Communist internationalism and the necessary awareness and consciousness of the state.' Dubček

[1] Smrkovský, *My 68*, v:4(1968), 7. The Košice Program was the platform of the post-war government, established in 1945 (in Košice) and which, among other things, promised autonomous Slovak organs, while in fact providing the basis for their subordination which followed.

[2] Anton Hykisch, 'The Everyday Routine of the Younger Brother,' *Plamen*, 10:1(1968), 22–9.

argued that national activity need not be divisive, for the more each was allowed to develop according to his own needs and traditions, the more he would feel at home, secure, and satisfied in the mutual state. This attitude was in keeping with Dubček's attitude towards democratization, i.e. only genuine and thorough democratization of the whole country could provide a guarantee for the rights and interests of the individual person or nation.

Some attempted to play down the 'nationalist' connotation of Slovak demands. For example, Husák made a somewhat dubious distinction at the 20 March Prague rally between 'a nationalism which is hostile to another nation and that which is a really justified call for a fresh solution to the relations between our nations.' Bil'ak was hesitant to use the word nationalism at all, and at Banská Bystrica Party conference (*Pravda*, 10 March 1968) he said that nationalism could not become a political platform in a country where the power rests in the hands of the Communists. These reactions must be seen, however, in the context of the political battle being waged within the Party. The conservatives, favoring the maintenance of strong centralized control (less from anti-Slovak sentiments than from the belief in dictatorship from one power center), condemned the Slovak demands as divisive bourgeois nationalism or separatism.[1] Thus the Slovaks had to be careful in using the term nationalism and sought to dissociate their position from any type of non-Marxist, separatist, or fascist nationalism of old.[2]

As to solutions of the Slovak problem, there were basically two alternatives: improvement of the existing system or adoption of a new system based on a new Constitution. The guiding principle of the existing system, at least until the pre-1968 reforms, had been the idea that nationalism was no more than a socio-economic problem; given the social reorganization of society and the economic development of Slovakia, the problem would disappear. The inadequacy of this concept was more or less conceded in the mid-1960s and some progress was made towards recognizing the legitimacy of Slovak political demands.[3] However, despite certain improvements in the status and jurisdiction of the Slovak organs, the basic political–administrative structure of the country remained unchanged.

[1] See, for example, Hagara in *Predvoj*, 8 February 1968.
[2] This included an effort to dissociate Husák from the idea of an independent Slovak state, proclaimed in the Slovak Communist Party program of 1941 and believed to have been supported by Husák as leader of the local Slovak Communists during the war, despite his denials of this charge when arrested in the 1950s. See Golan, *Czechoslovak Reform Movement*, for greater explanation.
[3] See Party resolution, *Rudé právo*, 7 May 1964 and *Sbírka zákonů*, No. 124/1964.

 Political reform and Slovakia

Indeed few were the voices which demanded a new Constitution, as most reformers seemed to hope that Slovak demands could be met merely by better application of the existing Constitutional arrangement.

In early 1968 the existing Constitutional arrangement came under severe criticism from Slovaks. This arrangement was known as the 'asymmetrical' model, since there were central state organs for all of Czechoslovakia, plus Slovak organs, but no counterpart Czech organs. In effect the Czechoslovak organs, based in Prague, provided the expression of Czech as well as state interests in an identity which gave the Czech interests dominance in the all-over state organs, Slovak interests being left to the subordinate Slovak organs. This asymmetrical model thus provided a two-thirds versus one-third rule, which mirrored not only the relative population ratio in Czechoslovakia but the administrative–political–power relationship as well. The socio-cultural sphere was similarly affected, Slovak cultural activities having been reduced to even less than a one-third proportion. The asymmetrical model had meant no more than Prague centralism, not unlike the practice of 'Czechoslovakism' in the pre-war Republic, which sought to build a new nation, at the expense, it was felt by the Slovaks, of Slovak national identity.[1]

Thus, it was pointed out, the Slovak organs had been gradually deprived of their rights from 1948 onwards, and, as Husák told the Prague rally, the Slovak National Council became 'a mere stage-prop' without right or means to govern; it had neither executive nor legislative nor judiciary powers. The 1960 Constitution abolished the Board of Commissioners of the Slovak National Council, thus eliminating the executive power of the SNC. The SNC lost control over the National Committees in Slovakia, when the latter were put under direct state control from Prague. The SNC, according to economist Viktor Pavlenda in *Pravda* (Bratislava), 12 March 1968, 'similarly lost its authority over the majority of other institutions in Slovakia, and where some authority was left, it was rather formal because the Slovak National Council did not have financial means to put its plans into effect.' The injustice of this situation was recognized by Prague in 1963–4, but, as Slovak historian Felix Vašečka pointed out, the agreement worked out then to expand the authority of the Slovak organs *was not embodied in the Constitution.*

In the search for a new solution the old Košice Program and the ideas accompanying its birth were analyzed once again. The Košice Program had indeed provided a good deal of the conditions demanded by the

[1] See, for example, *Pravda* (Bratislava), 6 and 12 March 1968; *Práca*, 11 March 1968; 2 April 1968; Hykisch, *Plamen*, 10:1 (1968).

Slovaks, particularly the recognition of Slovak sovereignty and the right to self-government. There were those who said that the problem was that this program had simply not been implemented, finally to be discarded even officially by the 1960 Constitution.[1] It was pointed out by others, however, that contrary to Slovak proposals and wishes, the Košice Program had in fact introduced the asymmetrical model. According to several historians, including the Czech Milan Hübl, it had been agreed in the 1943 talks in Moscow that there be equality of the two nations, i.e. Czech rule for Bohemia and Moravia (through the existing Czech National Council) and Slovak rule for Slovakia (through a Slovak National Council), with a common federal government and parliament.[2] According to Hübl, Beneš and the Czech National Socialists opposed this idea, and a compromise, proposed by Gottwald, was eventually accepted whereby Czech affairs would be handled directly by the Czechoslovak organs, though maintaining the Slovak National Council.[3] According to some Slovak Communist historians, for example Samo Falt'an, writing in *Rudé právo*, 8 April 1968, this compromise had been considered unsatisfactory, and it was expected that the Communist takeover in 1948 would bring about a full federal arrangement. Instead, however, the opposite direction was taken and even the positive points of the Košice Program were watered down until Slovak authority in Slovakia was dissipated and centralism opposed.

Husák confirmed that he and his colleagues had wanted a federal model in 1944–5 and he told a *Lidová demokracie* (22 March 1968) interviewer: 'In Slovakia opinion is unambiguously in favor of a federal solution.' The appearance of demands and proposals for a new Constitution based on a symmetrical model confirmed Husák's statement, though such demands were, upon occasion, from Czechs as well as Slovaks.[4] Hübl, and Husák, pointed to both Yugoslavia and the Soviet Union as models that might be copied in Czechoslovakia, although these models were criticized by Slovak economist Pavlenda on the grounds that they did not provide

---

[1] Jisl in *Reportér*, 28 February 1968; Prague radio, 20 March 1968 (Husák to Prague rally).

[2] *Pravda* (Bratislava), 6 March 1968; *Práce*, 21 February 1968 (Hübl); *Práca*, 2 April 1968; *Lidová demokracie*, 22 March 1968 (Husák).

[3] To prove National Socialist opposition to federation (and therefore the undesirability of additional parties), *Pravda* (Bratislava) published the National Socialists' 1946 proposals on the Slovak issue contained in a memorandum sent by the party to Gottwald in 1946 (29 March 1968).

[4] See, for example, *Práce*, 21 February 1968 (Hübl); *Rudé právo*, 4 April 1968 (Smrkovský to April plenum).

thorough symmetry, e.g. in economic affairs as well.[1] Neither model was widely discussed, however, and certain characteristics were overlooked. For example, while maintaining the structure and some practices of a federal system, the Yugoslavs had tried to solve their own chronic nationalities problem by bypassing, at least theoretically, the central and even national republic authorities and placing authority in the lower organs of self-government (the communes or even workers councils). The fact that this system had not solved the Yugoslav nationalities' problem may be the reason it was not widely discussed in Czechoslovakia. It may also have appeared too drastic a change for the Slovaks, who were seeking national self-expression rather than the dissipation of national units as such.

The demands for federation envisaged not only federalization of the Communist Party but also reinstatement of the Czech National Council and federalization of all the organs of the state, social organizations, and institutions. Each nation might have its own legislative body, and the Federal legislature would have to submit its laws for approval by the national legislatures, according to the suggestion of the Bratislava (Komenský) University Law Faculty contained in a *Pravda* (Bratislava) editorial of 10 March 1968. The creation of a second chamber in the Federal legislature based on equal representation of the two nationalities was also part of this suggestion. The Federal legislature would have its powers clearly defined by the Constitution, these being limited to fundamental questions of economic policy, defense, and foreign policy. Husák mentioned that one should not be afraid of returning the Slovaks the right to their flag, while many urged equality for Slovaks in the diplomatic service, the Army and security forces, and so forth.[2] Hübl said that Slovaks should be permitted to hold even the highest state and Party functions, although neither Czechs nor Slovaks should be permitted to monopolize all the top jobs at one time. The Slovak National Council Presidium endorsed these demands in a resolution calling for federation (carried by *Pravda* (Bratislava), 15 March 1968). It also decided to recall Michal Chudík as SNC chairman. Chudík was not only a Novotný man, often suggested by the latter as a replacement for Dubček in the Slovak leadership, but an opponent of federation as well.

[1] *Kultúrny život*, 23 February 1968 (Husák); *Práce*, 21 February 1968 (Hübl); *Pravda* (Bratislava), 12 March 1968 (Pavlenda).

[2] Bratislava television, 20 March 1968 (Husák) and Bratislava radio, 11 March 1968 (Gašparík); *Smena*, 24 March 1968 (Foreign Ministry answer came in *Pravda* (Bratislava), 12 April 1968).

Both the SNC presidium resolution and the earlier *Pravda* editorial–Law Faculty proposals called for a Constitutional Law pending a new Constitution (preferably to be worked out by 1970). This law, they said, should provide, first, greater authority for the Slovak organs, with control of the National Committees in Slovakia; secondly, approval of the economic plan and control of the budget designed for Slovakia; thirdly, a Slovak branch of the Supreme Court for cases contested in Slovak courts (the position of the Slovak deputy to the Prosecutor-General should also be clarified); fourthly, the Board of Commissioners to be reestablished as the Slovak executive body with commissioners' offices as executive organs; fifthly, an increase in the number of Slovak Commissioners, including an Interior Commissioner corresponding to the Interior Ministry; and finally, the creation of 'Secretaries of State' in all state bodies which did not have Slovak counterparts.[1]

One dilemma was the economic arrangement of the country, for federation might imply two independent economies. While not opposing integration of the economies, the Slovak economists' association favored national responsibility in the economic sphere as well.[2] One Slovak pointed out, in *Práca* of 2 April, however, that the socialist model was an improvement over the 'old classic bourgeois federation' precisely because it provided for state-wide direction of the economy. The same Slovak feared 'dualism' also in the area of civil and criminal law, and said that the Federal government would have to have responsibility for more than defense, foreign affairs, and currency.

There were also demands for the creation of separate Moravian and Bohemian organs on the grounds that these were two separate 'lands.' These proposals came mainly from Brno, which sought to assert Moravian rights vis-à-vis Bohemia. The South Moravian regional National Committee actually passed a resolution calling for a tripartite arrangement, suggesting Moravia–Silesia as a third 'land' (according to *Práce*, 18 April 1968). The Silesians, however, demanded their own province with a capital in Opava, a university, and the Silesian district borders which existed prior to the 1960 administrative reform.[3] It was pointed out, however, that these demands called for a geographic division of the

---

[1] Some of the above were included in the 1964 SNC law but were now to be given force of Constitutional Law pending the new Constitution. Bratislava had been raised to the status of a region and capital of Slovakia and the SNC was given jurisdiction over funds allotted Slovakia by the State budget, by decisions in January 1968.

[2] See chapter 2.

[3] *Lidová demokracie*, 4 May 1968.

Republic – something entirely different from the *national* division demanded by the Slovaks.[1]

The Party's Action Program declared that the asymmetrical model 'was in itself incapable of expressing and ensuring Constitutional relations between two people with equal rights.' It explained that the efforts made in 1964 to expand the rights of the Slovak organs could not suffice because the asymmetrical model (and 'unhealthy elements in the political atmosphere') had prevailed. In keeping with the Slovak demands, the Action Program called for a Constitutional Law, in time for the next elections, along the lines suggested by the SNC presidium, until the federal settlement could be worked out in a new Constitution. One clause of the Action Program called for a safeguard against majority-rule decisions in matters concerning Czech–Slovak relations or the Constitutional position of Slovakia. This presumably meant a return to the provision of the 1946 Constitutional Act whereby any Constitutional decision regarding Slovakia needed 'the consent of the majority of the present members of the Constituent Assembly elected in Slovakia,' or something similar to this.[2] There was nothing in the Action Program regarding structural changes in the National Assembly, which in fact did come with the January 1969 federalization of the country. Moreover, although the Action Program recognized the injustice of the asymmetrical model and the fact that the Czech lands were ruled directly by the central organs ('which as all-state organs were superior to the Slovak organs'), it did not clearly state the need to create Czech organs as counterparts of the Slovak organs. Thus, despite the condemnation of the asymmetrical system, the only reference made to a model for the new arrangement was a reference to the Košice Program.

The Slovaks had already expressed their desire for more than a return to the Košice Program, and many were apprehensive that the regime did not intend to set up a genuine symmetrical model (with counterpart Czech organs). Some even claimed that the Czechs were deliberately delaying, if not obstructing, a fair solution. Slovak philosopher Jan Uher, for example, warned that an attempt to remedy the situation by some sort of improvement of the asymmetrical model would be 'playing with fire,' while former Slovak Writers Union chairman Mihálik alerted a Slovak Party central committee meeting to 'a certain prevarication on this [federation] question' in the Czech lands.[3] Slovak intellectual Milan

[1] See *Lidová demokracie*, 22 April 1968 (interview with Viktor Knapp).
[2] *Sbírka zákonů*, No. 65/1946.
[3] *Kultúrny život*, 12 April 1968 (Uher); *Pravda* (Bratislava), 18 April 1968.

Holub said that in response to the fears expressed by many Slovaks he decided to interview the liberal, Czech, Party presidium member František Kriegel. Kriegel, as quoted by Holub in *Predvoj* of 18 April 1968, said that he favored federation, but ' "we shall certainly not set up a Czech National Council or any similar agency...You can set up your own agencies and ministries, but what we do in the Czech lands is our own concern." ' Holub interjected: 'It would have been presumptuous for a young Communist journalist to explain to such a high official that the matter concerns both nations, that federation implies the establishment of parallel legislative and executive bodies on both sides, with a central authority if possible denied the power of making majority decisions, over them.' Kriegel, according to Holub, went on to say that the creation of Czech agencies would be contrary to Czech traditions and involve too many new offices and civil servants. Holub termed as 'two-facedness' this approval of only those practical measures which would merely expand the asymmetrical model, and he likened such thinking to the failure of the April Party plenum, which had approved the Action Program, to discuss the federation idea originally on its agenda.

Possibly in reaction to this interview, or to other similar statements, another Slovak journalist, *Rol'nícke noviny* editor Marian Sklenka, on 20 April condemned the tendency in Prague to preserve the asymmetrical model. He warned that if the delaying tactics in Prague continued, 'very little would be left to us Slovaks but to realize our demands ourselves... even if this means separation and foundation of an independent socialist state.' This was the first time in this discussion that a Slovak organ (the daily of the SNC's agricultural commission) raised such a suggestion, claiming it to be 'in harmony with Marxist–Leninist theory on national policy,' though it was to be considered only as a last resort. The same article spoke of written guarantees of equality, 'if the Slovaks give up their rights to form an independent state and agree to remain with the Czechs in a common state,' thereby asserting the Slovaks' right to independence and the need to give this idea serious consideration. Another Slovak daily, *Práca*, published a rebuttal two days later, calling for recognition of the limits of even democratic discussions: 'let nobody touch something as sacred as the inviolability of the unity of our State.' As might have been expected, *Práca* dismissed the idea of independence by use of the example of the fascist Slovak state of World War Two. The Slovak agricultural daily, however, condemned this as 'demagoguery,' saying that it was obvious that creation of a 'Ludák' Slovak state was hardly meant, pointing out that even *Rudé právo* had once recently expressed understanding of the possibility of a Slovak demand for an independent socialist, Marxist state ' "in view of the experiences of the Slovaks with Prague centralism." '[1] The daily then published a letter supporting the idea of an independent state as one of the possibilities to be held in reserve, if a mutually and equally advantageous solution could not be found.

The ever-present threat of separation remained, though it was never accorded as much prominence as in this decisive early period when the work on the new Constitutional arrangement was begun. On 29 May an article in the Czechoslovak Film and Television Artists Union journal criticized Czech intellectuals for concentrating on democratization to the exclusion of concern for the federation issue. It stated that federation was so much a part of Slovak demands that 'any wheeling-dealing or half-hearted measures on this question would have consequences so grave in Slovakia that they would probably lead to a break-up of the republic.' As late as 2 August, *Kultúrny život* editor, the liberal Communist Pavol Števček, called for a recognition of the one occasion upon which the Slovaks had had independence (1939–45). Števček conceded that this Slovak state had been an instrument of 'Big Power manipulation' which 'brought to the surface only the scum of what is in the Slovak nation.' He maintained, however, that it was important to realize that 'the idea or recollection of the Slovak state's independence is alive in the national memory. It cannot be ignored forever in examining the alternatives in the solution of the perspectives of a small nation.'

Another alternative touched on was that of confederation. Although not accorded much consideration as an end in itself, it was proposed at least as an intermediary step towards federation.[2] One journalist, Michal Nadubinský in *Smena* of 23 April 1968, believed that the atmosphere and heritage of mistrust and animosity was such that federation might result in difficulties over jobs, equal representation, economic matters and so forth. He, therefore, suggested that prior to federation each nation must learn to stand on its own feet, including in the economic sector. This would mean a period of loose confederation of two fully independent states in which each would prove that it could exist on its own, so that mutual suspicion might be converted to mutual esteem. Slovak writer Mihálik also, on at least one occasion, proposed a 'Czechoslovak confederation of two socialist republics, one Czech and one Slovak.'[3] He

[1] *Rol'nícke noviny*, 27 April 1968. The reference was to *Rudé právo*, 16 March 1968 (article by Jan Šindelka).
[2] See, for example, discussion in *Reportér*, 7 August 1968.
[3] *Predvoj*, 18 April 1968 (speech in *Pravda* (Bratislava), 9 April 1968).

called only for 'coordination' of such matters as defense and foreign affairs, with no mention of economic matters. Generally the term confederation was not used, but it was indeed difficult to determine just how independent the Slovaks intended their government to be within the proposed federation. Most indications were that, no matter what term they used, the Slovaks wanted a loose federation which would accord the component parts the authority granted in such confederative arrangements as the Swiss model.

Not only Czechs were criticized for neglecting the idea of federation, however. As we have seen the Slovak Writers Union underwent a crisis over this issue when a number of the more nationalist members left the Union's weekly and revived Husák's old journal *Nové slovo*. *Kultúrny život* was accused of placing its emphasis on democracy rather than federation or on the idea that the latter could not be obtained without the former.[1] Together with this dispute came claims from some Slovaks that Slovak leaders were emphasizing federation to the exclusion of pressing for a democratization of Slovakia itself. This contention was sufficiently widespread for Slovak Party organs to feel it necessary on a number of occasions to explain their efforts in the direction of democratization. They emphasized, especially, their previous efforts in this direction, claiming that this early start had reduced the tasks awaiting the Slovaks after January 1968.[2]

Demands for the speedy settlement of the federation issue led to the foundation of a government committee for the drafting of a Constitutional Law and the working out of the political aspects of a federal arrangement. A sub-committee for special problems, headed by Husák, began its work on 21 May 1968, and a draft bill was to be submitted to the National Assembly on the fiftieth anniversary of the Republic, 28 October 1968. On 29 May Dubček outlined to the central committee the arrangement envisaged under the new law.[3] There would be autonomous organs for both nations, including governmental, political, and social organs. This meant both the creation of Czech organs and the federalization of the Party, which was to be worked out at the extraordinary Party congress planned by this time for 9 September 1968. It was expected that the federalization of the Party would follow the same

[1] See, for example, Milan Šimeček, 'Why are Czech Intellectuals Silent,' *Filmové a televizní noviny*, II:11 (1968), 8; *Reportér*, 15 May 1968.
[2] *Pravda* (Bratislava), 10 April 1968 (Bil'ak to Slovak central committee plenum); *Kultúrny život*, 5 April 1968 (Strinka).
[3] *Rok šedesátý osmý*, 193–4.

lines as that of the state. Aside from the fact that economic matters would be handled by the central government, the actual scope of the all-state organs (either of the Party or the government) was not explained by Dubček. At this plenum the central committee urged the creation of a government committee to set up Czech national organs, and a Czech commission of the Party to aid in working out the federalization of the Party.[1] From this resolution there eventually emerged the provisional Czech National Council, under Čestmír Císař.

The new arrangement would mean some change in the administrative organization of the state, for the regional level of government would be superfluous once a national level was created for each of the two nations, over the existing districts. The desired development would be the upgrading of the district National Committees, in order to bridge the gap that would be left by the elimination of the regional National Committees, without, however, expanding the number of districts.[2] One of the problems created by this plan was that the position of Moravia would be 'downgraded' when in fact the Moravians were interested in becoming equal components of the federation. In response, the South Moravian regional committee at Brno resolved a second time, on 5 June, in favor of a tripartite federal arrangement with equal status for a Moravian–Silesian republic. The North Moravian region (Ostrava), however, resolved in favor of a nationally based federation of the two nations – Czech lands and Slovakia.[3] Brno's position was rejected by the commission instituting the federal arrangement (and apparently by the Party as well) as a purely territorial settlement of what was in fact a national issue. The status of Moravia, it was argued, might be worked out within the Czech set-up.[4] It was natural that the Slovaks would oppose a tripartite arrangement, for that would have had the effect of perpetuating the former two-thirds Czech or asymmetrical model. Their argument in favor of a solution along national lines was countered by the Moravians' sense of the traditional cultural importance of Brno as the capital of a former 'land' within the Austro-Hungarian Empire.

The above plan would also, most probably, have meant a denial of

[1] Ibid. 223–4. The 27 June 1968 session of the National Assembly resolved to elect 150 Czech National Council members on 10 July 1968 (Prague radio, 27 June 1968), which it did.

[2] Husák revealed that some sixty requests for the creation of new districts had been received from areas dissatisfied with the arbitrary reduction of districts and regrouping of the 1960 territorial reorganization. (*Reportér*, 26 June 1968 (interview with Husák).)

[3] Ibid. and Prague radio, 5 June 1968.

[4] *Rudé právo*, 6 June 1968 (Smrkovský to May plenum).

various national minorities' demands for autonomous districts. Husák, however, when interviewed on the work of his commission, conceded no more than a certain improvement of the minority nationalities' position and rights, although he defended these rights against infringements by the nine-tenths Czech–Slovak majority of the country. The solution in this matter, as finally introduced by the Constitutional Law passed in October 1968, accorded *every* nationality the right to schools in their native tongue, the right to address officials in their native tongue, the right to national–cultural associations, and the right to their own press.[1] They were not, however, granted self-government or autonomous districts, as many of them had demanded.

The federal arrangement given the most attention called for a bicameral Federal parliament: one chamber elected on the basis of one-man, one-vote from the whole country; the second chamber a House of Nations, composed of equal representatives from the Czech lands and Slovakia. Bills would need approval by both chambers. This was apparently a compromise worked out after a stalemate in Husák's commission over the one-man, one-vote principle advocated by some Czech representatives.[2] The suggested creation of state secretaries in addition to ministers in all Federal organs was also considered. The Federal government would be responsible for foreign policy, foreign trade, defense, economic policy, finance, and other areas to be worked out. The arrangement introduced by the Constitutional Law of October 1968 adopted the bicameral arrangement and gave the Federal government exclusive jurisdiction in the areas of defense, foreign policy, material resources of the country, and protection of the Federal Constitution.[3] The Federal authorities were to share their responsibility with the national organs in the spheres of economic planning, currency, prices, transport, industry, agriculture and food, posts, labor, wage and welfare policies, security, press and other information matter. Other matters, such as legislation on association, assembly, education, civil and penal law, religion and certain other areas, would also fall under Federal jurisdiction, although the central organs might delegate these powers to the national parliaments.

It is difficult to determine if the post-invasion provisions were in fact

---

[1] *Sbírka zákonů*, No. 144/1968.

[2] Bratislava radio, 5 July 1968. Husák, at a Bratislava Party conference, employed this crisis as a reason for convoking an extraordinary Slovak Party congress, *before* the fourteenth congress rather than after as previously decided. (Slovak Party central committee decision, 20 June 1968, *Pravda* (Bratislava), 22 June 1968.) For the Czech view see ČTK, 6 July 1968, Bohumil Šimon speech to a Prague Party conference.

[3] *Sbírka zákonů*, No. 143/1968.

identical to the law envisaged by the pre-invasion committee. The new law seriously limited the legislative authority of the national organs, granting these organs extensive executive powers in return. While the nations each had their own court system, the Constitutional Court was federal, meaning that the central court could determine the Constitutionality of laws passed by the national courts. While the Constitutional Law was promulgated on time, probably indicating a Soviet desire to woo the Slovaks, and their leader Gustav Husák, in hopes of splitting the reform forces, some of the powers demanded by the Slovaks were left to the Federal authorities and a relatively centralist document passed after all. Subsequent practice, at least, followed this pattern.

9

Political Reform and Foreign Policy

Foreign policy was never a major concern of the reform movement, though foreign policy considerations, including relations with the international Communist movement, came in for scrutiny once the reformers came to power. To a large extent the new-found interest was a result of outside pressures, primarily from the Soviet Union, which prompted Czechoslovak pronouncements and actions which may not otherwise have appeared. It is indeed difficult to judge what turns Czechoslovak foreign policy might have taken over the years had the Soviet Union refrained from interfering, although one might argue that such interference was inevitable given the nature of the reform movement in Czechoslovakia. Insofar as it is possible, however, we shall try to distinguish between the foreign policies advocated by the reform and those demands which developed as a result of the outside pressures.

From the outset the new regime declared that there would be no change in Czechoslovakia's system of alliances, and the reform leadership maintained this position to the end. In his brief speech to the central committee plenum which elected him, Dubček clearly stated his continued loyalty to and belief in the 'socialist principles of internationalism' and the firm link with the Soviet Union.[1] A few days later, on 10 January 1968, *Rudé právo* scoffed at any idea of change in the 'decisive features' of Czechoslovak foreign policy, especially the alliance with the Soviet Union and relations with the two Germanies. Nevertheless, on 17 January it published an editorial which contained a number of formulations new in tone if not in substance, in speaking of the then forthcoming Budapest consultative meeting for the preparation of an international Communist conference. In language that was new for Prague, it referred to the absolute independence and sovereignty of each Party with regard to internal affairs, emphasizing the need for a democratic formulation of bloc unity, and the legitimacy of differences of opinion *and* of policies, as a result of specific conditions in each country. Thus there was the hint that Prague would demand a change in inner-bloc relations, a change which would grant equality of status and freedom of action, *within the socialist alliance*, for the pursuit of internal policies.

[1] *Rok šedesátý osmý*, 6.

This idea was spelled out in an article by Jan Mentel in the Ministry of Defense journal *A-revue* in January 1968. Mentel criticized the idea of laying down one line for the whole movement and sympathetically described the conviction of several Parties, specifically the Italian Communist Party, that each Party had to mould its policies to its own specific conditions. His conclusion was that

'the old type of relationship – which was covered in the documents issued in 1957 and 1960 – is no longer applicable...After all, the 20th Congress of the CPSU condemned monolithism in the international Communist movement and clearly indicated that the period of a leading Party and a leading state is passed.'

Mentel also implicitly criticized the USSR for continuing to champion the 1957 and 1960 documents, which, as he pointed out, proclaimed a non-existent unity, condemned Yugoslavia, and failed to take into consideration either local conditions or other progressive though non-Communist forces. A further sign that these were not simply isolated articles was a commentary on Prague radio, on 18 February, which singled out Romania for supporting the idea of diversity and equality as distinct from one Party's holding 'a privileged position.' This commentary condemned, as Stalinism, the demand for subservience of Parties to the CPSU, though in a more cautious vein it did add that the Soviet Union no longer demanded hegemony. Nonetheless, the radio advocated a 'revision' of the old documents and ideas, calling for a voluntary unity which respected the 'differences and national peculiarities, interests, and needs' of the various Parties.

While these comments were concerned with the nature of relations within the alliance, an article, though less authoritative than the above, appeared in the youth daily *Mladá fronta* on 14 February, which dealt with the specific (and delicate) issue of relations with West Germany. The article called for a 'normalization' of relations with Bonn, the very term used by Novotný a few years earlier when he was seeking an agreement with Bonn along the lines of the Polish–West Germany trade agreement of 1964. Novotný's efforts, born principally of economic demands, had been dropped, partially due to Soviet compliance with East German objections, partially due to what seemed to be West German ambivalence as well. Only after Poland and Hungary had improved their relations with Bonn, and Romania had actually opened diplomatic relations with West Germany, did Czechoslovakia sign a limited trade agreement in 1967. A reopening of the efforts to improve relations with West Germany was now demanded, on the grounds that changes had occurred in Bonn.

Mladá fronta argued that Bonn's new Eastern policy, which had led to improved relations with Bucharest and Belgrade, was in fact a concession which placed *East* Germany in a better position, for it meant the abandonment of the Hallstein Doctrine. Černík too, according to the Bavarian radio, 7 February 1968, had implied a renewed interest in West Germany when, on the occasion of the ratification of the 1967 trade agreement, he termed the treaty 'an important step towards the normalization of relations' with West Germany.

Dubček outlined the general lines of the foreign policy he envisaged for his regime on the occasion of the anniversary of the 1948 coup. Reiterating Czechoslovakia's continued friendship and alliance with the Soviet Union, Dubček nonetheless emphasized that relations with the socialist bloc must be 'based on the principles of equal rights, mutual advantage, respect,' though he ended this list with the familiar expression of 'firm international solidarity.'[1] While in fact he said little more on relations within the bloc, he did imply that 'specific conditions' must be taken into consideration. He also said that Czechoslovakia had the task, in the international movement, of demonstrating the possibilities for socialism in an economically and culturally mature country. This reference to Czechoslovakia's implicitly unique attributes in the Communist world was offered in direct support of the idea that Czechoslovakia might, therefore, forge its own way to socialism. Another idea introduced by Dubček in the same speech was Czechoslovakia's interest in Europe 'in the center of which our country is located.' He said that a normalization of relations with the countries of Europe – regardless of social systems – and cooperation between states were to be goals actively pursued in Prague's foreign policy. Concerning West Germany, however, Dubček maintained the earlier line on revanchism in Bonn and unflagging loyalty to the GDR.

In subsequent weeks the continuation of the alliance with the Soviet Union and the Warsaw Pact was advocated on a number of grounds. Some referred to being realistic, specifically with regard to geography; others emphasized Czechoslovakia's desire to be socialist and, therefore, part of the socialist camp; others, including Smrkovský on at least one occasion, emphasized the need for an ally against revanchist plans in Bonn.[2] Nonetheless, there were those who asked that this alliance be placed on a more voluntary basis with the character of an equal partner-

[1] *Rudé právo*, 23 February 1968 (22 February 1968 speech).
[2] ASHAI (Tokyo), 22 March 1968, (Goldstücker interview); *Pravda* (Bratislava), 21 March 1968; Prague radio, 25 February 1968; and Prague radio, 20 March 1968 (Smrkovský at Prague rally).

ship.[1] A Prague radio commentary on 7 March ventured the opinion that if the Soviet Union were unwilling to commit itself to nuclear defense of her allies, Czechoslovakia might be wise to reconsider the nature of her commitment to the Warsaw Pact in much the way De Gaulle had reconsidered his commitment to NATO. Goldstücker called for an independent diplomatic policy while not forgetting 'our realistic foundation, that is the Warsaw Pact.' Miroslav Galuška expressed the belief that one could remain faithful allies of the Soviet Union without abandoning the right to one's own foreign policy. In this regard he mentioned the likelihood of a resumption of relations of Czechoslovakia with Israel.[2] This same issue was raised in a Prague radio commentary, 25 February 1968, which urged a rethinking of Czechoslovakia's foreign commitments and policies so as not to be in the position of supporting nations which were not 'friendly to our ideas and permanent interests' or, more explicitly, sought to 'destroy some state and massacre its citizens.' This same commentary said: 'who can decide today whether justice is on the side of the Nigerian Government or on the side of Biafra?' Commentators began to speak also of a 'return to Europe,' calling it foolish to ignore the tendency in Western Europe to improve relations with the socialist countries.[3] It was argued that improved relations with Western Europe would 'restrict the chances of anti-communism' there, not fortify them, if one were to seek not only improved state relations but also closer collaboration with Western 'Marxist' parties, trade unions, and 'the European socialist tradition.'[4] In this spirit, recognition of and cooperation with progressive elements in Bonn was urged.[5]

Within the international Communist movement itself, Czechoslovakia showed signs of a more independent attitude in two specific matters. At the Warsaw Pact meeting in Sofia in early March, Dubček referred to Romania's reservations about the non-proliferation treaty as 'not unrealistic,' according to Bratislava radio, 8 March 1968. At the Budapest consultative meeting preparatory to the world conference, the Czechoslovak delegation led by conservative Vladimír Koucký, dissociated itself from the anti-Yugoslav aspects of the 1957 and 1960 Moscow declara-

---

[1] For example, commentary, Prague radio, 25 February 1968; *Pravda* (Bratislava), 21 March 1968.

[2] Prague radio, 20 March 1968 (Prague rally). This response was greeted with prolonged applause.

[3] See *Pravda* (Bratislava), 21 March 1968 or Šimeček, in *Kultúrny život*, 15 March 1968.

[4] Ibid. and *Rudé právo*, 22 March 1968.   [5] *Rudé právo*, 16 March 1968.

tions.[1] While this was in keeping with the general Soviet–Yugoslav détente, it was nonetheless a unique action at the meeting.[2]

These and similar statements did not go unnoticed in the rest of Eastern Europe. The Yugoslavs commented favorably that 'new ideas have also penetrated the foreign policy of Czechoslovakia and the international activity of the Party which, together with the state, wished to enjoy greater freedom of action in foreign and bloc policy.'[3] The Soviet Union and some of its allies also deduced this, for, although far from the major reason, Czechoslovakia's attitude towards its alliances was at least part of the reason Dubček was called to account at a meeting in Dresden on 23 March 1968. Romania, an advocate of liberalization of the Warsaw Pact and the prime example of independent foreign policy within the bloc, was not invited.[4] The suggestions heard in Czechoslovakia, however, had centered on the nature of the alliance rather than the fact of the alliance itself, and it was to be expected that Dubček would once again pledge loyalty to the Warsaw Pact. A disturbing sign, however, and one probably designed to bring direct controls on Czechoslovakia, was the reference in the Dresden communique to 'practical measures in the immediate future to consolidate the Warsaw Pact and its armed forces,' according to TASS, 24 March 1968. The reference was to a strengthening of the political consultative committee of the Pact, which might serve as the missing coordinating–controlling instrument for the Soviet Union. The idea was not new and the Romanians had been fighting it for some time with their own counter-proposals for liberalization and rotation of command.[5] In an interview upon his return from Dresden, Dubček intimated that only military coordination was intended in the strengthening of centralization of the Pact.[6] As to other aspects of Czechoslovak moves in the foreign policy sphere, e.g. efforts to improve relations with Western Europe, specifically West Germany, the worried allies were able to get

[1] Prague radio, 1 March 1968.

[2] Foreign Minister Hájek reportedly suggested improved relations with China but the Party presidium feared Soviet reaction.

[3] *Nedeljne informativne noviny* (Belgrade), 17 March 1968.

[4] Presumably Romania was not invited also because of her strong objections to outside interference in a country's internal affairs.

[5] This issue was one of the reasons for the Sofia meeting in early March, where it was decided to refer the issue, for six months' study, to the countries involved. The Dresden meeting would appear to have ignored this decision and gone ahead without Romania. (See Agerpres (Bucharest), 27 April 1968 (Ceausescu speech).)

[6] ČTK, 26 March 1968.

Dubček to agree to derogatory mention of Bonn in the communique, though apparently no promises were extracted.

In response to the Dresden meeting, such leaders as Císař and Goldstücker again expounded the inviolability of Prague's ties with the Soviet alliance system, despite accusations to the contrary, particularly from East Germany.[1] At the same time, however, Císař emphasized the principle of equality and sovereignty, and Smrkovský went further when he told the April plenum that 'our relations to the socialist camp and the rest of the world cannot be based on any principle other than that of mutual respect for national independence and state sovereignty.' Bohumil Šimon in *Večerní Praha* of 5 April 1968 added the idea that economic relations need not always follow political orientations of foreign policies or alliances. Another sign that the reformers were not silenced by Dresden was an article by the more radical philosopher Ivan Sviták in *Student*, 10 April, condemning the subservience of Czechoslovak foreign policy to the Soviet line. Sviták pointed to the dangerous manifestations of this, e.g. 'the sincere statements of support for the fascist-like Arab regimes of Nasser's type... The supply of war material, financed so readily by irretrievable credits, [which] directly served Arab imperialist policies.'

There were also suggestions regarding the formulation of foreign policy, such as a *Mladá fronta* article of 25 March which demanded that the Party also withdraw from this area. The paper claimed that while Dubček urged an 'active' foreign policy and the Communists of the Foreign Ministry a 'Czechoslovak' foreign policy, one must also have a 'democratized' foreign policy. The government and the elected organs, particularly the National Assembly foreign relations committee, should have their proper say in the determination of foreign policy. The population too should be permitted a voice, through discussion and meetings, dependent, of course, on the free flow of information. The paper bemoaned the fact that the population had been kept ignorant of developments in China, Romania, Cuba, and problems in CEMA. It called for freedom for commentators, editors, and the plain citizen to air their views in the mass media instead of the situation wherein even an attempt to explain, for example, the complex situation in the Middle East could bring upon an editor any number of accusations and reprimands – if not worse.

The Party's Action Program, approved just one week after the Dresden meeting, responded to these demands. It categorically declared that Czechoslovakia '*will formulate its own stand on basic issues of world policy*, based on the actual relations of international forces and on our awareness

[1] Prague radio, 8 April 1968 (Císař); *Volkstimme* (Vienna), 7 April 1968 (Goldstücker).

that our own stand is an active component of the revolutionary process in the world.' Only after stating this principle did the Program assert that the fundamental orientation of policy would be based on the alliance with the Soviet Union and the other socialist states. While expressing the goal of deepening ties and cooperation with the other socialist states, CEMA, and the Warsaw Pact, the Program proclaimed that the basis for these strengthened relations must be 'mutual respect, sovereignty, equality of rights, mutual esteem,' and only last in this list, 'international solidarity.'[1] A new formulation also appeared with regard to the developing countries. While Prague was to continue to participate in the struggle against imperialism or neo-colonialism, aid to these struggles would be 'within the limits of [Czechoslovakia's] ability and opportunities.' In this same context the Program condemned 'American aggression' in Vietnam but was unusually mild with regard to the Middle East, saying only that Prague would 'strive for a political solution to the Middle East crisis.' More explicit was the reference to the need for a 'more active European policy,' given Czechoslovakia's geographic position, and needs and opportunities as an industrial country. The Program stated that this would mean improved and increased relations with the countries of Western Europe – including 'the realistic forces in the German Federal Republic' (though not at the expense of 'the first socialist state on German soil,' the GDR) – and international organizations. The statement regarding Europe merely reflected Dubček's own numerous references to Czechoslovakia's position in the center of Europe and the need to give this position greater attention. The German statement, however, coming after Dresden, demonstrated Dubček's determination not to be intimidated. The Program gave due praise to East Germany and did mention neo-Nazi and revanchist trends in West Germany, but the reference to the latter came only *after* the stated intention of supporting the 'realistic' forces in Bonn. The other aspect of the 'return to Europe' idea was also supported by the Program, which advocated greater contacts and cooperation with all the progressive forces abroad.

The Action Program thus seemed to promise that Czechoslovak foreign policy would henceforth be more in keeping with the desires and needs of the Czechoslovak public. It went so far as to state that this would be the regime's goal, for it favored the 'democratization' advocated earlier. The Program called for initiative on the part of the Foreign Ministry, the National Assembly and its foreign relations committee, and the Party

---

[1] Emphasis mine. In his speech to the April plenum, Dubček had said 'based on principles of equality, mutual benefit, non-interference, and international solidarity.' (*Rudé právo*, 2 April 1968.)

central committee (as a larger body than the small group which had hithertofore determined foreign policy). Moreover, it called for dissemination of information concerning international relations so as to provide the public with the necessary tools for active participation in the formulation of policy.

The Action Program may have been the last official foreign policy declaration which could be considered uninfluenced by the growing pressures from the Soviet Union and other East European countries. The even tone of this document suggested that this was the policy guideline the new regime had decided upon before the Dresden meeting. From April onwards, however, the pressures were such that one could no longer be sure if Czechoslovak statements were merely reactions to these pressures or genuine expressions of the program adopted by the reformers. As pressures grew Prague's reaction was both to reaffirm its devotion to its allies and to emphasize, increasingly, the principles of sovereignty, equality, non-interference in internal affairs, and 'many roads to socialism.' The two were not contradictory; they were indeed designed to reassure Prague's allies that they had nothing to fear from Czechoslovakia, for the latter was merely pursuing her own way to socialism within the overall framework of her alliance system.

Not all statements concerning non-interference, independent foreign policy, and the nature of the alliance with the Soviet Union were prompted only by the growth of outside pressures. There were demands for placing economic relations with the USSR on such a basis that Czechoslovakia would not be dependent and thus subservient to any one camp or country. A demand reminiscent of Yugoslavia *circa* 1947–8 called for the removal of another element of Soviet control, Soviet advisors, and the secret talks between Czechoslovak and Soviet statesmen in which Czechoslovakia received policy guidelines.[1] There were voices from below which went so far as to advocate neutrality, but this idea was apparently not seriously entertained by the reformers, including the intellectuals. Articles in *Mladá fronta* and *Práce* referred to such demands, but they rejected the idea as untenable given the division of the world into camps, Czechoslovakia's desire to remain socialist, its geographic position, and so forth.[2] The *Práce* article explained that neutrality was valid only if respected by others, and the case of Belgium was cited as an example of the futility of neutrality in the case of war.

If neutrality was not seriously considered, a change in relations with

[1] See *Pravda* (Bratislava), 31 May 1968.
[2] *Mladá fronta*, 14 June 1968; *Práce*, 15 January 1968.

Europe was, as we have seen. The new Foreign Minister, Jiří Hájek, told the Zagreb daily *Vjesnik* (25 May 1968) that while Czechoslovakia intended to continue and even strengthen her ties with 'our socialist friends,' she wished also to pursue the 'active and realistic' European policy already advocated by Dubček. Hájek explained that Czechoslovakia favored a minimization of the differences between the capitalist and socialist parts of Europe, at least to a degree sufficient to prevent the danger of war between the two camps in Europe. Czechoslovakia might help to bring about peaceful competition between the two halves of Europe, without weakening the strength of the socialist camp, through direct contacts with the Western European countries. Hájek saw a certain willingness in Western Europe to accept this idea of building 'a kind of infrastructure of various peaceful ties and relations which would lead to a general easing of tension in Europe.' He said that the West would be mistaken, however, to interpret this policy as a retreat from socialism or the USSR, or to claim that such a retreat was a prerequisite to the policy. Hájek most probably expressed widespread official feeling when he said:

'Please do not foster any illusions or false hopes, because we do not want to go with you (the West). You severed ties with us thirty years ago. I must always repeat that the West then told us that there was no place left for us in their world, that they wanted peace with Hitler, that they wanted to rule over Europe together with him, and that we were a hindrance on this road and must, therefore, go away. We do not forget this.'

Hájek thus made it quite clear that any resemblance of the European policy he outlined to that of Beneš' conception of World War Two and after of Czechoslovakia as a bridge between East and West, was valid only insofar as Czechoslovakia might act as a bridge *from* the socialist bloc, while her loyalties to the bloc were never in doubt.

Hájek said that Czechoslovakia would attempt to overcome the former socialist mistrust of the UN and would strive to increase its cooperation with it. In answer to a question regarding policy in the Middle East, he said that, despite rumors to the contrary, the Czechoslovak public did *not* favor resumption of relations with Israel, that over 50 per cent of the public considered Israel an aggressor and only 8 per cent thought the Arabs responsible for the 1967 Six Day War. Hájek did not reveal the source of his statistics, but his denials notwithstanding public opinion in Czechoslovakia did appear to favor resumption of relations with Israel. This was evidenced by the numerous occasions on which the question was raised and such actions as the student-circulated petition for resumption of relations.[1] Other such signs of interest were the visit to Israel by the popular radio commentator Vera Šťovíčková in June 1968. Known for her pro-Israel broadcasts (for example, on 28 April 1968), Šťovíčková received interviews with the highest Israeli officials and it was believed that her trip was at least in part supported by the Czechoslovak government. Objective and pro-Israeli articles appeared in various journals, including interviews with the Israel Foreign Minister Abba Eban and with Avigdor Dagan, once a leading Czech writer, then head of the East Europe department of the Israel Foreign Office, articles by visiting journalists Gabriel Laub and Alexander Kramer, as well as objective accounts of the Arab problem and articles by Israeli journalists.[2] According to *Práce* of 17 April 1968, journalist Stanislav Budín told a rally in Prague that Czechoslovakia had not broken off relations with worse aggressors than Israel, e.g. the US, and, therefore, he believed negotiations should be opened for resumption of relations. A sign that the Party was taking these voices seriously, Hájek's comments notwithstanding, was the slowdown, pending review, of Czech arms deliveries to Egypt in April – and to Nigeria.

On the issue of relations with West Germany, reformers such as German literature specialist Goldstücker were optimistic about the possibility of improving relations because of the progressive attitudes now appearing in West Germany.[3] Budín too was optimistic when he told the Prague meeting that he expected a Czechoslovak ambassador in Bonn within a year. Another sign in this vein was the objective stand adopted by the Czechoslovak press with regard to German problems. The crisis created by the East German refusal to permit access to Berlin to Bonn officials was not only objectively reported in the Czechoslovak Party daily but even implicitly condemned. A *Rudé právo* article on this subject on 3 May 1968 drew severe criticism from East Germany, particularly for referring to the four-power guarantee of free access to Berlin, and a later *Rudé právo* article 'corrected' this reference.[4]

The objective reporting, part of the idea of democratizing foreign policy decisions, involved other socialist countries as well. *Rudé právo* of 21 June, on the occasion of the anniversary of the Cominform decision

---

[1] *Student*, 29 May 1968. Young people also demonstrated in front of the Foreign Ministry against Czechoslovak arms shipments to the Middle East and Nigeria.

[2] For example, *Reportér*, 13 March 1968; 5 June 1968; *Student*, 13 March 1968; 26 June 1968; 3, 24, 31 July 1968; 7 August 1968; *Literární listy*, 13 June 1968; *Signál* (Eban interview), 8 June 1968.　　[3] *Rinascita* (Rome), 19 April 1968.

[4] *Rudé právo*, 29 May 1968. The East German ambassador protested to Hájek on 10 May 1968. (*Berliner Zeitung*, 11 May 1968.)

expelling Yugoslavia in 1948, was both favorable to Yugoslavia and pointed, with its implied references to present-day efforts of interference in the internal affairs of fraternal Parties. The exceedingly frank treatment of this event, similar to that of articles on the anniversary of the publication of the court verdict against Imre Nagy (17 June 1958) could but make the Soviet Union nervous over this indiscriminate revelation of material in many ways derogatory to people or ideas still powerful in the Kremlin. Events in Poland were also objectively reported, and support for the students and persecuted Jews in Poland was generated. Prague youths demonstrated in front of the Polish Embassy on 1 May 1968 and held a rally of several thousand on 3 May protesting the treatment of Warsaw students and criticizing the anti-semitism and anti-Zionism of the Polish leaders.[1] Several intellectuals publicly criticized developments in Poland, and the Faculty of Philosophy of Charles University invited persecuted Polish professors Leszek Kołakowski and Zygmunt Bauman to lecture in Prague, after an article by philosopher Karel Kosík urging such an invitation appeared in *Literární listy*.[2] On 27 April and 6 May the Poles officially protested what they called an 'anti-Polish campaign' in the Czechoslovak media.[3]

CEMA and the Warsaw Pact also came under criticism (for example, in *Práce*, 15 June), but only from the point of view of making them better organizations and not necessarily from the point of view of criticism of Czechoslovakia's membership in them. It is in this light that the much-publicized comments by Prchlík, the new Party security chief, must be seen. His suggestions for rotation of command and equality between Pact members were little more than the suggestions pressed by Romania for some time – without the Romanians' implied threat to leave these organizations.[4] Intentions notwithstanding, the frank discussion of international

[1] Prague radio, 1 and 3 May 1968.
[2] Prague radio, 18 April (Jiří Lederer said they did not receive the invitation); AFP, 25 April 1968 (Jan Procházka interview); *Literární listy*, 4 April 1968 and 16 May 1968; *Práce*, 4 May 1968 (Procházka, Kohout, and Lustig published an appeal to Polish Party and state leaders to be tolerant of the students and to put an end to the anti-semitic campaign); *Kultúrny život*, 26 July 1968.   [3] PAP, 6 May 1968.
[4] Prchlík press conference, 15 July 1968 (see next chapter). The memorandum of the Klement Gottwald Military–Political Academy urging a new look at the Warsaw Pact and investigating future possibilities for various European security arrangements was also picked up by the Russians as 'demands' for neutrality (*Pravda* (Moscow), 27 September 1968). The memorandum, however, was designed for limited distribution and according to its authors contained no more than had already been proposed in the Rapacki plan and other Polish and East German statements (*Obrana lidu*, 2 November 1968).

matters was probably bound to embarrass and annoy Czechoslovakia's allies to the point that they 'detected' efforts to weaken the socialist bloc or at the very least efforts to place Czechoslovakia above or even outside this bloc rather than adhere, as it had formerly, to the blind discipline known as international solidarity. It may be said that the reformers' demands for and Dubček's belief in a 'Czechoslovak' foreign policy tended to defy definition – leaving the way open for an interpretation that foresaw a Romanian-type of independent policy within the bloc or worse. There is no evidence, however, that anyone in any position of authority, including the leading intellectuals, envisaged abandonment of the Soviet military or economic alliance system, even if for no better reason than geo-politic necessity. That overwhelming public demands, in the atmosphere of democratization, would have come to this is mere speculation, though it may be argued that even the existence of an atmosphere which might permit the expression of such demands was intolerable in the eyes of some of Prague's allies.

'The Czechoslovak way'

Relatively early one began to hear references to a 'Czechoslovak road' to socialism, a 'Czechoslovak way,' or even a 'Czechoslovak model.' Josef Smrkovský was among the most important and earliest proponents of a Czechoslovak road to socialism. In terms not unlike those used by Gottwald over twenty years earlier to justify the Czechoslovak Party's evolutionary rather than revolutionary road to socialism, Smrkovský said as early as 9 February 1968 in *Rudé právo*, 'It lies with us, Czechs and Slovaks, to enter courageously into unexplored terrain and therein to search for *our Czechoslovak socialist road.*' This phrase then began to appear in speeches and articles, and the Yugoslav news agency even reported on 17 March 1968 that a leading politician (unnamed) in Prague had referred to the existence of the Soviet way, the Yugoslav way, and, now, a third, Czechoslovak way to socialism.[1] At the April central committee plenum, reform leader Josef Špaček directly and strongly urged a return to the 'Gottwald tradition of a specific Czechoslovak road to socialism, a tradition which, unfortunately, to the detriment of our country, our people, and all international socialism, was gradually abandoned after February 1948, and to which we have so reluctantly returned

---

[1] For example, *Reportér*, 14 February 1968; *Literární listy*, 14 March 1968 (spoke of Czechoslovakia's unique and new type of socialist democracy); Czechoslovak television, 20 February 1968 (interview with Kolder).

after long years.'[1] The Action Program and the speeches surrounding it also made countless references to the new model for socialist development, the need to find a new way, and so forth. Goldstücker explained that Czechoslovakia was entering a stage of socialism 'which no socialist society has reached so far' and, as he put it, one was entering 'virgin territory.'[2] Dubček too, at the April plenum, spoke of entering a new phase which demanded a new model of socialism or as the Action Program put it: 'a new road of socialist development,' 'a new model of socialist democracy.'

Thus the need for a new model was justified by the fact that Czechoslovakia had entered a new stage of socialist development. Socialist society had been established, class conflicts eliminated, and new social relations created. Yet there would appear little reason to demand a Czechoslovak model to accommodate this new situation, for, Goldstücker's above statement notwithstanding, the Soviet Union had already entered this stage and, theoretically, could continue to provide a model. A second justification of the need for a new model eliminated this apparent contradiction – and indeed placed in question the legitimacy of employing the Soviet model at *any* stage of socialist development in Czechoslovakia. Explaining the purpose of the Action Program, Dubček told the April plenum that it 'opens up scope for basic structural changes in our society and for the creation of a new dynamic of socialism which would be in harmony with the changed social, economic, and cultural conditions as well as with specific national conditions.' The Action Program said: 'We want to embark on the building of a new model of socialist society, one which is profoundly democratic and conforms to Czechoslovak conditions.' The key then to the need for a new model was that a *Czechoslovak* model was needed – a model in keeping with the specifically Czechoslovak reality.

Just what constituted this specifically Czechoslovak reality was frequently repeated: the country's progressive traditions, her democratic tradition, her humanistic traditions, her high cultural, educational, and economic level. Smrkovský once again was one of the first to refer to Czechoslovakia's 'progressive' or 'especially, democratic traditions,' in *Práce* of 20 January, and at the 20 March Prague rally. Dubček spoke of Czechoslovakia as 'an economically and culturally mature country' 'with its democratic tradition,' in his 22 February speech. Others explained that Czechoslovakia had started after World War Two from 'a good starting point of a relatively high industrial and democratic development,' and

[1] *Rudé právo*, 11 April 1968.
[2] *Volkstimme*, 12 April 1968 (Goldstücker interview).

Goldstücker, for example, explained that even before socialism in Czechoslovakia, the country had been highly developed politically, socially, economically, and culturally.[1] It was pointed out on Prague radio, 25 February 1968, that Czechoslovakia should never, for example, have built the 11-year unified school system which replaced 'one of the most highly rated school systems in Europe.' To this was added the fact that whereas the socialist revolution had first occurred in a country with no parliamentary traditions, Czechoslovakia, according to Colotka in *Život* of 17 April, 'in the past... belonged among the countries with the most developed parliamentary democracy' or, as Goldstücker said, Czechoslovakia was 'the only socialist country to have had a pre-socialist democratic tradition and experience deeply rooted in the people and in the working class.' In other references to 'Our history, so rich in democratic traditions,' humanitarianism was added to the list of national characteristics, e.g. Černík's reference to the 'deep humanistic feelings of our people.'[2] Špaček summed up the 'special preconditions in Czechoslovakia' as a mature economy and culture, the high educational level of the people, the democratic tradition, a large working class, and a strong, experienced Communist Party.[3]

Thus the reform leaders argued, according to Černík, that the accepted goal of socialism in Czechoslovakia must be reached through democratic means.[4] Only a democratic model of socialism or what was called both democratic socialism and socialism with a human face would correspond to the specific conditions of Czechoslovakia. It was argued in *Práce* of 15 June 1968 that because of its traditions or specifically Czechoslovak conditions, the Czechoslovak 'spring' was bound to occur, and that because of the 'Czechoslovak reality,' including the advanced economy, Czechoslovakia had the opportunity to create a unique and new type of socialist democracy.'[5] Goldstücker admitted in *Volksstimme* that the as yet unattempted task facing Czechoslovakia was 'to create as democratic a system as possible on the basis of socialism.' In response to the suggestion that Czechoslovakia was attempting something never 'dared' by another Communist Party, the linking of socialism with freedom, Smrkovský commented, for Hamburg television, 17 March 1968: 'You are right and

[1] *Pravda* (Bratislava), 21 March 1968; Goldstücker interview to *Volksstimme*, 7 April 1968 and ASHAI, 22 March 1968.
[2] *Rudé právo*, 24 February 1968 (editor Hanzelka); 7 June 1968 (Černík to May plenum); *Literární listy*, 4 April 1968 (Havel).
[3] *Rudé právo*, 11 April 1968 (to April plenum).
[4] *Rudé právo*, 7 June 1968 (Černík to May–June plenum.)
[5] *Literární listy*, 14 March 1968 (Kliment). See also *Predvoj*, 9 March 1968 (Kotyk).

we are aware of this.' He added at the Prague rally three days later: 'but we are also aware of the fact that we must not miss this chance if we do not want it to be the last one for a long time.'

If the *need* for a Czechoslovak road to socialism was defended on the grounds that Czechoslovakia had specific national conditions which demanded a certain socio-political–economic structure (democracy), the *right* to a specifically Czechoslovak road was defended on the grounds that every nation or every Party should be permitted to adapt Marxism–Leninism to local conditions. The right of Czechoslovakia to work out its own model was defended as early as a 17 January 1968 *Rudé právo* article which declared every Communist Party 'a quite independent and fully sovereign unit, independently deciding all questions of internal Party life and Party policy...[which] takes into account in socialist construction the specific conditions of its country.' At the April central committee plenum Smrkovský argued that different political systems corresponding to the traditions of the countries involved could legitimately exist within a socialist framework. 'Therefore,' he said, 'it is the concern of individual nations and states to solve their system in a way that suits them.'[1] Indeed, it was argued, the variety of resulting forms would be favorable rather than detrimental to socialism.[2] To support this point Luigi Longo was quoted in a *Rudé právo* article, 19 April 1968, which went on to assert that the position of the Czechoslovak Party was based on the principle that '*it is the inalienable right of every socialist country and Communist Party to determine its own road to socialism in its own country*, and to decide which combination of *national and international experiences* it regards as best suited to the interests of that country and of the whole movement.' Frequent references to Yugoslavia and the invalidity of the 1957 and 1960 Moscow declarations were simply added ammunition for this argument. Václav Kotyk did recognize (in *Predvoj*, 9 May), however, that Czechoslovakia's way might meet with disapproval in other Soviet bloc countries given the concept of rule employed there. While Dubček did not speak of the principle of many roads to socialism as such, he strongly reiterated the principle of non-interference in the internal affairs of other Parties at both the April and May–June plena. As we have seen, it was Dubček himself who added the element of 'national conditions' to the reasons for finding a new model for Czechoslovakia, and there can be little doubt that his repeated references to the right of each Party to operate without inter-

[1] *Rudé právo*, 4 April 1968.
[2] Černík, for example, to May–June plenum (*Rudé právo*, 7 June 1968).

ference meant that each Party had the right to forge its own internal policies or model as it saw fit.

Indeed Dubček maintained that it was through the free development of a Czechoslovak model that his country might make its contribution to or serve world Communism. This was a crucial question, for one might argue that different roads to communism (freedom to develop one's own model), could never be superior in importance to the interests of the world movement. Dubček argued that a Czechoslovak road to socialism, in accord with and precisely because of the special preconditions in that country, would benefit the international movement. As a minimum it would provide a test-case for the possibilities of socialism in an advanced, industrialized, democratic country; more than this it might provide a model for socialism in the advanced capitalist states. In one of his earliest speeches in power, 22 February, Dubček said that the fact that Czechoslovakia had begun the road to socialism already economically and culturally mature 'obliges us to demonstrate what possibilities socialism has in a country of such a type.' On 2 March 1968 he told Kladno workers that it was the very development of democracy which would make socialism more attractive in the world – particularly in the capitalist world – and Czechoslovakia's democratic traditions could contribute both to this development of socialism and to the making of socialism more attractive in the world. He added, later, that Czechoslovakia did not have exaggerated ambitions in this sphere, but, he believed, it could offer new experience and knowledge.[1] His cautiousness was necessitated by the danger that one might think that the Czechoslovak Party was defying the existing power structure within the world movement by proposing a new, better, or (even merely by implication) alternative model. There were indeed some who claimed that Czechoslovakia's experiments, particularly in the economic sphere, might be beneficial to the other socialist countries, since Czechoslovakia was trying to solve problems involved in the development of a *socialist* economy and a *socialist* democracy.[2] At the very least the Czechoslovak experiments might provide a contribution to international discussions of Marxism–Leninism.[3] Others echoed Dubček's suggestion of Czechoslovakia as a model for Western Europe, while still others believed that Czechoslovakia might make a contribution to the world at large, just as she had once been a country of widely respected

[1] *Rudé právo*, 21 April 1968 (to Bratislava conference).
[2] For example, *Rudé právo*, 17 January 1968.
[3] *Élet és irodalom* (Budapest), 4 May 1968 (Císař interview).

parliamentary democracy.[1] Indeed, they argued, if the world saw genuine democracy in Czechoslovakia (instead of the forced closure of a cultural journal or economic chaos or police methods against students) 'there would be...an impregnable socialist propaganda all over the world.'[2]

This positive line changed as the pressures on Czechoslovakia grew, specifically as the fears of other socialist states grew with regard to the influence Czechoslovakia's experiments could or possibly already were having in their own countries. Relatively early, in his Hamburg television interview of 17 March 1968, Smrkovský had cautiously asserted that, though the Czechoslovak experiment might prove an interesting example 'for comrades in other socialist countries,' it probably could not be carried out by any other socialist state. While this was an implied reference to Czechoslovakia's special preconditions, it may also have been intended as an assurance to Poland and East Germany, in particular, that Czechoslovakia did not intend to export its model anywhere except, possibly, to the West. Speaking to the Hungarian public, in his *Élet és irodalom* interview, Císař was even more explicit in stating that Czechoslovakia did not see itself as providing a generally valid model available for export. In the days of the intense battle of words with the other socialist states, Černík too underscored Czechoslovakia's modest intentions. Speaking at the May–June central committee meeting he said, 'We are not presenting our road to socialism as a model for others, nor do we present it as a renaissance of Marxism, because we are only at the very beginning.'

Thus as it turned out, an emphasis on the purely national character of the experiment in Czechoslovakia, although it might render Czechoslovakia liable to accusations of nationalism or sectarianism, was necessitated by the fears of certain other countries of infection from Prague. This need to play down the universality or usefulness of the Czechoslovak effort and to play up its purely local nature was probably not contradictory to the reform program, for the reformers were in fact almost entirely concerned with improving their own society. As we have seen they generally refrained from criticizing the Soviet Union, preferring to argue that the model used there was simply not suitable in Czechoslovakia. Yet there were several problems that the reformers either failed to see or perhaps left for later. One of these was the phenomenon that freedom of expression and information was bound to affect reporting, including critical comments, on the other socialist countries. This could but evoke

---

[1] See *Kultúrny život*, 15 March 1968 (Šimeček); Prague radio, 20 March 1968 (Smrkovský to Prague rally), *Život*, 17 April 1968 (Colotka).
[2] Prague radio, 25 February 1968.

the ire of the countries involved. A more serious problem was that for all that the Czechs and Slovaks may have wanted their ideas to stay at home, for all that they may have genuinely wanted to live in continued loyalty to and alliance with the socialist states, there was little likelihood – as is clear with the benefit of hindsight – that these states would tolerate within their midsts an alternative so alien to their concept of the requirements of socialist rule. In the end it was just this point which defeated Czechoslovakia: national development could not be permitted to endanger socialism, as conceived by Moscow, or the other socialist countries in the scheme of Brezhnev's enunciated policy of limited sovereignty. Whether for export or not, purely national or not, the Czechoslovak model evoked a strong and fearful reaction, and the Czechoslovak road to socialism was condemned – and executed – as inimical to socialism.

10

Crisis and Invasion

The internal political situation

The differences in approach, attitudes, ideas and goals of the various members of the reform regime gradually emerged throughout the spring, for the coalition which had formed to remove Novotný could hardly be considered a coherent or homogeneous group.[1] Individual stands on the specific points of the reforms have been pointed out in the discussions of the reforms themselves. Generally speaking three to four loose groupings or streams emerged within the Party after January. They represented the range of views from extreme conservative to radical, including what might be termed a conservative group and a moderate-liberal group. The first of these, the extreme conservative, could not in fact be considered part of the reform regime since they constituted that group of left-over pro-Novotný politicians altogether opposed to the January 1968 changes. Their continued presence was rendered exceedingly dangerous by the emergence of the divisions within the reform regime itself, for as a conservative wing emerged within the 'January' group, the genuine reformers found themselves battling against *two* groups of conservatives.

The extreme conservative group, which was said to command the support of approximately one-third of the central committee in the spring of 1968, was represented by a number of district and even regional Party officials, particularly in Slovakia (for example, Rudolf Cvik in central Slovakia, replaced only on 29 May 1968).[2] The major Novotný men (Chudík, Laštovička, Šimůnek and Novotný himself) were removed from the Party presidium at the April plenum, primarily at the demand of the March Party meetings throughout the country. Of this group only Kapek remained, as candidate presidium member, along with Lenárt who in the spring of 1968 tried to temper his earlier support for Novotný.[3] It was through Kapek, however, that the dogmatists around Josef Jodas sent

---

[1] Sources for this section, unless otherwise indicated, consist primarily of interviews of Czech and Slovak reformers who prefer to remain anonymous.

[2] *Smena*, 22 May 1968.

[3] Vaculík, who had reform tendencies when Party leader in Brno, supported Novotný in 1967 but returned to the reform attitude during the spring. Lenárt, who also vacillated, landed finally in the conservative camp.

their protest to the reform regime on behalf of the so-called 'Libeň group of old Communists' which met on 17 February 1968 and again at conferences of the Prague eighth Party district. This protest, known as the 'Jodas Letter,' was later sent to Party members throughout the country when *Rudé právo* refused to publish it.[1] The pressures for an early convening of the fourteenth Party congress developed in March and April so that the Party might have the opportunity to divest itself of this group. The activities of the extreme conservatives gained strength, however, prior to the May–June plenum, primarily because of the Soviet pressures on the reforms, but also, it is likely, because of the split amongst the reformers themselves. Thus, a certain amount of tension was attendant on this plenum, for it was believed that a showdown might be attempted in the form of an effort to organize the two-thirds majority necessary to oust conservatives from the central committee prior to a congress.

Trouble with the conservative wing of the reform regime, however, also began to take form prior to the May plenum. This tendency was most apparent among the Slovak Party representatives such as Bil'ak, Barbírek, Rigo, and probably included Piller, Indra, Lenárt, Švestka and Kolder. These were people who had joined the anti-Novotný front in December but eventually exhibited tendencies, of varying degrees, towards feet-dragging and even criticism of reform. Indeed, Slovak circles in general had been displaying less interest in reform (and more in federalization) than the Czechs – often justified by Husák with the claim that Slovakia had begun its liberalization in 1963.[2] Concern that this group might combine with the extreme conservative group, or at the very least, facilitate the latter's efforts by abandoning the reformers, was aggravated by the opposition of some of the 'new conservatives' (for example, Bil'ak and Piller) to the early convening of an extraordinary congress.[3] This opposition came mainly in response to the growing campaign in April, particularly among the 'radicals,' to force a decision for an early congress. The 'radical' group, insofar as one existed, was concentrated in the Prague city Party committee, headed by Bohumil Šimon, in Brno, headed by Špaček, and in Ostrava.[4] It is difficult to say just which reform leaders, such as

---

[1] *Rudé právo*, 18 March 1968. See also *Reportér*, 27 September 1969.

[2] That it had begun then was generally recognized but it was never fully implemented, leaving Slovakia in as great a need of democratization as the Czech lands. (See Manák in *Kultúrny život*, 26 April 1968; Kusý in *Politika*, 20 March 1969.)

[3] For example, Piller interview, Prague radio, 3 April 1968; Bil'ak to Slovak Party group, *Student*, 15 May 1968.

[4] See *Tribuna*, 5 February 1969 ('Report on the Current Political Situation in the ČSSR,' prepared by Jan Kašpar for use against the reformers).

Smrkovský, Kriegel or Slavík belonged to this group or the moderates of the Dubček tendencies, particularly since these two groups worked together on most issues. At the April regional Party conferences Prague and Brno unequivocally favored an early congress while the Slovak regions were strongly opposed.[1] This conflict came to a head at the 7–8 May 1968 session of the Party presidium when the conservatives (old and new) began to speak about 'anti-socialist forces' and 'dangers' to the leading role of the Party.[2]

Alarmed by this new turn of events, the radicals, i.e. the Prague city Party committee and the regional Party committees of Brno and Ostrava (the North and South Moravian regions), held a meeting on 9–10 May 1968 to discuss the immediate creation of the Czech Communist Party, previously envisaged as an eventuality with the federalization of the country, but urged now as a means to counterbalance the growth of 'conservatism' in the central committee. Dubček and the moderates, however, apparently decided not to press the issue openly at this point, possibly hesitant to provoke the conservatives at a time of growing outside pressures, and, therefore, the idea was dropped in favor of convening the fourteenth congress. The Ostrava region did not receive news of this decision in time, however, and proceeded to discuss the matter at its 16–22 May session (along with the idea for an early congress); but the proposal was not approved.[3]

The Slovak central committee plenum of 22–24 May reiterated the anti-socialist charges raised at the presidium meeting, but Dubček virtually agreed to these in his speech to the May–June plenum. Thus the May–June plenum, coming as it did in the midst of growing outside pressures, internal Party splits, and uncertainty as to the reformers' ability to defeat their opponents, promulgated what appeared to be a retreat on various reform issues. Thus, as we have seen, there was the condemnation of K-231 and the admonishing of the media, for example. More significant there was the admission by Dubček for the first time that 'anti-socialist forces' constituted the major threat to the progress of reform. Yet, the plenum was perceived by the reform leaders themselves as, on the whole, a success. The reference to 'anti-socialists' had been followed by a condemnation of 'sectarian' (read, conservative) elements and, as was pointed out critically by the post-Dubček leadership, Dubček had not admitted that the so-called right-wing anti-socialists had appeared in

[1] *Rudé právo*, 5 January 1971.   [2] Ibid.
[3] *Nová svoboda*, 23, 25 May 1968; Zdeněk Hejzlar, 'The Evolution of the Communist Party of Czechoslovakia,' unpublished paper (Reading, 1971), 13–14.

the Party itself. Of greater significance for the reformers and potentially more efficacious than the many pronouncements or verbal rebukes, however, was the decision taken by the plenum to convoke an extraordinary congress on 9 September. This decision, possibly the result of a compromise with the new conservatives on the other issues, was what the reform regime needed to go ahead with its plans in the knowledge that defeat of its major opponents was virtually imminent. In the meantime Novotný was expelled from the central committee and his most conservative collaborators Pavol David, Karol Bacílek, Viliam Široký, Bruno Köhler, Štefan Rais, and Josef Urválek (all demoted in the 1963 de-Stalinization for the roles in the 1950s trials) were suspended from the Party. The Slovak Stalinist Cvik resigned of his own volition as did former Defense Minister Bohumír Lomský and former Justice Minister Václav Škoda. The plenum also authorized the beginning of work on the Czech Party by creating a commission under Josef Špaček. Špaček was probably intended to head the new Party, but the original tactical intent of the reformers to create the Party quickly was ignored.

One should not exaggerate these 'successes,' for indeed many reformers were distressed by the compromises made, the '2,000 Words' being the most far-reaching example of this negative reaction. Yet, the district and regional Party conferences which followed the plenum, with the major purpose of electing delegates to the congress, demonstrated clear support for the reformers against even the new conservatives. The overwhelming majority of the elected delegates were pro-reform, as attested to by later conservative accusations regarding the dangers this would have entailed for their cause at the forthcoming congress.[1] Moreover, the slate drawn up for the new central committee contained only about 30 per cent of the then current members of the central committee. Conservatives such as Indra had difficulty getting elected to the congress, Kapek and Kolder were not elected delegates, and others such as Bil'ak, Švestka and long-standing conservative Vladimír Koucký (ambassador to the USSR) came in for criticism at these meetings.[2] The conservatives continued their activities throughout the summer as evidenced by comments such as that of Jiří Hanzelka, in *Nová svoboda* of 29 June 1968, that Indra was trying to organize a conservative wing in the central committee prior to the congress. Their activities were also evident in the stepped-up leaflet campaign (often anti-semitic) and efforts to link up with the outside harassment such as the letter from the militia to the USSR.[3] The radicals

[1] *Rudé právo*, 5 January 1971.   [2] Prague radio, 1, 6–8 July 1968.
[3] See 182.

for their part were active mainly in preparing alternative liberal documents for the September congress, although here and there they raised the demand for a convening of the Czech congress before the fourteenth Czechoslovak Party congress.[1] The new conservatives continued to urge more firm measures on the part of the Party to restrain the democratization from below. Some of the results were the near-split in the presidium over the answer to outside pressures and efforts in August to discredit Dubček, with the ultimate intention of replacing him.[2] These efforts did not, however, succeed in obtaining full support even among the conservatives, and the reform regime was able to maintain sufficient unity to answer the interfering Warsaw Pact nations with at least outward firmness.

Outside reactions

It is difficult to determine exactly when concern began to develop amongst Czechoslovakia's allies in the Soviet bloc. East Germany had in fact been watching Prague apprehensively since the beginning of de-Stalinization in 1963 and 1964.[3] The Soviet Union had been less concerned as we have seen, leaving the resolution of the 1967 crisis up to the Czechoslovak Party itself. In a 16 February speech, following the 29–31 January 1968 visit by Dubček to Moscow (and brief visits by both Kádár and Gomułka to Czechoslovakia, 4 and 7 February, respectively), Brezhnev reiterated his adherence to the idea that 'every Party determines its own political course absolutely independently,' calling for coordination only with regard to foreign policy ('the fight against the common enemy'). Although Brezhnev and the other Warsaw Pact leaders, all of whom were present at Dubček's 22 February speech in Prague, may have been disturbed by the new regime's announced ideas, Soviet public comments even up to the end of March remained friendly and conciliatory.[4] Even Soviet reporting on the March 1968 Party meetings in Czechoslovakia seemed to purposely emphasize the 'routineness' of these meetings, stressing only the comments regarding the strengthening of the leading role of the Party, the loyalty to proletarian internationalism, Marxism–Leninism and the USSR.[5] East Germany was the first to openly express concern, in the

[1] Prague radio, 7 July 1968; Prague city Party conference ('Stanovisko').
[2] Robert Littell (ed.), *The Czech Black Book* (New York, 1969), 26.
[3] See Sindermann's comments to SED central committee plenum in February 1964, cited by J. F. Brown, *The New Eastern Europe* (London, 1966), 154.
[4] Warsaw Pact Commander-in-Chief Yakubovsky made an unannounced trip to Prague on 28 February 1968, immediately after Šejna's defection.
[5] *Pravda* (Moscow), 14 March 1968, for example.

form of critical reporting of developments in Czechoslovakia in mid-March and, in particular, a speech by East German Party secretary Kurt Hager published by *Neues Deutschland* on 27 March 1968. It may well have been Ulbricht's concern rather than that of Moscow which prompted the bloc leaders to call Dubček to Dresden on 23 March 1968. In addition, the student disturbances in Poland earlier that month, with their pro-Dubček slogans, probably also contributed to the decision to undertake what was but the first of the bloc's formal attempts to influence developments in Czechoslovakia. Even *Pravda* (Moscow) of 25 March 1968 admitted that the meeting had dealt with internal Czechoslovak affairs.

At the Dresden meeting the 'allies' presented some of the complaints which were to become standard in the following months, specifically demands for certain personnel changes, and an offer of Soviet troops should Dubček desire these in order to preserve the Party's leading role.[1] Dubček politely declined this offer, assuring Brezhnev that the Party had matters entirely under control. Insofar as can be determined, and according to Dubček himself, no concessions or promises were made by him at this meeting; he apparently merely repeated his oft-declared loyalty to the Warsaw Pact and the USSR, as well as his contention that there was nothing in the present changes in his country constituting a threat to socialism.

The Russians did not comment publicly on the Action Program, which it would appear was not in itself altered by the calling of the Dresden conclave.[2] At the CPSU central committee plenum of 8–10 April, however, Brezhnev delivered something of a warning to Czechoslovakia and the following statement was issued (in reference to the Dresden meeting): 'The plenum reiterates our Party's readiness to do everything necessary for the constant and steady consolidation of the socialist community in the areas of politics, economics, and defense.'[3] According to *Mladá fronta* of 25 April 1968, this plenum was followed by Party conferences in the USSR at which members were informed that 'the principle of vigilance "against hostile infiltration" has been revived and, in connection with the last plenum, the general validity of the principles of Soviet socialist construction both at home and abroad are underlined. Any kind of expression

[1] For domestic consumption, Moscow radio, 27 March 1968, for example, emphasized the 'special need' for vigilence and proletarian internationalism because of West German revanchism.

[2] They did react favorably to Svoboda's assumption of the Presidency (*Pravda*, 26 March 1968; *Krasnaya zvezda*, 6 April 1968).

[3] TASS, 10 April 1968; *Pravda*, 11 April 1968.

of national individuality is examined rather for elements of imperialist ideological infiltration than for a personal evaluation of existing circumstances.'

By late April mild polemics began between Czechoslovakia on the one side and the USSR and East Germany on the other, centering both on Hager's earlier remarks and on a speech made by Moscow Party first secretary V. V. Grishin, carried in *Pravda* (Moscow), 22 April 1968. It was in May, however, that the crisis which was building up between Czechoslovakia and her allies became most apparent. The month opened with Dubček's 4 May talks in Moscow, presumably called to explain matters further, including Czechoslovak economic needs in hopes of obtaining a large foreign currency loan, and, as Dubček admitted, Soviet fears of 'anti-socialist' excesses in Czechoslovakia.[1] As Smrkovský told the National Assembly foreign relations committee afterwards, Moscow presented 'heaps of evidence' of the forces considered to be operating against socialism.[2] These talks in Moscow were followed by a meeting there between the Soviet leaders and Ulbricht, Zhivkov, Kádár and Gomułka. According to Prague radio of 12 May 1968, quoting *Borba*, this meeting was called at Ulbricht's request and the Hungarian Party was hesitant about attending because of its sympathy for the Czechoslovak reform movement.

Neither the Soviets nor their allies were, apparently, satisfied with the results of Dubček's visit, for immediately thereafter strong and active polemics against the Czechoslovak reform movement began, particularly in the Soviet and East German media. The polemics singled out Smrkovský, Ludvík Vaculík, Procházka and Havel (among others), the idea of opposition parties, the clubs, attacks on the militia and critical references to other socialist countries, particularly the revelations about Soviet advisors in the Slánský trials and possible Soviet involvement in the death of Jan Masaryk. The polemics also attacked the Czechoslovak student movement, perhaps because of fears of the effects it might have (or, was already having) on Soviet and Polish students, just as the policies towards the Ukrainians and the Uniates in Slovakia was feared for its effect on the Ukraine. A favorite theme was western exploitation of events in Czechoslovakia, remarks about which were usually accompanied by stepped-up criticism of Bonn. The major accusation, however, focused on the growth of so-called anti-socialist forces in Czechoslovakia and the 'threat' to the leading role of the Party.[3]

[1] Prague radio, 6 May 1968 (interview).   [2] *Mladá fronta*, 16 May 1968.
[3] For Soviet accusations see *Pravda, Trud, Komsomolskaya pravda, Literaturnaya*

Another phenomenon of the aftermath of Dubček's trip to Moscow was the appearance of rumors of a Soviet military build-up on Czechoslovakia's borders. Upon his return Dubček had made a vague reference to the necessity of joint Warsaw Pact maneuvers (just as NATO held[1]), but nothing more specific was said to deny these rumors. Alleged remarks by Soviet officers Yepishev and Konev did little to relieve the tensions. Visiting Czechoslovakia for Liberation Day celebrations, Konev urged Kladno workers to preserve the militant, revolutionary traditions of the proletariat, adding, according to Moscow radio, 13 May 1968, that the Soviet Union would not permit anyone to destroy the fraternal ties between the two countries. Yepishev, according to an officially denied account in *Le Monde* (4 May 1968), told the CPSU central committee (and later Czech soldiers, according to reports in *Literární listy*, 9 and 30 May 1968), that the Soviet army was 'ready to comply with its duty should loyal Communists in Czechoslovakia request help in safeguarding socialism.' On 10 May 1968, ČTK announced that there were indeed troop movements along the Polish–Czechoslovak border, connected with Pact maneuvers. A few days earlier (7 May), it had been announced on Czechoslovak television that general staff exercises were scheduled for the summer or fall. Amidst rumors of Pact plans to station troops in Czechoslovakia, Soviet Defense Minister Grechko led a delegation to Czechoslovakia on 17 May. A few days later, on 21 May, the radio carried an announcement by Czechoslovak Defense Minister Dzúr on the imminent beginning of Pact maneuvers in Czechoslovakia. Grechko did say, however, that 'the solution of the internal problems of the Czechoslovak Peoples' Army is the internal affair of Czechoslovakia', and together with official denials about the stationing of Soviet troops in Czechoslovakia this was, presumably, designed to assuage the population.[2]

Simultaneously with Grechko's trip, Kosygin arrived in Czechoslovakia, ostensibly to take a cure in Karlové Vary. While little is known of Kosygin's talks in Prague, aside from the fact that they also dealt with economic matters, the major result appears to have been a pause in Soviet and East European (though not East German) polemics. This lull in polemics created the impression, expressed, for example, on Prague radio

gazeta, Izvestia, May–June 1968. Moscow radio also increased its Czech–Slovak broadcasting from two to five half-hour programs as of 8 May 1968. One may assume that they were also disturbed by the articles on Trotsky, Gramsci, Marcuse, Rosa Luxemburg, Imre Nagy or Daniel Cohn-Bendit which appeared in *Literární listy* particularly, or Rudi Dutschke's visit to Prague.

[1] This phrase was omitted from the TASS (7 May) version.
[2] *Rudé právo,* 19 May 1968; Prague radio, 21, 22 May 1968.

8 June, that the 'allies' were beginning to be less alarmed by developments in Czechoslovakia. For their part, the Czechs made special efforts at conciliation. For example, Smrkovský led a twelve-day parliamentarians' visit to the USSR, during which he made numerous, almost obsequiously flattering speeches to the Soviets and denounced what he called anti-Soviet and anti-communist invectives which 'sporadically appear in the Czechoslovak press.'[1] Yet, the basic frictions remained, evidenced by the fact that Smrkovský was not received by any high Soviet Party officials until the very end of his stay. And in those last conversations, with Brezhnev, he received the impression that the Soviets were still dissatisfied and believed that Prague underestimated the anti-socialist tendencies, particularly in the media (according to a speech he made in Prague, 17 June 1968). Štrougal also led a delegation to Moscow for talks on economic affairs, without, however, any apparent success.

The problems seemed to burst into the open once again after *Lidová demokracie* of 5 June 1968 reprinted a *New York Times* article which claimed that Šejna had been given Soviet help in his flight from Czechoslovakia. The Soviet Foreign Minister protested to the Czechoslovak embassy in Moscow, only to have this protest protested, by both *Lidová demokracie* and *Svobodné slovo* of 11 June. Full-scale polemics were resumed with a 14 June 1968 *Pravda* (Moscow) attack on Císař, answered the following day by *Práce* and by Císař himself in *Rudé právo* of 22 June 1968, and followed by renewed accusations in other Soviet, Bulgarian, East German and Polish media. Polemics reached a near-frenzy peak in response to the publication of the '2,000 Words' at the end of June. The strong reaction to this document warned of the growing power and audacity of 'anti-socialist forces' in Czechoslovakia and focused on the demands for an opposition party.[2] Slightly less polemical but a clear indication of the basis for Soviet objections was a Moscow broadcast to Czechoslovakia on 4 July which recognized 'specific' and 'distinctive' roads to socialism, but it said:

'There is not and cannot be socialism without common ownership of production; there is not and cannot be socialism without participation of the masses in the direction of society and the state; there is not and cannot be socialism without the leading role of the Marxist–Leninist Communist Party imbued with the spirit of proletarian internationalism.'

[1] ČTK, 11 June 1968 (speech in Leningrad).
[2] For a comparison of polemics within the bloc and reactions to the '2,000 Words' see

While these polemics were gaining momentum, Dubček led a delegation to Budapest, from 13 to 15 June, to sign a new friendship pact
(ahead of schedule). The delegation was well received and Dubček re-
marked that Kádár and the Hungarian comrades were 'keeping their
fingers crossed for us that our cause should succeed.'[1] The Czechs and
Slovaks thus felt that the Hungarians (themselves reform-minded in certain spheres) were behind them, as were the Yugoslavs and Romanians,
the latter primarily because of their struggle for the right of each Party
to determine its own policies. Yugoslav support had, in fact, been apparent for years in the reporting of the Yugoslav press on the liberals'
struggle for reform in Czechoslovakia, and in the spring Tito expressed
his desire to pay an official visit to Prague. Support was also forthcoming
from the Italian Party whose leader had issued a statement (ČTK, 7 May
1968) after a visit to Prague on 6–7 May 1968, supporting the efforts of the
Dubček regime to build democratic socialism. This sympathy, however,
did not and probably could not forestall the crisis which followed, although Kádár is reputed to have tried to mediate during his trip to Moscow at the end of June.

Confrontation

On 8 July, with polemics still strong on both sides, the Czechoslovak
presidium gave an official reply to letters received from the East German,
Polish, Hungarian, Bulgarian, and Soviet Parties calling for a joint meeting in Warsaw.[2] Prague replied, according to Prague radio, 8 July 1968,
that it welcomed discussions but preferred to conduct them on a bilateral
basis (and to include talks with Romania and Yugoslavia), at an 'appropriate time' and in respect of mutual non-interference in internal affairs.
Another bid for a meeting was received from the five on 11 July and a
similar answer sent on 13 July, but the 'suggested' meeting was in fact
already getting under way in Warsaw. The Czechoslovak leaders cabled
the group not to discuss Czechoslovakia in their absence, but the convening first secretaries sent a formal letter to Prague on 15 July 1968.[3]
Pointing to the 'undermining' of the leading role of the Party in Czechoslovakia (with specific references to the media and the clubs), and stating

---

'Czechoslovakia: A Qualitatively Different Stage of Communist Relations?,' RFE,
25 July 1968.
[1] ČTK, 15 June 1968.
[2] According to a speech by Císař, ČTK, 9 July 1968.
[3] See Dubček speech to special plenum, *Rudé právo*, 20 July 1968 and *Rudé právo*,
18 July 1968, for text of letter.

that a 'threat' to socialism in one country constituted a threat to socialism in all the socialist countries, the Warsaw letter demanded of Prague the following: an attack on anti-socialist forces; a ban on all political organizations acting against socialism; the reestablishment of censorship; and the revival of democratic centralism.

The Czechoslovak Party presidium met on 16 July 1968 to discuss the Warsaw letter, and in its reply the Dubček regime maintained its firm line regarding non-interference. Although admitting the efforts of anti-socialist forces, it denied that these posed a threat to socialism in Czechoslovakia. It also mentioned the continued divisive efforts of the 'dogmatic–sectarian' forces whose work in the past had harmed the position of the Party. Prague recognized the importance of maintaining the leading role of the Party but argued that the only way to ensure this in Czechoslovakia was to implement the Action Program and thereby present a Party deeply rooted in and responsive to the demands of Czechoslovakia itself. The Czechoslovak reply again urged bilateral talks, after stating that 'the common cause of socialism is not advanced' by the judging of other Parties' policies in their absence.

Dubček's firm stand in reply to the Warsaw letter and throughout this period was a courageous and independent act. Whatever the indications of a retreat on the domestic scene and the leadership's genuine concern over the liberalization possibly getting out of hand, this most difficult stand was indicative of the degree of Dubček's commitment to the reform movement and his belief in its necessity as well as its viability. Particularly so in view of the fact that at the time of the above communications Pact troops were still on Czechoslovak territory, their withdrawal clearly having been delayed since the close of exercises on 30 June 1968. On 19 July the Russians suggested a meeting with the Czechoslovak presidium in the Soviet Union or Poland, but Dubček refused to meet outside Czechoslovakia (or, reportedly, to hold any talks) as long as Pact troops remained in the country.[1] He was also hesitant about the Soviet demand for a meeting with the whole presidium, for the latter still contained many conservatives (such as Bil'ak, Kolder, and Švestka). These people had dragged their feet regarding the reply to the Warsaw letter, and it was feared that Moscow would try to exploit these cracks in the Czechoslovak Party's unity to split – and thus discredit – the Dubček regime, specifically with the purpose of obtaining a postponement of the Party congress. Nonetheless, on 22 July TASS announced that the CPSU had agreed to

[1] According to Prague radio, 20 July 1968.

228

Confrontation

talks in Czechoslovakia and, on the same day, Prague radio reported the beginning of the withdrawal of Pact troops.

The period between the Warsaw letter and the opening of the Soviet–Czechoslovak talks on 29 July 1968 was one of increasing mutual recrimination between the Soviet Union and her allies on the one side and Czechoslovakia on the other. Immediately after the Warsaw meeting, the CPSU held a central committee plenum at which most of the time was given to speakers opposed to developments in Czechoslovakia (for example, Shelest), and a resolution was passed supporting the Warsaw letter. On 19 July *Pravda* reported the discovery of a cache of American arms in western Bohemia, and, according to *Svobodné slovo* of 24 July 1968, Moscow followed this with a note demanding that Prague take steps to protect its western border. Beginning with a 22 July editorial, *Pravda* published several alarmist articles on the growth of anti-socialism, the dangers to communism in Czechoslovakia, and particularly the danger to the leading role of the Party (already overthrown, according to *Pravda*, in the media). East German and Polish comments were equally vituperative and, together with remarks in the Bulgarian press, even went so far as to hint at intervention.[1] Even the Hungarian Party, in an editorial in its daily organ of 25 July 1968, warned the reformers that their situation (particularly in the media) was nearing the 'counter-revolutionary' potential of Hungary of 1956 and that events in Czechoslovakia could no longer be considered merely internal matters.

In this same period, Dubček appeared on television (18 July, followed by Černík on 19 July) to pledge his intention of carrying on the reform program, *in toto*, without retreat. A meeting of the central committee (to which representatives of the newly elected delegates to the congress were invited) was called on 19 July to vote on the presidium's reply to the Warsaw letter. Although there had been certain critical or hesitant stands expressed at the 18 July Slovak central committee plenum, and by Švestka in *Rudé právo* articles of 14 and 18 July, the central committee unanimously backed the presidium.[2] At this meeting, Dubček urged the media to bear in mind their power and their responsibilities – a warning which was passed on in the form of a directive against polemic-provoking or anti-Soviet reporting – and a few days later Zdeněk Hejzlar, a known and trusted reformer, was named chief of Czechoslovak radio. The media did respond with support for the presidium letter, increasingly emphasizing

[1] For example, *Trybuna ludu*, 25 July 1968; *Neues Deutschland*, 24, 25 July 1968; *Robotnichesko delo*, 21 July 1968.
[2] *Pravda* (Bratislava), 19 July 1968; *Rok šedesátý osmý*, 251–8.

229

in the weeks that followed, however, the idea of the nation's sovereignty and the need to stand firm.[1] This last, it was claimed, could be achieved if the regime would merely turn to, inform, and rely upon the public.[2]

In response to the polemics, military officials, on sundry occasions declared the Czechoslovak army and border units entirely capable of defending the western border.[3] Yet, Party security chief Prchlík's press conference of 15 July on the Warsaw Pact provided the Soviet opportunity to extract at least a symbolic compromise prior to the negotiations. Presumably in response to certain of Prchlík's comments on sovereignty and Soviet domination of the Pact, *Krasnaya zvezda* of 23 July attacked both Prchlík and his proposals. On 25 July the Czechoslovak presidium dissolved the central committee's eighth department – and with it Prchlík's job.[4] While dissolution of this powerful and oft-misused department was a progressive step, recommended by Prchlík himself, it bore the markings of a concession to Moscow. Indeed, subsequent disavowal by the presidium of Prchlík's Pact proposals and the ambiguity over his reassignment attested to this.[5] There are reports, however, that the real cause of his removal was the fact that he had presented plans for the defense of Czechoslovakia in case of Soviet invasion.[6]

The Czechoslovak presidium thus went to the negotiations in Čierná nad Tisou amidst an atmosphere of heated polemics and with many Soviet troops still on Czechoslovak soil, but, also, with the support of the public demonstrated in a massive signature campaign. The Russians came armed with accusations and quotations, and, reportedly, an exaggerated estimate of the strength of the conservatives in the Czechoslovak Party. The discussions, which took place from 29 July to 1 August 1968, were, according to all accounts, stormy and at times vindictive. Instead of talk of the western border or West Germany or other such pseudo-issues over which the Soviets had claimed concern, the discussions focused on censorship, personnel changes, and 'anti-socialist forces' in Czechoslovakia, i.e. the leading role of the Party, and the clubs, as well as the demand for postponement of the congress. In the midst of the talks, Brezhnev reportedly became more cooperative, according to one account

[1] For example, Václav Kotyk in *Práce*, 11, 20, 23 July 1968; *Literární listy*, 25 July 1968; *Obrana lidu*, 27 July 1968 ('The ČSSR is Not Going to Commit Suicide'); *Reportér*, 24 July 1968.
[2] See *Literární listy*, 11 July 1968 (Liehm); 25 July 1968 (Dalimil, Pithart).
[3] Prague radio, 23–25 July 1968.   [4] *Rok šedesátý osmý*, 262.
[5] Defense Ministry statement, ČTK, 15 August 1968; Prague radio, 5, 6 August 1968; *Práce*, 7 August 1968, for example.
[6] See *Reportér*, 16 January 1969 (Luděk Pachman), for a hint of this.

because letters from leading Communists such as Tito, Ceausescu, and the Spanish Party on behalf of eighteen European Communist Parties had alarmed Moscow. There are many reports that Suslov changed positions on the question of invasion – even making a speech conciliatory towards Prague at Čierná – presumably because of his responsibility for and concern over the forthcoming international conclave. Indeed a major factor in Soviet hesitation over invasion most probably devolved from the knowledge of what such a move would mean for this laboriously prepared conference, scheduled then for November 1968.

Both sides regarded the Čierná talks as their own victory, while Moscow was later to accuse Prague of having 'violated' a Čierná 'agreement' which Prague claimed never existed. Černík was later to explain (in a 21 September speech in Ostrava): 'We did not conclude any agreement at Čierná. We only informed the Soviet representatives of what our future procedure would be in order to prevent both right-wing and left-wing extremist action.'[1] This 'procedure,' apparently interpreted by the Russians as pledged action, included plans for controlling the media, dissolution of K-231, refusal to register KAN, prohibition of the revival of the Social Democratic Party, and certain personnel changes, according to Dubček.[2] The Czechoslovak presidium pledged once again its continued loyalty to the Warsaw Pact and CEMA, and the Russians, for their part, apparently pledged an end to polemics, and total withdrawal of the Pact troops still on Czechoslovak territory. The possibility of a Soviet loan was discussed, while the issue of the Warsaw letter, which Prague had wanted annulled, was dropped in view of Dubček's agreement to meet Moscow's allies in Bratislava two days later.

Even before their return, the Czechoslovak leaders telephoned to Prague for arrangements to ensure at least self-censorship on the part of the media. Despite an all-night meeting in Prague, little could be done by then about the issues of *Reportér* and *Literární listy* just out (the latter containing a caricature of Ulbricht), short of outright confiscation of the journals. This was a step the officials at home were not willing to take.[3] An agreement was worked out with the media, however, for forty-eight hours of respite, i.e. until after the Bratislava talks.

---

[1] The most detailed account of these talks may be found in Pavel Tigrid, *Why Dubček Fell* (London, 1971), 83–9.

[2] See Dubček's speech to September 1969 plenum, text in William Shawcross, *Dubček* (London, 1970), 274–98. Kriegel, Císař, and Pelikán were to be replaced ('Moravus', 'Shawcross' Dubček – A Different Dubček,' *Survey*, 17:4 (1971), 203–15.)

[3] According to one account (Tigrid, *Why Dubček Fell*, 88), Mlynář was willing, but Pavel refused; another account claimed Černík was willing.

The regime's relative optimism over the outcome of the Čierná talks was not echoed by the skeptical public, suspicious that some secret arrangement had been made at Čierná. On 2 August, demonstrations and meetings were held in Praque and other towns, generally demanding to know *all* that had been agreed to at Čierná. In response, Dubček appeared on television to repeat that no agreements had been made. The atmosphere of apprehension unquelled, the Dubček team went off to talks with Ulbricht, Zhivkov, Gomułka, Kádár, and the Soviet leaders on 3 August 1968. This meeting consisted primarily of arguments over the draft communique presented by Ulbricht upon his arrival. This communique, with its formulation of what has become known as the 'Brezhnev Doctrine,' similar to, but more vague than, the Warsaw letter's assertion of mutual responsibility for the preservation of socialist regimes, was finally approved that evening. The tone of the communique notwithstanding, no direct mention was made of Czechoslovakia (as promised by the Soviets), and Dubček, as well as other leaders, insisted on television on 4 August, that nothing had been agreed upon which would interfere with the continuation of the reform program. Tension over an immediate threat did recede in the following days (hundreds of thousands of people, including many leading intellectuals, went off on holiday), not only because of the regime's optimism but also because Soviet troops did finally leave the country and polemics ceased.[1] Nonetheless, efforts to seek the suspension of K-231, KAN, and the Social Democrats' activities, plus voluntary censorship (including rumors of a switch towards more conservative personnel in *Rudé právo*), together with other such acts as the curbing of the demonstration held in Prague on 8 August, the continued condemnation of Prchlík, and defense of the militia, preserved the state of apprehension.[2] Thus, many commentators who had welcomed the dénouement of Čierná and Bratislava, continued to warn of Czechoslovakia's vulnerable position and to condemn the Soviet attempts to interfere in Czechoslovak affairs.[3]

Morale was boosted somewhat by Tito's 9–11 August, Ceausescu's 15–16 August trips to Prague, and the Czechoslovak–Rumanian Friendship Treaty signed on 16 August.[4] Moreover, on 10 August the Party

[1] See *Zemědělské noviny*, 6 August 1968 or *Literární listy*, 8 August 1968 on reason having prevailed at Čierná.
[2] See *Rudé právo*, 11 August 1968 or Prague radio, 10 August 1968.
[3] See *Literární listy*, 8 August 1968; *Reportér*, 7 August 1968 (Ruml, Hochman).
[4] Tito declared support for the Czechoslovak position, but reportedly expressed reservations to Dubček about the lack of censorship and Party control (see Tigrid, *Why Dubček Fell*, 94).

published its draft statutes to be voted on at the forthcoming congress – a sign that the reform path was still being pursued. Counteracting these positive signs was the 12 August visit of Ulbricht to Karlové Vary, where he held talks with Dubček. This was followed, on 14 August, by the resumption of polemics from Moscow, in the form of an article in *Literaturnaya gazeta* attacking *Literární listy*, followed by several *Pravda* attacks which went so far as to accuse the Prague leaders of failing to defend socialism. In the midst of this renewed tension Dubček traveled to the Hungarian border for talks with Kádár (17 August) while the Party met with the intellectuals and journalists. At this meeting, journalists reportedly raised the possibility of invasion, as well as the idea of declaring a state of emergency under which the media would accept censorship in keeping with the amended Press Law. The regime leaders, however, were reluctant even to admit to such a pessimistic possibility (with the exception of Kriegel).[1]

It is difficult to fix the date of the Soviet decision to invade and, therefore, equally difficult to determine which events if any during the three weeks between Bratislava and the invasion were crucial to the final decision. The possibility of Soviet invasion had been rumored since May, when Warsaw Pact exercises were used as a psychological weapon. Exercises of one kind or another were carried out throughout the summer, but those begun on 22 July, designed to integrate reserves logistically, were qualitatively different, possibly marking the difference between pressures and actual preparation for invasion.[2] This would not necessarily mean that Čierná was a mere smokescreen; preparations for invasion may well have been undertaken prior to the final decision on invasion itself, so that the armies might act, before the fourteenth congress, if negotiations failed. Some trace the decision to the announcement on 5 August of the appointment of General S. M. Shtemenko as Warsaw Pact Chief-of-Staff instead of M. I. Kazakov.[3] On 13 August, Shtemenko turned up in Poland, meeting with Pact commanders on 16 August in south-west Poland where exercises were taking place.[4] This meeting included Grechko, Warsaw Pact Commander-in-Chief Yakubovsky and General Yepishev, and was said, by *Pravda* of 18 August, to be for the purpose of working out prob-

[1] Tigrid, *Why Dubček Fell*, 96 and private interviews.
[2] John Erickson, 'The "Military Factor" and the Czechoslovak Reform Movement: 1967–68,' unpublished paper (Reading, 1971).
[3] Malcolm MacIntosh, 'The Evolution of the Warsaw Pact,' *Adelphi Papers*, 58 (June 1969), 14–15.
[4] *Trybuna ludu*, 14, 17 August 1968.

lems of 'cooperation and coordination of the fraternal armies.' Two days later, Shtemenko, Grechko, Yakubovsky and Yepishev paid a similar visit to East Germany, meeting there with GDR Defense Minister Hoffman.[1] Thus, it may be that Shtemenko was brought in as an experienced officer to command the invasion. It has been suggested that Kazakov was replaced because he, and other military leaders, opposed the invasion out of fear of the long-term negative effects an invasion would have on the dependability of the Czechoslovak Army as a key member of the Pact.[2]

The final decision to invade may have been connected with the publication of the draft statutes on 10 August, which demonstrated to the Russians Dubček's intention of going ahead with the congress. Thus, it may have appeared to Moscow that its efforts at splitting the reform leadership, and hopes of postponement of the changes expected at the congress, had failed, necessitating stronger action.[3] In their renewed complaints, the Soviets themselves claimed that such things as the demonstration in front of the Prague central committee building on 8 August, the continued suggestions for an opposition party, and the 'polemics' against the 'allies,' combined with the attacks on the militia, all indicated non-fulfillment of the 'agreements' for a strengthening of the Party's role.[4]

The East Germans claimed that during his visit, Ulbricht came to the conclusion that the Prague leaders were not implementing the Bratislava decisions (specifically, the pledge to curb the media), the implication being that intervention then became the only alternative.[5] Resumption of polemics did occur just two days after Ulbricht's visit, but this was in a Soviet weekly, suggesting its preparation before Ulbricht would have had time to make his report. Whatever role Ulbricht's trip may have played, the CPSU politburo held a meeting on 16 July 1968, at which Brezhnev is said to have repeated Ulbricht's remarks to the March Dresden meeting: 'if Czechoslovakia continues to follow the January line,

---

[1] *Trybuna ludu*, 18 August 1968. TASS, 17 August omitted Shtemenko's name from the list of participants in this meeting.

[2] John Thomas, 'Soviet Foreign Policy and Conflict Within the Political and Military Leadership' (Research Analysis Corporation, 1970), 7–10.

[3] The only mention of the congress in *Pravda* prior to the invasion was a 20 August quote from *Borba* that only 'slightly more than 25%' of the then present central committee would appear on the ballot.

[4] *Pravda*, 16, 18, 20 August 1968. Also condemned were public protests, discussed by the Prague presidium on 13 August, to a letter sent to the USSR by 99 (of 4500) workers in a Prague plant complaining of the reforms.

[5] See *Neues Deutschland*, 25 August 1968.

all of us here will run a very serious risk which may well lead to our own downfall.'[1] It was at this meeting that the Soviet politburo made its final unanimous decision to invade, although Černík later told a government meeting that Suslov and Shelepin had reservations about the decision.[2] It was on the following day, Saturday 17 August, that Dubček held his meeting with Kádár, who reportedly tried to warn Dubček that non-fulfillment of the Bratislava undertakings would result in 'extreme measures' on the part of the Soviets. (Dubček later denied accusations that Kádár had informed him of the forthcoming measures.[3]) At 11 p.m. on Monday night, 19 August, Dubček received a letter from Moscow outlining its renewed complaints of Czechoslovakia's failure to abide by the so-called Čierná and Bratislava agreements. According to Dubček, the letter contained no ultimatum, i.e. no hint of an invasion. He read it to the presidium, however, only after the news of the invasion reached him.

The next day, Tuesday 20 August 1968, the presidium met to discuss preparations for the forthcoming congress; also discussed at this meeting was a paper prepared under the supervision of Kolder and Indra on the internal political situation since Čierná and Bratislava. The latter was a conservative document warning of the growth of counter-revolution in the country. Piller and presidium candidate Kapek defended the paper against the indignant attacks of Kriegel and Černík, and a clear split over the issue developed.[4] Subsequent reports on Kolder, Indra, Bil'ak and others strongly suggest that the paper was a tactical ploy designed to split the leadership and to provide a basis for inviting the Pact armies in to help put down the counter-revolution. Even if the conservatives failed to get the document through (only Rigo, Bil'ak, Švestka, and Kolder did vote for it, in fact; Barbírek and Piller did not vote with them), the conservatives could at least claim, as they later did, that the 'healthy forces' in the Party had warned the leaders of the danger of counter-revolution. Whatever the details of the plan, it was later revealed that Kolder and Indra, Bil'ak, Barbírek, Piller, auditing and control commission chief Jakeš, security chief Šalgovič, and possibly Švestka, along with the

---

[1] Pavel Tigrid, 'Czechoslovakia: A Post-Mortem II,' *Survey*, 74–5 (1968), 114.
[2] Prague radio, 28 August 1968.
[3] Tigrid, *Why Dubček Fell*, 96; Dubček to September 1969 plenum.
[4] The dispute concerned a more detailed report prepared by Jan Kašpar presented with the Kolder–Indra report and more explicit on the 'threat' to socialism in Czechoslovakia. (Text in *Tribuna*, 5 February 1969 and *Rudé právo*, 2 July 1969.) For information on this meeting see Littell, *The Black Book*, 23–9 and Dubček's September 1969 speech.

demoted conservatives Karel Hoffman, Miloš Marko, and Miroslav Sulek (former ČTK chief), were informed of the invasion, in some cases, at least one day in advance.[1]

At 11.40 p.m. Černík left the presidium meeting to receive one of many phone calls of the evening from Defense Minister Dzúr. When he returned he announced that the troops of the five Pact countries had crossed the Czechoslovak borders and were occupying the country.

There is a striking continuity in the history of the Czechoslovak Party and its relations with the international Communist movement. In the 1920s the Comintern saw fit to intervene in Czech Party affairs, conducting high-level purges in efforts to elicit a less gradualist–reformist approach from the Czech Communists. In 1947, the Cominform brought pressure to bear upon Gottwald and his colleagues to abandon their parliamentary 'Czechoslovak road to socialism' and take power in Prague. In 1968 the Warsaw Pact (minus Romania) intervened with force, with the same goal of putting a halt to the Czechs' democratic and permissive procedures and policies. This striking similarity should not limit us to perceiving events as specific – and inevitable – Czechoslovak phenomena, however, for the nuclei of reform movements exist in perhaps every Communist Party in Eastern Europe; indeed, they have come to the fore in at least two previous cases: Poland and Hungary, 1956. What was specific to the Czechoslovak Party was the nature of the difficulties the international movement almost continuously encountered regarding the Czechoslovak Party (particularly its Czech elements). It was not the case that the reformers were nationalistic and thus placed a longing for national independence before the interests of the movement, or anti-Russian to the extent of rejecting Moscow's leadership. As we have seen, prior to the interference from the Soviet Union and her allies, the reform regime was little concerned with its international position, foreign policy, or relations with the Soviet Union. Certain aspects of the reforms implicitly, and even explicitly, argued for independence, but these were mainly within the realm of establishing a viable economy, free of political encumbrances, whether internal or external. The talk of a 'return to Europe' was intended in terms of economic–political–diplomatic contacts, not direct political alliance or even neutrality. It is true that many of the reforms, both

[1] See Smrkovský talk with Kuznetsov, published in Tigrid, *Why Dubček Fell*, appendix. Strange behavior by some of these men over the preceding days had prompted Dubček to agree to declare an alert in Prague on the morning of 20 August for fear of a coup-attempt at the presidium meeting, according to 'Moravus,' *Survey*, 17, 4 (1972), 210.

economic and political, might eventually and perhaps inevitably have led to a desire for independence of a political–economic nature, since the principle common to most of the reforms was de-centralization of authority and a system based on the free expression of the real interests of the component parts. Indeed, in the summer months of 1968, as Soviet pressures increased, there were voices raised in this direction of national independence. But this was neither the point nor the intended goal of the proposed reforms. Until the summer of 1968, the cry for a Czechoslovak socialism was not intended nor even widely interpreted domestically as anti-Russian.

While reform rule in Czechoslovakia was designed to build a model of socialism suitable to the country's needs, realities, and traditions, this desire was not born of nationalism or abhorrence for things Russian. It was, rather, born of problems and developments within Czechoslovak society for which the prevailing model, that of the Soviet Union, proved inadequate. Indeed, there were but rare voices which emphasized the Russian source of the ruling model. There is nothing in either the actions or speeches of the reform leaders to indicate that they saw their own, new model as unobtainable within the framework of the Warsaw Pact–CEMA alliances.[1] Nor did they suggest, or intend, that their emerging model should be an alternative or a challenge to the Soviet model. It was, rather, Soviet, Polish, and East German fears of the nature of this model and its already apparent attraction for certain elements in their own countries, leading to their efforts to interfere in Czechoslovak affairs, which prompted the Prague reformers belatedly to insist upon full sovereignty *and* the purely Czechoslovak nature of their experiment.[2]

The Russians strove to create the impression, publicly, that their major concern was that Czechoslovakia was falling into the hands of persons who wished to take her out of the socialist alliance, to defy the Soviet Union, and to move towards the West. Indeed, they contrived a number of 'facts' (such as caches of arms) to create the impression that the bloc was in danger from West German exploitation of the weakening of socialism in Czechoslovakia.[3] That these were not the genuine causes of the Soviet concern was evidenced by the nature of the latter's demands in the various meetings with Dubček. Indeed, demands to station Pact

[1] For this contention see for example Dušan Hamšík's appraisal in *Listy*, 30 January 1969.

[2] This was pointed out by Petr Pithart in *Literární listy*, 25 July 1968.

[3] See Michal Lakatoš in *Studentské listy*, 1 April 1969 or 'SV' in *Politika*, 26 September 1968 on this tactic.

troops in Czechoslovakia well pre-dated the reform regime,[1] and as pointed out, there is some evidence that important elements among the Soviet military were among those opposing the invasion, in the belief that Czechoslovakia was a more dependable link in the Warsaw Pact under Svoboda and Dubček than it would be after an invasion.

The discussions of Dresden, Moscow, and Čierná, as well as the history of the Soviet conception of power, all point to a more complicated, doctrinally influenced explanation for the invasion. In 1968, as in 1929 and 1947, Moscow's concerns focused on Czechoslovakia's traditional tendencies to democratic socialism, with all their implications for the rest of the Communist world. Like the Comintern and Cominform before them, the dominant powers in the Warsaw Pact were unwilling to accept that this type of socialism could lead to and preserve Communism. Specifically, the concept of the leading role of the Party, as applied by the Soviets for some fifty years, had become so intricately connected with the concept of Communist rule that Moscow could not conceive a Communist Party's remaining in power if it were to abandon its leading role.[2] Moscow could not conceive of a Communist state without the unchallenged, dictatorial, ubiquitous authority of the Party. And if the Communist Party could not remain in power in any but the orthodox way, then indeed Czechoslovakia's remodeling of the leading role of the Party to permit a certain degree of pluralism and controls on central power constituted in Soviet eyes a danger to Communist rule in Czechoslovakia. The implications of such a danger were clear: pluralism in Prague – which could mean not only difficulties for Soviet dictation of policy for that country, but also the inevitable dissolution of Communist power and, therefore, of the Communist regime – might well spread to other countries. The fall of the Communist regime in Prague would mean the loss of Czechoslovakia as a reliable ally or even a friendly neighbor. Here the international power-motive returned, but only as a consequence of a much more basic and immediate concern: the possibility of Communism in a pluralistic-democratic socialist society.[3] It was the democratic nature and content of the Czechoslovak experiment, rather than some fabricated 'danger' of neutralism or pro-western tendencies which precipitated the invasion.

It was in this context that the Soviets elucidated their concept of

[1] Deputy Foreign Minister Václav Pleskot admitted this on Prague radio (interview in German), 22 May 1968.

[2] See Hamšík, *Listy*, 30 January 1969; Pithart, *Literární listy*, 25 July 1968; or Hochman in *Reportér*, 2 October 1968.

[3] See ibid. and Šik interview to *L'Espresso* (Rome), 1 September 1968.

limited sovereignty: the right of the socialist 'camp' to determine what constitutes a danger to Communism even within other socialist nations. While this may be a purely arbitrary concept, designed ultimately to preserve the Soviet empire, it conveys an important lesson for reform efforts within the context of Communism. There are certain tenets so intricately wedded to the Soviet concept of rule that even non-nationalistic, pro-Russian, loyally socialist movements cannot infringe upon them. There is every reason to conclude that the reform regime in Czechoslovakia believed it could realize its program within the context of Communism and alliance with Moscow. It was Moscow, not Prague, which said – perhaps proved – the contrary.

Occupation[1]

Dubček's response to the news of the invasion was:
> 'On my honor as a Communist, I declare that I did not have the slightest idea or receive the slightest indication that anyone proposed taking such measures against us...I, who have devoted my whole life to cooperation with the Soviet Union, now they do this to me! This is the tragedy of my life!'

Yet, he and his colleagues set about to protect the country in the way they saw fit, assuming, as Dubček later explained (in his speech to the September 1969 plenum), that a representative of the invading forces would contact him with terms, at which time the presidium would make further decisions. In the meantime, he ordered the army to remain in barracks and the militia to make sure that arms were not made available to 'unauthorized' persons. Shortly after 1 a.m., the presidium issued a statement to the population denying any foreknowledge of the 'allies'' intentions and calling this action 'contrary to the fundamental principles of relations between socialist states and a denial of the basic norms of international law.' There were four opposing votes to this statement, those of Bil'ak, Kolder, Rigo, and Švestka. Indra was only a Party secretary and therefore not a voting member of the presidium. He, for his part, reportedly went to see Svoboda a few hours later to demand the formation of a 'Revolutionary Workers and Peasants Committee,' i.e. a new government under Indra. Svoboda is said to have ordered him out of his office.[2] This was apparently the furthest the conservatives got towards forming a quisling government, although a group of conservative central committee members met the following day in the Praha Hotel. Under the direction of

[1] Unless otherwise stated, the source for this section is Littell (ed.), *The Black Book*.
[2] Joseph Wechsberg, *The Voices* (New York, 1969), 27.

Kolder, Bil'ak, Vilém Nový, Miloš Jakeš, Indra, Piller, and Karel Mestek, this group issued a proclamation calling for cooperation with the invaders, though claiming no foreknowledge of the planned invasion.[1] At approximately 3 a.m. Černík was arrested by Soviet troops at the government Presidium Building; at about 4 a.m. Czechoslovak security officers entered the central committee building and arrested Dubček, 'in the name of the Revolutionary Government.' What had preceded these arrests, and even the invasion, was a meeting at 4 p.m. on 20 August at which the security chief, deputy Interior Minister Šalgovič, had informed selected officers of the forthcoming occupation and their assigned tasks. It was thus that certain key facilities, such as Prague's international airport, were attended to in anticipation of the invaders' arrival. As it turned out later the security forces were split as to their loyalties and some, supporters of the liberal Interior Minister Pavel, were interned during the occupation by the collaborators, while others helped the population against the Russians' agents. Sufficient collaborators were found among the security officers during the night, however, to arrest Císař, Smrkovský, Kriegel, Špaček and Šimon as well. These leaders were interned in the central committee building until the afternoon, at which time they were flown, handcuffed, to Lehnice, then to the Ukraine, and later to Moscow. Císař managed to escape and, like Pavel and other reformers believed to be in danger, was hidden by the people.

After orders by former Cultural Minister Hoffman to close the main radio transmitter were countermanded by Smrkovský (prior to his arrest), Czechoslovak radio went on the air at its scheduled time at 4.30 a.m., 21 August. An hour and a half later a powerful transmitter (later discovered to be in East Germany), began broadcasting in poor Czech and Slovak under the name 'radio Vltava'. It broadcast the spurious proclamation of the invading countries that they had been called in by (unnamed) Party and government leaders of Czechoslovakia to 'render fraternal assistance' against the counter-revolutionaries (supported and aided by western imperialists).[2] Czechoslovakia radio, however, continued to broadcast appeals to the people, including one sent by Dubček, to maintain calm and order. At 8.15 it broadcast an address by Svoboda, and

---

[1] *Mladá fronta*, 23 August 1968 (in *Black Book*, 84–5) version of Vaculík speech to fourteenth congress. The Pelikán transcript of Vaculík's speech is slightly different (Pelikán, *Vysočany Congress*, 26–8). Barbírek was also at this meeting but withheld his support (*Ranni vydani spojenych deniku*, 23 August 1968).

[2] Bil'ak later revealed names to central committee (*Listy* (Rome), 1/1971, 12). The Soviet Journalists Union journal *Za rubezhom* admitted (10–16 January 1969) that the Czechoslovak leaders had opposed the invasion as an infringement on sovereignty.

shortly thereafter shooting could be heard over the air as the invading troops began to occupy Prague radio. The announcer described the scene and declared loyalty to Dubček; the national anthems were played and then, silence. This was the beginning, however, rather than the end, of one of the strangest and probably most heroic chapters in radio–television broadcasting of our time. Prague radio and television began broadcasting from improvised studios and borrowed transmitters throughout the country, including Slovakia. With the help of the army and militia, whose radio facilities were used along with those of audio-visual research and training institutes and factories, and with the aid of citizens throughout the country who provided food, transportation, and protection, the radio and television directed the country throughout the critical first week of invasion. In the absence of the government and Party leaders held in Moscow and the physical inability of the government to function normally, the radio and television 'led' the people, instructing them not only, for example, to avoid provocations or bloodshed, but where to secure food, which persons were in danger of arrest and by whom, which plants were to deliver what foods to which areas, which routes to follow, and so forth. They announced the one-hour general strikes of 12 noon on Thursday 22 August and Friday 23 August, and the various shorter protest strikes on other days. They suggested the changing of street names and elimination of street numbers to confuse the enemy; they urged the population to completely ignore the invaders even to the point of denying them food and drink unless directly threatened.

Broadcasting in eight languages, they kept the people informed insofar as possible, and they broadcast appeals abroad for aid against the 'illegal and unnecessary' infringement of Czechoslovak sovereignty. Whereas in normal times there were only two radio programs and one television channel, during this extraordinary week, there were five radio programs, often as many as nineteen different stations, and three television channels.

The press, too, continued to function in one way or another in these days, often putting out mimeographed issues, sometimes several newspapers together. Here, too, the public, workers and military, helped find facilities or distributed the precious issues. There probably was not a journal, paper, organization or group that did not issue words of encouragement to the public, support for the legitimate leaders of the country, and condemnation of the invasion. The historians of the ČSAV Institute of History collected these for a documentary history of the fateful week (published in the fall).[1]

---

[1] *Sedm pražských dnů* (Praha, 1968) and known as the *Black Book*.

From the early morning hours of 21 August and throughout the week, the National Assembly met in continuous session. It was also under seige, for tanks had surrounded all official buildings, and deputies feared that if they left they might not be permitted to reenter. Therefore, the deputies, of whom a majority managed to reach the building, slept there and were brought food and blankets from outside.[1] To the surprise of many, such known conservatives as former Defense Minister Lomský shared in this siege, voting for the proclamations produced by the Assembly which condemned the invasion and demanded release of the country's leaders and immediate withdrawal of the Pact troops.[2] The government, too, met almost continuously, sometimes under the leadership of the Minister for Consumer Industries, Božena Machačová, sometimes of deputy Premier Štrougal or others. Shortly after noon of the first day of the invasion it issued a statement supporting the nation's leaders and condemning the invasion as 'an illegal act, contrary to international law and the principles of international socialism.' It also sent notes from the Foreign Ministry to the governments of the five invading countries demanding immediate withdrawal of troops.

On Thursday 22 August the occupation forces issued an ultimatum that a new government be formed, to consist of Bil'ak, Oldřich Pavlovský, Barbírek, Kolder, Indra, and Lenárt and to exclude Dubček and his colleagues.[3] A deadline of 6 p.m. was given on threat of the formation of an occupation regime. Despite efforts by Bil'ak and Kolder to get Svoboda to agree to this, the ultimatum went ignored, and the government announced that Svoboda, along with Dzúr, and Husák would try to get to Moscow to negotiate the release of the country's leaders. Bohuslav Kučera was also selected as representative of the National Front. The following day Svoboda announced the inclusion of Piller, Bil'ak, and Indra in the delegation, at the behest of Moscow, he implied.[4] The Slovak National Front's delegate, Klokoč, was unable to join the group due to a mishap with Soviet troops at the airfield.[5] At 10.45 that evening, the radio carried a message from Svoboda that he had succeeded in having Dubček, Černík, Smrkovský ('and other comrades') included in the negotiations. This group was joined the following day by Barbírek, Rigo, Švestka, Jakeš, Lenárt, and Mlynář.

[1] 196 deputies were present by 24 August, 47 of whom from Slovakia.   [2] Contained in *Dokumenty o Národním Shromáždění ve dnech 21.—28. srpna 1968* (Praha, 1968).

[3] Littell, *The Black Book*, 103; Pelikán, *Vysočany Congress*, 46; Lenárt reportedly refused to cooperate (*Black Book*, 215).

[4] For confirmation of this, see government press conference, 24 August 1968.

[5] *Rol'nícke noviny*, 31 August 1968.

Occupation

The Party, too, was active during this period, particularly since before their arrests Šimon had proposed to Dubček (on behalf of the Prague city Party committee, which met almost continuously in the following days) that the fourteenth congress should be convened, and a general strike organized, and an appeal sent to the Communist Parties throughout the world. After Dubček's arrest Šimon went ahead with these plans, which were all implemented even after Šimon's arrest shortly thereafter. Through arrangements made by the radio and through individuals, the fourteenth Party congress was opened at 11.18 a.m., 22 August 1968 in the ČKD factory in the Vysočany section of Prague. Disguised as workers and protected by the militia, some 1192 of the 1543 delegates elected attended the one-day congress. Only fifty Slovak delegates were able to attend, while eleven others who arrived late because of obstructions to their progress along the way asked that they be considered as having participated. Husák was detained en route to the meeting, but, at least, he tried to get to the congress which he was later to declare invalid. The Slovak Party congress was held as scheduled (26 August) despite a call from Husák to postpone it, and on its first day supported the standpoint of the fourteenth congress.[1] The Vysočany congress elected a new central committee and presidium, which included almost all the known reformers. Věnek Šilhán[2] was given direction of the presidium until Dubček's return. The congress condemned the invasion and demanded immediate withdrawal of the troops and release of the country's leaders. A one-hour general strike was threatened for the next day if negotiations for the above and a statement by Dubček to the nation were not forthcoming within the next twenty-four hours. The threat was carried out at noon, 23 August 1968. The congress also sent a letter of support to Dubček saying: 'The repeated calls of "Dubček, Dubček" coming from our youth who carried through Prague the bloodied state flag bear ample testimony that your name has become the symbol of our sovereignty.'

The youth indeed were the other heroes of this week of invasion. They led the population at large in its activities of passive resistance, in the streets, exhibiting an exemplary discipline while carrying out the instructions of the radio. In isolated cases they gave their lives either by trying to bar the way of the invading tanks or simply by expressing their sentiments. The country was united in these days as never before in its history; the solidarity and mutual consideration were such that many were later to have called it the most exhilarating if tragic week of their lives. There

[1] *Smena*, 18 September 1969 (Bil'ak statement); Zdeněk Hejzlar, *Chronology 1968–69*, unpublished paper (Stockholm, 1970), 36.   [2] From the Prague city Party group.

was even humor in the people's resistance, as witnessed by slogans and jokes spread at the time.[1] The numerous symbolic strikes were total, the country literally ringing with the clanging of bells, horns, and even alarm clocks upon call from the radio.[2] But, equally spontaneously, workers appeared for work for what they called 'Dubček shifts' on Sunday 25 August. These actions had a demoralizing effect on the occupying troops, many of whom thought that they were in West Germany, or the Ukraine, or, at the very least, a Czechoslovakia racked by civil war and counter-revolution. There were some cases of suicides by these troops, but there were more cases of trigger-happy nervousness and callousness. Reports of Czech and Slovak lives lost range from 80 to 200, while damage to property, including the National Museum in Prague, and to the economy of the country, to say nothing of its feelings for Russia, was incalculable.

Three questions which present themselves – and continued to be debated in Czechoslovakia long after the invasion – were the following: why were no preparations made for such an eventuality; why were the people not warned of the seriousness of the situation; and, why did the regime not permit the people to fight. The answers are by no means simple and, in fact, may never be provided. One can only assume that Dubček (partially raised in the Soviet Union), and his colleagues could not bring themselves to believe that the Russians would actually invade and therefore could not even begin to think of preparation. Dubček seemed to believe that it was only a matter of making Brezhnev *understand* what the reforms were all about. Moreover, the more practical may have believed that preparations, such as apparently were suggested by Prchlík, would merely have provoked the Russians, who would see in them 'proof' of the counter-revolution they claimed was brewing in Czechoslovakia. There is also the possibility that the regime had simply not believed the situation to have been as critical as it was. Dubček later defended himself on this very point, his only answer being that he never believed the Russians would do such a thing. Why the country did not fight is a question which can easily be answered with cold logic: a small nation, even possessing a good army, cannot hope to survive the combined armies of five countries, one of which is a world power. Indeed, Hungary had taught the socialist world that even armed resistance would not stop the Russians. Moreover, the reasonable Czech nation had survived hundreds of years of outside domination, outliving their oppressors with their indomitable spirit

[1] For example, 'Soviet–Czechoslovak friendship has been growing deeper each year. Now it has reached rock-bottom' or 'Lenin! Wake up! Brezhnev's gone mad!'
[2] Such a demonstration was accorded the returning leaders on 27 August as well.

and patience. Thus, they knew from experience that they could survive, even without their national sovereignty, and perhaps once again 'wait it out' as they had under the Habsburgs. This tradition of passive resistance and patience probably operated subconsciously, but it was most likely present when Dubček made his decision – as Beneš had thirty years before – not to sacrifice the nation's blood for the sake of some abstract notion of honor. That this rational approach did not satisfy everyone, particularly the young, was apparent in the frequent efforts to justify the failure to fight (or to distinguish this decision from that of Beneš) which appeared in Czechoslovakia in articles and speeches, and in conversations over the following months.[1] Passive resistance, however, became the by-word and Schweikism was given an added dimension of daring during the days of the invasion – and the months that followed.

On 27 August 1968 the reform leaders returned to the country after three days of physical and spiritual humiliation and exhaustion, and three more days of painful negotiations. Through the arrival in Moscow of Svoboda and Mlynář (and the former's telephone call to his wife), the Czechoslovak leaders had some idea of the courageous stand being put up by the population at home. It is just this which prevented the achievement of the invasion's immediate political objective: the establishment of an anti-reform government. It was just this stand which forced the Soviets to release the very people they had already literally spat upon as counter-revolutionaries, and to negotiate with them. This in itself was an impressive achievement and the reform leaders, themselves divided as to the best approach to the Russians in their present position, gained what they could in the Moscow talks. Their refusal to return home without Kriegel, who had refused to sign the Moscow agreement, was a spark of defiance, the success of which may well have raised their hopes.[2] Just how much they had salvaged in Moscow would be clear only in the following weeks and months, but both Smrkovský and Dubček, addressing the nation upon their return via the 'free, legal' radio, appeared as courageous but beaten men.

[1] For example, Dzúr interview, Prague radio, 5 October 1968.
[2] The Russians reportedly made anti-semitic attacks on Kriegel and sought to detain him in Moscow. (Tigrid, *Why Dubček Fell*, 118–19.)

11

The End of Reform Rule

The political situation

The post-invasion period was to be one of successive crises culminating in the final removal of the reform leaders and the systematic destruction of their programs. It began, however, with a general state of shock, probably for the regime as well as the population at large. The returned leaders expressed their determination to continue what became known as the 'post-January policies,' albeit with qualifications due to what also became known as the 'complicated conditions' of the time. Just what was contained in the agreements signed by the Czechoslovak leaders in Moscow became known only gradually, and full information has never in fact been published in Czechoslovakia.[1]

The National Assembly, still acting as a free and independent body, unanimously declared on 28 August that it had a right to examine all agreements reached outside Czechoslovakia and that it continued to uphold its own decisions of the invasion week concerning the illegality of the occupation, the demand for total withdrawal of foreign troops, recognition of the fourteenth Party congress, and a return to freedom of the media and all Constitutional organs. Other groups too, including students, intellectuals, and workers, officially expressed their misgivings about the agreement, signed as Smrkovský himself admitted 'in the shadow of tanks and planes on our territory.'[2] These objections notwithstanding, the government, the Party central committee, and the National Assembly itself, accepted the *Moscow Protocol* at their meetings of 28 August, 31 August, and 13 September 1968.[3]

Dubček had warned even in his speech of 27 August that the agreement contained stipulations for the restriction ('temporary') of the freedom of expression, and the following day Černík explained that controls were to be introduced regarding the media. Both revealed that the foreign troops would be staying for an unspecified length of time. In his speech to

[1] For text published in the West, see Tigrid, *Why Dubček Fell*, 210–14.
[2] Smrkovský on Prague radio, 29 August 1968; Littell, *Black Book*, 292–314.
[3] The National Assembly did not actually vote on the Protocol, but it enacted legislation for its implementation.

the central committee on 31 August, Dubček revealed that the *Protocol* also placed a ban on 'political organizations violating socialist principles and attempts to set up political parties outside the National Front.'[1] As explained by Černík to the National Assembly on 13 September, this meant the end of KAN and K-231.[2] The appropriate bill for censorship was then passed by the National Assembly, as was the new National Front bill (with a new preamble referring to the above restrictions) and a bill on public order to control the right to assembly.[3]

The central committee plenum also implemented two more of the *Protocol* clauses: personnel changes and invalidation of the fourteenth Party congress.[4] It was only ten days later that Zdeněk Mlynář revealed in a television speech that the *Protocol* called for an 'assessment' by the Prague government of those of its members who were abroad after 20 August 1968; the rest of the personnel stipulations were not publicly revealed though they were to include Party and state organs and the media. Mlynář's speech, which reportedly provoked the ire of the Russians, merely confirmed a process of changes already fairly clear: reform leaders Šik, Kriegel, Hájek, Hejzlar, Pelikán, Císař, and Pavel were removed from most or all of their leading positions.

The reform leaders used the opportunity, however, to rid themselves of some of the more Stalinist conservatives or at least, hopefully, neutralize them by adding a large number of liberals to an enlarged plenum (of 21 instead of 11 members). Those dropped were Kolder, Švestka, and Rigo while Kapek, Chudík, and Barbírek were demoted.[5] In their places on the central committee such reformers as philosopher Karel Kosík, historian Milan Hübl, and theorist Radovan Richta were added, along

[1] Prague radio, 1 September 1968.

[2] Already on 5 September the Interior Ministry rejected their applications, declaring KAN a political organization and K-231 a duplication of already created government organs. K-231 was in fact disbanded on 19 September 1968 (*Práce*, 23 October).

[3] *Sbírka zákonů*, Nos. 126–8/1968. Although not stated in the National Assembly bill, no new political parties were to be permitted, even within the National Front, although new social organizations might apply for membership. (ČTK, 13 September 1968, interview with National Front deputy chairman Josef Zedník.)

[4] The Slovak Party congress, already on 27 August, reversed its support of the 14th congress (see 243). In his 11 October speech to Tesla plant workers Dubček conceded another Soviet demand: redrafting of the proposed Party statutes.

[5] Petitions were signed by thousands of their constituents demanding the resignations of Indra and Kolder from the National Assembly. Kolder refused but was sent to Bulgaria. Šalgovič was even defeated for presidium membership of the Slovak Anti-Fascist Fighters Union in February 1969. (*Nová svoboda*, 19 September; Tigrid, *Why Dubček Fell*, Smrkovský–Kuznetsov conversation, 222; *Práce*, 28 March 1969.)

with a large number of lesser known but reform-minded persons. Husák was finally brought into the presidium, having been elected Slovak first secretary at the Slovak Party congress of 26–29 August 1968, as were Zdeněk Mlynář, Václav Slavík, Bohumil Šimon, and Svoboda (honorary membership), among others.

The stated reason for these changes was to provide leadership by 'comrades enjoying universal confidence and the ability to lead the Party in the complicated situation without extreme actions and internal splits that would weaken the Party and lead to the inconsistent realization of the political line adopted.'[1] In fact, however, despite the majority achieved by the reformers, a serious split was beginning to take shape within the reformers' ranks. As distinct from the 'conservatives' such as Piller, Barbírek, and Biľak, and from the liberal reformers such as Dubček, Smrkovský, Šimon, and Špaček, a third, centrist group around Husák emerged, known as the 'realists,' because of their pragmatic more compromising attitude to the 'harsh realities' of the country's position.[2] Their views were reflected in the statements of the Slovak Party, beginning with its early invalidation of the fourteenth Party congress. This approach led to the earlier 'consolidation' of the situation in Slovakia, often explained by Husák as the result of the fact that the Slovaks, unlike the Czechs, had been able to hold their congress and, therefore, produce a unified leadership group.[3] Yet the issue of convening a Czech congress had been the very issue which had divided this centrist group from the more liberal Czechs in the spring, and in time the attitude to both this and the speedy convocation of the new fourteenth congress became the distinction not only between conservatives and reformers but also between 'realists' and liberals.

The split amongst the reformers was reflected more in tone than in substance during the first weeks of the post-invasion period. Husák tended to be more critical of the errors of the Prague spring, referring even to 'anarchist' as well as 'anti-socialist' tendencies, with particular criticism for the media and the clubs. He also seemed to register impatience with rumors and exaggerations being spread irresponsibly, claiming that 'no one has exerted any pressure on us to jettison the sound ideas of socialist democracy.' At the same time he warned against 'naïveté,' referring to 'existing facts which we cannot change.'[4] While even Smrkovský and

[1] Dubček, Prague radio, 1 September 1968.
[2] See Jiří Baudiss, *Práce*, 18 September 1968 for an early appraisal of this.
[3] Husák interview, Bratislava radio, 1 September 1968; *Politika*, 19 September 1968.
[4] Husák speech on Prague radio, 28 September 1968; speech to Slovak National Front, ČTK, 18 September 1968 or speech in Trnovec, *Pravda* (Bratislava), 21 October 1968.

Dubček were critical of excesses which they admitted had appeared in the spring, their language was not nearly as strong, and they specifically denied that the Party had been thereby weakened.[1] Their general emphasis was more optimistically forward-looking. They both spoke of the specific planks in the reform platform, such as rehabilitations, or public participation, and an open policy, while Husák tended to concentrate on federalization, as he had in the spring as well. In appraising the reasons for the invasion, Dubček saw the primary error not in the Party's having tolerated this or that group but in having underestimated the international interest in and consequences of political developments inside Czechoslovakia, leading to 'a reduction of the confidence of the CPSU leadership in the ability of our Party to solve the problems which had arisen.'[2]

Soviet supervision of the beginning of the 'normalization' undertaken by the Czechoslovak leaders was conducted primarily through Soviet deputy Foreign Minister Vasily Kuznetsov, dispatched to Prague during the first week in September. In meeting with officials at all levels, he conveyed Moscow's dissatisfaction over the progress of normalization and specific 'infringements' of the *Moscow Protocol*, such as the enlarging of the presidium without prior consultation with Moscow. In talks with Smrkovský, Kuznetsov criticized the continued outspokenness of the press, even of *Rudé právo*, particularly in 'harping' on the presence of the foreign troops.[3] He did say that matters were generally better in Slovakia, except for the press, but he was not pleased with the way Bil'ak, Kolder, and Indra were being treated.

Following a presidium meeting on 2 October, Dubček, Černík, and Husák set off for two days of talks in Moscow. The limited composition of the Czechoslovak delegation was not, however, a good sign, and, indeed, the Soviets heatedly reiterated their objection, conveyed earlier, by Kuznetsov, to the progress and interpretation of normalization in Czechoslovakia, and to specific comments made by Czech reformers, such as those of Mlynář and Smrkovský. Rumors to the effect that further personnel changes were agreed upon, were, however, repeatedly denied by the Czechoslovak leaders.[4] Nonetheless Mlynář submitted his resignation (accepted only a month later), reportedly because he considered it impossible to continue working fruitfully, particularly if Moscow's objec-

---

[1] For example, Dubček speech on Prague radio, 14 September 1968; Smrkovský to Záluží works, *Rudé právo*, 24 September 1968.

[2] To 31 August plenum, Prague radio, 1 September 1968.

[3] Tigrid, *Why Dubček Fell*, 215–29 (also *Der Spiegel*, 14 October 1968).

[4] Prague radio, 8 October; *Smena* and ČTK, 23 October 1968.

tions to him were not vigorously opposed. Following these talks, in his 11 October speech, Dubček repeated his belief in the possibility of continuing the post-January program, but he was more critical than previously of the excesses of the Prague spring, particularly of the media.

The presidium communique issued after the meeting even referred, for the first time, to 'anarchist' tendencies, and it mentioned only the January 1968 and critical May 1968 plena of the Czechoslovak Party as a basis for future actions, conspicuously skipping the all-important April plenum which had approved the Action Program. Despite emphasis in both statements on the need to strengthen the leading role of the Party, Dubček continued to espouse the idea of public participation, in what was clearly an effort to tread the fine line between his own conception of Communist rule and Moscow's demands. At the same time he had, also, to attempt to maintain unity within the Party itself.

This last task was rendered still more difficult by the organization of the 'ultra-conservative' forces at a meeting in the Prague suburb of Libeň on 9 October. According to Moscow radio on 11 October 1968, some 600 'old communists' adopted documents which not only approved the invasion and called for prosecution of various persons in the mass media but also blamed the 'ideological softness, weakness, and incompetence of certain members of the Presidium' of the Party for the activities of 'counter-revolution.' Among the many targets of the group's attack was Bohumil Šimon's radical Prague city Party organization. Providing clues to Moscow's demands, the group also rejected the convening of a Czech Party congress until after the fourteenth congress which, it said, should be postponed until thorough normalization had been achieved. This group, under the leadership apparently of Antonín Kapek, Karel Mestek, Josef Jodas, Vilém Nový, and, probably, Alois Indra, met a number of times in the course of the post-invasion period. Their meetings, however, always evoked public protests, from workers and intellectuals alike, and the Party as early as Dubček's 11 October speech declared its opposition to organized factionalism of this, or any other, kind. In this Husák and the 'realists' were willing to join, for theirs was the road of accommodation for the sake of a return to normal times, without terror or reprisals and without the return of Novotný's collaborators.[1]

[1] See, for example, *Pravda* (Bratislava), 24 October 1968. The formation of a Libeň-type group was also reported in Pilsen (*Rudé právo*, 25 October 1968). Possibly to counter this phenomenon, a conference of 'old Communists' was held on 6 November, at the initiative of the Party's secretariat and addressed by Dubček (and criticized by radio Vltava).

Moscow's opposition to the creation of a Czech Party was apparent not only in the Liben statement but also in the omission of any reference to it in the presidium's 8 October communique and Dubček's speech. Indeed on 22 October Prague radio announced that the presidium had approved a proposal for the creation of a central committee 'bureau' for the Czech lands, which was created the following month under the conservative Štrougal. Moreover, on 25 October Dubček announced that the fourteenth congress would not be held in 1968. Another matter conspicuously absent from the 8 October communique was that of the withdrawal of the Pact troops. This issue was settled within days, however, by the signing of the treaty on 16 October for the temporary stationing of Soviet troops in Czechoslovakia. This treaty provided for the total withdrawal of the Pact troops (which in fact began in late October), with the exception of Soviet troops of unspecified number, which were to remain in Czechoslovakia for an unspecified period. It was presented as a necessary link in the defenses against NATO, although Kosygin's speech in Prague, on the occasion of the signing of the treaty, referred to the Brezhnev Doctrine as well.[1] The treaty closely followed those covering Soviet troops elsewhere in Eastern Europe, including the clause that the country's sovereignty would in no way be affected and that the troops would not interfere in internal affairs.

The general reaction to the treaty was one of despondency, despite the regime's efforts to emphasize the withdrawal of most of the troops.[2] The ratification ceremony of the National Assembly was broadcast live, but it was marred by the continued independence of at least some delegates who either abstained (ten persons) or spoke out against the treaty (four, including long-time Communists Kriegel and Vodsloň).[3] Addressing the Assembly Černík admitted the blow to Czechoslovak sovereignty but claimed that sovereignty was 'a notion which in the contemporary world cannot be practically realized in its absolute meaning.' His lengthy remarks strove, however, to reassure the nation that there would be no return to the illegalities of former years.

These reassurances were necessary, for a certain uneasiness had set in since Dubček's trip to Moscow in the beginning of October, even pointed

---

[1] This reference was omitted from the ČTK and TASS versions but carried in the Moscow radio English broadcasts. See TASS, 18 October 1968, for text of treaty.

[2] For example, *Rudé právo* and *Lidová demokracie*, 21 October 1968; *Reportér*, 30 October 1968 (Hochman) and *Politika*, 31 October 1968 (Alois Svoboda).

[3] Prague radio, 18 October 1968; ČTK, 12 November 1968. For speech by Sekaninová-Čakrtová, one of the dissenting deputies, see *Reportér*, 30 October 1968.

out in a *Nové slovo* article on 24 October 1968. In anticipation of troubles with the beginning of the school year, regime leaders appealed to students to return quietly to their studies.[1] These efforts notwithstanding, on 28 October, Czechoslovakia's national anniversary, young people did demonstrate, some staging a sit-down in front of the Soviet Embassy. The tension continued into November, with further spontaneous demonstrations on the anniversary of the Bolshevik Revolution. The regime was thus faced with deteriorating public morale and heightened tension just at the time at which it had to formulate and present the 'appraisal' Moscow demanded of the Prague spring and an outline of policies.[2] Indeed the latter was already a domestic necessity, for critical comments, for example those at a north Bohemian regional Party meeting (*Rudé právo*, 25 October 1968), had begun to appear about the return to 'cabinet politics' or politics behind closed doors and the lack of information on what the regime would (or could) do. This was one of the reasons for the student unrest which, on the eve of the November plenum, was threatening to break into a nation-wide student demonstration or strike. The conservatives too added to the tension preceding the plenum by holding another meeting in Prague, on 10 November.

The conflicting views were building as well within the central committee and even in the presidium prior to the plenum.[3] The major issue seemed to be the degree to which the Prague spring was to be condemned (i.e. if any of it should be continued) and the danger of anti-socialism ('danger from the right') emphasized. The centrists around Husák, joined now by Černík, Svoboda, Sádovský and possibly Erban, had been criticizing both 'left' and 'right' more or less equally, but Dubček, joined by Smrkovský, Špaček, and Šimon sought to go forward with as few recriminations as possible and a vote of confidence in the Action Program.[4] Given the strength of the conservatives (Piller, Bil'ak, Barbírek, Lenárt, Štrougal), however, Dubček decided to avoid a conflict with the 'realists', joining forces with them on the drafting of the plenum's resolution. To ensure even this compromise, and to undermine the conservatives' opposition,

[1] Svoboda to student delegation, *Rudé právo*, 10 October 1968; Císař to Prague science students, Prague radio, 14 October 1968; Smrkovský to Law Faculty, Prague radio, 24 October 1968; Education Minister Kadlec on television, 3 October 1968.

[2] Expressed at 12 November 1968 presidium meeting (*Rok šedesátý osmý*, 332–3).

[3] See Hejzlar, 'Evolution of the Communist Party' (Reading, 1971), 17–18; interview with Erban, Prague radio, 18 November 1968.

[4] Husák called the spring the 'second period of deformation' in Czechoslovak society, the first having been the Novotný era, according to Bratislava radio (13 November 1968) version of 11 November speech at Nitra.

after the first day of the plenum, Dubček, together with Černík, and Husák, traveled to Warsaw on the evening of 15 November to gain approval from Brezhnev (who was attending the Polish Party congress).[1] While this tactic was relatively successful against the conservatives, it greatly strengthened the 'realists.' They gained a decisive majority on the new executive board (created presumably to counteract the enlargement of the presidium and consisting of Dubček, Smrkovský, Husák, Černík, Erban, Sádovský, Svoboda, and Štrougal).[2]

The resolution itself, published in *Rudé právo* of 19 November 1968, was broad enough to mean many things to many people, and, indeed, a conservative interpretation of it became the basis upon which Moscow pressed its demands when Dubček was finally ousted. It was critical of the situation before January 1968 and of the 'dogmatic–sectarian' forces in the Party, whose efforts, it was claimed, played into the hands of anti-communists. The major part of the criticism, however, was reserved for the 'right-wing,' 'anti-socialist' forces, manifest particularly in the media, but also in *Student*, K-231, KAN, the Church's Council of Revival, attacks on the militia, and the efforts to revive the Social Democratic Party. These forces were 'admitted' to have threatened the leading role of the Party at various times. The resolution did uphold the Action Program, although it seemed to dissociate the Party from it somewhat by emphasizing that this had only been a working document. Nonetheless, various sections of the resolution did refer positively to the spirit of the Action Program, outlining such positive innovations of the spring as the open search for solutions to society's problems; recognition of group interests; the increase in the activities of the workers and particularly of the youth; cadre changes (albeit with some 'serious mistakes'); preparation of rehabilitations; the development of Party democracy (though without a 'corresponding increase in Party discipline and...a strict adherence to democratic centralism'); and preparation for federalization of the state. Nowhere in the document did the Party either justify the invasion or admit to the existence of 'counter-revolution.' Nonetheless the overall impact was critical and the guidelines for future work emphasized Party control so strongly that the more liberal clauses permitting the continuation of some reforms (democratic participation, availability of information) were all but eclipsed.

[1] Hejzlar, 'Chronology,' 45.

[2] Štrougal was added to the presidium, and four new secretaries were added (Bil'ak, Penc, Kempný, Hetteš) of which two, possibly three could be considered conservative at the time. The secret ballot was replaced by a return to 'acclamation' voting at this session.

While the reformers may have seen the document as a compromise which at least recognized the possibility of continuing some of their program, the public did not receive the document with much optimism. The plenum did little to relieve the growing apprehensions, especially as the meeting had been preceded and accompanied by the suspension of two weeklies (*Politika* and *Reportér*) and the announcement of severe travel restrictions. The students went out on strike, supported in many instances by workers and other groups; Prague journalists as well as the Czech Coordinating Committee of Creative Associations held meetings demonstrating their concern. According to an article in *Reportér* on 13 December 1968 (after its resumption), 'several million people participated in the November political actions, especially... the signing of open letters and statements.' Party meetings were held throughout the country to explain the plenum, but the now-usual complaints of 'cabinet politics' continued to be vetted even there, prompted additionally by the scant coverage of the plenum's speeches.[1] Leading figures such as central committee members Martin Vaculík, Ivan Málek, Karel Kosík, Oldřich Starý, Jaroslav Kladiva, Cultural Minister Miroslav Galuška and many lesser known reformers expressed dissenting views.[2]

Having barely recovered from the reception afforded the November resolution, the country was faced with the beginnings of another crisis. On 7 December the Czechoslovak leaders journeyed to another meeting with the Russians, this time in Kiev, prior to their 12 December 1968 central committee plenum. This time, however, the Czechoslovak delegation consisted of Dubček, Černík, Husák, Svoboda, and Štrougal – without Smrkovský. This was interpreted in Czechoslovakia as a serious modification of the leadership group and a sign that the reformers were being eased out.

Rumors began to spread, according to *Práce*, 12, 13 December 1968, that the Russians had refused to talk with Smrkovský and were demanding his ejection. Although the rumors were denied publicly and privately by several leaders and even by Smrkovský himself on 10 December, the Anti-Fascist Fighters Union sent a delegation to the December plenum demanding that Smrkovský be kept as chairman of the parliament even in its new form as the Federal Assembly after 1 January 1969. On 19 December the 900 000 strong Czech Metal Workers Union passed a resolu-

---

[1] For example, at a meeting of leading Party secretaries, 19 November (*Rudé právo*, 20 November 1968).

[2] See, for example, *Rudé právo*, 18–27 November 1968, on plenum; *Svět práce*, 27 November 1968; *Pravda* (Bratislava), 27 November 1968.

tion to go out on strike should Smrkovský or any of the leaders enjoying the public's confidence be released from office.[1] In keeping with their alliance with the Metal Workers, the Czech Students Union also pledged itself to strike, as did at least two large plants. The threat of strike turned into a campaign just a few days later, when Husák put a resolution through the Slovak central committee calling for a Slovak to hold the top office of the about-to-be-created Federal Assembly.[2] Husák's subsequent comments merely fanned the flames, for he referred, for example, in his 25 December television address, to the organization of 'various pressure campaigns' by 'right-wing opportunist forces,' around the person of Smrkovský. In response, thousands of resolutions and letters poured into Party and press offices on behalf of literally millions of citizens and groups, demanding that Smrkovský retain his leading position. Since Husák had presented the issue as a 'national' Slovak demand, the ever-existent Czech–Slovak conflict was aggravated and the country sorely split over the issue, just on the eve of the federalization which was to take effect on 1 January 1969. The regime was faced with a serious crisis, for the people had been galvanized by this tangible threat to what little hopes remained for the pursuit of the post-January policies. Tinged with this agitation was frustration over the return to decision-making over the heads of and with complete disregard for the will of the people, and the apparent helplessness of the Prague regime to stand up to the Russians – as demonstrated, symbolically perhaps, by the continued dissemination in Czechoslovakia of the two 'anti-January' organs of the Warsaw Pact media, the journal *Zprávy* and radio Vltava.[3]

After the arrival of a Soviet delegation on 27 December and an all-night meeting on 2 January, the presidium issued a statement strongly condemning the 'campaign' (particularly in the media) which 'allows the activities of extreme forces' and even threats of strikes, in connection with the appointment of the Federal Assembly chairman. Calling on all organizations to act responsibly, the Party explained that there was no intention to remove Smrkovský from his functions or from political life; the statement did, however, condemn the accusations levied against

[1] Prague radio in English, 19 December 1968, in Czech only two days later. See below for details of Smrkovský campaign.

[2] When in power however Husák did not place a Slovak in this or the other top state jobs.

[3] Details below. Dubček reportedly raised this last issue at the Kiev talks. Excellent analyses of the political situation at the time may be found in *Zítřek*, 28 December 1968 (Havel) and 8 January 1969 (Lakatoš). An example of popular frustration was the joke currently circulating according to *Svobodné slovo*, 5 December 1968: ' "What state is the most neutral?" "Czechoslovakia. It does not interfere even in its own affairs." '

Husák for his role in the whole affair. Smrkovský went on television on 5 January to appeal for calm, assuring the public that 'no obligations were taken anywhere' regarding his continuation in office, and literally begging the public to reconsider the threats to strike in view of the consequences such action might bear 'for our state, its internal stability, and for its international relations.' This did not, however, significantly dampen the campaign, as evidenced, for example, by pro-Smrkovský statements issued by Party groups in both Brno and Pilsen.[1] The situation was not helped, either, by rumors that Soviet troops were reoccupying certain factories and offices (denied officially by the government on Prague radio, 6 January). Moreover, Husák, speaking to Slovak Metal Workers on 6 January 1969, persisted in his line that 'campaigns by pressure groups are creating tension.' On 7 January Prague radio announced that the same day the presidium proposed Peter Colotka as chairman of the Federal Assembly, recommending that Smrkovský continue in the leadership of the Party and be named chairman of the Peoples Chamber and first deputy chairman of the Assembly. This announcement was followed by an address by Dubček, who once again pledged implementation of the post-January policies. Pleading for understanding and faith in the leadership, despite the fact that 'it is not possible to fully report various confidential negotiations,' he pointed to forces inside and outside the country 'interested in bringing the situation to a head and to tragic consequences.' The tone of his appeal, and of his policy, was best summed up by his comment: 'that which we can save for the present and for the future is not without importance. That which we could lose is considerable, it is a lot.' *Rudé právo* of 9 January 1969 reported that Dubček, Černík, Smrkovský, and Svoboda then sent a letter to the Czech Metal Workers Union imploring them to call off their strike threat. This was in fact done, on 9 January, after certain unidentified leaders spoke with the Metal Workers in person, presumably revealing something more of the already mentioned 'confidential negotiations.'[2]

The atmosphere although defused remained tense, with both the Czech trade union congress and another Party central committee plenum about to convene. The public was disappointed and apprehensive, having seen in this defeat a significant retreat from January, one more in a chain of such retreats. The fear that this trend might well continue was buttressed

[1] Prague radio in German, 6 January 1969.
[2] Prague radio, 9 January 1969. On the same day Dubček met with the Soviet delegation, which had been moving around the country throughout the crisis, returning to Moscow on 10 January 1969 after a last talk with Svoboda and a televised speech by Katushev.

by the growing strength of Husák and his attacks on 'pressure groups.' On the other hand, the threat of a strike and the resultant crisis had demonstrated the potential strength of the public. To some it must have appeared crucial that the public must not be permitted to lapse into apathy, particularly so long as some leaders remained for whom the public will still meant something. These may have been the thoughts which passed through the mind of the 21-year-old history student Jan Palach when he contemplated his tragic deed of 16 January 1969. On that day, the first of the central committee plenum, Jan Palach appeared in Václavské náměstí, where, in front of the National Museum, he poured an inflammable liquid over himself and set himself on fire. He died three days later.

Palach's act was clearly political as the following note left by him indicated:

'Considering that our nations are standing on the brink of hopelessness, we have decided to express our protest and to awaken the people of this country by the following.

Our group consists of volunteers who are willing to set fire to themselves for our cause.

I had the honor to draw number one and thus won the right to write the first letter and to become the first torch.

Our demands are:
1. immediate abolition of censorship
2. banning of the distribution of *Zprávy*

If our demands are not met within five days, i.e. by 21 January 1969, and if the nation does not provide sufficient support (i.e. by a temporary, unlimited strike), other torches will be lit.

Torch No.1

P.S. Remember August. Room was made for us in international politics. Let us take advantage of it.'

The regime fully appreciated the political nature of the act and hoped to prevent both a general reaction and further tragedies. The spontaneous response of the public, however, forced the regime to give the affair significant attention, including publication of the letter (with its call for a strike), official comments (by the Czech and Slovak governments and by the Party), and radio or television appearances of various leaders, including the student leaders, and President Svoboda, to urge calm and prudence.[1] Thus once again the regime was faced with a crisis – one

---

[1] The Slovak Party and government statements differed from the first statements of the Czechs in that they spoke of extremist elements which exploited the situation, using

which Dubček termed 'perhaps the most serious' since August – for letters and resolutions of sympathy with Palach's demands poured in from all over the country. Students demonstrated in Prague, Brno, Bratislava, Olomouc and other cities, and fearing disorders, the Federal government announced special security measures on 24 January, including the intention of using the army if necessary to preserve peace and order. On the eve of the funeral, Dubček also made a radio appeal for calm, warning the public not to be provoked by 'extremist forces which could, in the present tense situation, misuse the emotions of honest people and lead to unforseeable consequences.' The students were given full responsibility for the peaceful conduct of the funeral procession and ceremonies, for which hundreds of thousands of people lined the streets of Prague on 25 January 1969. At the funeral, Oldřich Starý, university rector and an active reformist, delivered the eulogy while at least two government ministers and reform leaders such as Jiří Hájek, František Kriegel, and Vladimír Kadlec paid their last respects. Memorial ceremonies were held in other parts of the country and the day was turned into one of semi-official mourning.

Palach's note spoke of a 'group,' but investigations both by the government and, privately, by the students, uncovered no signs of such a group. Nonetheless, some eighteen persons were reported to have emulated Palach's act within two weeks, although it was claimed that few were politically motivated, according to Prague radio, 29 January 1969. Only a later one, the suicide of Jan Zajíc on 25 February 1969, was generally received as a political deed and taken up by at least part of one public.[1]

The whole of Czechoslovak society was indeed deeply stirred by Palach's act, so untypical of the orderly and 'reasonable' behaviour of the Czech people, yet symbolically reminiscent of the martyrdom of Jan Hus.[2] The students had asked that Palach's sacrifice be understood as a demand for 'deeds,' and Dubček, along with others, took up this very theme in subsequent weeks. Yet it is difficult to discern any concrete gains by the

the young to aggravate the political situation. (Bratislava television, 20 January 1969; ČTK, 20 January 1969 for Husák comments to Slovak presidium.) Svoboda, Černík, Dubček and Smrkovský sent condolences to Palach's mother.

[1] See *Listy*, 27 March 1969.

[2] For accounts of the reactions see *Lidová demokracie*, 27 January 1969; *Mladá fronta*, 25 January 1968; Dubček radio speech, 5 February 1968; Jan Kavan radio speech on behalf of the students, 19 January 1969. Kusý called the act: 'the extreme expression of passive resistance, with which our people have been defending themselves ever since the August events...A reminder addressed to the living.' (*Smena*, 29 January 1969.)

way of a change in the general direction of the regime's policies. As the Smrkovský case had shown, the post-invasion reformist regime was greatly limited in its possibilities for positive action. This was clearly pointed out by Smrkovský in an uncommonly (for him) pessimistic and despairing speech he delivered to Brno students just two days after Palach's self-immolation. Not even the rudimentary yet symbolically significant demands of Palach could be met, according to Smrkovský, 'even if we wish it deep in our hearts;' and he recalled the real danger of the 'reappearance of tanks in the streets...and much bloodshed,' should threats of strikes and demonstration and the like be carried out. Such brutal frankness could not be carried by the media (it was reported only in the London *Times* of 10 February 1969), but the three months of crises had brought the country to a point at which the truth had to be said.

The various political forces in the country, as well as Moscow, also reacted to the latest turn of events. Radio Vltava, together with Vilém Nový (in an *Agence France Presse* interview, 28 January 1969), developed a theory of a western-'anti-socialist forces' plan to which Palach had allegedly been forced to agree, after having been assured that the liquid to be poured over him would produce a 'non-burning flame.' This theory, which implicated several intellectuals and student leaders by name, was also perpetrated in one of the several illegal, often anti-semitic leaflets circulating in the country, which were themselves condemned by the public and the regime alike.[1] A particular target of these leaflets was Smrkovský, though Dubček too did not escape criticism.

While the conservatives continued their activities, the realists appeared to be quietly strengthening their forces. It was in this period following January 1969 that the Party sought to weaken the various groups which had emerged so powerfully (the press, the students, the unions), and, so it was rumored even then in Prague, lay the groundwork for a change in leadership.[2] The issue of the 'pressure groups' was a central one in this period despite the restrictions introduced in September and codified by the November resolution. In a sense it was thus that a major fruit of the

---

[1] See *Mladá fronta*, 4, 7, 12 February 1969; *Práce*, 4 February 1969; *Svobodné slovo*, 21 February 1969; *Reportér*, 20 February 1969 (Škutina); *Večerní Praha*, 27 February 1969 (Prague city Party meeting.) Kohout and Luděk Pachman began court proceedings against Nový for his accusations against them as having helped 'ensnare' Palach (*Svobodné slovo*, 22 March 1969). For survey of illegal pamphlets (170 reported by Interior Ministry, 29 January 1969) see *Reportér*, 20 March 1969 (Kalina).

[2] For a brief but penetrating analysis of the political situation at the end of February see Kusý in *Práce*, 27 February 1969 or in *Svět v obrazech*, 18 February 1969.

Prague Spring came to fruition, for the 'pressure groups,' i.e. the intellectuals, the students, and the workers, began to consolidate and to act in the ways merely demanded or envisaged for them in the pre-invasion period. Regardless of regime will or policy, the 'pressure groups' became a force which greatly affected the political situation in the country and the process of 'normalization' demanded by the Russians.[1]

The intellectuals

Given the invading countries' particular abhorrence for freedom of expression, as evidenced at the Čierná and Bratislava talks as well as by subsequent declarations, it was to be expected that the intellectuals would find it difficult to operate in the post-invasion period. Yet they were surprisingly successful in expressing themselves and maintaining their role as a pressure group, if not as the leading spokesman of the society's democratic aspirations. This success may be attributed in part to reluctance of certain reform leaders to abandon the open exchange of views envisaged by the reforms, but mainly to the courageous persistence of the intellectuals and their mutual cooperation. This cooperation was formally suggested by the Czechoslovak Writers Union in the form of a 'Solidarity Pact,' signed by most of the scientific–artistic unions in the country, and promising the defense of every Czech and Slovak intellectual 'wherever he resides' against persecution because of his opinions or work.[2] One of the main tasks was to defend themselves against the accusations of the 'allies,' but this was complicated by the restrictions apparently demanded in the Moscow talks. A directive went out to the media not to publish 'anything that could be taken as criticism' of the invader countries (and, among other things not to use the term 'occupation').[3] Nonetheless the intellectuals sought to clear their names first by demanding – and obtaining – recognition of the legitimacy of the efforts of the media during the invasion.[4] They also took official stands in answer to the accusations contained

---

[1] For a discussion of this see *Zítřek*, 18 December 1968 (Lakatoš) or comments by National Front chairman Erban, Prague radio, 24 September 1968; 14 October 1968; 19 December 1968.

[2] *Zítřek*, 13 November 1968 (meant to cover intellectuals who remained abroad after the invasion as well).

[3] See *Politika*, 18 September 1968.

[4] Decision of government committee for Press and Information, Prague radio in English, 24 September 1968. Radio and television workers, together with Dubček and Svoboda, received Czechoslovak Peace Award for their work during the invasion (*Pravda* (Bratislava), 5 November 1968).

in the Soviet booklet *On Events in Czechoslovakia* (known as the *White Book*) which constituted an indictment particularly of the Czechoslovak intellectuals – who were generally misquoted. In response to these continuing outside attacks, the Journalists Union in Prague, for example, accepted Foreign Minister Jiří Hájek as a member, the Czechoslovak Writers Union issued a statement defending Goldstücker (and kept his seat as chairman open, electing poet Jaroslav Seifert only acting chairman), and the ČSAV issued a statement defending Šik and Jiří Hájek – all gestures of solidarity.[1] Particularly abhorrent to the intellectuals was the continued broadcasting of radio Vltava and the illegal dissemination of *Zprávy*, the Czech-language journal published by the Soviet command in Czechoslovakia. Practically every journal and paper in Czechoslovakia objected to the continuation of these organs; *Rudé právo* (26 March 1969) even protested when copies of *Zprávy*, which it called 'illegal printed matter,' were inserted in the Party daily in certain areas. As a result of these pressures radio Vltava was finally closed on 13 February 1969, *Zprávy* continued until 10 May 1969.

The significance of the intellectuals' struggle against Vltava and *Zprávy* lay not so much in the degree of their success or failure but in their very persistence in the face of the regime's hardening line on the right of intellectuals, particularly in the mass media, to intervene in what were considered purely political matters.[2] This line was apparent in the retrospective declarations and resolutions of the regime which singled out the media for undisciplined, harmful, and even 'anti-socialist' behaviour in the January to August period. The model for such criticism was outlined by Dubček in his 11 October 1968 speech to Party workers at the Tesla plant in Prague, codified in the November resolution, and subsequently embellished upon. These condemnations were accompanied by restrictions beginning with those immediately upon the leaders' return from Moscow: the abrogation of the June 1968 amendment to the Press Law which had abolished preliminary censorship. This Act was contained in a bill passed by the National Assembly on 13 September 1968, presented as a temporary measure pending the still-promised new Press Law. The law also authorized the founding of a government Committee for Press and Information with Offices for Press and Information in Prague and in Bratislava to supervise the media. These new organs, under the respective direction of deputy Premier Peter Colotka (replaced by Jaroslav Havelka

---

[1] *Lidová demokracie*, 17 December 1968; *Listy*, 14 November 1968; *Věstník* (ČSAV), 5 October 1968. See also *Sedm pražských dnů* (Praha, 1968).
[2] See Justice Minister Kučera's statement, Prague radio, 13 December 1968.

in December 1968), Ondrej Čemen, and Josef Vohnout were already established by decree on 30 August, and on 3 September 1968 the Ministry of Culture and Information had already been changed to the Ministry of Culture, to accommodate the new arrangement.[1] According to the new regulations the Office for Press and Information gained the right to prevent dissemination of facts considered 'at variance' with the vital interests of domestic or foreign policy. Černík did promise, in his 13 September speech to the National Assembly, that 'all suitable forms of cooperation with the journalists' unions' would be used.

Indeed the new regulations did contain two points which marked a definite improvement over the pre-1968 censorship arrangements: the censorship organs, i.e. the Office for Press and Information, were under a government committee rather than the Interior Ministry, and the censors could be and were selected in consultation with and from among each journal's or organization's own editorial staff. Thus the regime was counting primarily on self-censorship, and it strove to demonstrate its reluctance at enacting the new law, emphasizing its temporary nature and the necessities imposed by the 'situation.'[2]

Additional changes came in the wake of the invasion, most notably the recall of the progressive chiefs of radio and television, Zdeněk Hejzlar and Jiří Pelikán. *Literární listy*, *Kultúrny život*, and *Student* all decided to suspend publication almost immediately after the invasion because of their reluctance to change their political line in keeping with the new situation. Their replacements, *Listy*, *Literárny život*, and eventually, *Studentské listy*, were to be non-political.[3] *Listy* appeared on 7 November, under a liberal editorial board headed by reformer Milan Jungmann; it survived until a month after the fall of Dubček in April 1969, although the daily it had planned to publish as of October 1968, *Lidové noviny*, was never permitted. *Literárný život* had a different fate, in part because of the divisions within the Slovak Writers Union, in part because of the more rapid deterioration of the democratization in Slovakia. Regime delays in registering the journal and attempts to dictate the composition of the editorial board led to the resignation of two successive and reform-

---

[1] Prague radio, 30 August, 3, 7 October 1968. The government committee included the directors of radio, television, and ČTK and two representatives of the National Front. The government recommended representation of the creative unions as well (Prague radio, 17 September 1968).

[2] For example, Colotka interview, Prague radio, 24 September 1968.

[3] Prague radio, 10, 25 September 1968; *Student*, 28 August 1968. *Kultúrny život* was, however, denied the possibility of publishing one last issue. (*Reportér*, 25 December 1968 (Pilátová).)

minded prospective chief editors. To bypass this regime interference the Slovak Writers Union decided on 13 December to resume publication on 1 January 1969 of *Kultúrny život* (until then merely voluntarily suspended) if *Literárny život* were not granted registration. Nothing came of this ultimatum, but finally, after several subsequent false starts, *Literárny život* appeared on 16 April 1969 (under the editorship of a moderate Husák supporter), only to be suspended the following day.[1]

Reportér, too, suffered in the post-invasion period, and was suspended for one month on 8 November 1968. After a popular outburst and a threat by the journalists to take the matter to court, the weekly was permitted to reappear three weeks later. Together with *Listy* it was finally banned in May 1969. *Politika* replaced the central committee weekly *Kulturní tvorba* on 18 September, only to be suspended for three months after only eleven issues. Its publication was then transferred to *Rudé právo*, but it was banned finally on 1 April 1969.[2] *Život strany* was to have been replaced by *Tribuna* as decided prior to the invasion, but the latter appeared in January 1969 as the organ of the new Czech Bureau of the Party and, under the editorship of Švestka, was clearly a platform for the conservatives. Praised by Moscow's *Pravda*, 27 February 1969, it was criticized by *Rudé právo* (15 February 1969) and *Život strany* (19 February 1969), and Party printers delayed publication of the first issue because of their refusal to print what they considered articles contrary to post-January policies.[3]

Several other earlier planned journals also appeared which maintained, however, most of the liberal profile originally envisaged for them. These included *Obroda*, the formerly suspended organ of the Peoples Party; *Zítřek*, a weekly of the Socialist Party; *Svět práce*, originally published by the Social Democrats and then the trade unions until 1954; *Tvář*, the controversial young writers' weekly banned by Novotný in 1966, and *Doba*, organ of the 'scientific–technical intelligentsia' – all registered on 1 October 1969.[4] *Plamen*, the journalists' illustrated weekly *Svět v obrazech*, *My 69* (the youth monthly), and the student journals *Studenské listy* and *Reflex* were all suspended in the spring 1969 crackdown;

---

[1] For details see, ibid. and see Števček in *Rol'nícke noviny*, 13 December 1968; Prague radio, 14 December 1968. It reappeared in June, and was banned finally in July 1969.
[2] *Politika*'s very motto was probably offensive to some: Gramsci's 'Truth is Revolutionary.'
[3] ČTK, 14 January 1969.
[4] *Rudé právo*, 2 October 1968. *Svět sovětů*, weekly of the conservatives' center, the Czechoslovak–Soviet Friendship Organization, changed its name to the presumably more palatable *Svět socialismu* at the end of December 1968.

Zítřek was then disbanded, and several other journals such as the satirical weeklies *Dikobraz* and *Roháč* were disciplined by the new regime.[1]

The intellectuals' efforts to withstand the post-invasion restrictions were largely channeled through their unions, which increasingly executed the task undertaken by them in the pre-invasion period of legitimate pressure groups. The Czech section of the Writers Union issued a number of statements from September and October onwards upholding the principles both of 'national sovereignty' and 'individual freedom' as well as 'collective responsibility' for the work of Union members.[2] Although operating mainly through its weekly, *Listy*, the Writers Union also took an official stand on such issues as Goldstücker's position, relations with writers unions of the invader countries, and Jan Palach's self-immolation.[3] The Czech writers were somewhat more active than the Slovaks as a group, primarily because of the serious division within the ranks of the Slovak writers and the identification of at least some of the latter with Husák and the realists. This division, a continuation of the split which emerged in the spring of 1968, was also a factor in the postponements of the fifth writers congress, scheduled to introduce formal federalization of the Czechoslovak Writers Union.[4]

The strength of the genuine reformers in the Slovak Writers Union (e.g. Števček, Ťažký, Tatarka, Jesenská) was evidenced by the continued refusal of *Literárný život* to accept personnel changes, but this refusal meant also that the reformers were denied their principal platform (while the realists had *Nové slovo*).[5] This problem, as well as the strength of the realists within the Union, led to what came to be known as the 'silence of the Slovak writers.' On 17 December 1968 nine (the 'realists') of the thirteen members of the Slovak Writers Union presidium, including chairman Miroslav Válek, resigned (specifically in response to criticism over their handling of the formation of *Literárný život*). The Union's committee then took over the executive functions (pending election of a new presidium at the next congress), with the liberal Ivan Kupec elected acting chairman.[6] The split thus freed the hands of the reformers to pursue their struggle for democratization in such ways as support for declarations of the Czech writers, the sending of an open letter to the Soviet Writers Union in defense of Czechoslovak intellectuals, and, of

[1] See *Smena*, 3 April 1969. [2] *Listy*, 7 November 1968.
[3] See *Rudé právo*, 22 December 1968 or ČTK, 22, 28 January 1969.
[4] See chapter 5. The congress, postponed from January 1969 to March to April, finally opened on 10 June 1969. [5] See *Reportér*, 8 January 1969 (Tatarka) for details.
[6] For details see Hykisch interview in *Mladá fronta*, 21 December 1968.

course, the efforts for publication of *Literárny život*.[1] Without a presidium, however, and in open conflict with the realists, whose power in the Party and the Slovak government was increasing, the Union was severely handicapped in its dealing with the regime.[2]

The journalists were able to preserve a greater unity of action, though amongst them, as well, the Czechs showed greater initiative than the Slovaks. Like the writers, the Czech and Slovak journalist unions proclaimed collective responsibility for their members; they officially pursued their particular demand for information as well as freedom to play an active and critical role in the political life of the country.[3] On 18 November the Prague section held a meeting of over a thousand journalists, which issued a statement warning against censorship and the loss of contact between the regime and the people.[4] They stressed their solidarity with writers and scientists and protested the suspension of *Reportér* and *Politika*. The Brno section of the Union immediately proclaimed support for the Prague statement, as did meetings of the committees of both the Czech and Slovak Journalists Unions (5 and 6 December respectively), although the Slovaks abstained from certain points.[5] The Prague meeting attracted much attention and could later point to the lifting of the ban on *Reportér* and the easing of restrictions on political reporting in radio and television as their achievements.[6] The journalists continued their struggle in meetings with regime officials and operated in coordination with the Slovaks in such joint meetings as that of 28 February 1969 in Ostrava.

The Coordinating Committee of Creative Associations, founded in May 1968, became increasingly important in representing all the related unions on political as well as cultural issues. On 22 November it held a meeting, in the presence of Party officials such as Evžen Erban and of representatives of the following unions: Czech Writers, Czech Journalists, Slovak Journalists, Czechoslovak Composers, Czechoslovak Film and Television Artists, Czechoslovak Theatre and Radio Artists, Czechoslovak Architects, Czechoslovak Music Hall Performers, Czechoslovak Painters

[1] See, for example, *Listy*, 6 March 1969.

[2] With federalization Válek became Slovak Minister for Culture; there was no Federal Ministry of Culture, above him, for it was deemed that Czech and Slovak cultures were two distinct entities. (Galuška, Prague radio in English, 18 September 1968.)

[3] See, for example, the Union presidium's declaration, Prague radio, 31 October 1968.

[4] See *Svobodné slovo*, 19 November 1968.

[5] *Zemědělské noviny*, 20 November 1968; Bratislava radio, 6 December 1968; Czechoslovak television, 11 December 1968.

[6] As they did at the presidium session of the Czech Journalists Union, 5 December 1968 (Prague radio, 6 December 1968).

and Sculptors, the new Czechoslovak Trade Union of Artistic and Cultural Workers, the preparatory committee of the Czechoslovak Scientific Workers; representatives of ČSAV and observers from the students. Conspicuous by their absence were the Slovak Writers, a fact later criticized within that Union.[1] After a break for a meeting with Dubček and others, the meeting adopted a resolution favoring a role as a pressure group ('like the students and the workers') in the struggle for 'an open and non-cabinet policy,' although – probably the result of the talks with Dubček – it implied the temporary nature of the restrictions on the intellectuals. The Committee, in which the Scientific Workers Union played a particularly important role, continued to act as representative of the intellectuals, for example, against attacks by Vasil Bil'ak or *Zprávy* and radio Vltava. As federalization reached this group as well, the Slovak coordinating committee withdrew somewhat from the main activities, concentrating on specifically Slovak problems such as *Literárný život* and Slovak cultural appointments.

Cooperation existed with other groups as well, on another level. For example, the Czechoslovak Journalists Union invited student representatives to its meetings, as did the Prague group; all member organizations of the Coordinating Committee signed agreements with the students; and both the Czechoslovak Writers Union and the Czech journalists established links with the workers. The journalists, for example, even signed an agreement with the Miners Union for cooperation in the struggle for information and freedom of expression.[2] Specific groups, such as the Composers Union, the Film and Television Artists, the Czechoslovak Architects, as well as the employees of the radio and television and groups in the various branches of ČSAV and the Socialist Academy were all active in issuing declarations and letters to the regime on such issues as Smrkovský's future, the holding of elections and a Party congress, unjustified criticism of the media and so forth.

It was primarily through their published organs and the mass media, however, that the intellectuals were able to bring their pressures to bear. Indeed, the very character of these organs testified to the relative success of the intellectuals' efforts to resist regime restrictions and to contribute to,

[1] For this meeting, see *Lidová demokracie*, 23 November 1968. For reference to this criticism, see *Mlada fronta*, 21 December 1968 (Hykisch interview). For a history and explanation of the Coordinating Committee see Ludvík Pacovský in *Politika*, 19 October 1968.

[2] ČTK, 1 April 1969; Prague radio, 27 February 1969. Ludvík Pacovský pointed out this general cooperation with workers in *Zemědělské noviny*, 12 November 1968.

if not lead, the efforts to save the 'January policies.' Almost every journal and daily objected repeatedly to censorship and the singling out of the media as the major culprits of the spring. *Listy* often added to this a defense of civil rights against censorship and surveillance of mail. Asserting their right to a political role, the press critically covered the growth of conservativism and 'realism,' often condemning the divisive actions of the former, in detail, and mentioning names. Indeed Miroslav Kusý lost his job as Slovak Party ideology chief on 17 February 1969 for articles he published on just this subject.[1] *Reportér* was particularly outspoken (especially in articles by Jiří Hochman) against the anti-semitic and near-farcical theses of the conservatives, pointing to their lack of strength among the population.

The line most characteristic of the non-Party press (and also *Nová mysl* and *Politika*) was their pursuit of the 'January policies.' This was evidenced by the campaign for Smrkovský, or the efforts against a return to 'politics behind closed doors' and public apathy, and solidarity with the martyrdom of Jan Palach. Even many of the specific planks of the reform program were pursued, although the more radical discussions on such things as political reform or the revelations of past errors almost entirely disappeared. What was said, however, was said openly and boldly – often in piercing satires the directness of which went well beyond the bounds of veiled opposition.[2] Almost the entire press, from that of the non-Communist parties (for example, *Svobodné slovo* and *Lidová demokracie*) to the youth and workers' dailies *Mladá fronta* and *Práce*, as well as the weeklies – most directly the instruments of the intellectuals – joined the struggle to salvage the Prague spring. In the non-Party daily press there was little difference, for example, between Czech and Slovak organs, despite stricter controls in Slovakia. *Smena* was no less outspoken than *Mladá fronta*, and for this received a reprimand from the Slovak Office for Press and Information.[3] Likewise there was little qualitative difference between *Práce* and its Slovak counterpart *Práca*. Even on the 'national' issue of Smrkovský *Smena* and *Práca* published at least some of the support for the Czech leader, although they generally expressed the Slovak view of the issue. *Roľnícke noviny*, the Slovak agricultural daily, was traditionally more interested in the Slovak

[1] For example, in *Smena*, 29 January 1969 or *Práca*, 2 February 1969.
[2] For example, the first suspension of *Reportér* came in response to its reproduction of a 1957 Soviet cartoon showing a western diplomat in Washington receiving his hat and coat from the cloakroom. The caption read 'After the Visit,' and had a reporter say to another: 'They return his hat, coat, and galoshes. As for sovereignty, he had to leave it…' (*Reportér*, 30 October 1968; *Listy*, 14 November 1968.)
[3] *Smena*, 28 November 1968.

national issue, rather than liberal politics, than its Czech counterpart *Zemědělské noviny*; nonetheless, it did occasionally lash out against the conservatives or censorship or other signs of retreat from the post-January line.[1] The most striking contrast, however, appeared in the weeklies, for having been denied an organ for the liberal writers, Slovak intellectuals had nothing equivalent to *Listy*, *Reportér*, *Zítřek*, or *Politika*. *Nové slovo* was the only Slovak journal of this category and it, from its inception, was identified with the nationalist cause, becoming in time the standard-bearer of the realists because of its connection with Husák. As long as Kusý was Slovak ideology chief, the journal did publish some of his pro-democracy, anti-conservative pieces. Pro-reform intellectuals in Slovakia – who were a majority in the Slovak Writers Union committee – were, however, invited to express themselves in the Czech journals, for example in *Listy*, 6 March 1969, so that they could continue as part of the general pressure group.

The Slovak Party daily presented a strange combination of reformism and conservativism through most of the post-invasion period. One could find on its pages defense of the banned Czech journals and, almost simultaneously, attacks on them; one found pleas for information and a free press almost side by side with criticism of such demands and appeals for restrictions. While it predictably supported the official decision demoting but praising Smrkovský, it also used the occasion to attack Czech intellectuals. There was strong criticism of many aspects of the Prague spring, particularly in the commentaries of Bohuš Trávníček, but there was also implied criticism of the Czechoslovak Party's absence (along with the invading countries) from the Yugoslav Party congress. The overall line was in fact moderate rather than liberal and explicitly pro-Husák, although these examples of ambivalence attested to the presence of liberals in the *Pravda* offices, at least until Leopold Podstupka became chief editor on 17 February 1969, and even slightly thereafter.

Rudé právo was on the whole more critical and reform-oriented, particularly more so than might have been expected of the Party's official organ.[2] The paper's editor, Jiří Sekera (who replaced the conservative Švestka on 2 September 1968) believed in criticism. On the pages of *Rudé právo*, he advocated the right to clashes of opinion and popular control of the political powers. Although he did so in mild terms, and urged responsibility on the part of the media, he did permit a great deal of

[1] For example, on 15 October 1968 or 13 December 1968. The same was true for *L'ud* in comparison with the Czech non-Communist party dailies.

[2] Pointed out on occasion, for example, 2 January 1969, by radio Vltava.

leeway in editorial policy, as evidenced in the treatment of the Smrkovský and Palach issues. While this was hardly radicalism, the paper's loyalty to the reform movement, and its offensiveness in the eyes of the realists as well as conservatives, was attested to by the lengthy attack (published in *Rudé právo* of 10 April 1969) on the editorial policies and character of the paper in this post-invasion period. This attack, written by two instructors at the Party school, was ominously reminiscent of Novotný's June 1963 attack on *Pravda* (Bratislava), with its references to particular articles and emphasis on the need for the Party organ scrupulously to serve the Party line. The attack itself was part of the spring crisis, but that a need for it was felt by the realists testifies to the persistence of the reformists on the paper.

Radio broadcasting followed patterns similar to the press, maintaining its frankness and critical approach even under its new director, Odon Závodský. As in the pre-1968 period the foreign-language sections were able to report more freely than the domestic programs, but newscasters were able to get around restrictions by, for example, amply reporting items from the local press. While the revealing and often controversial discussion programs of the Prague spring were reduced to a bare minimum and politicians permitted themselves to be interviewed less frequently, the radio was able to maintain its role as at least one spokesman (if no longer the leaders) of the reform-minded public. By its selection of items or quotation of the press and aggressive interviewing, the journalists in the Czech radio expressed their support of Smrkovský, their sympathy with the demands of Jan Palach, their opposition to politics behind closed doors and censorship. There were, of course, restrictions on the medium just as on the press, and more controversial reporters such as Karel Jezdinský (transferred to Yugoslavia shortly after the invasion) were denied a by-line. Bratislava broadcasting was on the whole more severely limited, and often failed to report in as detailed a manner as Prague, for example with regard to the events following Palach's death.

Television had greater difficulty in pursuing its reformist position, due in part to its new director Josef Šmídmajer. While there was some good and often provocative reporting on television,[1] the frequent complaints from the critics and in other media attested to the change which took place in television earlier than elsewhere. Bratislava television was, apparently, even more restricted than the Prague studios. For example, *Práca* reported on 22 January that on 19 January Bratislava television

---

[1] For example, 4 November 1968 interview with Kusý, 10 November 1968 report on press restrictions, 26 December 1968 commentary on the Soviet Union in the UN or 3 December 1968 program on *Zprávy*.

switched on its part of a newscast without any reference whatsoever to the topic of the preceding fifteen minutes of news from Prague on Jan Palach. A similar contrast occurred a few weeks earlier with regard to resolutions supporting Smrkovský.[1] The restrictions on the media had become so arbitrary by the spring that *Doba* announced in its 17 April issue that it could no longer publish its column on forthcoming radio, television, and theatre programs, since announced programs, particularly on television, were continuously being cancelled at the last minute. One of the examples given was the program 'The Curious Camera' which in 1968 had been one of the more popular and provocative television shows. Thus radio and television lost, in the post-invasion period, their vanguard role assumed in the January to August period (and culminating during the invasion). While radio probably did a better job of any of the media in keeping the public informed, the major platforms for the intellectuals became once again the press and particularly the weeklies, as in the pre-1968 period.

The publishing houses and theatres were not affected for some time by the new restrictions. Indeed a number of controversial books or controversial authors (including émigrés as well as westerners and Czechs and Slovaks) found their way to the public. The film-makers did not fare so well, although a number of films made in early 1968 did get released before the spring of 1969. The entertainment world experienced a new wave of satire, and records of protest songs were pressed, sometimes even legally. It was relatively typical, however, when the broadcast of a Bratislava song festival was cut off in the middle because of a protest song.

The general mood of the intellectuals expressed in the efforts described in the preceding pages could probably be summed up as one of controlled determination. It is difficult to gauge the degree of optimism the intellectuals actually felt regarding the possibilities for preventing a return to the old system of rule, and it is equally difficult to determine to what degree there was agreement on the methods to be used. Nonetheless they seem to have been acting with an eye towards history, as if duty bound – for the sake of Czech traditions and for the sake of their own integrity (which in some cases, had only been retrieved in 1968) – to salvage what they could of the reform program without doing violence to its basic principles.

Youth and students

While the intellectuals had in effect been operating as an almost traditional interest or pressure group even under the Communists, only

[1] 27 December 1968, reported in Hajek and Niznansky, 'Czech and Slovak Media: A Comparison' (RFE, 18 February 1969), 4.

gradually did certain youth groups, particularly the students, emerge as a powerful – and leading – force, realizing a potential which had been unfolding over the preceding five years. Organizationally much was to be accomplished in the post-invasion period since ČSM had virtually disintegrated with the desertion of some twenty sub-groups, and potentially the most powerful group, that of the students, had splintered on the issue of formal organization. Thus the new student unions, SVS and ZVS, had not attracted many members in the pre-invasion period and the two most influential student leaders in the country, Luboš Holeček and Jiří Müller, had accorded them only half-hearted support (due to their apprehensions concerning arbitrary or formal 'establishments.')[1]

The youth and students had played an outstanding role in the week of the invasion but they had done so spontaneously and as individuals or small groups. This situation persisted for some two months following the invasion and even the 28 October and 7 November disturbances in several cities were not formally organized or sponsored by more than small groups of, mainly, secondary school pupils and apprentices.[2] It was only after the signing of the troop treaty and the increasingly apparent wittling away of the reform program that the value of organization came to be recognized in connection with such things as the November plenum, for example.

The SVS held its first parliament in Pilsen from 31 October to 2 November with representatives from almost all the Czech faculties. At this time the more radical Prague students fought for a political rather than purely social-interest group organization (particularly since the banning of the clubs like KAN had deprived them of their informal political outlets). They obtained a compromise in the form of the replacement of chairman Rybář by Michal Dymáček, an assistant in mathematics from Brno who although a moderate rather than a 'radical' agreed that the SVS should represent the students vis-à-vis the political powers. Karel Kovanda of the 'radicals' was elected to the presidium. The SVS was to be plagued throughout its brief existence by differences between these two groups: the Prague 'radicals' and the moderates (more or less identified with Brno). Their differences were mainly over tactics, and similar but not identical to the differences of reformists and realists within the Party. The moderates

---

[1] See chapter 3.
[2] See Interior Minister Pepich's statement, Prague radio, 12 November 1968. Radio Vltava, 9, 13, 15 November 1968, nonetheless claimed they were organized by the students in an illegal organization linked with western journalists, Kriegel, and other 'anti-socialist' forces.

sought accommodation with the regime through discussions and quiet politiking; the 'radicals' sought challenges to the regime and action to push the reform policies forward. The moderates on the whole hoped to work through the Party and were only mildly interested in the alliance with the workers; the 'radicals' placed greater emphasis on the workers, with little to no faith in the Party.[1] In time the Prague radicals, with the advantage of their respected leaders and successful (or at least newsworthy) activities, gained the ascendency. This was evidenced by the policies pursued by the students, although the Prague students were not able to bring about all of their desired personnel changes at the second parliament, held in Prague on 13–15 December. The split finally burst into the open at the SVS third parliament in Brno, on 21–22 February 1969. The 'radicals' were unsuccessful in unseating Dymáček (who was finally reelected on the third ballot with only one vote to spare), and decided to resign the positions they had gained at the parliament (e.g. Holeček as political department chief, Müller as responsible for contacts with workers, Kavan as international department chief).[2] Kovanda had refused to stand for the presidium again and thus there were no 'radicals' left in that group. With this the Prague group abandoned SVS and worked through the Prague parliament, explaining its position and preparing materials towards a final resolution of the issue at the SVS April congress. Although Prague had the largest concentration of students in the country (24 000), it was not easy to determine how many of these were interested in student politics, much less were supporters of the Prague 'radicals.' The result of a poll reported on Prague radio on 13 February 1969 showed that as distinct from 5 to 10 per cent of students (interviewed in the pre-January era) who were politically committed, approximately 30 per cent were committed between January and August 1968 and 57 per cent in the post-invasion period, of whom 15 per cent favored radical forms of commitment.

The 'radicals' did indeed stage a victory at the April congress in Olomouc; the moderates' proposal to join the National Front failed (by a

---

[1] For expressions of different views see Dymáček in *Mladá fronta*, 15 January 1969; Holeček–Dymáček discussion, *Svobodné slovo*, 10 April 1969; and *Host do domu*, XVI:8 (1969), 20–4. There were subdivisions also, for example, the radical group in the Prague School of Agriculture led by Miroslav Tyl, and the still more radical group associated with Petr Uhl known as the Revolutionary Socialist Youth in the Prague Philosophy Faculty.

[2] Prague radio, 23 February 1969; Prague radio in English, 21 March 1969. Details on movement are also available in Miroslav Tyl, 'Rozbor studentského hnutí a návrh koncepce pro jistou část studentstva,' SVS, I/064/69, unpublished paper (Praha, 1969).

large percentage) to gain the necessary two-thirds majority and the issue was once again put off.[1] On the less crucial issue of international affiliation the congress recommended seeking only associate membership in IUS, although the final position was to be worked out together with the Slovak Student Union. The 'radicals' consolidated their victory at the fourth parliament (which opened the following day), by securing almost all the leading positions in the Union. The new chairman, Jozef Trenčanský, was a compromise choice for he was a moderate, but he was also a Slovak studying in Prague and acceptable to the 'radicals'. His deputy was the 'radical' Karel Kovanda. As a result of the congress, however, the moderates, under Dymáček, formed a coordinating body of faculties wishing to join the National Front, gradually assuming the character of a rival group, favored by the regime against the now radical-dominated SVS. In June this second group formed a preparatory committee for a new student union (under Trenčanský, who had resigned from his SVS office in May because of opposition to certain 'radical' activities). On 20 June the Interior Ministry banned the SVS and, despite an emergency parliament which supported the 'radicals' and appealed against the government decision, the SVS was outlawed on 29 August, to be replaced by a new regime-organized student union only on 2 February 1970.

The Slovak Student Union (ZVS) had a much less stormy history, primarily because of the absence of a strong radical group in the Slovak schools. Thus the ZVS had voted to join the National Front as early as its constituent congress in May 1968 and pursued the equivalent of the Brno moderates' policies, with the emphasis on Slovak rights.[2] While there was occasional cooperation or solidarity in the activities of the two student unions, there was very little contact organizationally. The presidia of the two groups did meet on 5 January 1969 in Brno and issued a joint statement on the political situation,[3] but collaboration between them was in fact more nominal than actual, especially with the rise of the Husák group in the Party and the concomitant radicalization of the Czech students.

The ČSM was not entirely moribund throughout this period, though its open rejection by the youth since early 1968 forced the organization to alter its structure and profile. At its 19–20 September 1968 meeting the ČSM central committee decided to create a preparatory committee for a new federation of youth groups which would loosely bind the various

[1] Vote was 70 against; 71 for; 27 abstentions (*Reuters*, 28 April 1969).
[2] Prague radio, 6 December 1968.
[3] 'Předsednictva SVS a ZVS předkládají fakultám společné hodnocení politické situace na kterém se obě shodly v Brně,' unpublished, 5 January 1969.

groups established in 1968 (including the Pioneers, Junák, Military Youth League, Campers Union, Committee of Farm and Country Youth, Committee of Secondary School and Apprentice Youth, Union of Youth Clubs, Union of Working Youth, and the Union of Polish Youth).[1] The ZVS also joined, but the Czech students agreed only to associate membership. The Hungarian Youth Union delayed its adherence owing to a dispute which had arisen between it and ČSM groups in several areas, according to *Új szó*, 5 and 9 October 1968. On 19 December 1968 and 4 February 1969 respectively the Czech Association of Children's and Youth Organizations and the Slovak Youth Union were founded, followed on 11 March by the founding of the Czechoslovak Association of Children's and Youth Organizations.[2] ČSM was formally abolished on 5 March 1969. The Czech union, at least, declared that it did not consider itself the sole spokesman for the youth of the country nor did it claim jurisdiction over non-members. Indeed in both the Czech lands and Slovakia the component groups of the new unions were formally constituted as independent groups, joining the National Front individually. Aside from this, the regime did have the all-encompassing association which it had sought, and the potential similarity to ČSM was apparent in the retention of the ČSM leadership under new titles (Zdeněk Vokrouhlický as Czech and Czechoslovak chairman, Robert Harenčár as Slovak chairman). Nonetheless, one event which indicated that the new group was perceived at least by some as an improvement over ČSM was the founding of a rival ultra-conservative group known as the Union of Youth. A preparatory committee for this group sponsored a meeting in Prague on 7 March 1969, which was attended by such arch-conservatives as Josef Jodas but closed to the press and representatives of other youth groups. Its expressed purpose was the creation of an organization similar to the Komsomol.[3] The constituent congress of the Czechoslovak Association of Children's and Youth Organizations condemned the creation of the 'Youth Union' and requested Party officials to look into the matter.[4] With the emergence of the 'realists' as the major power in the Party, the official

[1] Prague radio, 21 September 1968.
[2] The Slovak group did not include the Hungarian and Ukrainian youth groups at this time; together with the Poles they were also missing from the Prague radio list of members given on 11 March 1969.
[3] *Zemědělské noviny*, 12 March 1968; *Mladá fronta*, 21 March 1968.
[4] Prague radio in English, 12 March 1968. There were also conservative outposts of ČSM which refused to abandon their status as ČSM affiliates and refused to recognize the idea of other independent youth groups in their areas. (*Rudé právo*, 11 April 1969.)

association began to operate as a regime organ, and it absorbed the conservative union.

The first major activity of the youth was planned in the days preceding the November central committee plenum and was designed to bring pressure on the Party to refrain from further retreat from the principles of the Action Program. It consisted of a student strike planned for international student day, 17 November (which commemorated students who lost their lives in protest to the Nazi occupation in 1939 and the subsequent closure of the universities). On 12 November representatives of almost all the Prague faculties (and the Union of Secondary School Pupils and Apprentices and the Union of Working Youth) set up a demonstration action committee, which included Prague 'radicals' Holeček, Kovanda, Dolanský, three Slovaks studying in Prague and two newer student activists. The idea was apparently being considered in other cities as well, for on 12 November Bratislava University officials appealed to students to avoid 'undesirable or illegal action.'[1] On 13 November – which was also the day preceding the central committee plenum – Dubček, Černík, Svoboda, Smrkovský, Erban, and Pelnář met with a Prague student delegation to urge them not to demonstrate on the forthcoming students' day.[2] Before a decision was in fact made, students in Olomouc received an inaccurate report that the Prague students were already out on strike; therefore, on the morning of 14 November the Olomouc students began to strike.[3] Their impatience may have been due, in part, to the fact that 12 000 Soviet troops were garrisoned in Olomouc. Pressures upon the SVS were strong and its presidium joined forces with the Prague action committee, supplying the ten-point demands which became the official strike demands.[4] On 16 November the more radical Prague agricultural students began a one-week strike, and that afternoon the SVS presidium voted to declare a strike in all Prague faculties, beginning on 18 November.[5] Thus, after day-long meetings on Sunday 17 November the Prague Action Committee declared the beginning of a three-day strike. Their venture was quickly joined by the secondary school pupils

[1] Prague radio, 12 November 1968.
[2] *Mladá fronta*, 4 December 1968; Tyl, 'Rozbor,' 15. In fact the students' application to hold a demonstration was rejected (Prague radio, 16 November 1968).
[3] Tyl, 'Rozbor,' 16.
[4] These points demanded freedom of expression, travel, science, association; legal and personal security for all citizens; opposition to 'policy behind closed doors' and continuation in office of those who had lost the peoples' trust; establishment of enterprise councils; a foreign policy responsive to the peoples' will; and were based on the Action Program. (*Lidová demokracie*, 21 November 1968.) [5] Tyl, 'Rozbor,' 16.

and apprentices in Prague and students in Brno, Ostrava, Ústí nad Laben, Pilsen, Bratislava and towns throughout the country.[1] An estimated 60 000 students (out of a total of 92 000) went out on strike for from four to seven days.

The strike consisted of peaceful occupation of university buildings, and it met with enthusiastic support even from many unexpected quarters. Intellectuals such as Karel Kosík, and Party liberals such as Kriegel and Vodsloň, came to speak with the students, while university lecturers and students conducted open seminars on the political situation. Groups such as the chamber orchestra came to entertain at the faculties; food and cigarettes were brought in by people of all ages. Regular visits between the schools and factories took place, with workers declaring their solidarity with the students and support for their ten points.[2] Based as they were on the Action Program these ten points represented much more than strictly student demands, and for this reason the students' action was seen by the public as an expression of their own failing hopes.[3] The significance of the strike was summed up thus by *Lidová demokracie* of 21 November 1969: 'By their action, which took its course in a peaceful and orderly manner, the students proved that they are a force which must be taken into consideration both now and in the future, that they are people who have their own views and who can defend them.'

Indeed this was the conclusion the regime also seemed to have drawn, and it was subsequently under pressure from the Soviets to discredit the students' effort as an anti-socialist, western-inspired provocation.[4] The Party ordered an investigation and within a short time Education Minister Kadlec (who himself had visited the striking students) submitted a report which in fact upheld the sincerity and legitimacy of the students' endeavor.[5] The subsequent government resolution disapproved

[1] Prague radio in English, 18, 21 November 1968.
[2] Pilsen Škoda works, for example (Prague radio, 18 November 1968). See also *Práce*, 26 November 1968 and *Lidová demokracie*, 21 November on worker support. Five South Bohemian cooperatives even organized a gift campaign of eggs and chicken for the striking students. (*Zemědělské noviny*, 3 December 1968.)
[3] A ČSAV poll revealed that 86% of those interviewed sympathized with the striking students; 11% disapproved; and 3% did not reply. (Prague radio in English, 17 January 1969.) ČSAV itself issued a statement of support as did other groups of intellectuals. (ČTK, 20 November 1968; *Listy*, 14 November 1968; *Práca*, 21 November 1968.)
[4] Radio Vltava, 17, 20 November 1968. For the students' account of their motivation see Holeček, Klímová, Müller in *Reportér*, 13 November 1968.
[5] The Prague city Party committee as well as the Party's university committee declared the strike spontaneous and legal. (Prague radio in English, 19 November 1968.)

of the use of a strike, but recognized the justice of the students' views, their discipline and their dedication to the post-January policies of the Party, according to *Rudé právo* of 21 December 1968.

One of the most important achievements of the strike was, perhaps, the bond forged between students and workers. This alliance, a renewal of contacts begun with much less success in early 1968, was to become the major effort of the students and, in a sense, their most formidable accomplishment. The students had not sought collaboration with the workers regarding the strike, but they had made efforts to gain their understanding and support.[1] In this they succeeded beyond their expectations, probably due to the politization the workers themselves had undergone just prior to and particularly following the invasion. Contacts with the workers were at first on an individual basis or in the factories; students spoke in plants, some plants sent representatives to student meetings. Reminiscent of former purely formal activities, students went out to work 'Dubček' shifts in Olomouc, and in the Czech lands they helped mine the coal so that Slovak schools could reopen.[2] This time these efforts seemed to be genuine. After the strike, however, students began contacting the trade unions prior to the latter's forthcoming congresses. The first fruits of these efforts was an agreement signed on 19 December between Jiří Müller on behalf of the SVS and the 900 000 strong Czech Metal Workers Union at the latter's constituent congress, reported on 21 December by *Práce*. This was followed on 5 January 1969 by a similar agreement with the construction workers and, a few days later, with the mineralogical, geological, and gas workers, and on 23 January with the Printers Union. In time, there were agreements with the power-station workers, designer and civil engineers, lumber workers, the controversial locomotive workers, and still others.[3] The Czech Metal Workers Union was the largest union in the country and its agreement with the students served as a model (and, probably, an encouragement) for the subsequent compacts. It called for

[1] This was emphasized by the students because of Soviet accusations, for example in *Komsomolskaya pravda*, 22 December 1968, that they were inciting disorder. For an authoritative account of the alliance with the workers, see Pavel Tomalek, 'Czechoslovakia 1968–1969: The Worker–Student Alliance,' MIT paper, 1971.

[2] *Práce*, 20 November 1968; 18 December 1968. These schools had not reopened after the Christmas holidays because of the coal shortage. (Prague radio, 4, 10 January 1969.)

[3] Tomalek, 'Alliance,' 29. Černík reprimanded Müller for his initiative with the metal workers, on the grounds that the Party had been ignored, but in fact the regime had tactically erred for it had not deemed the Metal Workers congress sufficiently important to rate official Party representatives. (Private conversations.)

mutual support, consultation, cooperation and exchange of information in pursuit of the 'post-January policies,' defense of the media, calling of a Czech Party congress, and other specific demands.[1]

By and large these alliances held throughout 1968–9 though they were much criticized (and feared) by the conservatives in the regime.[2] In concrete terms, they led to the formation of worker–student action committees which coordinated efforts designed to salvage what was possible of the post-January policies.[3] In addition to providing workers' support for students' efforts and vice-versa, they also facilitated the promulgation of pro-reform materials such as speeches by liberals, discussion materials and the like. While the potential power created by this collaboration was never fully utilized, the alliance of two such powerful groups as the students and the workers enhanced the power of each as a pressure group. And if this alliance did not succeed in preserving the post-January policy, it did render its dismantling considerably more complicated and slower. The campaign to prevent the removal of Smrkovský was but one instance when the cooperating pressure groups brought the regime to the brink of crisis and galvanized the public.[4]

The Smrkovský issue was in fact a workers' campaign, but the students saw it as the first test of their alliance and, therefore, joined forces with the workers to save Smrkovský as a symbol of the January policies. The SVS agreed to join the workers if they went out on strike, and they were active in raising support for Smrkovský.[5] The Smrkovský campaign was also joined, spontaneously, by youth throughout the country. Even in Slovakia the Bratislava city committee of the Union of Working Youth wrote supporting Smrkovský and the youth daily *Smena* published at least some support for him on 22 December 1968 and 6 January 1969, for example. The Slovak students were not, however, as active as the Czechs in contacting or supporting the workers and, although ZVS leader Jozef Šesták did address the Slovak Council of Trade Unions congress on 29

---

[1] 'Dohoda o spolupráci Českého odborového svazu pracujících v kovoprůmyslu a Svazu vysokoškolského studenstva Čech a Moravy,' unpublished (Praha), 19 December 1968.

[2] See, for example, Husák speech, *Pravda* (Bratislava), 2 June 1969.

[3] Tomalek, 'Alliance,' 30.

[4] Students also led a campaign, joined by the intellectuals, to keep Education Minister Kadlec in office, although he himself said he wanted to resign because of the impossibility of pursuing reform. (Prague radio, 15, 27–29 December 1968; *Mladá fronta*, 20 December 1968.)

[5] For example, in meeting with government leaders, 3 January 1969 ('Zápis z jednání delegace předsednictva SVS na předsednictvu vlády dne 3.1.1969').

January 1969, he divorced himself from the Prague 'radicals' (and apparently from the Smrkovský campaign) by condemning 'ultimata.'[1] Another campaign, undertaken primarily by the Prague students, was connected with the Yugoslav Party congress in March 1969 – and Czechoslovakia's non-participation. On 14 March the students' parliament in Prague organized a demonstration of approximately 6 000 persons and the SVS, together with the Prague Union of Youth Clubs and the Prague Union of Secondary School Pupils and Apprentices, organized a meeting, both protesting the regime's boycott. At both the meetings and demonstration leading professors, journalists and others spoke, demonstrating once again the solidarity which had been achieved between the various groups.[2]

Another activity undertaken by the youth was the mass meeting of 15 January 1969 sponsored by the Prague Union of Youth Clubs (chaired by Josef Wagner), as a continuation of the rallies held during the Prague spring. It was addressed by such leading intellectuals as Pavel Kohout, Karel Kosík, and Vladimír Škutina, as well as chess master Luděk Pachman, and reformer František Vodsloň.[3] Indicative of the progress made over the past year at least on one front was the presence of representatives of trade unions. Also indicative of the change from the previous year was Husák's failure even to reply to his invitation.[4] A resolution was passed supporting the Action Program and demanding, among other things, the establishment of workers councils. An example of the frank contributions made at this meeting was the following exchange: question as to whether the job of ambassador to Mongolia would be suitable for Drahomír Kolder; answer: 'I have been to Mongolia; it is a beautiful country...I don't know what you have against it!'

The regular talks with regime leaders (part of the platform of the moderate students) proved frank and useful, at least in providing the students a direct way in which to express their ideas – and to some degree to gain information on regime thinking. The 'radicals' claimed that the talks were much less effective than their concrete activities (such as the worker alliance) which confronted the regime with the need to act – not

[1] Prague radio, 29 January 1969. See *Mladá fronta*, 3 January 1969 for plea by Prague lecturer Luboš Kohout to Bratislava students on behalf of Smrkovský.
[2] *Svobodné slovo*, 14 March 1969; *Zemědělské noviny*, 19 March 1969.
[3] *Lidová demokracie*, and *Svobodné slovo*, 16 January 1969.
[4] Smrkovský and Indra both declined their invitations, the latter later condemning the meeting as the work of provocateurs. (*Práce*, 17 February 1969.) See *Rudé právo*, 29 and 31 January 1969 for a dispute over comments allegedly made by Pachman to this meeting.

talk. They nonetheless participated in these talks (just as the moderates supported the links with the workers). A sample of one such meeting – between SVS leaders and Černík and Erban – was held two days after the signing of the alliance with the Metal Workers. Here the students raised such issues as the return to 'cabinet politics,' accumulation of leading official functions, the flow of information, a congress of the Czech Party, Smrkovský's continuation in office, Bil'ak's unsuitability for high office, and the November resolution. They argued with Erban over adherence to the National Front and, for example, when Holeček explained that the students were not fighting *against* the leadership but *for* something, Černík challenged him by quoting one of the agricultural students' strike slogans, which said: 'a critical confrontation of powers is approaching,' and Erban said that the student–worker alliance made the '2,000 Words' look like 'an innocent ditty.'[1] In these meetings the students frankly – and often aggressively – presented their views, but in time they found themselves (rather than the regime) on the defensive for various activities attributed to them. This shift, however, was mainly a function of the changing balance of forces within the Party and the decline of those leaders who had valued such talks as a means of bringing the youth into political affairs. Indeed the whole idea was dropped after Husák took over in April, in direct reaction to the refusal of the SVS congress to join the National Front.

The students' 'international relations' were a topic of one of the meetings with the government, particularly after the students were accused by conservatives (specifically by Indra) in speeches on 11 February 1969 (reported by *Práce* the next day), of being directed from outside. 'Radical' leaders Kovanda and Kavan were accused of disseminating materials abroad and taken to task for participation in the January 1969 European students' conference in Budapest.[2] In Budapest Kavan delivered a measured but open attack on the invasion of Czechoslovakia and the presence of Soviet troops in the country, categorically denying either the existence of counter-revolution in Czechoslovakia or the claim of an invitation to the invading countries to intervene. With the help of the Yugoslav delegation the meeting was disrupted and split on the issue of Czechoslovakia, preventing even the passage of a final communique.[3] The students tried to mend fences with the Communist world, in what was at

[1] 'Zápis z jednání s předsedou ÚV NF E. Erbanem a předsedou vlády ing. O. Černíkem dne 21.12.1968.'
[2] See SVS defense of Kovanda and Kavan, *Studentské listy*, 4 March 1969.
[3] *Smena*, 16 January 1969. See Kavan interview, *Mladý svět*, 5 February 1969.

least a gesture, by sending a delegation from the Czechoslovak student center (the coordinating body for the SVS and ZVS) to Moscow from 16 to 20 December 1968. Its reception was far from warm, however, and the group was accused by the Russians of *not* enjoying the confidence of the students.[1]

The students also tried to use their meetings with the regime to secure the publication of a journal to replace *Student*. The new SVS weekly, *Studentské listy*, finally did appear with a special issue marking the death of Jan Palach and then regularly from 25 February 1969. The Slovak students began publishing *Reflex* on 7 April 1969, but both journals were banned in the spring.

The student contacts with the regime were probably most efficacious with regard to the handling of the response to Palach's self-immolation. The act of Jan Palach cannot be regarded as one of the students' activities, for Palach apparently acted alone, in a manner the students, however radical, would not have presumed to recommend. Nonetheless the students saw this as an act of one of their own, expressive of their own feelings, and a moral call to which they must respond by assuming responsibility at least for the reaction. Again the Prague students – the 'radicals' in and with the SVS leadership – took the lead by totally identifying Palach's motives with their own goals. In daily meetings with the government (primarily Czech lands Premier Rázl) and in their activities they sought to achieve three things: understanding of Palach's act, i.e. that it should not be belittled or slandered as the desperate act of a madman or criminal or as an ordinary suicide; public recognition of the deed, i.e. that it should not be silenced or ignored by the regime; and efficacy, i.e. that the act should not have been in vain. Thus in their talks with Rázl the students demanded publication of Palach's letter, permission to make a public statement, and the meeting of Palach's demands regarding *Zprávy* and censorship.[2] The government agreed to permit a minimum of publicity, including an SVS statement (subject to government approval). The statement, prepared by Kavan and Holeček with the help of the young lecturer Petr Pithart, called for 'deeds' (as distinct from indifference or mere words or promises) as the only fitting response to Palach's demands.[3] The government balked at this, but when a spontaneous procession and meetings took place amongst Prague students on Saturday 18 January, the government agreed to the statement – presumably having recognized the need for the cooperation of the students if

---

[1] 'Zápis,' 21 December 1968.   [2] Ibid. 17 January 1968.
[3] Broadcast, 19 January 1969; complete text, special issue *Studentské listy*, undated, 1969.

order were to be kept. On Sunday 19 January the students organized a dignified and peaceful procession in Prague, from Václavské náměstí to the Philosophy Faculty, which was joined by over a hundred thousand of Prague residents. After speeches from students and faculty, and representatives of the various trade unions and plants allied with the students, the Square of Red Soldiers, in front of the Philosophy Faculty, was renamed in honor of Jan Palach, according to Prague television, 20 January 1969. The funeral too was conducted (by the students without employment of the police or militia) in this spirit, constituting an impressive demonstration of discipline and dignity. Throughout the country students and young people, like their elders, expressed their sympathy with Palach's deed. Prague radio reported that students held meetings or marches (often together with workers) in Brno, Ostrava, Pilsen, České Budějovice, Pardubice, Ústí nad Labem, Hradec Králové, Bratislava, Nitra, Banská Bystrice, Košice, and other towns. While the ZVS did not itself organize the activities in Slovakia, it did issue a statement carried by Prague television, 24 January 1969, which characterized Palach's suicide as an act of 'extreme civic courage' and declared its intention to hold a Slovak student parliament to discuss the political situation and demands of the students. The Slovak authorities did not, however, cooperate to the extent of their Czech counterparts; traffic was not rerouted for the processions, and demonstrations were ordered confined to university facilities, according to Košice radio, 20 January 1969.

The regime had ordered the area cleared after the funeral, and the police enforced this even to the point of making arrests.[1] There was also a wave of self-immolations and suicides in various parts of the country, suspected of or claiming to be prompted by motives similar to those of Jan Palach. While the regime denied that any of them might have been politically motivated, in one case the students sought recognition of what was generally considered a genuine 'political' suicide: the death of Jan Zajíc, an 18-year-old student at the higher school of railway transport in Sumperk (Moravia); he set himself on fire on Prague's Václavské náměstí on 25 February 1969, the anniversary of the Communist takeover in 1948 and one month, to the day, after Palach's funeral.

The organization of Palach's funeral, together with the alliances signed with the workers in January and February, seem to have marked the high point of student activity. While the Prague 'radicals' did stage subsequent major successes within the student movement, no subsequent activities

---

[1] Prague radio, 27, 29 January 1969; *Svět v obrazech*, 18 March 1969 (interview with Interior Minister.)

matched the scope and importance of the above two. Having as it were measured both the students' strength and the latters' hesitancy to exploit it fully (for example, the students' refusal of workers' offers to strike in sympathy with Palach), the regime began to crack down on the radical students. It exploited the split in the SVS, as well as the differences between this group and the less radical Slovak students, and it strove to discredit the 'radicals' among the workers.[1] While none of these efforts was entirely successful, they must be seen in the light of the growing mood of hopelessness in the country and the dominance of the realists in the Party. Young people remained defiant, if scattered, organizing protest wherever and however possible. Yet student power never again achieved the dimensions it exhibited in the winter of 1969.

Workers

More than any other group in society, the workers came into their own in the period following the invasion. From an attitude of indifference (bordering on hostility) to the reforms in the pre-1968 period, to an attitude of interest and support in the January–August period, the workers joined the ranks of the most active proponents of the movement following the invasion. The explanation of this genesis probably lay in the fact that the abstract ideas of the intellectuals – even in the economic sphere – had little meaning for the workers. Encouraged by the regime to disdain the intellectuals and frustrated over the years to such an extent that the only safe or efficacious concern was their own material welfare, it took the *actual* changes of 1968 to show the workers that this movement might bode some good for them as well. Having only just embraced the new ideas, the workers were galvanized to action as a result of the blow struck by the invasion to their national and human pride. This activity took place at both the formal trade union level and at the lower, more individualistic plant and local level. At both levels, however, the activity was the result of spontaneous changes and decisions as distinct from the formerly imposed modes of behavior.

At its 25–26 September 1968 plenum the ROH central council affirmed its intention of carrying on with its envisaged reforms by approving the statutes drafted in the summer. These statutes recognized the ROH as a unit organized according to and dedicated to the interests of its members, claiming its right to defend and champion 'the legitimate *political*, eco-

---

[1] See, for example, Nový and Indra speeches, *Svobodné slovo*, 21 February 1968; *Práce*, 12 February 1968.

nomic, social, and cultural interest of its members' through 'an independent policy towards the state and the political parties.'[1] Organizing
according to interests meant that the ROH would permit the creation of
autonomous unions according to professional interests (albeit in accordance with the one enterprise, one union rule), with the right to formulate
their own statutes and programs.[2] This was to replace the former system
of some twelve multi-industrial unions amalgamated in ROH. Membership in the ROH was to be by individual union, which, it was decided
after some hesitation, would affiliate with an independent national (Czech
or Slovak) ROH center.[3] Individual unions might create federal committees to operate for them on a state-wide level, just as the central ROH
council would do for the movement as a whole (representing the unions on
questions of state legislation and so forth.) While individual unions were
to be financially independent, the regime's desire to preserve a unified
trade union movement was manifest in its ambivalence towards the
constituent assemblies of the new unions.

The statutes closely followed those proposed for the Party, emphasizing
democratization of the organization (omitting any reference to democratic
centralism) and the rights of members, though opposing factions. Indeed
the seventh state-wide ROH congress, held on 4–5 March 1969, was a
manifestation of the new democratic procedures – and the political role
accorded by the statutes as well. Three-quarters of the delegates had been
elected by individual unions, all delegates were selected by secret ballot
and both the discussions and resolutions were democratically and boldly
formulated.[4] It is difficult to determine if the congress or Poláček, its
reelected chairman, could have operated otherwise, given the spontaneous
activities of the workers and the strength of the newly created unions over
the preceding months.

The Czech and Slovak trade union councils were established at constituent congresses in January 1969, with Rudolf Pacovský and Vojtech
Daubner, respectively, elected chairmen (by secret ballot). Criticism of
the 'lack of democracy' and apolitical attitude of the Slovak congress was
raised by its own daily, *Práca*, on 1 February 1969, thus contrasting (in

---

[1] Emphasis mine. See *Práce*, 4 October 1968 for statutes.

[2] Statutes were to be subject to approval by the national union council.

[3] Alternate wording of this clause envisaged *one* union with two 'national' branches.
(Prague radio, 3 October 1968.)

[4] See Poláček speech and congress resolution, *Práca*, 11 March 1969 and reports in
Prague radio, 6, 7 March 1969 or *Rudé právo*, 5 March 1969. An article against 'anar-
cho-syndicalism' in *Pravda* (Moscow) on the eve of the congress was taken as criticism
and strongly attacked in *Práce*, 5 March 1969.

the labor field as elsewhere) with the more active Czechs.[1] Constituent congresses also took place in the fall and winter for fifty-seven new unions: thirty Czech, twenty-five Slovak, and two state-wide unions (for civil employees of the army and employees of the security forces.) Some ninety additional applications were rejected, according to ČTK, 25 November 1968, most notably that of the controversial Federation of Locomotive Crews. This group, having been rejected before the invasion as a legitimate union (because of the one enterprise, one union rule) had sought registration as a social-interest group, only to be turned down in September on the grounds that their activities were those of a trade union. By then a dues-collecting, 24 000 strong concern indeed operating as a union, the Federation declared itself an independent trade union, outside ROH. It planned a one-hour protest strike for 13 December, which it cancelled when promised renewed negotiations, but it continued to exist – illegally – even after condemnation by the Czech and Slovak railway workers' unions and by ROH chairman Poláček at the March congress.[2] The Federation attracted a great deal of worker interest and support, for, as *Lidová demokracie* of 18 March 1969 explained, it had become a 'test case for democracy.' The Action Program ruled against 'monopolization,' but the failure to legislate a law protecting freedom of association prior to the invasion left the way open for the banning of the union, as did the ROH statutes. The continued albeit illegal functioning of the Federation throughout Dubček's rule, however, attested to the latter's hesitation to force a showdown with the newly powerful workers over an issue which violated the spirit of the reform movement.

The largest and perhaps most radical union created was the 900 000 strong Czech Metal Workers under Vlastmil Toman. Not all of the new unions were radical, however; *Rudé právo*, 14 January 1969, claimed that 60–70 per cent of the new central committees' members were Communists. The diversity of the political leanings amongst the unions was demonstrated by the voting at the March congress: both radical leader Toman and the moderate-to-conservative Slovak leader Daubner were reelected to the ROH central council with the smallest majorities.[3] (Although *Práce* of 16

---

[1] The Czech Trade Union Council demanded, for example, that as long as censorship prevailed, the unions should exercise full control over their organs. (*Práce*, 25 January 1969.) With the new arrangement it was not certain if *Práce* would remain with the ROH central council or go to the Czechs.

[2] ČTK, 4 March 1969. For full story of the Federation see also chapter 3 and *Rudé právo*, 13 December 1968; *Zítřek*, 11 December 1968 and *Reportér*, 25 December 1968.

[3] Toman, 951 out of 1441 voting; Daubner 1062 out of 1441. (ČTK, 7 March 1969.)

March 1969 claimed that spontaneous applause demonstrated the general agreement with many of Toman's views.) The ROH leadership itself, under Poláček, was moderate, bordering on radical. It carefully explained that it had no intention of constituting an 'aggravation' to the regime, although it did intend to disagree and propose alternative ideas when the interests of the workers so dictated.[1]

There was a large number of issues on which the unions either individually or together took a position, from demands for elections and a Czech Party congress to support for an 'open policy' and protection of basic civil rights, and demands for the retirement of conservatives such as Bil'ak and Krček. A major campaign was waged by the ROH central council and the Czech Trade Union Council for workers councils. On 11 November 1968 ROH leaders complained to the government about the decision of 24 October 1968 to halt the creation of new councils, at which time 113 councils existed, though only 46 were functioning and 140 more were in the preparatory stages.[2] When the draft of the enterprise bill was circulated in February, the ROH and the Czech Trade Union Council led a heated debate in their journals and at their various meetings, particularly opposing the alternative proposal submitted by the Czech government. While expressing strong reservations about the enterprise bill itself (the Metal Workers Union, for example, wanted a larger percentage of workers in the councils of all three types of enterprises), the ROH and Czech Trade Union Council were willing to accept it as a 'minimum.'[3] Fearful that the Czech bill would be carried, they sought the immediate passage of the enterprise bill, recording their position in standpoints adopted by the Czech Trade Union Council and the ROH congress in March 1969. The Federal bill was indeed redrafted, however, and after Husák took over the bill was dropped altogether. Thus ended the reform program in that sphere and the 500 workers councils set up during Dubček's rule.[4] Despite this failure, the unions' campaign produced what

[1] *Práce*, 17 December 1968; Poláček speech (Prague radio, 7 March 1969). Poláček's speeches from September through March exhibit an evolution to an almost radical position.

[2] Poláček to ROH central council, ČTK, 5 December 1968.

[3] *Práca*, 18, 19, 26 February 1969 (Toman); ČTK, 25 February 1969; *Svět práce*, 26 February 1969. The ROH understandably preferred the arrangement it had proposed on 5 July 1968 (see chapter 2 for the various proposals.) Arguing that workers' rule would not mean management by unqualified persons M. Bárta reported in *Politická ekonomie*, XVII:8 (1969), 49, that 73% of those elected to the workers councils were engineers, 29% university-educated, for example.

[4] Figure supplied by Černík in speech to ROH congress. (Prague radio, 6 March 1969.)

was probably the most lively, open, and critical debate on proposed legislation in Czechoslovakia since 1948.

The unions, led by the ROH council and its chairman Poláček, also conducted a less dramatic but no less diligent, open campaign against the 1969 price rises which, they claimed, were in contradiction of union-government agreements.[1] It was only after Dubček's fall that the regime insisted that the unions abandon these claims to protect workers' wages and return to the concept of their primary task as that of protecting the country's all-over economic interests.[2] The unions also strove to protect their right to strike (recognized semi-officially in the 1968 spring), and most of the new unions, as well as the new ROH statutes, included strike provisions, defended even by Slovak labor leaders as late as the March 1969 ROH congress.[3]

Use of the strike weapon was threatened on a number of occasions, most notably the struggle led by the Czech Metal Workers to maintain Smrkovský in office. In response to rumors about Smrkovský's future, the constituent congress of the Czech Metal Workers resolved on 19 December to stage a protest strike should Smrkovský or any other leading official enjoying the confidence of the working people be demoted. After the Slovak central committee proposal for a Slovak as Federal Assembly chairman, the Union's central committee sent appeals to the National Assembly and the Slovak Metal Workers and passed a resolution calling on all the Union's basic organizations to support Smrkovský (if necessary by strike) as Assembly chairman until democratic elections could be held.[4] After Husák's speech of 25 December, Union chairman Toman published an indignant letter to Husák in *Práce* of 3 January 1969, reiterating the Union's opposition to changes in leadership at such a critical time. He strongly criticized Husák's preference for 'narrow nationalist questions' over the 'interests of the working class and socialism' and warned him that 'you cannot force your subjective view on our

---

[1] See, for example, *Práce*, 26 September 1968, and 26 March 1969; ČTK, 14 March 1969; Prague radio, 7 December 1968 and 12 January 1969.

[2] See *Práce*, 8 October 1969 account of Czech Trade Union Council plenum, still under Rudolf Pacovský.

[3] *Práca*, 28 November 1968; Pacovský favoring right to strike at Czech Trade Union Council congress (Prague radio in English, 21 January 1969); Poláček supporting political use of strike weapon, *Rudé právo* interview, 1 March 1969; see also Jan Duži, deputy chairman of ROH council (Prague radio in German, 5 March 1969, excluded from Czech version of speech). In June 1970 the strike provisions were removed from the ROH statutes.

[4] *Práce*, 28 December 1968.

whole people.' An extraordinary outburst from a man who had spent a good part of his life as an ROH official, it was the result of a mandate not only from a near-million strong union but from people throughout the country. Such unions as the 330 000 strong Czech Building Workers, the 200 000 Czech Farmers the 180 000 Czech Railway Workers, the Czech Union of Assembly and Suppliers Organizations, and many others declared support for Smrkovský.[1] Prague radio reported on 11 January 1969 that the Czech Union of Press Workers had elected him their honorary chairman. The ROH presidium supported the demands to maintain Smrkovský at least until general elections, and suggested to regime leaders on 3 January 1969 that Slovaks should chair both houses of the parliament.[2] Further ROH support also came in the form of permitting its organs to publish the many declarations and articles favoring Smrkovský, including one of 30 December by Czech National Council deputy chairman Zdeněk Jičinský.

Following the Party presidium statement on 3 January 1969, Svoboda, Dubček, Černík and Smrkovský dispatched a letter to the Metal Workers asking for understanding and warning against the dangers (to the whole country) of political crisis and tensions caused, it claimed, by the campaign and threat of a strike.[3] Regime officials then met with the Union's central committee on 9 January (presumably revealing more of the limits placed upon the reform regime by Russia). The Union then called off its strike threat, inasmuch, it claimed, as Smrkovský's replacement (Colotka) was also a reformer, and on the condition that Smrkovský must nonetheless be considered when democratic elections were held for the office by the deputies themselves.[4] The Metal Workers rejected, however, the implication that they were responsible for the tense situation in the country and adopted a standpoint which attributed this tension to the lack of information and, as Toman later said, to 'those who began to seek right-wing and extremist workers among the metal workers.'[5] The immediate crisis past, Toman nonetheless repeated the Union's fears regarding the future of those leaders considered symbols of the 'post-January policies' and pledged his group's intention to continue its pursuit of political goals.

[1] Prague radio, 20, 21, 29 December 1968; 3, 5 January 1969.
[2] *Práce*, 4 January 1969; Prague radio, 3 January 1969.
[3] *Rudé právo*, 9 January 1969.
[4] Prague radio, 9 January 1969.
[5] Speech to Czech Trade Union Council congress (ČTK, 22 January 1969); a reference to Husák's 25 December 1968 speech that 'right-wing extremists' were behind the Smrkovský campaign.

Another political campaign undertaken by the unions was the struggle against the dissemination of 'anti-January' materials. The workers, particularly the metal workers, joined the intellectuals' struggle against *Zprávy* and radio Vltava; Poláček even protested directly to Shelepin during an ROH council delegation's visit to Moscow in November 1968, *Práce* revealed on 4 December 1968. The Czech Union of Press Workers supported the refusal of Party printers in Prague to set type for the first issue of *Tribuna*, resolving at their constituent congress, 10–12 January 1969, not to take part in publication of materials the contents of which disagreed with the post-January policies or the November and December 1968 resolutions.[1] The printers' was one of the few successful such actions, for, as Císař admitted, the Party agreed to revise the contended issue of *Tribuna* before publication.[2]

Shortly thereafter another Prague printing plant refused to publish a Bulgarian journal because of an offensive cartoon on Jan Palach, according to Prague radio in English, 6 February 1969. This fulfillment of the printers' congress resolution was upheld and reconfirmed at the ROH congress. Demanding the disbanding of *Zprávy*, Zdeněk Spolek, chairman of the new federal committee of printers' unions, said that printers had been told by their unions to check the contents of material to be published so as to prevent another case such as the pamphlets defaming Smrkovský (for which printers had been employed under false pretences).[3]

Among the activities on other issues, the Czech Trade Union Council sent greetings to the Yugoslav Party congress, in clear defiance of the regime's boycott of the event, and *Práce* of 21 March 1969 objected to what people saw as discrimination against the Yugoslavs because of their 'independent, undogmatic, and creative approach' to socialism or discourtesy to a 'fraternal Party, which despite old Cominform injuries, stood by our state and people at the worst time.' The Czech Metal Workers published a letter in *Práce* on 20 December protesting Bil'ak's comments in an American Communist paper; the Czech Union of Health Workers objected to the severe restrictions placed on professional trips abroad; and the Czech Printers Union went on record repeatedly against censorship of domestic news.[4]

The unions also collaborated with the youth and intellectuals, de-

[1] Prague television, 11 January 1969.
[2] Prague radio in English, 12 January 1969.
[3] Prague radio in English, 5 March 1969.
[4] *Práce*, 3 December 1968; Prague radio, 12 January 1969. The Czech health workers elected Kriegel chairman at their January 1969 constituent congress.

veloping a relationship for which the groundwork had been laid in the spring and making it an integral part of the workers' policies. Thus over a dozen unions, for example the Czech Press Workers, the Czech Metal Workers, and the Czech Miners, supported the students and their demands, some, as we have seen, even entering formal alliance with the SVS.[1] A number of unions, such as the Czech Lumber Workers, the Czech Farmers, and the Czech Union of State Employees, defended the intellectuals against the attacks on the media and the Czech Metal Workers identified themselves with the intellectuals' demands of 26 November.[2] The Czech Press Workers and the Czech Miners, for example, also signed alliances with the journalists union.[3] Czech Trade Union Council chairman Rudolf Pacovský called on the unions to expand relations with the intellectuals and the congress resolution enlarged this to include the youth as well as the women's and farmers' groups.[4] The ROH council also maintained contacts with the intellectuals, and the ROH congress expressed support for them, asserting its willingness to strive for 'real freedom of journalistic work,' according to *Práca* of 11 March 1969.

These were not merely formalistic statements; they reflected a working relationship which had been steadily growing between the intellectuals, students, and workers. This relationship was manifest in the mutual support given for such specific interests as the intellectuals' freedom of the press, demanded by the workers and students in almost all their declarations, enterprise councils and the Smrkovský campaign, supported by the students and the intellectuals in their media, for the students' strike demands and the reaction to Palach's death, expressed by the workers and the intellectuals. Representatives of the students, journalists, and writers addressed the workers' conferences, and consultation took place at all levels including coordination between the ROH central council and the Coordinating Committee of Creative Associations, as *Práce* of 13 March 1969 reported. This collaboration provided dissemination of such materials as speeches by Kriegel, Kyncl, Vodsloň and others, unpublished because of censorship.[5] The solidarity was based on more than tactical considerations; they had discovered a mutuality of interests or, as

---

[1] Prague radio, 18, 21 December 1968 and 5 January 1969; *Lidová demokracie*, 21 November 1968.
[2] Prague radio, 20, 21 December 1968 and 9, 16 January 1969.
[3] Prague radio in English, 12 January 1969 and 27 February 1969.
[4] Prague radio in English, 21 January 1969; *Práce*, 25 January 1969.
[5] Tomalek, 'Alliance,' 31.

Ludvík Pacovský of the intellectuals' Coordinating Committee put it, 'their mutual need and mutual taste.'[1]

The Slovak unions were not as active as the Czechs in all of these activities, in part because of the more rapid deterioration of the reform movement in Slovakia, the backbone of the realists. Moreover, many of the post-invasion issues were easily side-tracked by the conservatives (and the realists) along national lines. This was the case, according to *Práca* of 27 January 1969, with the demand for a Czech Party congress, the fourteenth congress, and, most notably, the Smrkovský affair. On this last not one Slovak union was willing to join the Czechs' campaign, despite individual Slovak workers' declarations of confidence in Smrkovský. The Slovak Council of Trade Unions even condemned the 'ill-considered' Czech workers' decision, although it did cite lack of information as one of the causes of the crisis, according to Prague radio, 2 January 1969. Slovak labor leader Daubner and the Slovak unions generally concentrated on the problems of federalization (as *Práce* of 26 November 1969 pointed out) or limited themselves to the economic sphere (in which they firmly defended the workers) and the realist line promulgated by Husák, according to *Práce* itself, 1 February 1969. There were exceptions, of course, as for example, the chairman of the Slovak Union of Workers in Art and Culture, who spoke out against the attacks on 'rightist' forces, on the grounds that many people who had long ago lost the confidence of the workers, remained in union jobs.[2] Daubner, on the occasion of the congress of the Slovak Council of Trade Unions, expressed 'surprise' that the Slovak National Council had not sent a representative, and he later demanded a mutual flow of information if there were to be successful cooperation between the government and the unions.[3]

In many of the actions outlined above the unions were but responding to still more radical demands and actions from 'below,' from local union groups, individual plants and workers. Most notable was the perseverence and boldness with which the workers pursued their goals, anxious that the reform regime demonstrate the same qualities. They even went so far as unofficial strikes, although it is difficult to determine just when and where this weapon was used.[4] In addition to the tenaciously promoted wage-price demands, which might have been expected, on the whole the

[1] *Zemědělské noviny*, 12 November 1968.
[2] Bratislava radio, 28 January 1969.
[3] Bratislava radio, 27 February 1969 and 31 March 1969.
[4] See, for example, *Práce*, 10 October 1968 or *Zítřek*, 2 March 1969 (the latter mentioned a strike which closed the uranium mines for two weeks following the invasion).

workers concentrated on political–reform oriented issues. Acting spon-taneously and in defiance of government orders (though with ROH approval), workers continued to elect workers councils or preparatory committees for councils in many plants. The two mammoth plants, Škoda in Pilsen and Slovnaft Chemical Works in Bratislava even got so far as workers council elections for plant directors, ČTK of 26 February 1969 reported. On 9–10 January 1969 Škoda hosted a state-wide meeting of representatives of workers councils and preparatory committees from some two hundred plants, which elected a coordinating body which was eventually to set up an association of councils.[1] Černík rejected this last idea, at the ROH March congress, but workers continued to create councils and press for passage of the enterprise bill, both individually and through the coordinating committee.[2]

Opposition to *Zprávy*, radio Vltava, and the slanderous pamphlets circulated was expressed in plant after plant, including the East Slovak Iron Works, the ČKD tractor plant in Prague, the České Budějovice auto factory, the Communist group in Pilsen Škoda, as well as by hundreds of letters to the press and a meeting with regime leaders at the Mladá Boleslav Škoda plant in March 1969.[3] The union committee of the Svoboda publishing house refused to print certain articles of *Svět socialismu* and requested the journal be published elsewhere, *Práce* of 14 March 1969 reported. Demands for information and an 'open policy' as well as defense of the media were also expressed by local union resolutions and letters to the press, for example, the demands of 2500 Záluží Chemical Works employees or the Communists in the Šverma Iron Works in Slovakia.[4] Both *Práce* and *Reportér* received scores of letters condemning the suspension of *Reportér* in November 1968, and workers in several plants met with journalists, as well as students, on a regular basis.[5] Spontaneous support for the students' strike was manifest in such things as a fifteen-minute work stoppage in a Prague transport plant.[6] Com-munist workers in the Tisová power plant threatened to stop paying dues

---

[1] *Práce*, 9 January 1969; Prague radio, 9 January 1969.
[2] Prague radio, 21 February 1969; *Práce*, 3 December 1968 and 22 March 1969, for example.
[3] *Práce*, 10, 27 September; 5, 10, 11, 16, 22 October 1968; 5, 10 December 1968; January 1969; 22 March 1969; *Práca*, 10 September 1968; *Rudé právo*, 21 March 1969.
[4] *Rudé právo*, 4 November 1968; Prague radio, 7 February 1969.
[5] See *Práce*, 12 and 27 November 1968, for example, and Prague radio in English, 22 October 1968 and 28 February 1969.
[6] *Lidová demokracie*, 21 November 1968. See also *Práce*, 26 November 1968.

and even resign in protest to the regime's boycott of the Yugoslav Party congress, according to *Rudé právo* of 24 March 1969.

The biggest single issue, however, was that of Smrkovský. Indeed a number of plants even preceded the metal workers' call for support for Smrkovský, and at least two large plants, the Kladno steel works (through their local union) and the Chomutov iron works (union, Party committee, and *management*) threatened to strike.[1] The media, including, for example, *Rudé právo* of 29 December 1968, reported receiving thousands of letters, calls, cables, and delegations – even during the Christmas holidays – in support of Smrkovský (often criticizing Husák's speech.) The list of supporting resolutions was a long one and included such large groups of workers as the 50 000 strong Pilsen Škoda plant, 40 000 miners of the Most coal basin, the 40 000 strong Vítkovice steel works in Ostrava, and so forth. Even certain Slovak groups rose above the nationality issue and joined the campaign, for example, the Nováky chemical works, the Turčanské Strojárne engineering works in Martin, and the Union of Working Youth in the Bratislava Slovnaft plant.[2] Although this campaign did not end successfully, it left the workers in a tense mood, on the brink of utter frustration combined with total involvement, which was climaxed in the massive outpouring of solidarity with Jan Palach's tragic plea.

Often workers merely addressed letters or resolutions stating no more than their support for the 'post-January policies.' This phenomenon tended to reach peaks during periods of crisis, but appeared throughout the year. There was, for example, the letter in *Práce* on 10 October 1968, of a cutter in the Tatra Smichov plant who said he was for Dubček 'because no other politician throughout his career could accomplish what Dubček has accomplished in six months,' or that of 732 workers in a Hostivař plant, in *Práce* of 4 October 1968, pledging full support for the regime in its efforts to safeguard 'the sovereignty of the ČSSR and its further successful road toward democratic socialism with human features.' There were letters of support for individuals, such as the one signed by twenty-nine employees of a plant in Krnov congratulating Kriegel on his award from the Czechoslovak Society for Human Rights, complimenting him for 'combining the meaning of our revolutionary and Hussite traditions of democracy with the attitude of a genuine Communist–Marxist.'[3]

Other political demands called for a renewal of state sovereignty and withdrawal of the Pact troops, including one moving appeal in *Práce* of 1 October 1968, from 'a simple worker' that the Pact troops be replaced by

[1] *Práce*, 28 December 1968.   [2] Prague radio in English, 29 December 1968.
[3] *Mladá fronta*, 28 February 1969.

workers who would see with their own eyes that the country wanted to build socialism but must do this 'in the spirit of our traditions and conditions. We want nothing else.' There were, according to a Party official writing in *Práce* of 2 December 1968, thousands of demands for the holding of the fourteenth Party congress, for example, the standpoint of 2500 Communist workers in the Záluží chemical works, or the creation of a Czech Party (over which Communist workers in the steel shop of the Nová Huť' plant in Ostrava-Kunčice withheld their Party dues), or the holding of elections.[1] Indeed there was even a rise in resignations from the Party among workers, due in many cases to these specific issues, according to *Rudé právo* of 3 December 1969 and later ČTK reports.

There were also expressions of conservative views by workers, sometimes quite vituperative (and often anti-semitic), but these came almost entirely in the form of anonymous letters to the press. One such letter, from Communist 'Novák, Prague,' accusing *Práce* editor Velenský of having been a Gestapo agent, forecast almost to the day that 'our time will come. Perhaps as soon as in two months!'[2] In the East Slovak Ironworks, the conservative Emil Rigo was reelected chairman of the Party committee, from which he had been recalled in August, according to *Smena* of 3 March 1969.

A much larger number of letters and worker statements, however, rejected these conservative expressions, deploring both their anonymity and frequent vulgarity or racism.[3] There were also demands for the removal of conservative officials, specifically Kolder, Kapek, and Biľak, as well as the more general condemnations of the fact that persons who had long ago lost public confidence, claimed to represent the people or the workers.[4] The Libeň meeting was strongly condemned as illegal factionalism; and its leaders were taken to task by name. Indeed this reaction approached near campaign proportions, particularly in Slovakia, with resolutions or meetings by Communists in at least a dozen large plants.[5] The large Slovak participation in this particular protest was probably

[1] *Rudé právo*, 4, 13, 30 November 1968; 21 March 1969; *Pravda* (Bratislava), 5 November 1968.

[2] *Práce*, 1 February 1969. See also on this subject, *Práce*, 9 November 1968; *Rudé právo*, 22 October 1968; *Pravda* (Bratislava), 17 December 1968.

[3] According to *Pravda* (Bratislava), 4 November 1968; see also *Rudé právo* or *Práce*, 22 October 1968.

[4] See *Smena*, 2 April 1969; *Práca*, 23 September 1968; *Práce*, 13 November 1968; *Lidová demokracie*, 21 March 1969.

[5] See, for example, *Pravda* (Bratislava), 4, 5, 7, 8 November 1968 or *Práca*, 6, 7 November 1968.

indicative of the fine distinction insisted upon by the Slovak realists, between them and the ultra-conservatives, especially as it came at a time when the liberals had allied with the realists in the central committee in connection with the then forthcoming November plenum.

Workers in the post-invasion period seemed to awake, stirred by a national pride in a way that they had not earlier been stirred by politico-economic interest, to take their place at the head of the pressure for reform. Joining forces amongst themselves, restaffing and working through their unions, collaborating with the intellectuals and students, they represented a force of which the regime was clearly fearful. As with the other groups, they did not utilize this force to its fullest, apparently because of the innate 'realism' or rationality even of the Czech workers, once convinced of the irrevocable inability of the regime to rule against Moscow's wishes. As Ludvík Pacovský said in *Zemědělské noviny* of 12 November 1968:

> 'If after January it was above all the members of the intellectual strata who expressed the most radical opinions, then today the picture has completely changed. Manual workers are speaking the most clearly, the most forcefully, and with the most anger...It is certainly essential to know that the workers have today become by far the strongest pressure group.'

And replying to Husák's use of this last term pejoratively, Czech National Council deputy chairman Jičinský said, in *Práce* of 30 December 1968 of the workers' activities: 'If this is regarded as a so-called pressure group, then it must be said that it is in order and it is democratic.' Thus it was only after the invasion, as *Práce* pointed out on 4 January 1969, that 'the true kernel of January was (*sic*) now clearly recognizable,' having finally borne its fruits.

Crisis

February and March 1969 saw a slight reduction of tensions inside Czechoslovak society, despite the outspokenness of the ROH March congress, the demands for elections, for workers councils, for more information and the like. Even the suicide of Jan Zajíc at the end of February and the demonstrations against Czechoslovakia's non-attendance at the Yugoslav Party congress in March did not return the country to the crisis atmosphere of the November–January period. At most they served to remind both population and regime alike that 'normalization' had not yet been achieved.

Some of the planks of the Action Program had been implemented, but generally in a manner adjusted to the demands of Moscow, often divesting the measures of their original significance. Thus federalization – the most extensive reform permitted after the invasion – was more a hollow sop for the Slovaks than the genuine autonomy hoped for in the spring. The rehabilitation program continued, with the naming of judges to special rehabilitation courts, but the whole process slowed down, grinding almost to a halt by the spring, the military rehabilitation tribunals and the draft law on extra-judiciary rehabilitations never having come into effect.[1] In February a defense council was set up, composed of government, military and Party officials responsible to the Federal Assembly for the military policies of the country. This was in a sense a return to a similar pre-war council, but when proposed by the reformers in the spring of 1968 it was to have included control functions over the security as well as military organs and, presumably, to have been more independent from the Party.[2] Defense and security committees were set up in the new parliamentary chambers, as recommended in the spring, but their powers did not exceed those of the Party's security department as envisaged by the reforms.

A barometer of public preferences from the invasion to the spring crisis could be found in polls conducted in this period. Immediately after the invasion the following results were received from a sample of 200 persons in Prague on the question: who are the three personages in public life today whom you trust most? In order of the number of times mentioned: Dubček, 90%; Svoboda, 81%; Černík, 41%; Smrkovský, 33%; and Císař 22%.[3] In a poll taken two months later, in Slovakia, 94.2% listed Dubček; 91.8%, Svoboda; 60.5%, Smrkovský; 57.8%, Černík, and 34.9% Husák (lowest even in Slovakia).[4] By March, in a ČSAV poll of 1635 persons throughout the country, Svoboda, Dubček, Smrkovský, and Černík remained in the highest places, Smrkovský third in the Czech lands (63%) and fourth in Slovakia (36%) with Černík third in Slovakia (42%) and fourth in the Czech lands (39%); Husák was only fifth in Slovakia (24%) and still lower, ninth, in the Czech lands (only 2%).[5]

---

[1] *Rudé právo*, 27 March 1969; *Smena*, 11 April 1969 and ČTK, 26 March 1968 for complaints on this issue.
[2] See chapter 7. The Party first secretary was now chairman and, in fact, the council was heavily staffed by the Party. (*Pravda* (Bratislava), 4 February 1969.)
[3] *Reportér*, 18 September 1968.
[4] *Práca*, 29 December 1968.
[5] ČTK, 2 April 1969. A ČSAV poll a year earlier had registered Dubček, 50%; Smrkovský, 32%; Husák, 20%; Husák in Slovakia, 53.5%. (ČTK, 27 March 1968 and Prague radio, 28 March 1968.)

Inside the Party conservatives and realists seemed to be gaining strength; the former appeared to have gained control of the police and security forces, the latter seemed to be espousing an increasingly conservative position, as attested to by Husák's speech to the Slovak central committee plenum of 12 March 1969.[1] Moreover, in Slovakia, among the workers as well as the students and intellectuals, reform activities had been more or less paralyzed. It took an issue of national pride once again to unite the population and to bring it into the streets – not so much with political demands as with the pent-up frustrations of an increasingly bleak horizon.

This 'issue' was the ice-hockey victories of Czechoslovakia over the Soviet Union in Stockholm on 21 and 28 March 1969 (the championships were to have been played in Prague but were transferred at the latter's request in September 1968 because of the disruptions caused by the invasion).[2] There had been few opportunities for celebrating in Prague in that period, and a victory of any kind over the Russians provided an emotional uplift of extraordinary dimensions. The press received the victories with headlines of 'What David Did With His Sling, We Did With A Puck,' 'They Left Pieces of Their Heart on the Ice,' 'A Sensation for the World, A Disaster for the Rival, Everything for Us, Yes, It is True.' Reporting referred to the players as 'fighters' and the press reported comments such as, this was proof 'that we can get even with every reality, however harsh,' 'sometimes even a small nation is great,' 'continue to fight in the spirit of our traditions,' 'Thank you, you have told them everything,' and 'Long live the victory of Athens over Sparta.' Congratulations were sent to the team from factories and newspapers, groups and individuals, and even the country's officials, Černík and Dubček.[3]

Following each victory people gathered in the streets to celebrate, but it was after the second victory, the evening of 28 March, that 100 000 to 150 000 people packed the Václavské náměstí.[4] These celebrations and others throughout the country, including Slovakia, quickly took on an anti-Soviet character and culminated, in Prague, in the damaging of the Aeroflot offices, in Bratislava and elsewhere, in attacks on Soviet soldiers

[1] See *Práca*, 1 April 1969; *Práce*, 2 April 1969, or Mináč in *Nové slovo*, 3 April 1969.
[2] Prague radio, 17 September 1968.
[3] See all papers of 29, 30 March 1969 and Prague radio, 30, 31 March 1969.
[4] ČTK, 29 March 1969. The Slovak Interior Minister revealed that 8000–10 000 people had demonstrated in Bratislava after the first victory, threatening the Soviet military headquarters there. (ČTK, 1 April 1969.)

and installations.[1] While there was talk later of provocations, the massive pouring into the streets and even the rush of anti-Soviet sentiment were clearly spontaneous, even if one were able to find provocateurs behind, for example, the attack on Aeroflot. Although the Interior Ministry band was one of the many to contribute to the celebrations in Prague, and members of the armed forces in various places also joined in, clashes led to sixty-five police wounded and thirty-nine arrests in Prague alone.[2]

Expressing understanding of and sympathy with the celebrations, the government issued a statement on 29 March condemning the excesses which had led to vandalism and damage to Soviet installations. In what was a relatively mild reprimand, the government referred only in passing to possible activities of 'provocateurs and anti-socialist criminal elements,' attributing most of the damage to 'citizens who [were] unable to control their actions,' according to Prague radio, 29 March 1969. Two days later, however, the tone changed somewhat as indicated both by the Interior Ministry statement, which emphasized the idea of 'provocateurs, offenders, and criminal elements,' and by a *Pravda* (Moscow) article on 31 March which attributed the events to 'right-wing anti-socialist forces' which as in November and January 'once again seek to aggravate the situation in Czechoslovakia.' Blaming the media for 'stirring up public passion,' and inciting people to demonstrate even after the first victory, *Pravda* added an ominous remark of 'surprise' that the Party's leadership had done nothing 'against these unhealthy and dangerous phenomena.' Asserting that the 28 March demonstrations were 'directed by certain people,' the paper claimed that Smrkovský 'who, as is well known, more than once before has been involved in similar actions,' was among the participants on 28 March.[3] On the day of this article, Soviet Defense Minister Grechko and deputy Foreign Minister Semyonov arrived in Czechoslovakia. After this statement of the Russian view, the Czechoslovak press and various government, Party, and social organs began to condemn the acts of vandalism.

Under the direct pressure of an ultimatum delivered by Grechko on 1 April in talks with Dubček, Černík, and Svoboda, the presidium issued a statement which generally echoed the line taken by *Pravda* with regard to

[1] In Mladá Boleslav, Ústí nad Labem, Liberec, Olomouc, Jaroměř, Košice, Bratislava, and Brno, for example.
[2] *Lidová demokracie*, 29 March 1969; Defence Ministry statement, ČTK, 9 April 1969; Interior Ministry statements, ČTK, 31 March and 3 April 1969.
[3] The Federal Assembly issued a denial, saying that Smrkovský had had to detour between meetings because of the crowds. (*Rudé právo*, 1 April 1969.)

'anti-socialist' forces, the media, and organized anti-Sovietism. Also in keeping with Moscow's line, the presidium singled out Smrkovský for having failed to abide by the November resolution. The statement announced that measures would be taken to ensure public order and to guarantee the political line of the media. With this the country moved into full crisis. Meeting after meeting, of government and Party organizations throughout the country, as well as the two most powerful union groups, the Czech Metal Workers and the Czech Trade Union Council, took place during the next few days, all condemning the anti-Soviet outbursts.[1] On 3 April Dubček addressed the country, hinting several times at the possibility of a second Soviet intervention. He called not only for prudence and discipline but cooperation in carrying out the new restrictions since 'the time we have for consolidation is not unlimited.' Inasmuch as the damage was already done, the demonstrations having been a spontaneous phenomenon which calmed within hours, Dubček's speech seems to have been designed rather to demonstrate to the Russians, by demonstrating to his own people, the seriousness with which he regarded these events and particularly any future repetition of them. It probably also served to explain to the public the measures he had been forced to take, and possibly might yet have to take, for it was in keeping with Dubček's entire approach to believe that understanding would bring cooperation.

The arrival of Grechko and Semyonov, together with the presidium reprimand of Smrkovský, led to rumors of impending personnel changes in the leadership. In particular Grechko's visits with Štrougal, Kempný, Husák, and military leaders, in addition to visits by Svoboda to various military units including the Brno Military Academy (with Černík, Husák, and Czech National Council chairman Rázl, without Dubček) gave rise to the story that Svoboda was going to form a new government with the help of the military.[2] Another form of the rumored coup had it that Grechko demanded that Svoboda and the military take over but that Svoboda refused.[3] In the midst of these rumors the Czechoslovak Party presidium met on 8 April; it announced that measures would be taken against specific journalists, and scheduled a central committee plenum for 17 April.[4] It also prepared the answer to Grechko's ultimatum to the

[1] One paper, at least, was willing expressly to deny the charges of an organized 'anti-socialist' action: *Zemědělské noviny*, 2 April 1969.
[2] ČTK, 2 April 1969; Tanjug, 3 April 1969.
[3] See 'The Military Coup That Never Was' (RFE, 6 June 1969).
[4] Prague radio, 8 April 1969.

Czechs to put their house in order. On the same day Czechoslovak Ambassador to Moscow, Koucký, met with Kosygin. Then Svoboda set out for a two-day visit to Slovakia, setting off another series of rumors, denied by *Rudé právo* of 12 April 1969. On 11 April, in a speech to farm officials in Nitra, Husák delivered a scathing and quite direct attack on Dubček, stopping short only of mentioning his name.[1] He blamed the past year's tensions and crises on weak, poor, undecided leadership which had led to disunity in the top organs of the Party and thereby allowed 'free scope' to the 'anti-socialist and hostile forces,' particularly in the media. Recognizing that it was a mistake not to have spoken out sooner, Husák called for a leadership capable of acting decisively and of putting decisions into practice. Concluding in terms dangerously reminiscent of Novotný, Husák played on the masses' old distrust of intellectuals by condemning the idea of 'elites' and called for a class concept of freedom.

Husák's speech bore all the signs of a deal between him and the conservatives to replace the Dubček leadership, a deal if not engineered at least supported by the Soviets. Indeed on the very day of this speech Štrougal was meeting with Semyonov and the Soviet ambassador, while the Czech ambassador in Moscow was meeting with Brezhnev. After a side-trip to Soviet forces in East Germany, Grechko returned to Prague in time for a 12 April meeting of the Party executive board which discussed the forthcoming plenum, particularly the resignation of Dubček. The following day Warsaw Pact maneuvers were announced by Prague radio for 14 to 16 April, and on 14 April Grechko left Czechoslovakia, leaving Semyonov in Prague. Adding to the mounting tension, Prague radio on 14 April announced a government communique that additional Soviet troops were to arrive, only to retract the announcement an hour later as having, 'in view of changed circumstances, no foundation in truth.' On 15 April the Slovak Party daily published an article critical of Smrkovský, criticized by the Party presidium for earlier references to the danger from dogmatists in the Party. One day before the plenum, the executive board issued a statement defending these same dogmatists: Rigo, Indra, Bil'ak, Barbírek, Kolder, Piller, Švestka, Kapek, Lenárt, and Jakeš, and exonerated them for their collaborationist roles in August. Thus the stage was set for the changing of the guard, Smrkovský having engaged in self-criticism on the pages of *Rudé právo* on 16 April, the paper itself having engaged in self-criticism four days earlier. It was, in

[1] Bratislava radio, 11 April 1969.

fact, the 14–15 April 1969 session of the Party presidium that approved the replacement Dubček by Husák.[1]

The public did not remain indifferent to these increasingly clear signs of imminent changes. Students of the radical agricultural college in Prague went out on strike on 14 April, while other students threatened to strike in the event of personnel changes.[2] Prague journalists, writers, and workers met with students in a day of discussions on the situation also on 14 April.[3] The Czech Trade Union Council issued a statement of solidarity with the workers in the media and its chairman, Rudolf Pacovský, declared continued confidence in the nation's leaders.[4] The regime was taking no chances, however. On the night of 16 April, prior to the opening of the plenum, some 894 persons were taken into custody, of whom 103 were detained, in the Czech lands; 2300 were taken in Slovakia, of whom 135 were detained, Prague radio reported on 17 April. While these were not political arrests (the detained were reported to be criminals and vagrants) they were a show of police strength – and regime willingness to use the means at its disposal. The central committee met, briefly, on 17 April 1969 and carried out its prepared changes: Husák replaced Dubček as Party first secretary; the executive board was abolished and the presidium reduced to eleven persons (once again,) consisting of Bil'ak, Colotka, Černík, Dubček, Erban, Husák, Piller, Sádovský, Svoboda, Štrougal, and Karel Poláček. Smrkovský was the only member of the former executive board not included in the new presidium, which also excluded liberals Šimon, Slavík, and Špaček, among others.

The whole crisis, however, had something artificial about it. The demonstrations after the ice-hockey games had almost none of the potential dangers characteristic of the several crises in the post-invasion period. The populace was not organized into active groups around specific demands with threats of greater action if satisfaction were not forthcoming. Neither the unions nor the intellectuals nor the students nor individual factories or organizations brought pressures to bear as they had at the time of the Smrkovský affair or even in reaction to Jan Palach's death. Indeed all of these usual channels of pressure acquiesced to the regime's demand for condemnation of vandalism, recognizing that dis-

---

[1] According to one report Dubček had his opposition to Husák's nomination registered in the minutes of this meeting, his choice having been Černík (once he believed that he himself had no chance of staying in). ('Moravus,' *Survey*, 17:4 (1971), 213.)

[2] Tanjug, 17 April 1969; Prague radio, 14 April 1969.

[3] Ibid. See also Prague radio, 17 April 1969, Prague city Party statement on 'pressures.'

[4] Prague radio in English, 15 April 1969.

orders were likely to do little to remove the Russians from the country. At the very least one can say that these still relatively powerful groups were caught 'unprepared' for the spontaneous demonstrations and, after the fact, did not see in them the stuff of which to make a crucial stand. On the other hand, the anti-Russian outburst (even if partially triggered by provocateurs) was symptomatic of the deep-seated fury and disillusionment amongst the population, which, in the eyes of Moscow, was not sufficiently controlled by the Dubček regime and, therefore, constituted a continuous threat to the very goals of the Soviet invasion. For those in Czechoslovakia who had been struggling to gain power over the reformers, this was the perfect opportunity; Moscow's strong reaction gave them the backing they needed. They did not squabble too much among themselves over the distinctions between 'realism' and 'conservativism;' the aim was to gain power, after which one could decide on just which variant of anti-reform would rule. For these elements in the Party the situation was favorable, for the population was *not* organized for crisis, ready to strike in defense of its reform heroes as it had been upon occasion in the preceding months. For the Russians, too, the situation was convenient, for finally they had had an open and even violent defiance of the Soviet Union – much easier to dub anti-communist and dangerous than the Communist reform movement they sought to eliminate.

Thus the Soviet Union achieved, albeit belatedly, a significant part of its objectives of August 1968: a leadership willing to dismantle the reform program and return to the type of dictatorial Party rule identified by the Soviet Union with Communism. Yet even with this change the Soviet Union did not receive its 'normalization,' for the reform movement had taken root too deeply and too broadly throughout the population to be easily exorcised. Husák, having himself been a victim of the terror of the 1950s, understood the pitfalls of the policies advocated by the conservatives. Moscow too recognized this and, therefore, permitted Husák his systematic yet measured dismantling of the reforms which only a year later saw the total discrediting of Dubček and only two years later tentative trials of some of the 'guilty.'

Bibliography

SELECTED CZECH AND SLOVAK LANGUAGE NEWSPAPERS AND JOURNALS

Acta Universitatis Carolinae, A-revue, Československý časopis historický, Czechoslovak Economic Papers, Czechoslovak Foreign Trade, Czechoslovak Life, Czechoslovak Sociological Society Bulletin, Dějiny a současnost, Dikobraz, Divadelní noviny, Divadlo, Doba, Ekonomiká revue, Ekonomický časopis, Ekonomický ústav, Hospodářské noviny, Host do domu, Katolické noviny, Knižní kultura, Kulturní noviny, Kulturní tvorba, Kultúrny život, Lidová armáda, Lidová demokracie, Listy, Literární listy, Literární noviny, Literárny život, Ľud, Mezinárodní politika, Mezinárodní vztahy, Mladá fronta, Mladý svět, My 68, My 69, Nová mysl, Nová svoboda, Nové slovo, Novinář, Noviny vnitřního obchodu, Noviny zahraničního obchodu, Nový život, Obrana lidu, Otázky marxistickej filosofie, Plamen, Plánované hospodářství, Politická ekonomie, Politika, Práca, Práce, Pravda, Právnické štúdie, Právník, Právny obzor, Predvoj, Příspěvky k dějinám KSČ, Reflex, Reportér, Roháč, Roľnícke noviny, Rovnost, Rudé právo, Sborník historický, Sešity pro mladou literaturu, Slovanský přehled, Slovenské poľľady, Smena, Smer, Socialistická škola, Socialistické zemědělství, Statistika, Student, Studentské listy, Svět práce, Svět socialismu, Svět sovětů, Svět v obrazech, Svoboda, Svobodné slovo, Tribuna, Tvář, Tvorba, Učitelské noviny, Universita Karlova, Večerní Praha, Večerník, Věda a život, Věstník ČSAV, Vlasta, Výběr, Zemědělské noviny, Zítřek, Život, Život strany.

SELECTED SOVIET AND OTHER EAST EUROPEAN NEWSPAPERS AND JOURNALS

Berliner Zeitung (East Germany), *Borba* (Yugoslavia), *Élet és irodalom* (Hungary), *Izvestia* (USSR), *Komsomolskaya pravda* (USSR), *Krasnaya zvezda* (USSR), *Literaturnaya gazeta* (USSR), *Nedeljne informativne noviny* (Yugoslavia), *Népszabadság* (Hungary), *Neues Deutschland* (East Germany), *Polityka* (Poland), *Pravda* (USSR), *Robotnichesko delo* (Bulgaria), *Trybuna ludu* (Poland), *Trud* (USSR), *Vjesnik* (Yugoslavia), *Za ruzbehom* (USSR), *Zprávy* (Soviet command in Czechoslovakia).

SELECTED PERIODICALS APPEARING IN THE WEST

Primarily *East Europe, Problems of Communism, Studies in Comparative Communism, Listy* (Rome), *Survey, Svědectví*; occasionally *American Political Science*

Bibliography

Review, Canadian Slavonic Papers, Die Zeit, The Economist, Encounter, Foreign Affairs, Jews in Eastern Europe, Les Temps Moderns, Orbis, Rinascita, Soviet Studies, Volkstimme, World Politics and the monitoring services of the BBC, FBIS, and RFE; the analyses by RFE.

SELECTED BOOKS AND PAMPHLETS

Bystřina, Ivan, 'K otázkám pluralitního politického systému socialismu,' unpublished paper (Mannheim, 1968).

Československo 1968 (Praha, 1969).

ČSSR : The Road to Democratic Socialism (Prague, 1968).

Czechoslovak Political Science at the IPSA Congress in Brussels (Praha, 1968).

The Czechoslovak Trade Unions (Brussels, 1970).

Deyl, Z., Belda, J., Bonček, M., Klimeš, M., *Na rozhraní dvou epoch* (Praha, 1968).

Documents Tchécoslovaques (Paris, 1969).

Dubček, Alexander, *Du Printemps à l'hiver de Prague* (Paris, 1970).

  K otázkam obrodzovacieho procesu v KSČ (Bratislava, 1968).

  O národnostní otázce (Praha, 1968).

Ello, Paul, *Czechoslovakia's Blueprint for Freedom* (Washington, 1968).

Erickson, John, 'The "Military Factor" and the Czechoslovak Reform Movement,' unpublished paper (Reading, 1971).

Falt'an, Samo, *Slovenská otázka v Československu* (Bratislava, 1968).

Feiwel, George, *New Economic Patterns in Czechoslovakia* (New York, 1968).

Fiblich, Jan, *K otázkám byrokracie a byrokratismu* (Praha, 1968).

Garaudy, Roger, *La liberté en soucis* (Paris, 1968).

  Toute la verité (Paris, 1970).

Gitelman, Zvi, 'Public Opinion and Political Reform in Czechoslovakia,' unpublished paper (University of Michigan, 1971).

Golan, Galia, *The Czechoslovak Reform Movement* (Cambridge, 1971).

  and Shafir, Michael, *Bibliography for the Study of the Communist World* (Jerusalem, 1970).

Goldman, Josef, and Kouba, Karel, *Economic Growth in Czechoslovakia* (New York, 1969).

Hamšík, Dušan, *Spisovatelé a moc* (Praha, 1969).

Hejzlar, Zdeněk, 'Chronology 1968–69,' unpublished paper (Stockholm, 1970).

  'The Evolution of the Communist Party of Czechoslovakia,' unpublished paper (Reading, 1971).

Hromádka, Josef, *Thoughts of a Czech Pastor* (London, 1970).

Husák, Gustáv, *Projevy a stati 1969–70* (Praha, 1970).

James, Robert (ed.), *The Czechoslovak Crisis* (London, 1968).

Jodl, Miroslav, *Teorie elity a problém elity* (Praha, 1968).

K událostem v Československu (Moskva, 1968).

Bibliography

Kaplan, Karel, *Znárodnění a socialismus* (Praha, 1968).

Kdo je kdo v ČSSR (Praha, 1969).

Klokočka, Vladimír, *Volby v parlementních demokraciích* (Praha, 1968).

Kosík, Karel, *Dialektika konkrétního* (Praha, 1963).

Kusín, Vladimír, *The Intellectual Origins of the Prague Spring* (Cambridge, 1971).

Kusý, Miroslav, *Filosofie politiky* (Bratislava, 1966).

Lakatoš, Michal, *Úvaha o hodnotách demokracie* (Praha, 1969).

Liehm, A. J., *Trois Générations* (Paris, 1970).

Littell, Robert (ed.), *The Czech Black Book* (New York, 1969).

Löbl, Eugen, *Sentenced and Tried* (London, 1969).

  Svedectvo o procese s vedením protištátneho sprísahaneckého centra v čele s R. Slánskym (Bratislava, 1968).

  Úvahy o duševnej práci a bohatstve národa (Bratislava, 1969).

London, Artur, *L'Aveu* (Paris, 1969).

Lukaszewski, Jerzy (ed.), *The Peoples Democracies After Prague* (Bruges, 1970)

M, *A Year in Eight Months* (New York, 1969).

Machonin, Pavel, *Sociální struktura socialistické společnosti* (Praha, 1966).

Machovec, Milan, *Tomáš G. Masaryk* (Praha, 1968).

Mackintosh, Malcolm, *The Evolution of the Warsaw Pact* (Adelphi Papers, London, 1969).

Mandrou, Robert, *Les sept jours de Prague 21–27 Aout 1968* (Paris, 1969).

Mimoriadny zjazd KSS 26–29-9-1968–Protokol (Bratislava, 1968).

Mlynář, Zdeněk, *Stát a člověk* (Praha, 1964).

Mňačko, Ladislav, *The Seventh Night* (New York, 1969).

On Events in Czechoslovakia (Moscow, 1968).

Pelikán, Jiří (ed.), *The Czechoslovak Political Trials* (London, 1971).

  The Secret Vysočany Congress (London, 1971).

Procházka, Jan, *Politika pro každého* (Praha, 1968).

Remington, Robin (ed.), *Winter in Prague* (Cambridge, Mass., 1969).

Richta, Radovan, *Civilizace na rozcestí* (Praha, 1968).

Rodnick, David, *The Strangled Democracy* (Lubbock, Texas, 1970).

Rok šedesátý osmý v usneseních a dokumentech ÚV KSČ (Praha, 1969).

Sbírka zákonů Československé socialistické republiky (Praha, 1968–9).

Schöpflin, George, *The Soviet Union and Eastern Europe, A Handbook* (London, 1970).

Schwartz, Harry, *Prague's 200 Days* (New York, 1969).

Sedm pražských dnů (Praha, 1968).

Selucký, Radoslav, *The Plan That Failed* (London, 1970).

Shawcross, William, *Dubček* (London, 1970).

Šik, Ota, *Ekonomické zájmy* (Praha, 1968).

  Fakta o stavu ČS. národního hospodářství (Praha, 1968).

  Plán a trh za socialismu (Praha, 1968).

Bibliography

IV. Sjezd svazu československých spisovatelů (Praha, 1968).

Slánská, Josefa, *Report on My Husband* (London, 1969).

Šlingova, Marian, *Truth Will Prevail* (London, 1968).

'Stanovisko komunistů mimořádné městské konference k obecným politickým problemům' (Praha, 1968).

Statistická ročenka Československé socialistické republiky (Praha, 1968–9).

Suda, Zdenek, *The Czechoslovak Socialist Republic* (Baltimore, 1969).

Sviták, Ivan, *The Czechoslovak Experiment* (New York, 1971).

Svoboda : The Press in Czechoslovakia 1968 (Zurich, 1969).

Tatu, Michel, *L'Hérésie impossible* (Paris, 1968).

Theiner, George (ed.), *New Writing in Czechoslovakia* (London, 1969).

Thomas, John, 'Soviet Foreign Policy and Conflict Within the Political and Military Leadership' (Research Analysis Corporation, 1970).

Tigrid, Pavel, *Kvadratura kruhu* (Paris, 1969).

Le printemps de Prague (Paris, 1968).

Why Dubček Fell (London, 1971).

Tomalek, Pavel, 'Czechoslovakia 1968–1969: The Worker–Student Alliance' (MIT paper, 1971).

Tyl, Miroslav, 'Rozbor studentského hnutí a návrh koncepce pro jistou část studentstva,' unpublished paper (Praha, 1969).

The Use of Anti-Semitism Against Czechoslovakia (London, 1969).

Wechsberg, Joseph, *The Voices* (New York, 1969).

Windsor, Phillip, and Roberts, Adam, *Czechoslovakia 1968* (London, 1969).

Zartman, William, *Czechoslovakia. Intervention and Impact* (New York, 1969).

Zeman, Z. A. B., *Prague Spring* (London, 1969).

Index

Academic Council of Students, 73, 75

Action Program: adoption of, 57, 194, 250; and agricultural problems, 46–8; on anti-semitism, 93; on consumer goods, 33; on courts and judges, 185; on currency, 35; and the 'Czecho-slovak way to socialism,' 212; on dictatorship of proletariat, 134, 145n, 158; and Dubček, 212, 252; on economic cooperation with bloc, 37–8; and economic reforms, 27–35, 38, 42, 46–9, 53, 55; and employment, 55; on elected organs of government, 149, 153; and enterprise independence, 27–30, 33, 46–8; and federalization, 49, 193; on foreign policy, 205–7; on foreign trade, 27, 35, 38; on freedom of association, 58, 65, 78, 84; and freedom of expression and information, 117; on government, 149; on government and economic reforms, 27–33; on inner Party democracy, 140; on intellectuals, 53; on interest groups, 57–8; and leading role of Party, 134–5, 146, 158; and legal system, 185; and management, 42, 46–8; and market economy, 27, 30–3, 46–8; on mass organizations, 58–9, 65; and National Assembly, 149, 193; and National Committees, 149–50, 153; and National Front, 153, 156–7, 167; and national minorities, 99–100, 102; position towards, after invasion, 250, 252–3, 275–6, 275n, 279, 296; and possibility of opposition, 157–8, 157n, 161; and prices, 27, 31–3, 35; on private sector, 33–4, 48; on security organs, 185; and separation of Party and state, 146; and 'Slovak Question,' 49, 193; on small enter-prises, 33–4; and Smrkovský, 252; and socialist society, 212; and Spaček, 252; on state, 134; on trade unions, 42, 62, 68; and USSR, 223; on wages

and salaries, 31–2; and workers, 42, 53; on workers councils, 42, 45; and youth, 77, 275; other references, 18, 29, 83, 133, 153, 163, 228, 285

Action Program of Ministry of Education, 103n

Action Program of student organization, 75

Agence France Presse, 259

Agricultural Production Administrations (APA), 25

agriculture: and Action Program, 46–8; and economic reforms, 22, 25–7, 27n, 46–8, 55, 67–8; enterprise independence in, 25–6, 46–8; management in, 25–6, 46–8; organization of, 25–6, 46–8, 66–8, 198; private sector in, 26–7, 68, 69n; trade union in, 25n, 26, 47, 66–9, 288, 290; other references, 55

Anti-Fascist Fighters Union, 80, 254

anti-semitism: Action Program on, 93; and Arab–Israeli conflict, 15, 91–4, 108; of conservatives, 93n, 108n, 259, 267, 294; and purge trials, 91–3, 108, 170; and Slovak nationalism, 91, 93–4; other references, 128, 245n

Arab–Israeli conflict, 15, 15–16n, 91–4, 107–8

A-revue, 201

army: and December 1967 political crisis, 16, 183–4, 183n; Main Political Directorate of, 16, 184; and reforms, 182–5, 296, 296n; other references, 241, 285

Association of Land Conservation Co-operatives, 48

Association of Socialist Youth, 77

associations and trusts, 9–10, 21–5, 27–9, 44, 47

Auersperg, Pavel, 121

Austria, 39, 52

Austro-Hungarian Empire, 197

Auto Club of Czechoslovakia, 79

Index

Chudík, Michal, 5n, 191, 218, 247
Chytilová, Věra, 14
Čierná nad Tisou conference, 228–33, 235, 238, 260
Cíganik, Ivan, 139
Circle of Independent Writers, 82, 106, 160
Císař, Čestmír: at central committee plenum of May–June 1968, 164; and the 'Czechoslovak way to socialism,' 215n, 216; and leading role of Party, 135; official positions of, 5, 14, 69, 116, 164, 197, 247; and Party and possibility of opposition, 164; popularity of, after invasion, 296; and students and youth, 69, 77, 152–3, 252n; and USSR, 226, 231n; other references, 89, 122, 205, 227n, 240, 289
Civil Code (1964), 12n, 175n
Čivrný, Lumír, 126
Clementis, Vladimír, 4, 186
Club of Critical Thought, 82
Cohn-Bendit, Daniel, 224–5n
Colotka, Peter, 147, 162, 213, 256, 261, 288, 301
Cominform, 170–1, 209–10, 236, 238, 289
Comintern, 236, 238
Committee of Farm and Country Youth, 274
Committee for Press and Information, 261, 262n
Committee for Scientific Management, 45n
Committee of Secondary School and Apprentice Youth, 274
Constitution (1960), 2, 14, 84, 95–6, 144, 152, 179–80; and Slovakia, 189–90
Constitution (new), 13–15, 102, 132–3, 135, 147–9, 154, 167, 188–93, 196
Constitutional Act (1946), 193
Constitutional Court, 179, 185n, 199
Constitutional Law, 185n, 192–3, 196–9
consumer goods, 9, 32–4
Coordinating Committee of Creative Associations, 110, 265–6, 266n, 290–1
Council for Mutual Economic Assistance (CEMA): and the reforms, 37–8, 40, 237; suggestions for reform in, 37–8, 41, 210; other references, 205, 206, 231
Council of Revival, 253
courts and judges: Action Program on,

185, administrative courts, 12, 12n; criticism of, 92, 172, 179; Constitutional Court, 71, 179, 199; reform of, 10, 12, 12n, 168, 176, 178–9, 192; and Slovakia, 192, 199; State Court, 175; Supreme Court, 74n, 175–6, 177n, 192; other references, 74n, 115, 175, 180n, 263, 296
CPSU, 3–4, 201, 249; central committee of, 223, 225, 228–9, 234–5
credits: and economic reforms, 9–10, 26, 32, 44, 49–50; foreign, 36, 39–41, 205, 224, 231
Cuba, 205
Cultural Association of the Hungarian Working People in Czechoslovakia (Csemadok), 94–8, 100–1, 102n, 152
currency, 35–40, 50, 112, 198
Cvik, Rudolf, 218, 221
Czech Association of Children's and Youth Organizations, 274
Czech Communist Party: 19, 143, 220–1, 294; congress of, 222, 248, 250–1, 278, 280, 286, 291
Czech Coordinating Committee of Creative Associations, 254
Czech Farmers Union, 67–8, 288, 290
Czech Journalists Union, 109, 265, 265n
Czech League for Human Rights, 83n
Czech National Council, 190–1, 194, 197, 197n
Czech Trade Unions Council, 284–6, 287n, 289, 299, 301
Czech Union of Assembly and Suppliers Organizations, 288
Czech Union of Building Workers, 288
Czech Union of Health Workers, 289
Czech Union of Lumber Workers, 290
Czech Union of Metal Workers, 254–6, 280, 285–90, 299
Czech Union of Miners, 290
Czech Union of Press Workers, 288, 290
Czech Union of Printers, 289
Czech Union of Railway Workers, 288
Czech Union of Secondary School Pupils and Apprentices, 279
Czech Union of State Employees, 290
Czech Union of Working Youth, 275
Czech Union of Youth Clubs, 279
Czech Writers Union, 265
Czechoslovak Academy of Sciences (ČSAV), 14, 52, 81, 84, 106, 241, 261, 266; polls of, 152n, 276n, 296, 296n

Index

Ecumenical Council of Churches, 91
Ecumenical Movement of Students and Intelligentsia, 89
educational system: and national minorities, 95–6, 198; organization and nature of, 11, 103n; reform of, 11, 69, 103n; and religious education, 86–7, 90, 92–3; Soviet model for, 11, 213
Egypt, 209
Eichler, Benjamin, 92
electoral laws, 13, 75–6, 106, 150, 152–3, 167–8
electoral system, 14, 150–3, 157–9, 167–8
Élet és irodalom, 122, 135, 216
enterprises: independence of, 9–10, 20–3, 25–35, 42–4, 46–50; public (state), 29, 45–6, 286; shareholder, 29, 29n, 34, 45–6, 286; social, 29–30, 45–6, 286
Erban, Evžen, 252–3, 260n, 265, 275, 280, 301
Estetika, 106

Falt'an, Samo, 129, 190
Farmers Union, 67–8; *see also* Czech Farmers Union, Slovak Farmers Union, trade unions in agriculture
Feder, Richard, 92
Federal Assembly, 148n, 191, 198, 254–6, 287, 296, 298n
federalization: Action Program on, 49, 193; of Czechoslovak Writers Union, 264; and economic reforms, 49–50, 192; and government, 190–2, 195–6; and National Assembly, 149, 193, 197n, 198–9, 254–6, 287; and National minorities, 95, 197–8; of Party, 19, 143, 191, 196–7, 220–1; and 'Slovak Question,' 15, 49–50, 71, 71n, 107, 107n, 190–9, 219, 249, 255–6, 287–8, 291; of trade unions, 64–6, 284–5; tripartite, demands for, 192–3, 197; other references, 253, 255, 265n, 296
Federation of Locomotive Crews, 65, 285, 285n
Federation of Machine Drivers, 65
Fierlinger, Zdeněk, 50
Fischl, Otto, 177
Fojtík, Jan, 132n
foreign policy, 36–41, 71, 92–3, 108, 156, 198; Action Program on, 205–7; and political reforms, 200–17, 236; *see also individual countries*
foreign trade: Action Program on, 27, 35,

38; and CEMA, 37–41, 205–6, 210, 231, 237; and economic reforms, 9–10, 20, 22, 33, 35–41, 47, 47n; joint-stock companies, 22, 22n, 35, 35n; political aspects of, 7, 36–41, 201; and USSR, 2, 37, 39–41, 52, 201, 224, 231; and West Germany, 201–2; other references, 92, 93, 198
France, 71
Freemasons, 90
Fuchs, František, 92

Galuška, Miroslav, 116–18, 203, 254
Goldmann, Josef, 7n
Goldstücker, Eduard, 5n, 17, 70n, 79–80, 103–5, 114, 173; attacks on, 93, 128, 261; and the 'Czechoslovak way to socialism,' 212–13; on foreign policy, 202n, 203–5, 209; and leading role of Party, 133–4, 162–3; on non-Communist political parties and possibility of opposition, 162–4; on youth and students, 71, 77
Gomułka, Władisław, 222, 224, 232
Gottwald, Klement, 2, 101, 132, 170–1, 190, 190n, 211, 236
government: Action Program on, 149; during invasion, 241–2; and economic reforms, 9, 12–13, 21–33, 42, 44, 46–50, 192; and elected organs of government, 13, 13n, 144, 146–50; formation of new, 6, 19; and federalization, 190–2, 194–6; and National Assembly, 13, 13n, 144, 146–9, 152, 205–6; and political reforms, 71, 148–52, 154–68, 196–9; and Slovak organs, 13, 15, 50–1, 107, 186, 189–94, 196–9; and trade unions, 10, 62–4, 286–7, 291–2; *see also* state
government, elected organs of: Action Program on, 149, 153; and electoral system, 150–2; and economic reforms, 12–13; and government, 13, 13n, 144, 146–50; and leading role of Party, 148–50, 153; and Party, 147–53, 185–205; and political reforms, 147–53, 185, 198–9; Slovak, 149, 191, 193–4, 196, 198–9; *see also* state, National Assembly, National Committees
Grafik, Michal, 99
Gramsci, Antonio, 224–5n, 263n
Grechko, A. A., 225, 233–4, 298–300
Grishin, V.V., 224

313

Index

Index

Index

Zajac, Ladislav, 62
Zajíc, Jan, 258, 282, 295
Za rubezhom, 240n
Závodský, Odon, 269
Zemědělské noviny: post-invasion, 268, 295, 299n; pre-invasion, 48, 67, 82, 123, 127, 152
Zhdanovism, 170

Zhivkov, Todor, 224, 232
Zingor, Viliam, 176
Zionism, 91, 170, 210
Zítřek, 263–4, 268
Zivot, 147, 162, 213
Zivot strany, 101, 263
Zprávy, 255, 257, 261, 266, 269n, 281, 289, 292